PATERNOSTER BIBLICAL MONOGRAPHS

For Whom Did Christ Die?

PATERNOSTER BIBLICAL MONOGRAPHS

For Whom Did Christ Die? The Extent of the Atonement in Paul's Theology

Jarvis J. Williams

MILTON KEYNES, UK

Copyright © Jarvis J Williams, 2012

First published 2012 by Paternoster

Paternoster Press is an imprint of Authentic Media
52, Presley Way, Crownhill, Milton Keynes, MK8 0ES

09 08 07 06 05 04 03   8 7 6 5 4 3 2 1

The right of Jarvis J Williams to be identified as the author of this work has been asserted by him in accordance with the Copyright, Designs and Patents Act 1988.

All rights reserved. No part of this publication may be reproduced, stored in a retrieval system, or transmitted, in any form or by any means, electronic, mechanical, photocopying, recording or otherwise, without the prior permission of the publisher or a license permitting restricted copying. In the UK such licenses are issued by the Copyright Licensing Agency, 90 Tottenham Court Road, London W1P 9HE.

British Library Cataloguing in Publication Data
A catalogue record for this book is available from the British Library

ISBN 978–1–84227–730–0

Typeset by Jarvis J Williams
Printed and bound in Great Britain
for Paternoster Publishing
by Lightning Source, Milton Keynes, UK

PATERNOSTER BIBLICAL MONOGRAPHS

Series Preface

One of the major objectives of Paternoster is to serve biblical scholarship by providing a channel for the publication of theses and other monographs of high quality at affordable prices. Paternoster stands within the broad evangelical tradition of Christianity. Our authors would describe themselves as Christians who recognize the authority of the Bible, maintain the centrality of the gospel message and assent to the classical creedal statements of Christian belief. There is diversity within the constituency; advances in scholarship are possible only if there is freedom for frank debate on controversial issues and for the publication of new and sometimes provocative proposals. What is offered in this series is the best of writing by committed Christians who are concerned to develop well-founded biblical scholarship in a spirit of loyalty to the historic faith.

Series Editors

I. Howard Marshall	Honorary Research professor of New Testament, University of Aberdeen, Scotland, UK
Richard J. Bauckham	Professor of New Testament Studies and Bishop Wardlaw professor, University of St Andrews, Scotland, UK
Craig Blomberg	Distinguished Professor of New Testament, Denver Seminary, Colorado, USA
Robert P. Gordon	Regius Professor of Hebrew, University of Cambridge, UK
Stanley E. Porter	President and Professor of New Testament, McMaster Divinity College, Hamilton, Ontario, Canada

To Ana, Jaden, and Elba ("Ita") for all of their prayers, love, support, help, and encouragement

Table of Contents

ABBREVIATIONS

PREFACE

1. Introduction, Thesis, and History of Research..............................1

2. Humanity's Spiritual Plight in Paul's Anthropology....................32

3. Divine and Human Agency in Paul's Soteriology......................105

4. The Purpose of Jesus' Death in Paul's Atonement-Theology........189

5. Conclusion...215

Abbreviations

ANTC	Abingdon New Testament Commentaries
AThR	*Anglican Theological Review*
ATR	*Australasian Theological Review*
BJRL	Bulletin of the John Rylands University Library of Manchester
BN	*Biblische Notizen*
BThSt	Biblisch-theologische Studien
CBQ	*Catholic Biblical Quarterly*
ConBNT	Coniectanea neotestamentica or Coniectanea biblica: New Testament Series
CTJ	*Calvin Theological Journal*
EvQ	*Evangelical Quarterly*
EvT	Evangelical Theology
FRLANT	Forschungen zur Religion und Literatur des Alten und Neuen Testaments
HDR	Harvard Dissertations in Religion
HTR	*Harvard Theological Review*
JETS	*Journal of the Evangelical Theological Society*
JRT	Journal of Religious Thought
JSNT	*Journal for the Study of the New Testament*
JSNTSup	Journal for the Study of the New Testament: Supplement Series
JSOT	*Journal for the Study of the Old Testament*
JTS	*Journal of Theological Studies*
LNTS	Library of New Testament Studies
LXX	Septuagint
MT	Masoretic Text
MBT	Münsterische Beiträge zur Theologie
MNTC	Moffatt New Testament Commentary
NIB	*The New Interpreter's Bible*
NovT	*Novum Testamentum*
NPNF	Nicene and Post-Nicene Fathers
NTD	Das Neue Testament Deutsch
NTS	*New Testament Studies*
NTM	New Testament Monograph
OTM	Old Testament Monograph
PTR	*Princeton Theological Review*
SBFLA	*Studii biblici Franciscani liber annus*
SBL	Society of Biblical Literature
SBLDS	Society of Biblical Literature Dissertation Series
SBLSP	*Society of Biblical Literature Seminar Papers*

SCS	Septuagint Commentary Series
SNT	Studien zum Neuen Testament
SNTS	Society for New Testament Studies
SNTSM	Society for New Testament Studies Monograph
SNTSMS	Society for New Testament Studies Monograph Series
TrinJ	Trinity Journal
WMANT	Wissenschaftliche Monographien zum Alten und Neuen Testament
WTJ	*Westminster Theological Journal*
WUNT	Wissenschaftliche Untersuchungen zum Alten und Neuen Testament
WW	*Word and World*

PREFACE

"Will I finish this monograph before my deadline?" This is the question that constantly lingered in the background of my thinking as I relentlessly worked on each chapter. As each of the two previous monographs that I have written, this book has been both a challenge and a joy to write. It has been a challenge because numerous obstacles arose during the writing process that constantly slowed me down or set me back throughout the approximate two years that it has taken me to write and complete it (e.g. teaching 48 hours in one year, getting ill, numerous speaking engagements, etc.). It has been a joy because this book has allowed me to offer critical reflection upon Paul's soteriology and the extent of the atonement in Paul's theology for nearly two years, an exercise that has both strengthened my mind and my soul.

There are numerous people to thank, for whom and to whom I am extremely grateful, for their labors in helping me firstly get this monograph in print and secondly for sparing me from many other mistakes (either exegetical or clerical) in addition to the ones that readers will likely find as they read the book. However, space allows me only to thank a few. Although I am extremely grateful to those who have made this work better than it would have otherwise been, I alone am absolutely responsible for any error or deficiency that readers may find in this book.

I owe many thanks to Dr. Robin Parry (editor for Pickwick) and to the members of Paternoster's peer reviewing committee for New Testament monographs. When I initially submitted the proposal for this monograph in the fall of 2009, Robin was the managing editor at Paternoster. He and his colleagues thoroughly reviewed my proposal, and their diverse committee of international scholars did not allow their own theological perspectives of the extent of the atonement to influence whether they would accept or reject my proposal. Instead, they accepted it based on the potential promise of the work, and they encouraged me to write the best scholarly, New Testament monograph that I could possibly write in defense of what I thought was Paul's view of the extent of the atonement. In addition, Robin worked laboriously to inform me and other Paternoster authors of the status of our monographs during the press's transition from one owner to another and from one managing editor to another, and he specifically worked to ensure that the new editor would continue to go forward with the publication of this work. Robin's efforts in favor of this monograph, his friendship, and his hilarious British sense of humor are greatly appreciated!

I owe many thanks to Dr. Mike Parsons (commissioning editor for Paternoster) for his careful, editorial eye and for his help with Paternoster's house style throughout my writing of this monograph. Mike also deserves thanks for handling the transition at Paternoster with grace and communicating with me soon after he began his new editorial post that he was very excited to be editing and publishing my manuscript. I greatly appreciate his work on behalf of this monograph and his encouragement throughout the writing process.

I owe many thanks to Dr. Simon J. Gathercole for the time that I was able to spend with him in November 2010 at Campbellsville University. Simon graciously accepted my invitation to participate in our department's Biblical and Theological Lectures in November 2010 during the same week of the national meeting of the Society of Biblical Literature in Atlanta, GA in spite of his busy schedule. A late flight from Cambridge, England to Louisville, Kentucky, a long drive with me from Louisville to Campbellsville, and very little sleep did not keep him from investing much time and effort into the lectures. Simon's keen intellect, his scholarly care, his gentle spirit, and his willingness to invest much time and energy into our students and faculty in two (too short!) days during chapel, during lectures, during a luncheon, and in the classroom were greatly appreciated by both my students and by me. I am especially grateful for the encouragement and helpful advice that he offered me (a young scholar) during our individual times together by answering my many questions about research, writing, publication, and the pursuit of novelty in the field of New Testament Studies.

I owe thanks to Campbellsville University and to Dr. John E. Hurtgen, my dean at Campbellsville University, for their continued support of me and of my work. I especially owe many thanks to Dr. Hurtgen. From my very first day at Campbellsville University, he has given me his full support to pursue with great passion and zeal the work to which God called me at the university. Even when we have disagreed, he has always supported my teaching in the classroom, my research, my writing, and my other scholarly endeavors. I am so grateful to Dr. Hurtgen for entrusting me with his confidence and for granting me the freedom to do my part in serving the Biblical Studies program, the School of Theology, and the university community in the ways in which I am equipped to do so. I also appreciate the way that he works to treat everyone at our university and in our department with grace!

I owe many thanks to Daniel Motley, my research assistant. Although Daniel has graduated from Campbellsville University and is no longer one of my students, he continues to serve as my research assistant while pursuing his graduate degree elsewhere in Biblical and Theological Studies. Daniel graciously completed the abbreviations page, the bibliography, the subject index, and he checked to ensure that the footnotes and the bibliography harmonized. I appreciate his careful work, his perpetual willingness to take on "boring" clerical tasks for me that very few students (if any) and that very few scholars (if any) enjoy, and I am thankful for his friendship.

I owe thanks to Ian Lawrence, my dear friend and co-teacher at Clifton Baptist Church, for completing the scripture index. Ian without hesitation was willing to assist me with the manuscript in spite of the fact that he and his wife were expecting their second child shortly before I was able to give him a completed copy. His assistance with the manuscript and his friendship are greatly appreciated!

I offer many thanks to my Biblical Studies students and colleagues at Campbellsville University from 2008-2010 for enduring lectures and paper presentations that related to this book. I especially thank my students in my spring 2010 Intertestamental Judaism class and in my fall 2010 Studies in Paul class, in the latter of which much of chapter 2 was presented as lectures, for their hard work, for their stimulating questions and discussions, and for their eagerness to embrace my constant push to consider carefully what the ancient texts actually say and for their irrevocable commitment to push back to challenge me to do the same.

Finally, I offer many, many, many thanks to my family! My dear wife of 10 years, Ana, and our beautiful and very energetic three year old son, Jaden, have been tremendous sources of joy and strength for me. I do not exaggerate when I say that this book would not have been written if it were not for God's grace through them. I also offer many thanks to Ana's mother (or as my son says "my Ita"), Elba, for her love, support, and help around the house during her four week visit with us from Costa Rica during the summer of 2011. As I was finishing this monograph, I became ill with numerous, unexpected physical problems, and (to be quite blunt) I thought that my death was near! I nearly emailed my editor on more than one occasion to inform him that I did not want to continue writing the monograph due to health issues since I did not (at the time) see an end of them in sight. Yet, God used Ana, Jaden, and Elba to encourage me to keep hoping in God, to keep persevering in my writing, and they reminded me that I was not as sick as I thought. Thankfully, they were right, and by God's grace he restored my health and enabled me to continue writing and to complete this monograph. God used their prayers and love to pull me through (what was for me at that time) the most difficult physical struggle that I have ever experienced in my 33 years of life! It is, therefore, a great honor and a great joy to dedicate this book to Ana, Jaden, and Elba for all of their prayers, love, support, help, and encouragement.

Jarvis J. Williams
Louisville, Kentucky (USA)
July 2011

Chapter 1

Introduction, Thesis, and History of Research

For whom did Christ die? This question has been the subject of intense debate especially since the Reformation.[1] Although this question did not experience dispute until late in the sixteenth century, the issue can be traced back to the earliest days of the Christian church.

Thesis
I will argue in this book that according to Paul, Jesus died exclusively for all elect Jews and Gentiles to achieve their salvation. As I argue this thesis, the book will attempt to show that the extent of the atonement is not simply an abstract theological discussion, imposed on the text by theologians, and void of a biblical or exegetical foundation. Instead, I will argue that this discussion is biblical and Pauline, and that an answer to the question for whom did Christ die can be detected in Pauline theology by means of a careful, exegetical analysis of the relevant Pauline texts and of the relevant texts in the Old Testament and Second Temple Judaism.

Purpose
The book's purpose is to offer a detailed, exegetical investigation of selected texts in Paul and in early Judaism that shed light on Paul's view of the extent of Jesus' death. In the last few years, New Testament scholars have shown an increasing interest in Jesus' death,[2] but no one has focused exclusively on providing an answer to the singular question for whom did Jesus die according to Paul's atonement-theology. New Testament scholars have neither provided a monograph that exegetically argues that Paul believed that Jesus died exclusively for all elect Jews and Gentiles who unite themselves with Jesus and identify with the Christian community.

---

[1]Jonathan Rainbow, *The Will of God and the Cross: An Historical and Theological Study of John Calvin's Doctrine of Limited Atonement* (Allison Park, PA: Pickwick, 1990); Raymond A. Blacketer, "Definite Atonement in Historical Perspective," in *The Glory of the Atonement: Biblical, Theological, and Practical Perspectives*, eds. Charles E. Hill and Frank A. James III (Grand Rapids: Baker, 2004), 304-23.
[2]See history of research below.

History of Research

Many scholars would argue that biblical interpreters did not begin to discuss particular atonement until the late sixteenth century.[3] It is true that Christians did not formulate and defend particular atonement with sharp precision until the sixteenth century during the debates between the Calvinists and the Arminians and during the debate at the Synod of Dort (1618-1619). However, it is historically inaccurate to assert that no Christian writers discussed the extent of the atonement nor argued for particular atonement until the sixteenth century. The Synod of Dort affirmed (what was eventually called) particular atonement (Canons of Dort articles 8-9), but Christian exegetes in the earliest days of the church discussed the extent of the atonement and appeared to argue for or against such a doctrine before the theological debates and controversies of the 1600s.[4]

The history of research will not attempt to document every place in the history of the church where discussions of the extent of the atonement have occurred. In this regard, the history of research will not be exhaustive. Instead, it will briefly and selectively trace the trajectory of the discussion pertaining to particular atonement from its earliest occurrences until the current discussion in contemporary scholarship. It will particularly argue that discussions regarding particular atonement appear quite early in Christian literature outside of the New Testament. The history of research will also argue that although particular atonement can be detected in early Christian literature outside of the New Testament as early as the first century CE and although much literature has been written since the Synod of Dort in defense of particular atonement, my current book is distinct from any biblical monograph that has been previously written in defense of particular atonement in biblical scholarship, for it is (to my knowledge) the only monograph that concerns itself exclusively with arguing in favor of particular atonement from the Pauline letters by means of exegetical rigor. As the history of research will suggest, much of the scholarly work on the extent of the atonement that argues for particular atonement has primarily approached the topic from the perspective of systematic theology, even when such works have appealed to New Testament texts.[5]

---

[3] For sources, see Blacketer, "Definite Atonement," 304-23.

[4] Relying upon other scholars, Blacketer ("Definite Atonement," 304-05) asserts that definite atonement or particular redemption better explains the Synod's view than the phrase limited atonement. See Richard A. Muller, *Dictionary of Latin and Greek Theological Terms* (Grand Rapids: Baker, 1985), esp. 273; Roger Nicole, "Particular Redemption," in *Our Savior God: Man, Christ, and the Atonement*, ed. J.M. Boice (Grand Rapids: Baker, 1980), 165-78.

[5] In fact, one of the strongest defenses of particular atonement is John Owen's, *The Death of Death in the Death of Christ* (Edinburgh: Banner of Truth, 1959). Owen's book primarily addresses the extent of the atonement with philosophical and theological categories and not by a careful and detailed biblical exegesis of the relevant texts. For a better exegetical investigation of the extent of the atonement, see John Murray, *Redemption—Accomplished and Applied* (Grand Rapids: Eerdmans, 1975).

Introduction 3

Patristic Discussions of Particular Atonement (CE 90-451)[6]
1 Clement (CE 95-98)
In 1 Clement, after Clement urges the Corinthians to abandon empty and futile thoughts and to embrace what is good (7.1-3), he exhorts them to fix "their eyes on the blood of Christ and let us understand that it is precious before his Father" (ἀτενίσωμεν εἰς τὸ αἷμα τοῦ Χριστοῦ καὶ γνῶμεν ὡς ἔστιν τίμιον τῷ πατρὶ αὐτοῦ) (7.4), "because, being poured out for our salvation, [Christ's blood] won for the whole world the grace of repentance" (ὅτι διὰ τὴν ἡμετέραν σωτηρίαν ἐκχυθὲν παντὶ τῷ κοσμῷ μετανοίας χάριν ὑπήνεγκεν) (7.4) (brackets mine). This statement sheds light on the extent of the atonement and especially seems to affirm particular atonement, for Clement suggests that Jesus' blood was for "our salvation" (τὴν ἡμετέραν σωτηρίαν) and that his blood "won for the whole world the grace of repentance" (παντὶ τῷ κοσμῷ μετανοίας χάριν ὑπήνεγκεν). The phrase τὴν ἡμετέραν σωτηρίαν can only be applied to the author (Clement/the Romans) and the audience (the Corinthians) since he states in 7.1 that "we write" to admonish "you" (i.e. the Corinthians) and to remind "ourselves" (both the author and the audience) (ταῦτα ἀγαπητοί οὐ μόνον ὑμᾶς νουθετοῦντες ἐπιστέλλομεν ἀλλὰ καὶ ἑαυτοὺς ὑπομιμνήσκοντες). Clement's exhortation exclusively applies to Christians, for he uses the vocative ἀγαπητοί in 7.1 before he offers his admonishment to the Corinthians and because he reminds himself and fellow believers in Corinth and Rome of the value of Jesus' death.

Furthermore, Clement states that Jesus' blood was poured out to accomplish salvation and to grant the grace of repentance for παντὶ τῷ κοσμῷ ("the whole world"). This phrase must be limited to those who believe (which would include Clement/Romans and his audience), because Clement has already stated that Jesus' blood was for "our salvation" and since the "our" exclusively refers to the ἀγαπητοί (i.e. both Clement/Romans and the Corinthians) in 7.1. Moreover, Clement's statement also seems favorable toward particular atonement, for not everyone in the world actually experiences the grace of repentance (not even in Clement's day), but only those who believe.

Clement affirms the particularity of repentance and qualifies the scope of his earlier statement regarding the efficacy of Jesus' death in accomplishing repentance for the "whole world" when he says "let us go into all the generations and let us teach that from generation to generation, the Master has given an opportunity for repentance to those who desire to turn to him" (διέλθωμεν εἰς τὰς γενεὰς πάσας καὶ καταμάθωμεν ὅτι ἐν γενεᾷ καὶ γενεᾷ μετανοίας τόπον ἔδωκεν ὁ δεσπότης τοῖς βουλομένοις ἐπιστραφῆναι ἐπ' αὐτόν) (7.5). With the latter statement, Clement defines παντὶ τῷ κοσμῷ μετανοίας χάριν from 7.4. That is, the whole world for

---

[6]Throughout the book, I will use the term "definite" or "particular" atonement to refer to limited atonement and "general" and "universal" atonement to refer to unlimited atonement.

whom Jesus' blood has won repentance is none other than those who desire to turn to him in 7.5. Clement's words in 7.6-7 support this interpretation. He appeals to Noah and Jonah who preached repentance (7.6), and he asserts that only those who "obeyed" Noah's message were saved (7.6). Regarding Jonah, Clement asserts that only "those who repented of their sins made atonement to God by their prayers and received salvation, even though they had been [previously] alienated from God" (7.7) (brackets mine). Thus, the repentance for the whole world and the salvation, mentioned in 7.1-4, are not in fact for the whole world, but only for those who repent, believe, and are saved.

Particular atonement also arises to the surface in other parts of 1 Clement. In 8.5, Clement asserts that God "desires all his beloved to participate in repentance" and that he established repentance for his "beloved by an act of his almighty will" (8.5). The "beloved" are Christians and more specifically the "elect" whom Clement mentions earlier when he asserts that the "elect" were joined to Peter and Paul on account of their exemplary lives for Christ (5.1-6.1, esp. 6.1). In 1 Clement 12.7, commenting on the blood of the old covenant, Clement states that "through the blood of the Lord," redemption will come to all who hope and believe in God. He states elsewhere that Jesus "bears our sins and suffers pains for our sakes" (16.4).

Commenting on Isaiah 53, Clement says that Jesus was wounded "because of our sins (16.5)," "afflicted because of our transgressions" (16.5), "delivered for our sins" (16.7), and that he came to earth to die for "the transgressions of [God's] people" (16.9) (brackets mine). In 21.6, Clement urges "let us regard the Lord Jesus Christ, whose blood was given for us" (τὸν κύριον Ἰησοῦν Χριστόν οὗ τὸ αἷμα ὑπὲρ ἡμῶν ἐδόθη ἐντραπῶμεν). In 29.1, Clement commands the Corinthians to pursue holiness and love God "who made us to be an elect portion for himself" (ὃς ἐκλογῆς μέρος ἡμᾶς ἐποίησεν ἑαυτῷ). In 36.1, Clement speaks of the salvation that believers have found in Jesus Christ (αὕτη ἡ ὁδός ἀγαπητοί ἐν ᾗ εὕρομεν τὸ σωτήριον ἡμῶν Ἰησοῦν Χριστόν). In 38.1, while exhorting the Corinthians to pursue unity with one another, he explains that the physical body needs all of its parts and commands the "whole [physical] body" to be saved "by means of Christ Jesus" (σῳζέσθω οὖν ἡμῶν ὅλον τὸ σῶμα ἐν Χριστῷ Ἰησοῦ). In 46.4, Clement refers to the elect of God. In 46.6, Clement urges the schismatic Corinthians to know that "we" (i.e. the elect) have one God, one Christ, and one Spirit. Then he asks how can "we" divide the body of Christ, which he calls "one's own body" (τὸ σῶμα τὸ ἴδιον) (46.7). In 49.1-50.1, Clement connects God's love for the elect and God's reception of the elect with Jesus' vicarious death for their sin. In 49.5, Clement states that God made the "elect of God" (οἱ ἐκλεκτοὶ τοῦ θεοῦ) to be perfect in love, and in 49.6 that Jesus received us in love and that "because of the love, which he had toward us, Jesus Christ, our Lord, gave his blood for us by means of God's will, and [he] gave his flesh on behalf of our flesh and [his] soul on behalf of our souls" (διὰ τὴν ἀγάπην ἣν ἔσχεν πρὸς ἡμᾶς τὸ αἷμα αὐτοῦ ἔδωκεν ὑπὲρ ἡμῶν Ἰησοῦς

Introduction

Χριστὸς ὁ κυριὸς ἡμῶν ἐν θελήματι θεοῦ καὶ τὴν σάρκα ὑπὲρ τῆς σαρκὸς ἡμῶν καὶ τὴν ψυχὴν ὑπὲρ τῶν ψυχῶν ἡμῶν) (brackets mine).

In 50.2, Clement states that those who are found in God's love are those whom God considers worthy. In 50.3, he declares that "our" sins are forgiven through love (cf. 50.6). In 50.6-7, he states that those to whom God does not reckon sin are blessed and that such a declaration of blessedness "came upon those who have been elected by God through Jesus Christ, our Lord. . ." (οὗτος ὁ μακαρισμὸς ἐγένετο ἐπὶ τοὺς ἐκλελεγμένους ὑπὸ τοῦ θεοῦ διὰ Ἰησοῦ Χριστοῦ τοῦ κυριοῦ ἡμῶν). Thus, in light of the above evidence from 1 Clement, Jesus' death and its benefits are limited only to the elect who believe, because it only saves the elect, the very ones who will repent, believe, and obey.

2 Clement (CE 95-98)

In the second letter to the Corinthians ascribed to Clement, the author urges the Corinthians to esteem Jesus with the same level of reverence as God and that they should not belittle their salvation (οὐ δεῖ ἡμᾶς μικρὰ φρονεῖν περὶ τῆς σωτηρίας ἡμῶν) (1.1). The author, then, states that "Jesus endured to suffer many things on account of us" (ὅσα ὑπέμενειν Ἰησοῦς Χριστὸς παθεῖν ἕνεκα ἡμῶν) (1.2). The author immediately states that Jesus "saved us," that "we" cannot repay him for what we received (1.4), and that he "showed us mercy and saved us because he had compassion on us" (1.7). Finally, chapter 1 culminates with the author stating that Jesus "called us when we were not, and he willed us into existence when we were not." (1.8). The author's point here cannot simply refer to physical creation since he speaks earlier about the Corinthians' calling in the context of salvation and Jesus' death for those whom he has saved (1.1-5; cf. 9.1-11).

Rather, by calling "us" into existence, the author must be referring to God's effectual calling whereby he converted the Corinthians from the state of unbelief to belief in Christ. This interpretation especially fits with the author's statements that Jesus "saved us while we were perishing" (1.4) and that God saved us while "we were blind with respect to understanding" (1.6), while we worshiped idols (1.6), and while we were trapped in darkness (1.6). In 2.1-6, the author expresses that God willed to save "the church" (2.1), those who "believed" (2.3), and those "who were perishing" (2.7). Each of these groups refers to the "sinners" whom Jesus called into spiritual existence (2.4; cf.14.5). In 17.4-5, the author applies redemption to believers by stating that the Lord will return and redeem "each of us according to our deeds" (17.4) and that unbelievers will be astonished when they see Jesus reigning in his kingdom, because they did not believe the message of salvation (17.5). The author applies the soteriological privileges, which result from Jesus' death for sin, mentioned in chapter 1 to refer exclusively to the believing community of faith: i.e. to those who have been saved. He does not speak about the universal efficacy of Jesus' death, but seems to affirm particular atonement.

Ignatius's Letters (CE 117-138)

Ignatius composed his letters during a difficult time of persecution, but he exhorts the churches to remain steadfast in their loyalty to the bishops and to the Lord Jesus Christ. Regarding particular atonement, in his greeting to the church at Ephesus, Ignatius professes that the Ephesian church is "predestined before the ages" and elected for eternal life (τῇ προωρισμένῃ πρὸ αἰώνων εἶναι διὰ παντὸς εἰς δόξαν παράμονον ἄτρεπτον ἡνωμένην καὶ ἐκλελεγμένην) (Ign. *Eph. Salutation*). Ignatius, then, applies the blood of Christ to the salvation of the elect when he states that the Ephesians "took on new life by means of the blood of God" (ἀναζωπυρήσαντες ἐν αἵματι θεοῦ) (Ign. *Eph.* 1.1).

Later in the same letter when speaking of the Ephesians' love for sound doctrine and their rejection of evil doctrine, Ignatius describes their faith in metaphorical language. He declares that the Ephesians are stones of a temple and have been uplifted by the crane of Jesus Christ: viz., the cross (Ign. *Eph.* 9.1). He refers to Jesus' cross after he describes the Ephesians as stones, "which have been prepared beforehand" (ὡς ὄντες λίθοι ναοῦ προητοιμασμένοι εἰς οἰκοδομὴν θεοῦ πατρός ἀναφερόμενοι εἰς τὰ ὕψη διὰ τῆς μηχανῆς Ἰησου Χριστοῦ ὅς ἐστιν σταυρός) (Ign. *Eph.* 9.1; cf. Rom 9:23). Thus, Jesus' cross, says Ignatius, and the Spirit enable the Ephesian believers (temple-stones which God prepared beforehand) to circumvent evil doctrine.

That Jesus' cross only benefits believers is clarified by Ignatius's command in Ign. *Eph.* 10.1 when he states that the Ephesians should pray that "the rest of mankind would find God, for there is hope for repentance for them." In light of Ignatius's previous soteriological statements about the Ephesians in Ign. *Eph. Salutation* where he says that believers are "predestined and elect before the ages for eternal life" and in Ign. *Eph.* 9.1 where he says that believers are "temple-stones prepared beforehand," "the rest of mankind" in Ign. *Eph.* 10.1 must only refer to unbelievers. Moreover, Ignatius states that Jesus was crucified for "faith in God" (Ign. *Eph.* 16.2) and that he embraced the ointment of death upon his head "so that he would breath immortality on the church" (Ign. *Eph.* 17.1). Here Ignatius applies the benefits of Jesus' death exclusively to the one who has faith and to the church, not to every person without exception. Likewise, Ignatius states once more to the Ephesians that Jesus' cross grants salvation and eternal life to believers (Ign. *Eph.* 18.1).

In his letter to the Trallians while Ignatius urges them to be obedient to their bishop, he states that subjection to the bishop is as subjection to Jesus and that when they are subject to the bishop, they demonstrate that they live in accordance with the standard of Jesus, "who died for us so that you would flee death if you believe in his death" (τὸν δι' ἡμᾶς ἀποθανόντα ἵνα πιστεύσαντες εἰς τὸν θάνατον αὐτοῦ τὸ ἀποθανεῖν ἐκφύγητε) (Ign. *Trall.* 2.1). Ignatius here limits the benefit of one's escaping death by means of the death of Christ to those who believed in his death, and those who believed in his death are in fact the ones who would flee death, for their belief in his death

Introduction

delivers them from death. Since belief in Jesus' death enables those who trust in his death to escape death, Ignatius seems to affirm that the death of Christ was particularly for those who would believe. This is supported by a later statement that Ignatius makes that Jesus calls the Trallians (believers) through his cross and suffering (Ign. *Trall.* 11.2). Evidence of a particular atonement arises elsewhere in the letters of Ignatius. While seeking to convince the Smyrneans that Jesus died and resurrected in the flesh, Ignatius connects Jesus' death with the salvation of his church (Ign. *Smyrn.* 1.1-2). He is explicit that Jesus suffered and died for his church "so that we might be saved" (Ign. *Smyrn.* 2.1; cf. 6.2).

The Letter of Polycarp (CE 1st Century)

While praising the Philippians for their faithfulness to God, Polycarp states that the Philippians are "chosen by God" (Pol. *Phil.* 1.1) and that he rejoices because they remain firmly established in their efforts to bear fruit to the Lord Jesus, "who endured for our sins until death" (Pol. *Phil.* 1.2). He, then, states that the Philippians "have been saved by grace" (Pol. *Phil.* 1.3). In these brief, introductory remarks, Polycarp applies Jesus' death for sin to the salvation of the elect with the words "chosen by God" (Pol. *Phil.* 1.1), "who endured for our sins until death" (Pol. *Phil.* 1.2), and we "have been saved by grace" (Pol. *Phil.* 1.3). As a means by which to compel the Philippians to live exemplary lives of righteousness, Polycarp appeals to (as he calls them) the martyrdoms of Ignatius, Zosimus, Rufus, and the apostle Paul. He reminds the Philippians that these martyrs did not love the present world, "but the one who died for us and for us who arose by means of God" (Pol. *Phil.* 9.2). With the latter statement, Polycarp applies Jesus' death and resurrection exclusively to Christians, and not to the present world.

The Martyrdom of Polycarp (CE 155-180)

The Martyrdom of Polycarp is a description of both the execution of Polycarp for his devotion to Jesus and a description of other faithful Christians. As the author(s) describes the events surrounding Polycarp's execution as he was burning from the fire, the author(s) states that the death of the "elect" (ἐκλεκτῶν) is quite different from unbelievers. He asserts that Polycarp demonstrated that he was certainly one of the "elect" because of the manner by which he died (Mart. *Pol.* 16.1-2). The author(s), then, discusses the concern that Polycarp's executioners had that some Christians would worship Polycarp instead of the Christ, because of whom he became a martyr (Mart. *Pol.* 17.1-2). However, the author(s) clarifies that Polycarp's executioners did not understand that Christians will neither be able to forsake Christ "who suffered on behalf of the salvation of all of the world, namely, [on behalf] of those who are saved; [that is], the blameless one [suffered] on behalf of sinners, [and] nor [are Christians able] to worship any other [person]" (τὸν ὑπὲρ τῆς τοῦ παντὸς κόσμου τῶν σῳζομένων σωτηρίας παθόντα ἄμωμον ὑπὲρ ἁμαρτωλῶν οὔτε ἕτερόν τινα σέβεσθαι) (Mart. *Pol.* 17.2) (brackets mine). Thus, there is a connection in the Martyrdom of Polycarp between the salvation of the elect and the death of Jesus. In fact, the Martyrdom of Polycarp qualifies the scope of Jesus' death for the "whole world" as a death for "all of those who are saved" by placing the genitival construction τῆς τοῦ παντὸς κόσμου τῶν σωζομένων σωτηρίας after the construction τὸν ὑπὲρ τῆς τοῦ παντὸς κόσμου (Mart. *Pol.* 17.2).

As he bids his farewell, the author(s) concludes the letter by urging his audience to walk in accordance with the gospel with respect to the word of Jesus Christ, "with whom glory [be] to God because of the salvation of the holy elect" (μεθ᾽ οὗ δόξα τῷ ἐπὶ σωτηρίᾳ τῇ τῶν ἁγίων ἐκλεκτῶν) (brackets mine) (Mart. *Pol.* 22.1). This statement makes it clear that from the perspective of the author(s) of the Martyrdom of Polycarp, salvation is for the elect. Based on the letter's earlier statements about the death of Christ (Mart. *Pol.* 17.2), we can infer that this text affirms that Jesus' death was only for the holy elect, which results in the salvation *only* of the holy elect.

The Epistle of Barnabas (CE 130-131)
The Epistle of Barnabas largely concerns itself with exhorting its readers to abstain from ungodliness, to pursue obedience to Jesus Christ, and not to imitate Israel's disobedience (*Barn.* 1.1-4.14). The author often urges his audience to do the preceding by means of an allegorical exegesis of the Old Testament (cf. *Barn* 11.1-12.11). Regarding the extent of the atonement, Barnabas states in 5.1 that the Lord died, "so that we would be purified by means of the forgiveness of sins, which is by means of the blood of his purification" (εἰς τοῦτο γὰρ ὑπέμεινεν ὁ κύριος παραδοῦναι τὴν σάρκα εἰς καταφθοράν ἵνα τῇ ἀφέσει τῶν ἁμαρτιῶν ἁγνισθῶμεν ὅ ἐστιν ἐν τῷ αἵματι τοῦ ῥαντίσματος αὐτοῦ). With this statement, Barnabas suggests that Jesus died exclusively so that sinners would be purified (i.e. forgiven) from their sins (*Barn.* 5.1). With a relative clause (ὅ ἐστιν ἐν τῷ αἵματι τοῦ ῥαντίσματος αὐτου), he explains that this forgiveness comes to sinners "by means of the blood of his purification" (ὅ ἐστιν ἐν τῷ αἵματι τοῦ ῥαντίσματος αὐτου). Barnabas later states that Jesus suffered "so that his wound would give us life" (ἔπαθεν ἵνα ἡ πληγὴ αὐτοῦ ζωοποιήσῃ ἡμᾶς) and that he suffered "for us" (δι᾽ ἡμᾶς) (*Barn.* 7.2). One can be certain that from Barnabas' perspective, those for whom Jesus suffered in order to give life are none other than those who would believe and be saved, for Barnabas states in the same context that Jesus offered his flesh for the sins of his new people (ὑπὲρ ἁμαρτιῶν μέλλοντα τοῦ λαοῦ μου τοῦ καινοῦ προσφέρειν τὴν σάρκα μου) (*Barn.* 7.5), while affirming that a sacrificial goat in the Old Testament was a type of Jesus, which was set forth for the church (πῶς γὰρ ὅμοιος ἐκείνῳ εἰς τοῦτο ὁμοίους τοὺς τράγους καλούς ἴσους ἵνα ὅταν ἴδωσιν αὐτὸν τότε ἐρχόμενον ἐκπλαγῶσιν ἐπὶ τῇ ὁμοιότητι τοῦ τράγου οὐκοῦν ἴδε τὸν τύπον τοῦ μέλλοντος πάσχειν Ἰησοῦ τί δὲ ὅτι τὸ ἔριον εἰς μέσον τῶν ἀκανθῶν τιθέασιν τύπος ἐστὶν τοῦ Ἰησοῦ τῇ ἐκκλησίᾳ θέμενος) (*Barn.* 7.10-11).

That Barnabas seems to affirm a particular atonement is further supported when he states that Jesus established a covenant with his people in that "the Lord himself gave to us [a covenant] as a people of an inheritance because he endured for us" (αὐτὸς δὲ ὁ κύριος ἡμῖν ἔδωκεν εἰς λαὸν κληρονομίας δι' ἡμᾶς ὑπομείνας) (*Barn.* 14.4) and when he states that Jesus "was made manifest so that these would be perfected with respect to sins and so that we would also receive the covenant of our Lord Jesus by means of the one who inherited [it], who was prepared for this reason: [namely], so that he himself would confer in us a covenant by means of a word, and he was manifested and redeemed from darkness our hearts which were already freely spent in the realm of death and which were handed over in the realm of lawlessness, [namely], deception" (ἐφανερώθη δὲ ἵνα κἀκεῖνοι τελειωθῶσιν τοῖς ἁμαρτήμασιν καὶ ἡμεῖς διὰ τοῦ κληρονομοῦντος διαθήκην κυρίου Ἰησοῦ λάβωμεν ὃς εἰς τοῦτο ἡτοιμάσθη ἵνα αὐτὸς φανεὶς τὰς ἤδη δεδαπανημένας ἡμῶν καρδίας τῷ θανάτῳ καὶ παραδεδομένας τῇ τῆς πλάνης ἀνομίᾳ λυτρωσάμενος ἐκ τοῦ σκότους διάθηται ἐν ἡμῖν διαθήκην λόγῳ) (*Barn.* 14.5) (brackets mine).

Barnabas continues by asserting that "the Father gave orders to Jesus to prepare a holy people for himself, and he redeemed us from darkness" (*Barn.* 14.6) and that his death for others is effectual for everyone for whom he died (*Barn.* 14.7-9). The latter point is evident from the discussion in *Barn.* 14.7-9 regarding the benefits and the efficacy of Jesus' death "for us," which is mentioned in *Barn* 14.5. In *Barn.* 14.7-9, the author declares that God gave the people, for whom Jesus died, Jesus as a covenant to open their spiritually blind eyes and to redeem them. Barnabas follows this statement with the assertion that Jesus' redemption of a people enables them to be the means by which salvation reaches the ends of the earth (*Barn. 14*.8) and that Jesus was appointed to proclaim the favorable year of the Lord (*Barn.* 14.9). The proclamation of the good news to the spiritually blind and captive delivers from blindness and releases from captivity only those who believe, and those who believe (according to Barnabas) are the "us" for whom the Father sent Jesus to die and to whom he sent him to proclaim the good news of salvation. Thus, according to Barnabas, Jesus' blood actually achieved purification, forgiveness of sins, and redemption for those whom he died.

Epistle to Diognetus (CE 155-225)
The Epistle to Diognetus seems to affirm particular atonement. The author clearly asserts that God created and designed the heavens and the earth and everything in them for his purposes (*Diogn.* 7.2). In *Diogn.* 8.1-9.2, the author discusses that God (the Master and Creator of the universe), after conceiving a "great" and "imperishable" plan, communicated this plan to Jesus and sent him into the world to save those who were living in accordance with unrighteousness. The author's discussion of God's plan for the unrighteous culminates with a discussion of Jesus' death for the ungodly. He states that God did not "hate us," neither "reject us," nor "hold a grudge against us," but he was patient: "he, himself, accepted our sins; he, himself, gave up his own son [to

be] a ransom for us, the holy one for the lawless ones, the one without evil for the evil ones, the righteous one for the unrighteous ones, the immortal one for the mortal ones, the imperishable one for the perishable ones" (οὐκ ἐμίσησεν ἡμᾶς οὐδὲ ἀπώσατο οὐδὲ ἐμνησικάκησεν ἀλλὰ ἐμακροθύμησεν ἠνέσχετο αὐτὸς τὰς ἡμετέρας ἁμαρτίας ἀνεδέξατο αὐτὸς τὸν ἴδιον υἱὸν ἀπέδοτο λύτρον ὑπὲρ ἡμῶν τὸν ἅγιον ὑπὲρ ἀνόμων τὸν ἄκακον ὑπὲρ κακῶν τὸν δίκαιον ὑπὲρ τῶν ἀδίκων τὸν ἄφθαρτον ὑπὲρ τῶν φθαρτῶν τὸν ἀθάνατον ὑπὲρ τῶν θνητῶν) (*Diogn.* 9.2) (brackets mine).

In *Diogn.* 9.3-4, the author implies with two rhetorical questions that only Jesus' perfect obedience in death covered "our sins" and that the lawless ones were justified by means of the only son of God. Those for whom Jesus died are the same group as the lawless ones since the author states that Jesus covered "our sins" by his death and that his death justified the lawless ones. He concludes his discussion of the soteriological benefits of Jesus' death in *Diogn.* 9.5-6 by asserting that the justification of sinners through the blood of Christ was a "sweet exchange" and that it saves the powerless, and he further states that God has "willed us to believe" (ἐβουλήθη πιστεύειν ἡμᾶς) (cf. *Diogn.* 9.6). The author connects his comments about God's comprehensive sovereignty over all things (*Diogn.* 8.1-9.2) with comments about the penal and the ransoming natures of Jesus' death for the sins of others (*Diogn.* 9.2) and with comments about God's willing of certain individuals to believe, and he states that Jesus' penal death for the sins of others actually (not hypothetically) affects justification for the lawless ones in that it provides salvation for them (*Diogn.* 9.3-6). Thus, according to Diognetus, one can conclude that Jesus' death was specifically for those whom God willed to believe and these are the ones whom the blood of Jesus justifies.

Jerome (CE 342-420)

Francis Turretin (CE 1623-1687) argues that Saint Jerome was the first exegete to argue specifically for particular atonement.[7] Commenting on Matthew 20:28 ("just as the son of man came not to be served but to serve and to give his life as a ransom for many"), Jerome emphasizes that Jesus came to serve and to give his life as a ransom for redemption "for many." Jesus did not say (Jerome asserts) that he gave his life as redemption for all, but "for many." That is, he gave his life "for those who wanted to believe."[8] Although Jerome's statement is fairly ambiguous in that it does not explicitly state that Jesus died exclusively for the elect, Turretin interprets Jerome's statement to refer exclusively to the

---

[7]Francis Turretin, *Institutes of Eclectic Theology*, trans. George Musgrave Giger, ed. James T. Dennison, Jr. (Phillipsburg, NJ: P&R, 1994), 2:462.
[8]St. Jerome, *Commentary on Matthew*, trans. Thomas P. Scheck (Washington, DC.: The Catholic University Press of America, 2008), 228-29.

Introduction

elect since he (Turretin) states that those who would believe would be none other than the elect.[9]

Augustine (CE 354-430)
Some say that Augustine was the first Christian exegete to argue that Christ specifically died to redeem the elect.[10] Since Augustine nowhere explicitly states that Christ died to redeem the elect alone, to appeal to Augustine as the earliest Christian exegete who affirmed particular atonement is potentially problematic. Still, Calvinistic scholars rightly argue that Augustine makes numerous statements about the efficacy of the blood of Christ for the elect that seem to support that he believed and taught what eventually became known as particular atonement.[11]

For example, commenting on John 10:26, Augustine boldly asserts that Jesus understood the Pharisees to be "predestined to everlasting destruction, not won to eternal life by the price of his own blood."[12] An implication of this statement is that Jesus' blood paid for the salvation of those who were predestined to eternal life. Commenting on the "many mansions" of John 14:2, Augustine notes that "those whom [Christ] has redeemed by his blood, he shall then have delivered up to stand before his Father's face" on the last day (brackets mine). Augustine makes a connection between Christ's blood, redemption, and being delivered over to the Father. For Augustine, "those whom Christ had redeemed by his blood" are the same ones who will be "delivered over to the Father" on the last day.[13] Commenting on John 17:11-12, Augustine pens that "those, therefore, are understood to be given to Christ who are ordained to eternal life. These are they who are predestined and called according to the purpose, of whom, not one perishes."[14] With these words, Augustine connects Jesus' death for the salvation of others with those whom the Father gave to Jesus (i.e. the elect), and he affirms that the elect are in fact those who will not perish since Jesus died specifically for them. Commenting on 1 John 2:2, Augustine states that Jesus' death was an atoning sacrifice "for the whole world" in that he both atones for the sins of the "church in all nations" and "the church throughout the whole world."[15]

---

[9]Turretin, *Institutes*, 2:462. Of course, Turretin's interpretation of Jerome does not prove that Jerome affirmed particular atonement.
[10]Millard Erickson, *Christian Theology*, 2nd ed. (Grand Rapids: Baker, 1998), 845; Blacketer, "Definite Atonement," 308-09.
[11]Blacketer, "Definite Atonement," 304-05; Rainbow, *The Will of God*, 9-22. Cf. J. Pohle, *The Catholic Encyclopedia* (New York: Encyclopedia Press, 1913), 6:700a.
[12]The citations from Augustine and the entire structure of this paragraph come from Blacketer, "Definite Atonement," 308-10. For the primary texts, see Augustine, "Tractate on John's Gospel," in *Nicene and Post-Nicene Fathers*, series 1, ed. P. Schaff (1186-89, repr. Peabody, MA: Hendrickson, 1994), 7:267. Henceforth NPNF.
[13]NPNF 7:504.
[14]NPNF 5:480.
[15]NPNF 7:465.

In addition, Augustine also seems to affirm particular atonement when he argues against Pelagius' interpretation of 1 Timothy 2:4 ("God desires all men to be saved and to come to the knowledge of the truth"). Augustine suggests that, on the one hand, it is wrong to affirm that God desires every person to be saved but that, on the other hand, his divine will is frustrated by the free choice of sinful humanity, because the gospel is foolishness to those who perish but the power of God to those who are saved (cf. 1 Cor. 1:18). The latter group are the very ones to whom Paul refers in 1 Timothy 2:4. These are the ones whom God instructs to come to Jesus, and he wills all of these to come to the knowledge of the truth. Therefore, Augustine affirms that Paul argues "that no man is saved unless God wills his salvation: not that there is no man whose salvation he does not will, but that no man is saved apart from his will."[16] Regardless of whether Augustine's exegesis of the above texts is correct, he seems to argue in favor of particular atonement.

In his other anti-Pelagian writings, Augustine makes other statements that appear to affirm particular atonement.[17] While affirming original sin and the universal condemnation of humanity, Augustine states that those who are delivered from God's just condemnation by grace are vessels of mercy by the work of Christ not based on their merit (*Augustine on Nature and Grace* 5). With the phrase "work of Christ," Augustine refers to Jesus' death, because he mentions the "blood of Christ" both earlier in his anti-Pelagian writings (*Augustine on Nature and Grace* 4) and later after the phrase "work of Christ" (*Augustine on Nature and Grace* 6-7). Regarding particular atonement, Augustine says "but of whose mercy, if not his who sent Christ Jesus into the world to save sinners, whom he foreknew, and foreordained, and called, and justified, and glorified" (*Augustine on Nature and Grace* 5). An affirmation of particular atonement is evident here since Augustine affirms that Jesus came to save "sinners" and since he defines these sinners whom Christ came to save as those whom God "foreknew," "foreordained," "called," "justified," and "glorified." In other words, Augustine expresses that those for whom Christ came to die were in fact the elect.

Less explicit allusions to particular atonement also occur in Augustine's writings, but they are allusions to particular atonement, nonetheless. In his anti-Pelagian writings, Augustine asserts that Jesus died to "redeem us from death" and that the human will does not naturally want such a ransom "to be translated from the power of darkness and of him who has the power of death into the kingdom of Christ the Lord" (*Augustine on Nature and Grace* 26). An allusion to particular atonement is evident in Augustine's connection of Jesus' ransom "for us" with one's transferal into Christ's kingdom. Thus, one can infer from this connection that in Augustine's view, the ones whom Christ ransomed are the ones whom he transfers into his kingdom. Augustine also connects the sufficiency of Jesus' cross both with the

---

[16] Blacketer, "Definite Atonement," 310.

[17] Citations from Augustine's writings come from *Basic Writings of Saint Augustine*, vol 1, ed. Whitney J. Oates (New York: Random House, 1948).

Introduction

foolishness of the preaching of the cross of Christ that heals believers and with justification (*Augustine on Grace* 47).

Another allusion to particular atonement occurs in Augustine's letter to Januarius. When explaining to Januarius why the annual celebration of the Lord's passion (i.e. Easter) does not fall on the same day each year, Augustine connects Jesus' death for sin with those who believe and with eternal life and the resurrection. He states that Christ died "for our transgressions" and that he rose "for our justification." He later states in the same letter that Jesus taught that "the one who believes in him will pass from death to life." He further states that the Lord's passing from death to life "is now being carried out in us by faith—faith in the forgiveness of our sins in hope of eternal life—when we love God and neighbor."[18] Augustine further says that those who believe are buried with Christ through baptism and that those who believe in Christ have been saved for hope. So, Augustine appears to interpret the benefits of Jesus' death to be efficacious only for those who believe.

Augustinian Disciples
Augustine's disciples were more explicit than their teacher in defending particular atonement. Prosper of Aquitaine (CE 390-465), for example, affirms that Jesus died for everyone in that he takes on himself humanity's nature. This nature is common to everybody because the entire scope of humanity mutually shares in a fallen condition and because he paid a valuable price on the cross for sin. Prosper writes that Jesus "was crucified only for those who were to profit by his death," which can only be the elect who would be saved. Pelagian and Semi-Pelagian responses to both Augustine and his disciples and his disciples' critique of them support that other interpreters of Augustine and his disciples perceived them to affirm particular atonement. Both the Pelagians and Semi-Pelagians responded to the arguments of Augustine and his followers with regard to particular atonement.[19] For example, Faustus (a Pelagian) says that Augustinians "wander far from the path of piety who say that the Savior did not die for all" (De Gratia Dei et Libero Arbitrio 1.4). Hincmar states that one of the errors of Gottschalk of Orbais (a ninth century monk) was that he preached that Christ died only for the elect, not for the salvation of all men. The Council of Arles, which was a Semi-Pelagian council, as recorded in the letter of Faustus similarly critiqued the Augustinian tradition of particular atonement.[20] Commenting on the remnants of the Pelagian heresy, however, Prosper says in a letter to Augustine that "this is their definition and profession that Christ died for the whole human race and that no one is excluded from the redemption effected by his blood" (*Letter to Augustine* 6). Prosper also notes that the Pelagians assert that one of Augustine's damnable errors was that he

---

[18] All citations from Augustine's letter to Januarius come from *Letters of Saint Augustine*, ed. John Leinenweber (Tarrytown, NY: Triumph Books, 1992), 75-77.
[19] Ibid.
[20] The above discussion and the cited patristic texts can be found in Turretin, *Institutes*, 2:455-56.

taught that "Christ did not die to accomplish the redemption of the whole world."

Medieval Discussions of Particular Atonement (500-1500)[21]
Peter Lombard (CE 1100-1160)

Peter Lombard contrived an important formulation of the extent of the atonement that proved to be both the standard way of articulating the extent of the atonement for centuries and the starting point for debates during the early stages of Reformed orthodoxy.[22] Lombard acknowledges that Jesus' death could have certainly covered the sins of every individual without exception, but his death is efficacious only for the elect. That Lombard affirmed particular atonement is strengthened by his acknowledgement that Jesus' death benefits only those who believe (*Distinction XIX*.1.55.1-3). This is evident by his connection of redemption, Christ's death, and justification with faith. Lombard states that "we are freed by Christ's death from the devil and sin because, as the Apostle says, in his blood we are justified; and since we are justified, that is, released from our sins, we are freed from the devil who kept us in the bonds of our sins" (*Distinction XIX*.1.55.1).

In response to his own question how are "we released from our sins by his death" (*Distinction XIX*.1.55.2), Lombard states that sinners are released from their sin "because by [Jesus'] death, as the Apostle says, charity toward us is commended, that is, God's charity toward us is revealed as most excellent and commendable, since he handed over his son to death for the sake of sinners" (*Distinction XIX*.1.55.2). He immediately thereafter asserts that "since token of such great love toward us has been shown, we are moved to, and kindled with, love of God, who has done so much for us. . ." (*Distinction XIX*.1.55.2). Particular atonement most clearly comes through in the latter statement since Lombard connects Jesus' death for sinners and their justification with the individual love for God shown by those sinners for whom Jesus died. In other words, those sinners for whom Jesus died are the very ones who are moved to love God. Lombard goes on to say that those for whom Jesus died and who therefore love God are also the ones whom God justifies by Jesus' blood and the ones whom Jesus' blood cleanses from sin (*Distinction XIX*.1.55.2-3). Lombard asserts that Jesus functions both as a priest and as a sacrificial victim in order to achieve reconciliation for those whom he died. With respect to sufficiency, he offers himself as ransom "for all," but his ransom is only efficient for the elect because his death affects salvation exclusively for them.

Commenting on Augustine's exegesis of Romans 5:9 that we have been reconciled to Christ by his death, Lombard interprets Augustine to teach that Christ did not reconcile "us" in such a way that after this reconciliation he

---

[21]For this point, see also Rainbow, *The Will of God*, 25-32; Carl Trueman, *The Claims of Truth: John Owen's Trinitarian Theology* (Carlisle: Paternoster, 1998), 199-226.

[22]Peter Lombard, *The Sentences: Book 3—On the Incarnation of the Word*, trans. Giulio Silano (Toronto: Pontifical Institute of Mediaeval Studies, 2008).

began to love us, whereas before he hated us, as if an enemy has been reconciled to an enemy, so that two who were formerly enemies have now become friends (*Distinction XIX*.3.6.2). Instead, "we" were reconciled to God who already loved "us," for God did not begin loving "us" at the moment that he reconciled "us" to himself by the blood of Jesus, but God loved "us" before the creation of the world. That is, God loved "us" before we were anything at all. Lombard, then, poses the question: "how then were we reconciled to God, who already loved us?" Lombard's answer is that we were God's enemies because of sin, but God still only had love toward "us" even when "we" sinned against him (*Distinction XIX*.3.6.2).

The "us" and "we" for whom Christ died are exclusively the elect according to both Augustine and Lombard, for these alone are the ones for whom God's love overcomes his hatred, whereas God still hates those who are not reconciled to God by the blood of Jesus. That this is especially true with regard to Lombard's understanding of the extent of the atonement seems right because he alludes to Ephesians 1:5-6 when he states that God loved "us" before the foundation of the world. Ephesians 1:4-6 states that God chose "us" in Christ before the foundation of the world and that he predestined "us" in Christ in love. Lombard asserts elsewhere that Jesus offered himself in death to God with regard to the sufficiency of the price "only for the elect with regard to its efficacy, because he brought about salvation only for the predestined" (*Distinction XX*.3.5.66.1). That Augustine refers to the elect in the text that Lombard cites in *Distinction XIX*.3.6.2 is supported by Augustine's statements and Lombard's interpretation that God never really hated those whom he reconciled to himself through the blood of Jesus. Regardless of whether Augustine and Lombard are correct, the implication of their statements is that although God's love was always present for those whom he has currently reconciled to himself through the blood of Jesus, his divine hatred was current and still remains present *only* over those whom he will not reconcile to himself through the blood of Jesus. For Augustine and Lombard, these people who receive God's eternal love both before and after his act of reconciliation through the blood of Jesus are the elect (Augustine *Tractate on John's Gospel* 7.267, 465, 480, 504; Augustine *On Nature and Grace* 4-7, 26, 47; cf. *Letter to Augustine* 6; Lombard, *Distinction XIX*.3.6.2; XX.3.5.66.1).

Thomas Aquinas (CE 1225-1274)
Thomas Aquinas had an Augustinian understanding of election. He would have, therefore, had little sympathy for the Remonstrant theology. For example, contrary to the Remonstrants, Aquinas rejects the belief that God based his election of some to be saved on his foreknowledge of a person's merits. He rejects that God elects based on any foreseen faith.[23] Rather, he suggests that predestination is based exclusively on God's will. Alluding to 1 Timothy 2:4, Aquinas suggests that God does not will everyone to be saved, for he says that

---

[23] *Summa Theologiae* 1, Q23, article 5.

the text "can be understood as applying to every class of individuals, not to every individual of each class."[24] This would mean that "God wills some men of every class and condition to be saved, males and females, Jews and Gentiles, great and small, but not all of every condition."[25] While discussing the Lord's Supper, Aquinas says that "the blood of Christ's passion has its efficacy not merely in the elect among the Jews, to whom the blood of the Old Testament was exhibited, but also in the Gentiles."[26] In other words, according to Aquinas, Jesus' blood is for every class of people, not only for Jews. When speaking of union with Christ, Aquinas states "the head and members are as one mystic person, and therefore Christ's satisfaction belongs to all the faithful as being his members."[27] This statement again seems to support particular atonement since Aquinas connects Christ's satisfaction to the faithful members of the body of Christ who have union with him.[28]

Reformation Discussions of Particular Atonement (1500-1750)
Martin Luther (CE 1483-1546)

Luther embraced an Augustinian particularism. Arguing in favor of predestination in his lectures on Romans, Luther indirectly seems to affirm particular atonement by rejecting a universalistic interpretation of 1 Timothy 2:4: "For these verses must always be understood as pertaining to the elect only, as the apostle says in 2 Timothy 2:10 'everything for the sake of the elect.' For in an absolute sense Christ did not die for all, because he says: 'this is my blood which is poured out for you' and "for many"—he does not say: 'for all—'for the forgiveness.'"[29]

---

[24] *Summa Theologiae* 3, Q78, article 8, ad. 8.
[25] Ibid.
[26] Ibid.
[27] *Summa 3*, Q48, article 2, ad. 1.
[28] Blacketer ("Definite Atonement," 312-13) points out, however, that Aquinas also spoke of the atonement in general terms. For example, speaking of two wills of God, Aquinas states that God willed salvation for everyone without exception according to his antecedent will, but the salvation of the elect according to his consequent will. Aquinas also seems to affirm Lombard's earlier suggestion that Jesus' death was sufficient for all but efficient for the elect: "Christ's passion sufficed for all, while as to its efficacy it was profitable for many." For references in Aquinas' works, see *Summa Theologiae* 1, Q19, article 6, objection 1; *Summa Theologiae* 3, Q78, article 8, objection 8; *In ad Thom*. I, at 1 Tim 4:10. On Aquinas' view of predestination and atonement, see Jill Raitt, "St. Thomas Aquinas on Free Will and Predestination," *Duke Divinity School Review* 43 (1978): 188-95; Lee H. Yearly, "St. Thomas Aquinas on Providence and Predestination," *AThR* 49 (1967): 409-23; Rainbow, *The Will of God and the Cross*, 34-38; Carl Trueman, "Puritan Theology as Historical Event: A Linguistic Approach to the Ecumenical Context," in *Reformation and Scholasticism*, 253-75, esp. 269-71.
[29] Luther's Works, American edition, ed. H.T. Lehmann, et al. Vol 25 (St. Louis: Concordia), 1955-86, scholia in Romans 8, II.

Introduction

John Calvin (CE 1509-1564)

Some scholars within the Reformed tradition oppose particular atonement.[30] They justify their position by arguing that John Calvin himself did not affirm particular atonement.[31] If Calvin's view of election sheds any light on his view of the extent of the atonement, then one can be certain that Calvin affirmed that Jesus exclusively died to atone the sins of the elect, for Calvin strongly believed that God predestined only some to salvation while he predestined others to damnation.[32] Nevertheless, one cannot point solely to Calvin's obvious predestinarian theology to argue that he likely supported particular atonement since (1) many scholars agree that Calvin's view of the extent of the atonement is not particularly clear from his larger writings and (2) since many scholars identify with the Calvinist tradition and Calvin's view of predestination but reject particular atonement. Thus, to discern Calvin's view of the extent of the atonement, one needs to analyze thoroughly his predestinarian theology and his discussions of the atonement throughout his larger writings and his sermons and from this analysis infer whether Calvin's soteriology and atonement theology support that he affirmed particular atonement. Since such an analysis is outside of the purview of both this history of research and this monograph, a few observations of Calvin's view of the extent of the atonement from selected portions of his writings must suffice.

Due to the work of some scholars, the premise that Calvin affirmed universal atonement is now believed to be doubtful, and for good reason.[33] Commenting on 1 John 2:2, Calvin rejects the argument that this text extends salvation to the reprobate. On the one hand, he affirms Lombard's earlier assertion that Jesus' death was sufficient for all but efficient for the elect. But, on the other hand, Calvin does not think that this truth applies to 1 John 2:2.

---

[30]E.g. M. Charles Bell, "Calvin and the Extent of the Atonement," *EQ* 55 (1983): 115-23; Basil Hall, "Calvin against the Calvinists," in *John Calvin*, ed. G.E. Duffield (Grand Rapids: Eerdmans, 1966): 19-37; Brian G. Armstrong, *Calvinism and the Amyraut Heresy* (Madison: University of Wisconsin Press, 1969); Holmes Rolston III, *John Calvin versus the Westminster Confession* (Richmond, VA: John Knox, 1972); R.T. Kendall, *Calvin and English Calvinism to 1649* (New York: Oxford University Press, 1979); J.B. Torrance, "The Incarnation and 'Limited Atonement,'" *EQ* 55 (1983): 83-94.

[31]Kendall, *Calvin*, 212. For a recent critique of Kendall's thesis, see Jonathan D. Moore, "Calvin Versus the Calvinists? The Case of John Preston (1587-1628)," *RRR* 6.3 (2004): 327-48; P.L. Roumendal, "Calvin's Forgotten Classical Position on the Extent of the Atonement: About Sufficiency, Efficiency, and Anachronism," *WTJ* 70 (2008): 317-35.

[32]For example, see John Calvin, *Concerning the Eternal Predestination of God*, trans. J.K.S. Reid (Louisville: Westminster John Knox, 1997).

[33]Paul Helm, *Calvin and the Calvinists* (Edinburgh: Banner of Truth 1982; reprint Edinburgh: Banner of Truth, 1998); Roger Nicole, "John Calvin's View of the Extent of the Atonement," *WTJ* 47 (1985): 197-25; idem, "John Calvin's View of the Extent of the Atonement," in *Standing Forth: Collected Writings of Roger Nicole* (Fearn, Ross-shire, Christian Focus Publications, 2002), 283-312; Frederick S. Leahy, "Calvin and the Extent of the Atonement," *Reformed Theological Journal* 8 (1992): 54-64; John Murray, "Calvin on the Extent of the Atonement," *Banner of Truth* 234 (1983): 20-22.

Rather, when John states that Jesus was the propitiation for our sins and for the sins of the "whole world," he means that Jesus' death benefits the "whole church." Thus, "whole world" does not include the reprobate, but exclusively refers to those who were scattered throughout various regions of the world." According to Calvin, Christ is the savior of the world in that he saves all who are saved. Consequently, one can infer from Calvin's statements here that he limited Christ's propitiation to the elect.[34] In addition, when Calvin speaks against the sacramental theology of Heshusius, who taught that Jesus is bodily present in the elements, Calvin boldly states that "I should like to know how the wicked can eat the flesh of Christ which was not crucified for them? And how can they drink the blood which was not shed to expiate their sins?"[35] This statement affirms that Jesus' blood was not shed for everybody and did not expiate the sins of everybody, but only some.[36]

When speaking of Christ's redemption as securing salvation, Calvin asserts that dead and lost sinners ought to seek salvation in Christ, for Jesus' name was given to him by the will of God to save "his people from their sins" and that Jesus has the office of redeemer so that he would be "our" Savior (*Institutes* 2.1).[37] Calvin continues that "redemption would be defective if it did not conduct us by an uninterrupted progression to the final goal of safety" and that salvation only comes to those who rest in Jesus (*Institutes* 2.1). Three statements above seem to limit the extent of Jesus' death to the elect: (1) The dead and lost should seek salvation in Christ. (2) Jesus died to save his people from their sins. Certainly, Matthew 1:21 means by this statement that Jesus came to save Jews. However, the important point for my observation is that when speaking of Jesus' office of redeemer and the purpose for which the name Jesus was given to him, Calvin cites a text that limits salvation to a specific group (namely, Jews) instead of a general group. (3) Jesus' redemption guarantees final salvation for those who rest in him.

When speaking of God's reconciliation of sinners to himself by Christ, Calvin asks: "For how could [God] have given us in his only-begotten Son a singular pledge of his love, if he had not previously embraced us with free favor" (*Institutes* 2.2)? God's pledge of which Calvin speaks is election, for he states later, after discussing how God can hate those whom he now loves in Christ, that Paul says that God "has blessed us with all spiritual blessings in the heavenly places in Christ: according as he has chosen us in him before the foundation of the world (Eph. 1:3-4)" (*Institutes* 2.4). In support of the latter

---

[34]See Calvin's commentaries on 1 John 2:2.
[35]See John Calvin, *Tracts and Treatises*, trans. Henry Beveridge (Edinburgh: 1849), 2:527.
[36]Against Bell, "Calvin and the Extent of the Atonement," 119-21; Rowendal, "Classical Position," 331.
[37]All citations from Calvin's Institutes come from *Institutes of the Christian Religion*, trans. Henry Beveridge (Grand Rapids: Eerdmans, 1997). For a classic discussion of Calvin and Calvinism, see Benjamin B. Warfield, *Calvin and Calvinism*, vol. 5 in the Works of Benjamin B. Warfield (Grand Rapids: Baker, 2003).

Introduction

interpretation, Calvin quotes a text from Augustine that discusses how God shows love by reconciling sinners to himself through the death of Christ:

> Incomprehensible and immutable is the love of God. For it was not after we were reconciled to him by the blood of this Son that he began to love us, but he loved us before the foundation of the world, that with his only-begotten Son we too might be sons of God before we were anything at all. Our being reconciled by the death of Christ must not be understood as if the Son reconciled us, in order that the Father, then hating, might begin to love us, but that we were reconciled to him already, loving though at enmity with us because of sin. To the truth of both propositions we have the attestation of the Apostle, 'God commends his love toward us, in that while we were yet sinners, Christ died for us' (Rom 5:8). Therefore, he had this love towards us even when, exercising enmity towards him, we were the workers of iniquity. Accordingly, in a manner wondrous and divine, he loved even when he hated us. For he hated us when we were such as he had not made us, and yet because our iniquity had not destroyed his work in every respect, he knew in regard to each one of us, both to hate what we had made, and love what he had made" (*Institutes* 2.4; cf. Augustine *Tractates on John 110*).

The "love" to which Augustine and Calvin refer throughout the above quote is the death of Christ, for Calvin cites Romans 5:10 and he discusses at great length in book 2 that Jesus' death expiated sins, propitiated God's wrath, and reconciled to God those who were once hated by him (cf. *Institutes* 2.1-19).

Francis Turretin (CE 1623-1687)

During the 1600s due largely to the debates between the Calvinists (Synod of Dort) and the Arminians (the Remonstrants), discussions regarding the extent of the atonement became more precise. For example, after briefly discussing the views (as he calls them) of the Pelagians, the Jesuits, the Lutherans, the Arminians, and the Universalists,[38] Francis Turretin arduously defends particular atonement with 10 distinct arguments.[39] Due to space constraints, I will only mention a few of his most convincing comments to support his view. Turretin argues that Christ's death is restricted to certain ones in the New Testament.[40] The mission of and death of Jesus are restricted to "his people," "his sheep," "his friends," "his church," or "his body," but never extends to all men collectively. Thus, Christ is called Jesus because he will save his people from their sins (Matt. 1:21). More, Paul calls Jesus the Savior of "his body" (Eph. 5:23), and John calls him "the good Shepherd who lays down his life for the sheep" (John 10:15) and "for his friends" (John 15:13). The New Testament

---

[38] Turretin, *Institutes*, 2:455-59.
[39] For all of Turretin's arguments, see *Institutes*, 2:459-82.
[40] Ibid., 2:459.

also suggests that Jesus died so that he would gather together as one God's children who were scattered abroad (John 11:52), and he died to purchase the church of God with his own blood (Acts 20:28; Eph. 5:25, 26). In light of the above evidence, Turretin asks: "Now if Christ died for each and every one, why do the Scriptures so often restrict his death to a few? How can he be said to be the Savior of his people and of his body simply if he is the Savior of others also? How can he be said to have laid down his life for his sheep, for the sons of God, and for the church if (by the counsel of God and the intention of Christ himself) he died for others also?"[41] Turretin continues by saying that when Paul says that Christ was delivered over for him (Gal. 2:20), he does not exclude others from a fellowship in the same love. However, all of the above passages, Turretin asserts, "if not explicitly yet implicitly include an exclusion in the description of those for whom Christ died (which cannot pertain to others)."[42] They all have in common the same endeavor of amplifying the remarkable love of Christ to his sheep for whom he delivered himself up to death.[43]

Commenting on 1 Timothy 4:10 ("God is the Savior of all men, but especially of those that believe."), Turretin says that "it is gratuitous to say that Christ is the Savior of those for whom salvation is indeed acquired, but to whom it will never be applied."[44] The phrase "to save" denotes the actual communication of salvation, and the Christ is Jesus, because he is willing and able to save sinners, because he takes away all obstacles of salvation from those whom he saves, and because he actually saves his people by applying it directly to them, "which was the intention of God in sending Christ and the end of his mission (as the angel clearly imitates by the imposition of the name Jesus)."[45] Commenting on Ephesians 5:25 and Titus 2:14, Turretin argues that Christ delivered himself on behalf of his church and excludes those who are not part of the church and that Christ's giving himself up for his church results in the church's sanctification. Commenting on the fact that Jesus died for those whom the Father gave him (cf. John 17:2, 6; 6:37), Turretin asserts that Paul speaks of these people as "the people whom [God] foreknew" (Rom. 11:2), "heirs and children of promise" (Rom 9:8), "the seed of Abraham" (Rom. 4:13), and that Jesus died for Jews and Gentiles (Gal. 3:8, 16) (brackets mine).[46] He further points out that Christ "died for our sins and was raised for our justification" (Rom. 4:25),[47] that he died and rose again so that all for whom he died would live for God and not for themselves (2 Cor. 5:14-15),[48] that God freely gave him up to death for us (Rom. 8:32),[49] and that the gift of the Son and the Spirit

---

[41] Ibid., 2:459-60.
[42] Ibid., 460.
[43] Ibid.
[44] Ibid.
[45] Ibid., 461.
[46] Ibid., 463.
[47] Ibid., 464.
[48] Ibid.
[49] Ibid., 465.

Introduction

are given by God to us for salvation and both the gift of the Son and the gift of the Spirit are always presented together in Scripture as cause and effect (John 16:7; Gal. 4:4, 6; Rom. 8:9; 1 John 3:24).[50] In addition, Christ is the foundation of all spiritual blessings in Christ (Eph. 1:3), the first of which is faith.[51]

Turretin continues further and states that when Paul affirms that Jesus "died for all" (2 Cor. 5:15), he means that Jesus died for those "who are also dead, not with a death in sins, but with spiritual sin."[52] Paul's point here is not to prove that the individuals are corrupt, but to demonstrate the obligation with which believers are duty-bound—"whether as to justification through the imputation of the merit of Christ's death (as if they had made satisfaction in their own persons) or as to sanctification through the crucifixion of the old man by the efficacy of the cross of Christ, who lived not unto themselves, but unto Christ; for whom Christ not only died, but also rose again and whom the love of Christ constrains."[53] Paul's rhetoric here suggests, Turretin says, that these expressions of grace belong to only the elect and believers since only they both die in and with Christ (cf. Rom. 6:6, 8); the elect are the very ones whom Paul believes are justified by the obedience of the one man Jesus (Rom. 5:18-19; 1 Cor. 15:22), and they are the "all" and the "whosoever" ones that will call upon the Lord to be saved (Rom. 10:11; Col. 3:11; 1 Tim. 2:4-6). These are the same ones whom God promised to Abraham would be blessed through Abraham's seed (Gen. 12:3; 15:1-5; 22:18; 26:4; Rom. 4:16; 9:7; Gal. 3:8, 16).[54] These are not condemned because Christ died for them (Rom. 8:34).[55]

Reformation Confessions on Particular Atonement

As can be seen from the above history of research, to say that discussions of particular atonement did not occur until the councils of the 1600s systematically began to argue that Jesus died for the elect is inaccurate. Instead, it is more accurate to say that certain Reformed councils and confessions argued more precisely in the 1600s for particular atonement in response to Arminian arguments about the extent of the atonement. Two examples of this precision are evident in the Reformed confessions of both the Canons of Dort (CE 1618-1619) and the Westminster Confession of Faith (CE 1647). The goal here is not to discuss every Reformed confession of the 1600s that argues for particular atonement, but I have representatively chosen the Canons of Dort and the Westminster Confession of Faith because they contain the type of language

---

[50]Ibid.
[51]Ibid., 468.
[52]Ibid., 472.
[53]Ibid.
[54]Ibid., 472-74.
[55]Ibid., 474.

that current advocates of particular atonement use to articulate their arguments.[56]

Canons of Dort (CE 1618-1619)
The Synod of Dort met in the city of Dordrecht in the Netherlands in 1618-1619. It was a national synod of the Reformed churches in the Netherlands with an international character since it had 26 delegates from 8 foreign countries. The fundamental purpose of the synod was to settle a debate in the Dutch churches that was precipitated by the increasing influence of Arminianism. Jacob Arminius, who taught theology at the University of Leiden, challenged the teaching of both Calvin and his followers on numerous points. After Arminius died, his followers presented five particular problems that they had with Calvin and his followers. The antagonists of Calvin and Calvinism were called the Remonstrants, and their writing against Calvinism inherited the title of the Remonstrance, which was published in 1610. In the Canons of Dort, Reformed churches rejected the five points of Arminianism.

Regarding the extent of the atonement, the Canons of Dort say the following:

> . . . it was the entirely free plan and very gracious will and intention of God the Father that the enlivening and saving effectiveness of his Son's costly death should work itself out in all his chosen ones in order that he might grant justifying faith to them only and thereby lead them without fail to salvation. In other words, it was God's will that Christ through the blood of the cross (by which he confirmed the new covenant) should effectively redeem from every people, tribe, nation, and language all those and only those who were chosen from eternity to salvation and given to him by the Father; that he should grant them faith (which, like the Holy Spirit's other saving gifts, he acquired for them by his death); that he should cleanse them by his blood from all their sins, both original and actual, whether committed before or after their coming to faith; that he should faithfully preserve them to the very end; and that he should finally present them to himself, a glorious people without spot or wrinkle (article 8).

> [The plan of saving God's elect], arising out of God's eternal love for his chosen ones, from the beginning of the world to the present time has been powerfully carried out and will also be carried out in the future, the gates of hell seeking vainly to prevail against it. As a result, the chosen are gathered into one, all in their own time, and there is always a church of believers founded on Christ's blood, a church

---

[56]Other helpful Reformed confessions that represent the arguments in the current discussion of the extent of the atonement are the Scots Confession (CE 1560) on election and the Belgic Confession (CE 1566) article 16 on election and article 21 on atonement.

which steadfastly loves, persistently worships, and—here and in all eternity—praises him as her Savior who laid down his life for her on the cross, as a bridegroom for his bride (article 9) (brackets mine).

Westminster Confession of Faith (CE 1646)

The Westminster Confession of Faith is a Reformed confession in line with the Calvinist tradition. The Westminster Assembly drafted the document in 1646. The confession articulates particular atonement in the following way:

> It pleased God, in His eternal purpose, to choose and ordain the Lord Jesus, His only begotten Son, to be the Mediator between God and man, the Prophet, Priest, and King, the Head and Savior of His Church, the Heir of all things, and Judge of the world: unto whom He did from all eternity give a people, to be His seed, and to be by Him in time redeemed, called, justified, sanctified, and glorified (8.1).

> The Son of God, the second person of the Trinity, being very and eternal God, of one substance and equal with the Father, did, when the fullness of time was come, take upon Him man's nature, with all the essential properties, and common infirmities thereof, yet without sin; being conceived by the power of the Holy Ghost, in the womb of the virgin Mary, of her substance. So that two whole, perfect, and distinct natures, the Godhead and the manhood, were inseparably joined together in one person, without conversion, composition, or confusion. Which person is very God, and very man, yet one Christ, the only Mediator between God and man (8.2).

> The Lord Jesus, by His perfect obedience, and sacrifice of Himself, which He through the eternal Spirit, once offered up unto God, has fully satisfied the justice of His Father; and purchased, not only reconciliation, but an everlasting inheritance in the kingdom of heaven, for those whom the Father has given unto Him (8.5).

> Although the work of redemption was not actually wrought by Christ till after His incarnation, yet the virtue, efficacy, and benefits thereof were communicated unto the elect, in all ages successively from the beginning of the world, in and by those promises, types, and sacrifices, wherein He was revealed, and signified to be the seed of the woman which should bruise the serpent's head; and the Lamb slain from the beginning of the world; being yesterday and today the same, and forever (8.6).

Post-Reformation Discussions of Particular Atonement and My Contribution to the Discussion

In both old and recent works on Jesus' death, scholars have focused on the background influences behind Paul's conception of atonement, the saving significance of his death in Paul's theology, or the meaning of sacrifice in Paul's theology.[57] Because of C.H. Dodd's work in the 1950s that argued

---

[57]Hastings Rashdall, *The Idea of Atonement in Christian Theology: Being The Bampton Lectures for 1915* (London: Macmillan, 1925); Ethelbert Stauffer, *The Theology of the New Testament*, trans. John Marsh (London: SCM, 1955), 185-334; T.W. Manson, "Hilastērion," *JTS* 46 (1945): 1-10; Leon Morris, "The Meaning of Hilastērion in Romans 3:25," *NTS* 2 (1955-1956): 3-43; K. Wengst, *Christologische Formeln und Lieder des Urchristentums*, SNT 7 (Gütersloh: Mohn, 1972); Sam K. Williams, *Jesus' Death as Saving Event: The Background and Origin of a Concept*, HDR 2 (Missoula: Scholars Press, 1975); I. Howard Marshall, "The Meaning of Reconciliation," in *Unity and Diversity in New Testament Theology: Essays in Honor of George E. Ladd*, ed. Robert A. Guelich (Grand Rapids: Eerdmans, 1978), 117-32; Robert J. Daly, *Christian Sacrifice: The Judaeo-Christian Background before Origen* (Washington, DC: The Catholic University of America, 1978), 236-50; Theofried Baumeister, *Die Anfänge der Theologie des Martyriums*, MBT (Münster: Aschendorf, 1980); Martin Hengel, *The Atonement: A Study of the Origins of the Doctrine in the New Testament* (London: SCM, 1981); Ralph P. Martin, *Reconciliation: A Study of Paul's Theology* (Atlanta: John Knox, 1981), 105-06; Seyoon Kim, *The Origin of Paul's Gospel*, 2nd ed., WUNT 2 (Tübingen: Mohr Siebeck, 1984); idem, "2 Cor 5:11-21 and Reconciliation," *NovT* 38-39 (1996-1997): 360-84; Nicole S.L. Fryer, "The Meaning and Translation of Hilastērion in Romans 3:25," *EvQ* 59 (1987): 99-116; Marinus de Jonge, "Jesus' Death for Others and the Death of the Maccabean Martyrs," in *Text and Testimony: Essays on New Testament and Apocryphal Literature in Honour of A.F.J. Klijn*, ed. T. Baarda et al. (Kampen: J.H. Kok, 1988), 142-51; reprinted in *Jewish Eschatology, Early Christian Christology and the Testaments of Twelve Patriarchs: Collected Essays* (Leiden: Brill, 1991), 125-34; idem, *Christology in Context: The Earliest Response to Jesus* (Philadelphia: Westminster Press, 1988); idem, *Jesus, the Servant-Messiah* (New Haven: Yale University Press, 1991), 37-48; idem, *God's Final Envoy: Early Christology and Jesus' Own View of His Mission* (Grand Rapids: Eerdmans, 1998), 12-33; G.K. Beale, "Reconciliation in 2 Corinthians 5-7 and Its Bearing on the Literary Problem of 2 Corinthians 6:14-7:1," *NTS* 35 (1989): 550-81; Cilliers Breytenbach, *Versöhnung: Eine Studie zur paulinischen Soteriologie*, WMANT 60 (Neukirchener-Vluyn: Neukirchener Verlag, 1989); idem, "Versöhnung, Stellvertretung und Sühne: semantische und traditionsgeschichtliche Bemerkungen am Beispel der Paulinischen Briefe," *NTS* 39 (1993): 59-79; David Seeley, *The Noble Death: Greco-Roman Martyrology and Paul's Concept of Salvation*, JSNTSup 28 (Sheffield: Sheffield Academic Press, 1990); George Wesley Buchanan, "The Day of Atonement and Paul's Doctrine of Redemption," *NovT* 32 (1990): 236-49; Wolfgang Kraus, *Der Tod Jesu als Heiligtumsweihe: Eine Untersuchung zum Umfelt der Sühnevorstellung in Römer 3:25-26a*, WMANT 66 (Neukirchener-Vluyn: Neukirchener Verlag, 1991); J.W. van Henten, "The Tradition-Historical Background of Romans 3:25: A Search for Pagan and Jewish Parallels," in *From Jesus to John: Essays on Jesus and New Testament Christology in Honour of Marinus de Jonge*, JSNTSup 84, ed. Martinus C. de Boer (Sheffield: Sheffield Academic Press, 1993), 101-28; idem, "Jewish Martyrdom and Jesus' Death," in *Deutungen des Todes Jesu im Neuen Testament*, WUNT 181, ed. J. Frey and J.

Introduction 25

against propitiation,[58] many academic and popular works in the 20th century focused on expiation and propitiation. Leon Morris and Roger Nicole especially offered a sharp response to Dodd's claims and strongly argued for propitiation.[59] Several works have also focused on a particular theory of the atonement (e.g. Christus Victor, penal substitution, moral influence theory, etc.).[60] In current scholarship, expiation and propitiation are often discussed in

---

Schröter (Tübingen: Mohr Siebeck, 2005), 139-68; Stanley Porter, *Katallassō in Ancient Greek Literature, with Reference to the Pauline Writings* (Cordoba: Ediciones El Almendro, 1994); Christopher A. Davis, *The Structure of Paul's Theology: "The Truth Which is the Gospel"* (Lewiston, NY: Mellen Biblical Press, 1995), 120-24; Bradley H. McLean, *The Cursed Christ*, JSNTSup 126 (Sheffield: JSOT Press, 1996); Kenneth Grayston, "Atonement and Martyrdom," in *Early Christian Thought in Its Jewish Context*, ed. John Barclay and John Sweet (Cambridge: Cambridge University Press, 1996), 250-63; Daniel P. Bailey, "Jesus as the Mercy Seat: The Semantics and Theology of Paul's use of Hilastērion in Romans 3:25" (Ph.D. diss., Cambridge University, 1999); Bernd Janowski, *Sühne als Heilsgeschen*, WMANT 55, 2nd ed. (Neukirchener-Vluyn: Neukirchener Verlag, 2000), 350-54; Thomas Knöppler, *Sühne im Neuen Testament*, WMANT 88 (Neukirchener-Vluyn: Neukirchener Verlag, 2001), 133-87; Daniel G. Powers, *Salvation through Participation: An Examination of the Notion of the Believer's Corporate Unity with Christ in Early Christian Soteriology*, Biblical Exegesis and Theology 29 (Leuven: Peeters, 2001); Daniel Stökl Ben Ezra, *The Impact of Yom Kippur on Early Christianity*, WUNT 163 (Tübingen: Mohr Siebeck, 2003), 198-202; Stephen Finlan, *The Background and Content of Paul's Cultic Atonement Metaphors* (Atlanta: SBL, 2004); Tom Holland, *Contours of Pauline Theology: A Radical New Survey of the Influences on Paul's Biblical Writings* (Scotland, UK: Mentor, 2004); Henk S. Versnel, "Making Sense of Jesus' Death: The Pagan Contribution," in *Deutungen Todes Jesu im Neuen Testament*, WUNT 181, ed. Jörg Frey and Jens Schröter (Tübingen: Mohr Siebeck, 2005), 213-94; Jarvis J. Williams, *Maccabean Martyr Traditions in Paul's Theology of Atonement: Did Martyr Theology Shape Paul's Conception of Jesus' Death?* (Eugene, Or: Wipf and Stock, 2010); idem "Martyr Theology in Hellenistic Judaism and Paul's Conception of Jesus' Death in Romans 3:21-26," in *Christian Origins and Hellenistic Judaism: Literary and Social Contexts for the New Testament*, eds. Stanley E. Porter and Andrew W. Pitts (Leiden: Brill, Forthcoming).

[58]C.H. Dodd, *The Bible and The Greeks*, 2nd ed. (London: Hodder and Stoughton, 1954).

[59]Leon Morris, *The Apostolic Preaching of the Cross*, 3rd ed. (Grand Rapids: Zondervan, 1965); idem, *The Cross in the New Testament* (Grand Rapids: Baker, 1965); Roger Nicole, "C.H. Dodd and the Doctrine of Propitiation," *WTJ* 17 (1954-1955): 117-57. Cf. Stanislas Lyonnet and Léopold Sabourin, *Sin, Redemption, and Sacrifice: A Biblical and Patristic Study* (Rome: Biblical Institute Press, 1970); I. Howard Marshall, "The Death of Jesus in Recent New Testament Study," *WW* 1 (1983): 12-21.

[60]For a few examples, see Benjamin B. Warfield, "Atonement," in the *Works of Benjamin B. Warfield*, vol. 9 (Grand Rapids: Baker, reprinted 2003), 261-309; James H. Cone, *God of the Oppressed* (Maryknoll, NY: Orbis, 1997) 42-52, 211-12; Delores S. Williams, "The Color of Feminism: Or Speaking the Black Woman's Tongue," *JRT* 43 (1986) 42-58; idem, *Sisters in the Wilderness: The Challenge of Womanist God-Talk* (Maryknoll, NY: Orbis, 1993); John Sanders (ed.), *Atonement and Violence: A Theological Conversation* (Nashville: Abingdon, 2006); Charles E. Hill and Frank A. James III (eds.), *The Glory of the Atonement* (Downers Grove, IL: InterVarsity Press,

the context of penal substitution.[61] Recent work has begun to focus again on the sacrificial nature of Jesus' death[62] and on the meaning and significance of his death,[63] while also seeking to redefine (what the authors deem to be) the appropriate Pauline and/or Christian understanding of atonement.[64]

2004); . Denny Weaver, *The NonViolent Atonement* (Grand Rapids: Eerdmans, 2001) 99-178; Michael Hardin and Brad Jersak (eds.), *Stricken By God? Non-Violent Identification and the Victory of Christ* (Grand Rapids: Eerdmans, 2007), 13-53; Jarvis J. Williams, "Penal Substitution in Romans 3:25-26?" *PTR* 13 (2007): 73-81; idem, "Violent Atonement in Romans: The Foundation of Paul's Soteriology," *JETS* 53 (2010): 579-99.

[61]Hill and James (eds.), *Glory;* Williams, "Penal Substitution ," 73-81; idem, "Violent Atonement, 579-99."

[62]Markus Barth, *Was Christ's Death a Sacrifice?* Scottish Journal of Theology Papers 9 (Edinburgh: Oliver & Boyd, 1961); Frances M. Young, *The Use of Sacrificial Ideas in Greek Christian Writers from the New Testament to John Chrysostom* (Philadelphia: The Philadelphia Patristic Foundation, 1979); Bradley H. McLean, "Christ as Pharmakos in Pauline Soteriology," *SBLSP* (1991): 187-207; idem, "The Absence of an Atoning Sacrifice in Paul's Soteriology," *NTS* 38 (1992): 531-53; Richard H. Bell, "Sacrifice and Christology in Paul," *JTS* 53 (2002): 1-27; Peter Lampe, "Human Sacrifice and Pauline Christology," in *Human Sacrifice in Jewish and Christian Tradition*, ed. Karin Finsterbusch, Armin Lange, and K. F. Diehard Römheld (Leiden: Brill, 2007), 191-209.

[63]Ernst Käsemann, "Some Thoughts on the Theme of the Doctrine of Reconciliation in the New Testament," in *The Future of Our Religious Past: Essays in Honour of Rudolph Bultmann*, ed. James M. Robinson, trans. Charles E. Carlston and Robert P. Scharlemann (London: SCM, 1971), 49-64; idem, "The Saving Significance of the Death of Jesus in Paul," in *Perspectives on Paul*, trans. Margaret Kohl (Philadelphia: Fortress, 1971), 32-59; James D.G. Dunn, "Paul's Understanding of Jesus' Death," in *Reconciliation and Hope*, ed. Robert Banks (Grand Rapids: Eerdmans 1974), 76-89; Gerhard Friedrich, *Die Verkündigung des Todes Jesu im Neuen Testament*, BThSt (Neukirchener-Vluyn: Neukirchener Verlag, 1982); Charles B. Cousar, *A Theology of the Cross: The Death of Jesus in the Pauline Letters* (Minneapolis: Augsburg Fortress, 1990); Morna D. Hooker, *Not Ashamed of the Gospel: New Testament Interpretations of the Death of Christ* (Grand Rapids: Eerdmans, 1994), 20-46.

[64]For a few examples, see Cynthia S.W. Crysdale, *Embracing Travail: Retrieving the cross Today* (New York: Continuum, 1999); Raymond Schwager, *Jesus in the Drama of Salvation: Toward a Biblical Doctrine of Redemption*, trans. James G. Williams and Paul Haddon (New York: Crossroad, 1999); idem, *Banished from Eden: Original Sin and Evolutionary Theory in the Drama of Salvation*, trans. James G. Williams (London: Gracewing, 2005); Anthony W. Bartlett, *Cross Purposes: The Violent Grammar of Christian Atonement* (Harrisburg, PA: Trinity International Press, 2001), esp. 198-220; John Dunhill, "Communicative Bodies and Economies of Grace: The Role of Sacrifice in the Christian Understanding of the Body," *Journal of Religion* 83 (2003): 79-93; Cynthia L. Rigby, "Taking Our Place: Substitution, Human Agency, and Feminine Sin," *International Journal for the Study of the Christian Church* (2004): 220-34; Kathryn Tanner, "Incarnation, Cross, and Sacrifice: A Feminist-Inspired Reappraisal," *ATR* (2004): 35-56; Stephen Finlan, *Problems with Atonement: The Origins of, and Controversy about, the Atonement Doctrine* (Collegeville, Minn.: Liturgical Press, 2005); S. Mark Heim, *Saved from Sacrifice: A Theology of the Cross* (Grand Rapids:

Introduction 27

Scot McKnight's recent book on Jesus' death discusses atonement theory by investigating how the historical Jesus envisioned his own death.[65] Most recently, work on Jesus' death in one stream of scholarship has become dominated with discussions on theological theories of atonement as scholars for[66] or against[67] penal substitution respond to each other's arguments. My two recent books on atonement in Paul discuss the background influences behind and the relationship between Jesus' death for sin and racial reconciliation.[68]

To my knowledge, no biblical scholar has ever devoted a single

---

Eerdmans, 2006); Robert J. Daly, "Images of God and the Imitation of God: Problems with Atonement," *Theological Studies* 68 (2007): 36-51; idem, *Sacrifice Unveiled: The True Meaning of Christian Sacrifice* (New York: T&T Clark, 2009); David A. Brondos, *Paul on the Cross: Reconstructing Paul's Story of Redemption* (Minneapolis: Augsburg Fortress, 2006); idem, *A Fortress Introduction to Salvation and the Cross* (Minneapolis: Augsburg Fortress, 2007); idem, *Redeeming the Gospel: The Christian Faith Reconsidered* (Minneapolis: Augsburg Fortress, 2010).

[65] Scot McKnight, *Jesus and His Death: Historiography, the Historical Jesus, and Atonement Theory* (Waco, TX: Baylor University Press, 2005).

[66] J. I. Packer, "What Did the Cross Achieve? The Logic of Penal Substitution," *Tyndale Bulletin* 25 (1974): 3-45; Derek Tidball, *The Message of the Cross* (Downers Grove: InterVarsity, 2001); James Beilby and Paul R. Eddy (eds.), *The Nature of the Atonement: Four Views* (Downers Grove: InterVarsity Press, 2006); Williams, "Penal Substitution," 73-81; Frank S. Thielman, "The Atonement," in *Central Themes in Biblical Theology: Mapping Unity in Diversity*, eds. Scott J. Hafemann and Paul R. House (Grand Rapids: Baker, 2007), 102-27; Steve Jeffery, Mike Ovey, and Andrew Sach, *Pierced for Our Transgressions: Rediscovering the Glory of Penal Substitution* (Nottingham, UK: Inter-Varsity Press, 2007); Mark Dever and J.I. Packer, *In My Place Condemned He Stood* (Wheaton: Crossway, 2007); I. Howard Marshall, *Aspects of the Atonement: Cross and Resurrection in the Reconciling of God and Humanity* (Carlisle, UK: Paternoster, 2008); Derek Tidball, David Hilborn, and Justin Thacker (eds.), *The Atonement Debate* (Grand Rapids: Zondervan, 2008); Williams, "Violent Atonement, 579-99."

[67] Joel B. Green and Mark Baker, *Rediscovering the Scandal of the Cross: Atonement in New Testament & Contemporary Contexts* (Downers Grove, IL: InterVarsity Press, 2000); Steve Chalke, *The Lost Message of Jesus* (Grand Rapids: Zondervan, 2003); idem, "The Redemption of the Cross," in *The Atonement Debate: Papers from the London Symposium on the Theology of Atonement*, eds. Derek Tidball, David Hilborn, and Justin Thacker (Grand Rapids: Zondervan, 2008), 36-45; Alan Mann, *Atonement for a Sinless Society: Engaging with an Emerging Culture* (Carlisle, UK: Paternoster, 2005); Brad Jersak, "Non-violent Identification and the Victory of Christ," in *Stricken by God?: Nonviolent Identification and the Victory of Christ*, eds. Brad Jersak and Michael Hardin (Grand Rapids: Eerdmans, 2007), 18-53; Scott McKnight, *A Community Called Atonement* (Nashville: Abingdon, 2007);
Stephen H. Travis, *Christ and the Judgment of God: Divine Retribution in the New Testament* (Peabody, MA: Hendrickson, 2008).

[68] Jarvis J. Williams, *Maccabean Martyr Traditions in Paul's Theology of Atonement: Did Martyr Theology Shape Paul's Conception of Jesus's Death* (Eugene, Or.: Wipf & Stock, 2010); idem *One New Man: The Cross and Racial Reconciliation in Pauline Theology* (Nashville: Broadman & Holman, 2010).

exegetical and biblical monograph to an investigation of the extent of the atonement in the Pauline corpus. Recent articles on Pauline Theology,[69] Pauline Theologies,[70] and New Testament Theologies[71] do not consider the extent of the atonement in Paul when these works discuss Paul's soteriology and atonement. The only recent book available that exegetically investigates the extent of the atonement in Paul is by Tom Barnes.[72] His thesis is that limited atonement is *the* biblical view of atonement and that this view strengthens the church. Barnes' work is helpful since he argues his thesis from many biblical texts, since he demonstrates how a correct understanding of limited atonement strengthens the church, and since he writes in a clear and accessible style for the popular Christian community.

However, from an academic perspective, Barnes' book has significant weaknesses. His work is exclusively written for a popular Christian and Evangelical audience instead of for the broader academic community, and he often assumes confessional presuppositions throughout the book without defending them. Consequently, he neither interacts with previous or contemporary scholarship on the extent of the atonement nor with previous or contemporary biblical scholarship on the atonement in Paul. Furthermore, since Barnes argues his thesis from a variety of biblical texts, his analysis of texts from the Pauline corpus lacks detailed exegesis. Once more, since Barnes is concerned with demonstrating that particular atonement is *the* biblical view of the atonement, he broadens his investigation to all of the relevant texts (not just the Pauline ones) that he deems to support his thesis. On the other hand, my current book investigates the extent of the atonement in Paul's theology by offering a detailed exegesis of all of the relevant Pauline texts and by critically

---

[69]E.g. Gerald F. Hawthorne, Ralph P. Martin, and Daniel G. Reid (eds.), *Dictionary of Paul and His Letters* (Downers Grove, IL: InterVarsity Press, 1993). This neglect was not rectified in the recent edition: e.g., Daniel G. Reid (ed.), *The IVP Dictionary of the New Testament* (Downers Grove, IL: InterVarsity Press, 2004).

[70]Herman Ridderbos, *Paul: An Outline of His Theology* (Grand Rapids: Eerdmans, 1966), 182-97; J.C. Becker, *Paul, the Apostle: The Triumph of God in Life and Thought* (Philadelphia: Fortress, 1980), 182-212; James D.G. Dunn, *The Theology of Paul, the Apostle* (Grand Rapids: Eerdmans, 1998), 207-33; Thomas R. Schreiner, *Paul: An Apostle of God's Glory in Christ* (Downers Grove, IL: InterVarsity Press, 2001), 219-36; Udo Schnelle, *Apostle Paul: His Life and Theology*, trans. M. Eugene Boring (Grand Rapids: Baker, 2005), 442-54.

[71]Rudolph Bultmann, *The Theology of the New Testament*, trans. Kendrick Grobel, First Published in 1951 and in 1955 as 2 vols (Waco: Baylor University, 2007), 63-345; George Eldon Ladd, *A Theology of the New Testament*, revised edition (Grand Rapids: Eerdmans, 1974); Adolf Schlatter, *The Theology of the Apostles: The Development of New Testament Theology*, trans. Andreas J. Köstenberger (Grand Rapids: Baker, 1999; First published in 1922), 228-51; Frank Thielman, *Theology of the New Testament: A Canonical and Synthetic Approach* (Grand Rapids: Zondervan 2005), 219-479; Thomas R. Schreiner, *New Testament Theology: Magnifying God in Christ* (Grand Rapids: Baker, 2008).

[72]*Atonement Matters: A Call to declare the Biblical View of the Atonement* (Webster, NY: Evangelical Press, 2008).

Introduction

engaging the relevant scholarship that is related to the book's thesis.

Many of the current works that argue in favor of particular atonement are systematic theologies. For example, the systematic theologies of Millard Erickson and Wayne Grudem discuss the extent of the atonement in ways that are helpful and informative, and Grudem in fact argues in favor of particular atonement.[73] Their method is true to the discipline of systematic theology in that they discuss the different views and in that they extrapolate from a variety of biblical texts to support the different positions. In light of such a systematic approach, there is a limit to the amount of detailed exegetical work that can be done in both these and other systematic theologies. Moreover, in light of the holistic approach of a systematic theology, such a work cannot alone concern itself with an investigation of a singular biblical author's view of any particular doctrine, not even an investigation of something as important as the extent of the atonement.[74] Therefore, those who desire to know a particular New

---

[73] Erickson, *Christian Theology*, 779-858, esp. 842-58. Wayne H. Grudem, *Systematic Theology* (Grand Rapids: Zondervan, 2000), 568-603, esp. 594-603. For similar methods of discussing the extent of the atonement in classic systematic theologies antecedent to Erickson and Grudem, see R.L. Dabney, *Systematic Theology*, 2nd ed. (St. Louis: Presbyterian Publishing Co., 1878), 518-28; Loraine Boettner, *Studies in Theology*, 4th ed. (Grand Rapids: Eerdmans, 1957), 315-339; Louis Berkhof, *Systematic Theology*, 4th ed. (Grand Rapids: Eerdmans, 1977), 392-99 (although as many Calvinists, Berkhof spends the majority of his discussion simply defending particular atonement).

[74] Recent Arminian responses to particular atonement have neither argued their case with detailed exegesis that allows the categories of a New Testament author's view of the extent of the atonement determine the categories by which these scholars argue in favor of general atonement. Rather, similar to their Calvinist interlocutors, Arminian interpreters have often disguised their systematic theological arguments in the costume of New Testament exegesis. Poor exegesis from Arminian critics is best illustrated in the most recent work of Kenneth Keathley (*Salvation and Sovereignty: A Molinist Approach* [Nashville: Broadman & Holman, 2010], esp. 191-210). After concluding the last chapter, Keathley states that "exegetically speaking, proponents of the limited atonement position are in a difficult spot." He then goes on to reject particular atonement. The problem with his chapter on the atonement (and with the entire monograph) is not that he disagrees with particular atonement, but that he does not offer a detailed exegetical critique of and response to it, while he simultaneously criticizes without substantiation Calvinistic exegesis. Rather, he simply cites a few texts that support the competing positions that he discusses and he asserts that universal atonement makes the best sense of all of the texts that seemingly support particular atonement. Even if Keathley is right (and I do not think that he is), his work is unconvincing due to its poor and (often) lack of exegesis. Arminians and Calvinists alike have been too occupied with refuting (Arminians) or vindicating (Calvinists) the TULIP with the result that they have failed to consider a basic and important question regarding the extent of the atonement: viz., what is a particular New Testament author's view of the extent of the atonement? As a result of neglect to this question, both Arminians and Calvinists have failed to let this question be the motivation behind their analysis and investigation of the biblical material. Instead, much of the works of Arminians and Calvinists on the extent of the atonement begin with the premise that the

Testament author's view of the extent of Jesus' death cannot solely look to any one systematic theology, but one must look to a work that rigorously engages the ancient texts with a detailed exegetical analysis of the relevant texts. In light of the absence of such a detailed investigation of Paul's letters that searches for his understanding of the extent of Jesus' death, this work seeks to fill this lacuna.

Chapter-by-Chapter Summary

Chapter 1 has introduced the thesis, method, purpose for writing the book, and my contribution to the discussion, and it has offered a selective history of research of both the discussion of the extent of atonement and atonement in Pauline scholarship. Chapter 2 (Humanity's Spiritual Plight in Paul's Anthropology) discusses Paul's perception of humanity in light of his conception of sin. I argue that Paul deems humanity to be completely corrupted by sin as a result of Adam's transgression and that this corruption destroys humanity's ability to respond to God's great act of salvation in Jesus.

Chapter 3 (Divine and Human Agency in Paul's Soteriology) discusses God's role and the human's role in salvation according to Paul's soteriology. I argue that Paul suggests that divine agency surrounds human agency in his soteriology. The chapter also investigates relevant Jewish texts that discuss both God's role and the human's role in salvation. This chapter serves to argue that Paul's conception of God's role in salvation has strong roots both in the Hebrew Bible and in Second Temple Judaism and that in Paul, the Hebrew Bible, and in certain fragments of Second Temple Judaism human agency is consequent to and the result of divine agency, and only those whom God has chosen to be part of the believing community receive God's soteriological benefits.

Chapter 4 (The Purpose and benefits of Jesus' Death in Paul's Atonement-Theology) argues that Paul suggests that Jesus' death both actually

---

TULIP is either right (Calvinists) or wrong (Arminians) or that the L in the TULIP is either right (Calvinists) or wrong (Arminians), and both interpreters approach the biblical material seeking to justify their premises *a priori*. For a few examples of this method from Arminians and Calvinists from recent publications, see Norman L. Geisler, *Chosen But Free*, 2nd ed. (Bloomington, Minn.: Bethany House, 2001); David Hunt and James White, *Debating Calvinism* (Multnomah, Or.: Multnomah, 2004); David Hunt, *What Love is This: Calvinism's Misrepresentation of God* (Bend, Or.: The Berean Call, 2004); Jerry L. Walls and Joseph R. Dongell, *Why I Am Not A Calvinist* (Downers Grove, IL: InterVarsity Press, 2004); David N. Steele, Curtis C. Thomas, S. Lance Quinn, *The Five Points of Calvinism: Defined, Defended, and Documents*, 2nd ed. (Phillipsburg, NJ: P&R, 2004); Duane Edward Spencer, *TULIP: The Five Points of Calvinism in Light of Scripture*, 7th ed. (Grand Rapids: Baker, 2007). For an Arminian effort to respond exegetically to a Calvinistic reading of atonement, see Ben Witherington III, *The Problem with Evangelical Theology: Testing the Exegetical Foundations of Calvinism, Dispensationalism, and Wesleyanism* (Waco: Baylor University Press, 2005).

Introduction 31

(not hypothetically) atones for the sins of Christian Jews and Christian Gentiles and that his death actually accomplished soteriological benefits for those for whom he died. The chapter also investigates the concept of atonement in the Hebrew Bible and in the various segments of Second Temple Judaism by looking at Leviticus 16 and 2 and 4 Maccabees. The chapter especially investigates the purpose and benefits of atonement in these Jewish texts, and it argues that these texts are the background in front of which interpreters of Paul should understand his atonement-theology. I also argue that Paul suggests that because Jesus' death actually atoned for the sins of all elect Jews and Gentiles and accomplished their salvation and because divine agency surrounds human agency in Paul's soteriology, Jesus' death serves as the foundational reason why all (and only those) Jews and Gentiles who express faith in Jesus will participate in God's great act of salvation in Jesus in Paul's atonement-theology.

Chapter 5 (Conclusion) ties together chapters 2-4 and infers implications from them. The concluding chapter suggests that Paul's anthropology, the Jewish background behind Paul's conception of atonement, his view of divine and human agency in the salvation process, his certainty that Jesus actually (not hypothetically) achieved atonement, forgiveness of sins, and salvation for those whom he died, and his certainty that Jesus' death will actually save from God's wrath everyone who believes suggest that Jesus exclusively died to atone for the sins of and to provide salvation for those elect Jews and Gentiles whom God predestined for salvation before the foundation of the world. These are the very ones whom Paul thought would believe the gospel and who would reap the soteriological benefits of Jesus' death. Chapter 5 also offers ways New Testament scholars and theologians can push forward the discussion of the extent of the atonement in Paul.

Chapter 2

Humanity's Spiritual Plight in Paul's Anthropology

Introduction

This chapter discusses Paul's perception of humanity's spiritual plight in his anthropology. I argue here that Paul deems the entire human condition to be under the power of sin as a result of Adam's transgression and that he deems such power destroys humanity's ability to respond by faith to God's great act of salvation in Jesus Christ.[1] The three major arguments that I put forth to advance the thesis of this chapter are as follows: (1) Paul interprets the defective spiritual condition of Jews and Gentiles to be a direct corollary of Adam's transgression. This argument is developed under the heading of the *nachwirgung* of Adam's transgression. (2) The law's entrance into salvation-history exacerbated the defective spiritual condition of Jews and Gentiles. This argument is developed under the heading of the *nachwirgung* of Torah's entrance into salvation-history. (3) Jews and Gentiles are slaves under sin's power.[2]

The *Nachwirgung* of Adam's Transgression[3]

The Universal Power of Sin
Romans 5:12-21 (esp. 5:12) is the classical text to which interpreters often point in the Pauline corpus to defend original sin.[4] In his radical rereading of

---

[1] Approaching Paul's soteriology from plight to solution has been strongly contested by E.P. Sanders, *Paul and Palestinian Judaism* (Minneapolis: Fortress, 1977), 442-515.

[2] A book length treatment either has been or could be devoted to many of the texts that I discuss throughout this monograph. Thus, this work will by no means attempt to offer a detailed exegesis of every text or attempt to survey all of the relevant secondary literature. For a detailed analysis and survey of all of the relevant literature, the reader should see the critical commentaries of the relevant texts and related monographs.

[3] Some of the material in this chapter overlaps with my book *One New Man: The Cross and Racial Reconciliation in Pauline Theology* (Nashville: Broadman & Holman, 2010). I have produced the overlapping material with their permission.

[4] For a discussion of Rom. 5:12 and original sin in Paul by the fathers, see David Weaver, "From Paul to Augustine: Romans 5:12 in Early Christian Exegesis," *St. Vladimir's Theological Quarterly* 27 (1983): 187-206; idem, "The Exegesis of Romans

Romans, Stanley K. Stowers vociferated against such an appeal by boldly stating that Paul is unconcerned in Romans 5:12-21 in demonstrating "a timeless psychology or anthropology of sin form the story of Adam's fall."[5] Although he (in my view) grossly overstated his case (since he surprisingly neither seriously interacted with the text of Romans 5:12-21 nor with arguments that counter his reading, but baldly asserted that the traditional reading is unviable and commenced to affirm his view based on this assertion), Stowers has a point. In Romans 5:12-21, neither Paul's main concern nor his argument has anything to do with original sin. Instead, he offers an Adam-Christ comparison and contrast with the intent of further developing the theme of the assurance of hope, an assurance possessed by all of those who have been justified by faith and an assurance that Paul began to expound in Romans 5:1-11.[6] But Paul discusses this hope as he presents the universal effects of Adam's sin upon the entire creation.

Paul's argument in Romans 5:12-21 is grammatically complex since he introduces the text in Romans 5:12 with the prepositional phrase διὰ τοῦτο, follows this phrase with the comparative adverb ὥσπερ, truncates the comparison in 5:13-17, and again takes up the comparison in 5:18-21.[7] The words διὰ τοῦτο and ὥσπερ in 5:12 and the two inferential particles ἄρα οὖν, another comparative adverb ὡς, and the comparative phrase οὕτως καὶ in 5:18 support that he introduces an argument in 5:12 that he truncates until 5:18. This presentation means that 5:13-17 is parenthetical material and is not central to the argument of 5:12-21. Διὰ τοῦτο in 5:12a is possibly both anaphoric and kataphoric,[8] for the phrase does not grammatically appear to connect explicitly with what precedes but with what follows while the text

---

5:12 Among the Greek Fathers and Its Implications for the Doctrine of Original Sin: The 5th-12th Centuries," *St. Vladimir's Theological Quarterly* (1985): 133-59. For original sin in Paul and for a bibliography, see Stanley E. Porter, "The Pauline Concept of Original Sin, in Light of Rabbinic Background," *Tyndale Bulletin* 41 (1990): 3-30.

[5]Stanley K. Stowers, *A Rereading of Romans: Jews Justice, and Gentiles* (New Haven: Yale University Press, 1994), 251-55.

[6]So Thomas R. Schreiner, *Romans*, BECNT (Grand Rapids: Baker, 1998), 245-49. Against James D.G. Dunn, *Romans 1-8*, WBC 38A (Nashville: Word, 1988), 1:242, 271.

[7]For a different reading of the syntax, see Peter J. Leithart, "Adam, Moses, and Jesus," *CTJ* 43 (2008): 264-65 n. 15.

[8]Against Karl Barth, *The Epistle to the Romans*, trans. Edwyn C. Hoskyns, 7th edition (Oxford: Oxford University Press, 1965), 164-65; Ernst Käsemann, *Commentary on Romans*, trans. Geoffrey Bromiley (Grand Rapids: Eerdmans, 1980), 141-42; Porter, "The Pauline Concept of Original Sin," 20-21; C.E.B. Cranfield, *Romans*, ICC, 11th edition (New York: T. & T. Clark, 2004), 1:271-72; Ben Witherington, III, *The Problem with Evangelical Theology: Testing the Exegetical Foundations of Calvinism, Dispensationalism, and Wesleyanism* (Waco: Baylor University Press, 2005), 12. So Anders Nygren (*Commentary on Romans*, trans. Carl C. Rasmussen [Philadelphia: Muhlenberg Press, 1949], 206-12) argues that 5:12-21 relates to the argument that precedes and follows 5:12.

thematically connects with the argument of Romans 1:18-5:11 and Romans 6:1-8:11.[9] If this is correct, Paul's words flow from 1:18-5:11 and anticipate in 5:12a the inference in 5:18-21. Paul's argument in the entire unit appears to be that just as Adam's disobedience introduced sin and death to all (exacerbated by the entrance of the law into salvation-history), so also Jesus' obedience conquered the power of sin introduced to humanity by Adam's disobedience and produced life for all (5:12-21).

As stated earlier, the concept of original sin is not Paul's central concern, but this idea nevertheless emerges from Romans 5:12.[10] Paul refers to the "one man" who sinned in 5:12, and he posits that this "one man" is indeed "Adam" in 5:14.[11] He continues by speaking of the "transgression of Adam" (5:14), "the transgression of the one" (5:15, 17), "judgment from the one" (5:16, 18), "the one who sinned" (5:16), the "reign of death through the one" (5:17), and "the disobedience of the one man" (5:19). He refers to Jesus' obedience as "the gift from the one man" (5:15, 17), "acquittal through the one man" (5:18), and "the obedience of the one" (5:19). Paul's use of the adverbs ὥσπερ (5:12, 19), ὡς (5:15-16, 18-19), and οὕτως καὶ (5:15, 18) throughout 5:12-20 elucidate the Adam-Christ comparative contrast.

Regarding the *nachwirkung* of Adam's transgression, Paul states that "sin entered into the world through one man, death through sin, and so death spread to all men with the result that all sin" (Rom. 5:12; cf. 2 Esdr. 3:7-8 [NRSV]; 4 Ezra 3:21). Since the "one man" who introduced sin to the creation is Adam (cf. 5:14), Paul here must be alluding to Genesis 2-3. Adam's disobedience introduced sin into God's good creation (cf. Gen. 1-3), and a universal reign of sin immediately followed his disobedience.[12] After Adam sinned, God first curses his good creation (cf. Gen. 3:14-21). This curse and the events that followed suggest that the human condition after the disobedience of Adam radically changed after his transgression. Prior to sin's entrance into the creation, Adam enjoyed God, his presence, and his creation, but after he sinned he fled from God's presence and he cultivated God's creation by the sweat of his brow (cf. Gen. 3). Because of his transgression, God cursed (1) the animals (Gen. 3:14), (2) the woman (Gen. 3:16), (3) the man (Gen. 3:17), and (4) the

---

[9]For examples of a kataphoric use of διὰ τοῦτο, see Matt. 13:13; 24:44; Mark 12:24; John 5:16, 18; 8:47; 10:17; 12:18, 39; Rom. 1:26; 13:6; Eph. 6:13; 1 Thess. 2:13; 3:7-8; 2 Thess. 2:11; 1 Tim. 1:16; 2 Tim. 2:10; Phlm. 1:15; Heb. 2:1; 9:15; 1 John 3:1.

[10]Unless I am misreading him, Witherington (an Arminian) basically understands the argument of the text the same as I, although we disagree on certain exegetical details and theological implications of the text. However, he reads an Arminian view of atonement and salvation into texts that say nothing about general atonement or hypothetical universal salvation, and he imports an Arminian interpretation of 1 Tim. 2:3-5 and Titus 3:5-6 on to Rom. 5:12-21. Based on his horizontal and retroactive reading of Paul, he suggests that interpreters should read Rom. 5:12-21 in light of 1 Tim. 2:3-5 and Titus 3:5-6. See Witherington, *Evangelical Theology*, 10-20, esp. 14-16.

[11]Unless otherwise indicated, all translations of biblical texts are my own.

[12]Similarly John Calvin, *Institutes of the Christian Religion*, trans. Henry Beveridge (Grand Rapids: Eerdmans, 1997), 2.1.5.

ground (Gen. 3:17-19). This universal curse fulfilled God's promise to Adam in Genesis 2:17 that if he should eat from the forbidden tree, he would certainly die.

God's curse was both physical and spiritual death. Physical death seems apparent in Genesis 3:19 by God's remarks to Adam and Eve that they would return to dust. But spiritual death was also part of God's promise in Gen 2:17 and part of the curse in Genesis 3. This is evident in the basic storyline of Genesis 3. Genesis 3:8 states that Adam and Eve fled from God after they sinned. Genesis 3:16 states that "enmity" would exist between "his seed" and between "her seed" and that the seed of the serpent would crush the heel of the "seed of the woman" while the "seed of the woman" would crush the head of the "seed of the serpent." Moreover, from Genesis 3 until the end of the Hebrew Scriptures, the story of humanity is one of perpetual spiritual failure, for spiritual death manifests itself by means of humanity's sinful actions. Examples from the Hebrew Scriptures are plentiful. For the sake of space, a few selected examples must suffice.

After Genesis 3, spiritual death first manifests itself through Cain. Eve conceived Cain and Abel after she and Adam transgressed God's command and thus introduced sin into God's good creation (Gen. 4:1, cf. 3:1-24). When Cain and Abel presented offerings to God, he rejected Cain's offering and accepted Abel's (Gen. 4:3-5). Genesis 4:7 supports that sin ruled over Cain since God informs Cain of the presence of sin in his life and since he exhorts him to master the power of sin. Cain became angry with God after he rejected his offering (Gen. 4:6). He killed his brother (Gen. 4:8), and he lied to God when he questioned him about Abel (Gen. 4:9).

Another example of spiritual death's manifestation through sinful actions occurs in Genesis 6. There the author states that the population had vastly increased (cf. Gen. 5:1-6:1). With humanity's numerical prosperity, sin likewise increased. The apex of humanity's sin in Genesis 6 is sexual relationships between the sons of God and the daughters of men (Gen. 6:2, 4). Although commentators do not agree on the identity of the sons of God since the text does not explicitly state their identity,[13] the text conspicuously states that the sexual relationships between the sons of God and the daughters of men offended God and provoked him to "blot out" humanity. Genesis 6:5-6 states that "the Lord saw that the evil of men increased in the land, and every form of thoughts in his heart was only evil all the day. And the Lord regretted that he made man in the earth, and he grieved in his heart."

Israel's constant disobedience to God in the wilderness suggests that Adam's transgression caused spiritual death. YHWH showed his power to Israel by judging Egypt with various plagues (Exod. 5-11), by delivering the nation from slavery (Exod. 12-13), and by destroying Pharaoh and his army in the sea (Exod. 14. Immediately after YHWH delivered Israel from slavery and destroyed Pharaoh in the sea (Exod. 12:33-14:31), Israel sang a song of praise

---

[13]For discussion of the sons of God and the relevant Jewish texts, see Kenneth A. Mathews, *Genesis*, NAC (Nashville: Broadman & Holman, 2003), 22-35.

to YHWH (Exod. 15:1-21). As the nation journeyed in the wilderness without food and shelter, the people grumbled against Moses (Exod. 16:2). They accused him of bringing them out of Egypt in order to kill them (Exod. 16:3).

Sin and thus spiritual stubbornness was the reason for Israel's grumblings against Moses. This is supported by the nation's attack against Moses. Israel's attack against him was an attack against YHWH himself since Moses led the people out of Egypt as he was instructed by Yahweh (Num. 11:1; 12:1-9). As Moses and Israel journeyed through the wilderness, the people again grumbled against Moses because they lacked water (Exod. 17:1-2). The people accused Moses of leading them out of Egypt in order to kill them in the wilderness (Exod. 17:3).

Israel's spiritual stubbornness is further evident when the spies returned to give a report about the land (Num. 13:25-33). The spies informed the people that they could not possess the land since its inhabitants were too large for Israel to overcome (Num. 13:32-33). Consequently, Israel cried out to YHWH and wept (Num 14:1). The sons of Israel subsequently "murmured" against Moses and Aaron (Num. 14:1; cf. 16:11, 41); they wished that they were still in Egypt (Num. 14:2); they accused YHWH of wanting to bring them out of Egypt to kill them (Num. 14:3), and they expressed that they preferred to return to Egypt rather than enter into the new land (Num. 14:3).

Israel became bitter. The nation desired to stone Moses and Aaron (Num. 14:10). YHWH's response to Moses' prayer reveals that the people's grumblings were not simply a matter of their questioning Moses' leadership or the leadership of Aaron. Rather, the people were refusing to trust YHWH (Num. 14:11). Israel responded this way on account of the nation's rebellious hearts (cf. Num .14:9). The people's response can *only* be accredited to their sin (Num. 14:18-19).

The Golden Calf incident also demonstrates the universal impact of sin. In Exodus 19:3, Moses went up to Mt. Sinai to converse with God. In Exodus 19:3-32:19, Moses spends much time on Mt. Sinai receiving YHWH's law for the people. Because of Moses' delay, the people became restless (Exod. 32:1). They summoned Aaron to make a god for them who would lead them through the wilderness (Exod. 32:1). Aaron appeased the people's request. He created for them a Golden Calf from the jewelry that they acquired while enslaved in Egypt (Exod. 32:2-4). Aaron erected the calf, and the people proclaimed: "These are your gods, Israel, who caused you to come up from the land of Egypt" (Exod. 32:4). Aaron encouraged the nation to worship the calf although this worship should have been ascribed only to YHWH (Exod. 32:5-6; cf. Exod. 20:3-6). Aaron built an altar before the Golden Calf (Exod. 32:5), held a feast in its honor (Exod 32:5), and allowed the people to bring burnt offerings and peace offerings to it (Exod. 32:5).

Israel's worship of the calf was idolatry. The nation's idolatry violated the first and second commandments (cf. Exod. 20:1-6), for the nation broke its covenant with YHWH, the very covenant that (without hesitation) it promised to honor (cf. Exod. 24). Exodus confirms sin's impact on Israel in Exodus 32:7-8 when YHWH tells Moses that Israel "has acted wickedly" and that it has turned aside from obeying him to worship false gods. YHWH further reveals Israel's stubbornness in Exodus 32:9 when he states that the nation was a "stiff-necked-people."

The universal impact of sin is evident in the constant failure of Israel's dynasty. This is evident from the life of Saul. He had a great beginning, but a tragic end. He was a handsome Benjamite (1 Sam. 9:1-2), Israel's first king (1 Sam. 9:15-16; 10:17-24; 15:1), and he defeated Israel's enemies (e.g., 1 Sam. 11; 14:47-52). However, he often disobeyed YHWH and Samuel, YHWH'S prophet. Saul's digression is especially seen toward the end of his life.

In 1 Samuel 15, YHWH commands Saul to destroy Amalek and his property (1 Sam. 15:1-3). Saul disobeyed this command. He ambushed the Amalekites (1 Sam. 15:6), but he spared the Kenites (1 Sam. 15:6) and Agag, the king of the Amalekites (1 Sam. 15:8-9). Saul's actions might at first appear to be acts of mercy toward those whom he spared, but Samuel's response to Saul suggests that Saul sinned against YHWH. YHWH said that he regretted that he made Saul king, "for he has turned from after me, and he has not caused my word to rise" (1 Sam. 15:11). Samuel later states that Saul's actions were evil (1 Sam. 15:19). Samuel's other statements in the text imply that Saul was rebellious, insubordinate, and that he rejected YHWH's word (1 Sam. 15:23). After Samuel rebuked Saul, Saul responds by saying "I have sinned because I have transgressed the mouth of YHWH and your words, because I feared the people and listened to their voice" (1 Sam. 15:24).

Samuel tells Saul that he "has rejected the word of YHWH" (1 Sam. 15:25). Consequently, "YHWH will reject" him as Israel's king (1 Sam. 15:26). More than once the author states that an "evil spirit of YHWH" came upon Saul (1 Sam. 16:14-15; 18:10; 19:9; cf. 16:16, 23).[14] Saul failed to protect Israel from Goliath (1 Sam. 17). He spent most of his kingship relentlessly pursuing David's life (1 Sam. 18:10-19; 19:2; 24:1-22; 26:1-25), and he sought help from the occult instead of from YHWH (1 Sam. 28:1-25).

Certain aspects of David's life reveal the devastating effects of Adam's sin. The chief example of the effect of sin in David's life is his episode with Bathsheba. David committed adultery with and impregnated Bathsheba (2 Sam. 11:1-5). David attempted to cover up his sin by summoning Uriah from war (2 Sam. 11:6). He sought to persuade Uriah to abandon his military responsibilities and sleep with his wife during the time of war in order to cover up his sexual sin with Bathsheba (2 Sam. 11:8-13). David executed Uriah by placing him on the frontlines of war (2 Sam. 11:14-17). The author concludes the narrative in 2 Sam 11:27 with the following words: "But the thing which David had done was evil in the eyes of YHWH."

The effect of Adam's transgression can be seen through the lives of the various kings that succeeded David. When David died, Solomon assumed his father's throne (1 Kgs 1:38-53). Solomon brought much success to the kingdom (1 Kgs 6-8). However, as with David, his father, sin impeded Solomon's reign and brought devastating consequences upon the dynasty.

---

[14] 1 Sam. 16:14 especially states that "the Spirit of YHWH turned away from Saul."

YHWH blessed Solomon's reign. He blessed Solomon with wisdom (1 Kgs 3:16-28), with royal officials (1 Kgs 4:1-19), with wealth (1 Kgs 4:20-34; 2 Chr. 1:14-17; 2 Chr. 8:13-30), with alliances with other kings (1 Kgs 5:1-12), and with a temple (1 Kgs 6:1-8:66; 2 Chr. 2:1-7:10). However, Solomon's demise and the demise of his kingdom began when Solomon married many foreign women (1 Kgs 11:1). YHWH commanded Solomon to obey his law and to walk faithfully before him (1 Kgs 9:4). YHWH likewise warned Solomon that if he disobeyed him by breaking the covenant, he would expel Israel from the land (1 Kgs 9:6-7). Part of YHWH's covenantal stipulations was a prohibition against idolatry (1 Kgs 9:6; cf. Exod. 20:2-3), but Solomon broke the covenant by marrying foreign women who worshipped other gods and by turning his heart after their gods (1 Kgs 11:4-13).

Solomon's sin divided the kingdom between Israel and Judah (1 Kgs 12:16-24). Many of the people in both the northern and southern parts of the kingdom rebelled against YHWH. Kings-Chronicles record the spiritual decline of the kingdom and the apostasy of the kingship. There was conflict both within and without Solomon's kingdom on account of Solomon's sin. YHWH raised up adversaries against Israel (1 Kgs 11:14-25). Those within Solomon's own house rebelled against Israel (1 Kgs 11:26-40). Furthermore, virtually all of the kings who succeeded Solomon were evil and rebelled against YHWH. They practiced idolatry (1 Kgs 12:1-15:3 [2 Chr. 10:1-19], 26, 34; 22:51-53; 2 Kgs 3:2-3), committed evil in the sight of YHWH (1 Kgs 16:7, 30-32; 2 Kgs 13:2; 15:8-9, 17-18, 23-24, 27-28; 16:1-2; 21:1-9, 19-22; 23:31-32; 24:8-9; 2 Chr. 11:14-17), and led the kingdom away from YHWH (2 Kgs 17:7-23).

The universal impact of sin is also evident from the prophets. Isaiah and Jeremiah warn Israel and Judah of exile because of their sin. Isaiah states that Israel is a sinful nation, weighed down with iniquity, an offspring of evil doers, and sons who act corruptly (Isa. 1:4). Isaiah also states that Israel abandoned YHWH, despised him, and turned from him (Isa. 1:4; 65:1-3). Isaiah even calls Israel a harlot on account of the nation's spiritual infidelity (Isa 1:21). Jeremiah prophesies that evil overtook the nation (Jer. 2:3), because it did not walk in accordance with YHWH's stipulations (Jer. 2:2-37). Jeremiah calls Israel a spiritual harlot and a spiritual adulteress because of its disobedience to YHWH (Jer. 3:6-10).

Ezekiel's prophesy came to him when the nation was in exile because of its sin (Ezek. 1:1-3). YHWH informs the nation through Ezekiel that he would judge the people because of the nation's sin against him (Ezek. 5:1-7:19). Israel defiled the temple (Ezek. 7:20) and endorsed evil (Ezek. 11:2). The nation's religious leaders were corrupt; the prophets were false prophets (Ezek. 13:2); the elders were idolaters (Ezek. 14:1-11; cf. 22:1-31), and the religious shepherds were faithless (Ezek. 34:1-10).

Hosea depicts Israel as a spiritual harlot, and he compares the nation's sin to Adam's transgression (Hos. 6:7). Amos states that YHWH will judge the nation because of its transgression and that YHWH will judge the nation for its iniquities (Amos 2:6; 3:3). Micah speaks of those who scheme iniquity (Micah 2:1). Habakkuk laments because of the iniquity that surrounds him (Hab. 1:3).

Humanity's Spiritual Plight 39

The universal impact of sin was also evident and acknowledged in certain factions of Second Temple Judaism. The Qumran sectarians, for example, expressed that the "flesh" is in bondage to sin's power (1QS 4:20-21). Mankind commits iniquities, rebellions, sins, has a perverse heart, and walks in darkness (1QS 11:9-10; 1QH 2; cf. 4 Ezra 4, 7, 8). According to some in the community, there are two types of people: people of darkness (in contrast to the people of God) and the people of light. The people of darkness are cursed and unclean (1QM 13:5).[15] In addition, other Second Temple texts assign blame for sin's power. The author of Jubilees 3:17-32 blames Adam, Eve, and the serpent for sin. The author of Sirach 25:24 only blames Eve. The author of Wisdom 2:24 blames only the devil. The author of 2 Baruch 54:19 asserts that Adam is responsible for his own sin, but everyone else is his own Adam.[16]

In light of the above, Paul's sentiment that "sin entered the world through one man and death through sin, and death spread to all men with the result that all sin" (Rom. 5:12) refers to the universal impact of sin that resulted from Adam's transgression. Thus, the *nachwirgung* of Adam's transgression is evident amongst Jewish communities in the Old Testament and in certain factions of Second Temple Judaism. Paul confirms the universal impact of Adam's sin with the phrases εἰς τὸν κόσμον and εἰς πάντας ἀνθρώπους in 5:12. Adam's sin produced death into the world to all people. Paul also expresses in Romans 5:12 that the agent through whom sin and death entered the world was Adam and the manner by which sin entered the world and brought a universal curse upon the entire creation was his disobedience.[17] Paul's logic runs as follows: (1) Adam's sin → into the world = death for Adam and the world, (2) Adam's sin → spread of death into the world = the spread of death to all men, and (3) Adam's sin → the spread of sin and death to all men = humanity's bondage to the power of sin.

The latter clause (translated above as "with the result that all sin") in Romans 5:12b has been the subject of intense debate among New Testament scholars because of the prepositional phrase ἐφ' ᾧ that introduces the relative clause ἐφ' ᾧ πάντες ἥμαρτον. There are numerous translation options.[18] Some interpreters suggest that ᾧ is a masculine pronoun, whose antecedent is an implicit νόμος,[19] θάνατος,[20] or ἄνθρωπος.[21] The Adamic interpretation

---

[15]Similarly Udo Schnelle, *Apostle Paul: His Life and Theology*, trans. M. Eugene Boring (Grand Rapids: Baker, 2003), 504-05. Paul's explanation of the origin of sin and death is similar to the author of 4 Ezra (4 Ezra 3:7-22), but differs from other factions of early Judaism.
[16]References from Witherington, *Evangelical Theology*, 13.
[17]I take καὶ οὕτως in a modal sense (cf. Acts 7:8; 27:44; Rom. 11:26; 1 Cor. 11:28; 14:25; 15:11; Gal. 6:2; 1 Thess. 4:17; Heb. 6:15; Jas 2:12; Rev. 9:17).
[18]For a recent summary of the interpretive options, see Brian J. Vickers, *Jesus' Blood and Righteousness* (Wheaton: Crossway, 2006), 125-41; idem, "Grammar and Theology in the Interpretation of Rom. 5:12," *TrinJ* 27 (2006): 271-88.
[19]Frederick W. Danker, "Rom V.12: Sin under Law," *NTS* 14 (1967-68): 428.

has its origins in Augustine who could not read Greek well but relied on the Latin translation *in quo* ("in whom").[22] He interpreted Adam to be the antecedent of ᾧ and the clause ἐφ' ᾧ πάντες ἥμαρτον to mean "in whom" (i.e. in Adam) "all sinned." Accordingly, Paul expresses that Adam was humanity's federal head in that he represented them. Thus, when Adam sinned, all sinned in Adam and all sin originated in Adam.[23] Others have interpreted ᾧ as a neuter word, and they have taken the phrase ἐφ' ᾧ as a conjunction.[24] With this reading, the phrase could be translated as "because"[25] or "so that."[26] Advocates of this reading interpret ᾧ to refer to humanity's participation in Adam's sin with the result that he inherits his depraved nature and the universal curse that resulted from his disobedience.[27] Robert Jewett posits that ἐφ' ᾧ refers to "the realm in which humans were sinning, that is, the κόμος ('world') that is mentioned in vv. 12 and 13."[28] His reading suggests that Adam influences the fate of humanity, and humanity is responsible for its sins that it commits in the world (2 Apoc. Bar 54:15, 19).[29]

That an implicit νόμος is the antecedent of the relative pronoun is possible since Paul has spent Romans 2:1-4:25 discussing the role of Torah in judgment and justification and since he begins to discuss the exacerbation of sin in light of Torah's entrance into salvation-history in Romans 5:13. But this option should be rejected because Romans 5:12 is concerned with Adam's role in introducing sin and death into the world, not with Torah. That θάνατος is the antecedent of the relative pronoun is possible since the term occurs twice in 5:12 and since its last occurrence is in close proximity of the relative pronoun. Nevertheless, the context of 5:12 speaks against this interpretation because Paul states that death is the consequence of Adam's sin, not the reason for which

---

[20]Rudolph Bultmann, "Adam and Christ according to Romans 5," in *Current Issues in New Testament Interpretation: Essays in Honor of Otto A. Piper*, eds. and trans. W. Klassen and G. F. Snyder (New York: Harper & Brothers, 1962), 143-65, esp. 153.

[21]J. Cambier, "Péchés des hommes et péches d' Adam en Rom v. 12," *NTS* 11 (1964-65): 246-53.

[22]Weaver ("From Paul to Augustine," 203 n. 52) asserts without argumentation that some evidence suggests that Augustine's knowledge of Greek improved throughout the course of the Pelagian controversy.

[23]John Murray, *The Imputation of Adam's Sin* (Phillipsburg, NJ: P&R, 1959).

[24]Dunn, *Romans*, 1:273; Joseph Fitzmyer, *Romans*, ABC 33 (New York: Doubleday, 1993), 416; idem, "The Consecutive Meaning of ἐφ' ᾧ in Romans 5.12," *NTS* (1993): 321-39.

[25]Dunn, *Romans*, 1:273; Käsemann, *Romans*, 148.

[26]Fitzmyer, *Romans*, 416; idem, "The Consecutive Meaning," 321-39.

[27]This appears to be Cranfield's view (*Romans*, 1:274-79). However, Cranfield conflates the view that understands ἐφ' ᾧ as a conjunction and that understands humanity to have sinned in their own person since humanity has inherited Adam's sinful nature.

[28]Robert K. Jewett, *Romans*, Hermeneia (Minneapolis, Fortress, 2007), 376. I apologize to both Robert K. Jewett and Paul Jewett for erroneously confusing them and their publications in my previous publications in 2010.

[29]Jewett, 376.

humanity sins. The phrase ἑνὸς ἀνθρώπου could be the antecedent of the relative pronoun, but its distance from the relative pronoun speaks against it. Likewise, κόσμος is a possible antecedent of the relative pronoun if the latter should be understood as a masculine singular, but this understanding is also unlikely on account of both the noun's distance from the relative pronoun and because Paul seems to be expressing a more profound thought in 5:12 besides the idea that humans sin in the world. This more profound idea is that sin universally reigns over the entire creation as a result of Adam's transgression.

The ἐφ' ᾧ construction only occurs in Paul in the New Testament (Rom. 5:12; 2 Cor. 5:4; Phil. 3:12; 4:10). In each occurrence outside of Romans 5:12, the phrase should be interpreted as a conjunctive construction, for the relative pronoun does not point to a grammatical antecedent. Thus, those who interpret ἐφ' ᾧ to have a conjunctive force in 5:12 are on firm ground, for the phrase and the relative pronoun do not point to a singular, grammatical antecedent but to the entire theological concept in 5:12: namely, sin entered the world through Adam, death through sin, and Adam's sin that leads to death results in the fact that all sin.[30] Both the other Pauline uses of the phrase (2 Cor. 5:4; Phil. 3:12; 4:10) and the argument of 5:13-21 support the conjunctive reading.

Paul states in Romans 5:13-14 that the entrance of the law into salvation-history exacerbated the problem of sin, for he states that sin was in the world even before the giving of Torah and that it was not counted as transgression, whereas sin's universal reign over the entire creation was still evident even before the giving of Torah since death reigned from Adam until Moses.[31] Paul's argument in Romans 5:15-21 contrasts Jesus' obedience with Adam's disobedience in order to highlight the superiority of the gift of justification provided through Jesus' obedience over the universal condemnation of sin resulting from Adam's disobedience.[32] Paul first pits Adam's transgression against Jesus' gift in Romans 5:15. He asserts that God's gift, provided through Jesus' obedience, will supremely abound for many since "many died because of the transgression of the one man." Since the grace and gift of God that come to humanity as a result of the obedience of the "one man" in Romans 5:15 refer to justification and eternal life (Rom. 5:17), the death that all died as a result of Adam's sin must include spiritual death in Romans 5:12, for Paul states that the transgression of the one man results in condemnation for all in 5:16.

---

[30]For a detailed discussion of ἐφ' ᾧ that resists committing to any antecedent, see D.L. Turner, "Adam, Christ, and US: The Pauline Teaching of Solidarity in Romans 5:12-21" (Th.D. diss, Grace Theological Seminary, Winona Lake, Ind., 1982), 129-49. This reference is cited in Daniel B. Wallace, *Greek Grammar Beyond the Basics: An Exegetical Syntax of the New Testament* (Grand Rapids: Zondervan, 1996), 342-43, esp. 343 n. 75.
[31]Against Leithart, "Adam, Moses, and Jesus," 257-73, who argues for a positive role of Torah's entrance into salvation-history.
[32]Similarly Cranfield, *Romans*, 1:270.

Romans 5:16-21 affirms the universal impact of Adam's transgression on humanity. Here Paul contrasts Jesus' gift with Adam's sin. Judgment comes as a result of the one who sinned, but the gift results in acquittal "from many transgressions" (ἐκ πολλῶν παραπτώματων) (Rom. 5:16).[33] Prior to Romans 5:16, Paul has only spoken of transgression in the singular, for the singular transgression was another way of referring to Adam's sin (Rom. 5:12-16a). But now, Paul mentions in Romans 5:16 Adam's sin (ἑνὸς ἁμαρτήσαντος) and the judgment that comes as a result along side of the phrase "from many transgressions." This suggests that the "many transgressions" do not refer to Adam's sins, but to the transgressions of all who sin because of Adam's transgression. Paul makes this certain when he contrasts the penalties of the transgression of the one (death, judgment, bondage to sin) with the blessings of the obedience of the one (justification, eternal life, and freedom from sin) in 5:12-21 and with the argument of 5:17-21.[34]

The γὰρ in Romans 5:17 explains 5:16. In 5:17, Paul begins to speak of Adam's sin, because he again speaks of transgression in the singular (παραπτώματι). He states that if death reigns through the transgression of the one, those who receive the gift of righteousness would receive eternal life through Jesus (5:17). Because of the διὰ τοῦτο and ὥσπερ in 5:12, the inferential particles ἄρα οὖν, the adverb ὡς, and the adverbial phrase οὕτως καὶ in 5:18, the latter text continues Paul's initial thought in 5:12 by inferring from Romans 5:15-17 that the gift of Jesus' obedience and the curse of Adam's disobedience are completely antithetical to one another. Paul mentions in 5:18 that "condemnation" comes to all as a result of Adam's sin and that "justification" comes to all as a result of Jesus' obedience. Paul reiterates this contrast in Romans 5:19 by stating that Adam's disobedience made many sinners, and Jesus' obedience made many righteous.

Paul makes a similar argument in 1 Corinthians 15:21-22 with the intent of defending the veracity of a future resurrection (1 Cor .15:1-58). He affirms that Jesus has been raised from the dead (1 Cor. 15:20). To defend this, he then offers an Adam-Christ comparison and contrast in 1 Corinthians 15:21-22. He states since death entered through a man, then resurrection from the dead enters through a man (1 Cor. 15:21). The comparison is that a man brought death and a man brings life, but the contrast is seen in that death comes as a result of the disobedience of the one man but life as a result of the obedience of the other. Paul spends the rest of 1 Corinthians 15 arguing that although death reigns because of Adam's sin, death is not the final word (1 Cor. 15:23-58). Paul affirms that the man who brought death is Adam and the man

---

[33] J.R. Daniel Kirk argues that *dikaiōma* means "reparation" accomplished by a convicted person who satisfies the court and justifies the defendant. In his view, the term should not be translated in Rom 5:16 as justification, but as "reparation," which leads to justification. See "Reconsidering *Dikaiōma* in Romans 5:16," *JBL* 126 (2007): 787-92.

[34] The δικ-word group in Rom 5:16-21 suggests a connection with Rom. 1:16-5:11, for this unit uses the δικ-word group throughout.

Humanity's Spiritual Plight

who brings resurrection-life is Christ when he states "just as" (ὥσπερ) "in Adam all died, thus also" (οὕτως καὶ) "in Christ all will be brought to life" (1 Cor. 15:22).

Finally, Paul concludes the unit of Romans 5:12-21 in Romans 5:20-21 by stating that the law made sin worse; grace abounded over sin through Jesus; sin abounded in death because of Adam, but grace abounded much more resulting in eternal life through Jesus' obedience. Thus, according to Paul in both Romans 5:12-21 and 1 Corinthians 15:21-22, Adam's transgression has a spiral effect upon the entire world (Rom. 4:25; 4 Ezra 3:21). Adam sinned; his sin introduced sin and death into the creation; death reigns over the entire universe, and everyone after Adam personally sins and transgresses, so that everyone is responsible for his individual sins (Rom. 3:23; 4:25).

Sin as Power

The *nachwirgung* of Adam's transgression is further seen in the universal power of sin.[35] Sin in Paul should not only be conceived of as individual transgressions, but as a dominating power. Paul's personification of sin as a power that reigns (Rom. 5:14, 17, 21; 6:12), as an organism that grows and springs to life (Rom. 5:20; 7:9), as a master to which we are enslaved and from which we need emancipation (Rom. 6:7-9, 14-16, 18-19, 22; 7:23, 25; 8:2), as an employer that compensates with death (Rom. 6:23), as a deceiver and executioner that seizes an opportunity to kill its victim (Rom. 7:8, 11; 8:10), as a master under which one lives (Rom. 7:14; Gal. 3:22), as a resident who makes his abode in a community (Rom. 7:17, 20), and as a power that uses the law to produce death (1 Cor. 15:56) support that Paul perceives of sin as a power. Paul discusses the power of sin in Romans 6 while he makes the argument that Christians are no longer slaves to its power. In light of the great promise of Romans 5:21, that Christ conquered the power of sin when the power of sin began to increase after the Torah entered into salvation-history, Paul anticipates a possible inference in Romans 6:1 from the promise of Romans 5:21. He asks: should Christians continue in sin? He forcefully argues in Romans 6:2-8:17 no because Christians have been liberated from sin's power through Christ's death and resurrection and because they too await their final redemption along with the entire creation.

By the question in Romans 6:1, Paul likely intends to ask whether Christians should continue to be dominated by the power of sin, not whether they should commit individual sins. This interpretation seems right, for Paul states that "we died to sin," testified to by our water-baptism (Rom. 6:2-4), "we should walk in newness of life (Rom. 6:4), "our old man has been crucified together with Christ" (Rom. 6:6), "our sinful body has been abolished" (Rom.

---

[35]For a recent work on sin as power in Paul, see T.L. Carter, *Paul and the Power of Sin*, SNTSM 115 (Cambridge: Cambridge University Press, 2003). He argues that Paul's concept of sin as power should be understood to communicate the point that the Torah-observant Jew had no advantage over the law-free Gentile since both groups are under sin's power.

6:6), "we no longer serve sin" (Rom. 6:7), "we died with Christ" (Rom. 6:8), "we should consider ourselves to be dead to sin" (Rom. 6:11), "sin should not reign in our mortal body" (Rom. 6:12), "sin no longer rules over" us (Rom. 6:14), and "we are no longer slaves to sin" (Rom. 6:14-20) but "we have been freed from sin" (Rom. 6:15, 20-22). That sin is a universal power is further supported when he asserts that sin uses the law to increase its power (Rom. 7:7-24) and when he speaks of creation being "under sin" (Rom. 3:9; 7:14; Gal. 3:22) and "in sin" (Rom. 6:1; Eph. 2:1, 5; Col. 2:13). This latter point is especially evident when Paul speaks of the "longing" of creation (Rom. 8:19), the "groaning" of creation (Rom. 8:22), and the "crying out" of creation (Rom. 8:23) as a woman who cries out in labor because of her birth pains. Paul personifies the creation in this manner because it awaits its final emancipation and redemption from sin's power (Rom. 8:21-23). In addition to the above descriptions of sin as power, Paul states that Christ "died to sin once and for all" (Rom. 6:10). The latter statement cannot mean that Jesus died to his personal sin, because the consistent and incontrovertible presentation of Jesus in the New Testament is that he did not sin (2 Cor. 5:21; 1 Pet. 2:23-24).

Paul also speaks of sin as a power when he discusses one's pre-conversion spiritual condition. He speaks of being "in the flesh" (Rom. 8:8-9) as opposed to being "in the Spirit" (Rom. 8:9; Gal. 5:17) or "in Christ" (Rom. 6:11, 23; 8:39; 12:5; 1 Cor. 1:2, 30; 2 Cor. 2:14; 5:17; Gal. 1:22; 2:4; 3:28; 5:6; Eph. 1:3; 2:7; 3:6; Phil. 1:1; Col. 1:2; 1 Thess. 4:16). Scholars have debated for years the meaning of Paul's anthropological terms.[36] The evidence seems to suggest that Paul uses σάρξ in different ways throughout his letters.[37] The contexts in which the term occurs should be the deciding factor in determining its meaning. For example, σάρξ refers to one's physical existence (Rom. 7:18, 25; 1 Cor. 6:16; 7:28; 2 Cor. 4:11; 12:7; Gal. 2:20; Phil. 1:22). In this regard, it can be synonymous with σῶμα. Σάρξ can also refer to one's ethnic heritage (Rom 1:3; 9:5, 8), circumcision (Rom. 2:28), humanity (Rom 3:20; 1 Cor. 1:29; Gal. 1:16; 2:16; Eph. 6:12), the physical body of either animals or humans (1 Cor. 15:39-40, 50; Gal. 4:13-14; 6:12-13; Eph. 2:14; 5:29, 31; 6:5), works (Rom 4:1; Gal. 3:3; 4:23, 29), an ethnic group (Rom. 9:3; 11:14; 1 Cor. 10:18; Eph. 2:11), and the sinful passions (Gal. 5:16). Σάρξ can also refer to sin as a power (Rom. 7:5).

In Romans 7:5, Paul states that "we were in the flesh." That Paul refers to the time when believers were under the power of sin and not simply to

---

[36] For an analysis and bibliography, see Robert K. Jewett, *Anthropological Terms: A Study of Their Use in Conflict Settings* (Leiden: Brill, 1971).
[37] See Rom. 1:3; 2:28; 3:20; 4:1; 6:19; 7:5, 18, 25; 8:3-9, 12, 13; 9:3, 5, 8; 11:14; 13:14; 1 Cor. 1:26, 29; 5:5; 6:16; 7:28; 10:18; 15:39, 50; 2 Cor. 1:17; 4:11; 5:16; 7:1, 5; 10:2-3; 11:18; 12:7; Gal. 1:16; 2:16, 20; 3:3; 4:13 14, 23, 29; 5:13, 16-17, 19, 24; 6:8, 12-13; Eph. 2:3, 11, 14; 5:29, 31; 6:5, 12; Phil. 1:22, 24; 3:3 4; Col 1:22, 24; 2:1, 5, 13, 18, 23; 3:22; 1 Tim. 3:16; Phlm. 1:16.

Humanity's Spiritual Plight

individual sins is evident from the argument of Romans 7:1-6.[38] The fundamental issue in these verses is that those who have been united to Jesus by faith are no longer under the power of Torah because they have died to its power (Rom. 6:1-7:6). To defend this premise, Paul uses an illustration of a woman who is bound to her husband by the Torah as long as the husband lives (Rom .7:2), but Torah no longer binds the woman to her husband when he dies (Rom. 7:2). However, if the woman should marry another husband while her current husband lives, then she is guilty of adultery since she would still be obligated to the law regarding her husband (Rom. 7:3), but she is free to marry whomever she pleases whenever the husband dies (Rom. 7:3). Paul concludes from this that the Jews who were under Torah have died to its power through Jesus' body (i.e. his death) and that they have been joined to him who was raised from the dead so that they would bear fruit to God (Rom. 7:4). That Paul directly addresses Jews in Romans 7 is supported by γινώσκουσιν νόμον λαλῶ ("to those who know the law") (Rom. 7:1). In Romans 7:5, Paul speaks of being under the power of the law by speaking of being "in the flesh." For Paul, subjection under the power of Torah is equivalent to subjection under the power of sin (Rom. 3:9; 6:14-15; Gal. 3:22-23), for one needs redemption from Torah just as he needs redemption from sin (Gal. 3:10-13; 4:4-25).

Romans 7:5 further explains 7:4. This seems right because of the γὰρ that connects Romans 7:5 with 7:4 and because of the conceptual parallels in the two verses: "death to the law through the body of Christ" (Rom. 7:4) versus "sinful passions through the law working in our members" (Rom. 7:5), "united to another person" (Rom. 7:4) versus being "in the flesh" (Rom. 7:5), and "so that we would bear fruit to God" (Rom. 7:4) versus "so that we would bear fruit to death" (Rom. 7:5). Paul concludes the argument of Romans 7:1-6 in 7:6 where he applies the analogy of 7:1-5 to Jewish Christians. He states that Jews in Christ have been severed from Torah's power because they died to Torah (just as the wife of a deceased husband is no longer bound to the law of her husband) with the result that they serve "by means of the newness of the Spirit and not by means of the oldness of the letter" (Rom. 7:6). In other words, when Jews in Adam under Torah were outside of Christ, they were under the power of Torah and thereby under the power of sin, i.e., in the flesh, but in Christ they serve not in the flesh/in the letter of the law, but by means of the power of the Spirit.

Furthermore, Paul states in Ephesians and Colossians that Jewish and Gentile Christians were "dead in transgressions and in sins" prior to their conversion (Eph. 2:1; cf. 2:5; Col. 2:13).[39] If the datives τοῖς παραπτώμασιν and ταῖς ἁμαρτίαις in Ephesians 2:1 and τοῖς παραπτώμασιν in 2:5 are

---

[38] I offer a more extensive exegesis of Rom. 7 below during my discussion of the *nachwirgung* of Torah's entrance into salvation-history.

[39] As scholars know well, Ephesians and Colossians are two of the disputed Pauline letters. Even if it can be proven that Paul did not write Ephesians and Colossians, my appeal to these texts does not hinder my argument, for they could have been written by a Pauline disciple who reflected Paul's theology.

construed as causal datives, Paul means that transgressions and sins are the reason that these Jews and Gentiles were spiritually dead prior to their conversion. Regardless of the function of the datives, that Paul views sin as a power that dominates in Ephesians 2:1 and in 2:5 is likely because he states that the Ephesians formerly walked in their sins "in accordance to the ruler of the authority of the air, the spirit which is now working in the sons of disobedience" (Eph. 2:1). Although Paul states here that the ruler of the air and his spirit are ruling and working in the sons of disobedience instead of transgressions and sins, he still depicts sin as a power because these Gentiles were formerly under the authority of the ruler of the air when they were dead in trespasses and sins, and they were dominated by the power of sin and subjugated under the ruler of the air because they lived disobediently in sin (Eph. 2:2-3). Thus, sin in Paul should not only be understood as individual transgressions, but also as a dominating power that reigns. Yet, sin manifests its dominating power both in and over the lives of its subjects through their individual sinful actions.

Sin as Disobedience

The dominating power of sin through sinful actions is evident in the ensuing argument of Romans 1:18-3:20 after Paul briefly discusses the reason why he is eager to preach the gospel in Rome (Rom. 1:15-17).[40] Paul states that he is eager to preach the gospel to the Roman Christians (Rom. 1:15), because he is not ashamed of the gospel and because the gospel is God's power that produces salvation for all who believe (Rom. 1:16). Paul explicates the saving power of the gospel in Romans 1:17 by stating that God's saving righteousness is revealed in it by faith. Romans 1:18-3:20, then, places the saving power of the gospel alongside of the universal power of sin that results in God's current and eschatological judgment.

Paul states that God's wrath is revealed in the current age upon every form of ungodliness and upon every person who suppresses the truth (Rom. 1:18). God's wrath in Paul is primarily eschatological (Rom. 2:5-16; 3:5; 4:15; 5:9; Eph. 2:3; 5:6; Col. 3:6; 1 Thess. 1:10; 2:16; 5:9),[41] but his wrath (ὀργὴ θεοῦ) in Romans 1:18 refers to his personal, retributive wrath that he unleashes in the current age upon those who suppress his truth. Because he based his

---

[40]Against G. Röhser, *Metaphorik und Personifikation der Sünde* (Tübingen: J.C.B. Mohr, 1987), who argues that sin in the Pauline corpus should not be referred to as a power, but as personified deed. In response to Röhser, see H. Umbach, *In Christus getauft—von der Sünde befreit: Die Gemeinde als sündenfreier Raum bei Paulus* (Göttingen: Vandenhoeck & Ruprecht, 1999). But he too overstates his case in the opposite direction, for he argues that sin in Paul is always a power to which all in Adam are subjected and must be freed by the Spirit and that Paul avoids ἁμαρτία outside of Romans when he talks about deviant behavior since the term conveys the deeper meaning of sin as power.

[41]A.T. Hanson (*The Wrath of the Lamb* [London: SPCK, 1957], 84-85) altogether limits God's wrath to the present age; he denies any eschatological aspect of God's wrath.

argument largely on Romans 1:18-32, C.H. Dodd argued in the middle of the 20th century that God's wrath was not personal, but that it was simply the result of sin taking its full effect in the lives of those who suppressed the truth.[42] Although somewhat disagreeing with Dodd that God's wrath is impersonal, Stephen H. Travis recently argues in a revised work that God's wrath in Romans 1:18-32 is not retributive. He contends instead that God brings judgment upon individuals from within by allowing the transgressions of the offender to reach their full measure. At least Travis is correct to point out that God's wrath in Romans 1:18-32 refers especially to the full outworking of the offender's sins and to God's personal judgment of the offender in his giving him up to commit various sins, but he reads this understanding into texts in Romans (e.g. Rom. 2:6-10) where God's external payment after measuring one's deeds seems to be in view.[43] As I have argued elsewhere,[44] both Dodd and Travis fail to realize that God's handing over of the offender to commit various sins in Romans 1:18-32 is in fact a personal (against Dodd) and a retributive (against Travis) act of God, for his handing over of the offender to commit various sins is his personal and retributive payment for the offender's offense.[45] In the text of Romans 1:18-32, God judges the offender by handing him over to the desires of his heart *after* he suppresses the truth (Rom. 1:18-20), *after* he fails to honor God (Rom. 1:21), and *after* he exchanges the truth of God for a lie (Rom. 1:23).[46]

Paul states that the reason God's wrath is revealed upon those who suppress the truth is because God revealed his eternal power and divine nature to them by means of his creation (Rom. 1:19-20). Instead of worshipping the sovereign God of creation, those who suppress the truth reject God and worship his creation, thereby committing idolatry (Rom. 1:21-23). Paul, thus, states in Romans 1:24, 26, and 28 that God's wrath is revealed in the current age against those who suppress the truth in that God gave them over to a depraved mind to commit various sins to practice a sinful and rebellious lifestyle against God.

---

[42]C.H. Dodd, *The Epistle of Paul to the Romans*, MNTC (London: Hodder & Stoughton, 1932), 21-24; idem, *The Bible and the Greeks*, 2nd ed. (London: Hodder & Stoughton, 1954), 82-95.
[43]Stephen H. Travis, *Christ and the Judgment of God: The Limits of Divine Retribution in New Testament Thought* (Peabody, MA: Hendrickson, 2008), 60-70, 74-84.
[44]Jarvis J. Williams, *Maccabean Martyr Traditions in Paul's Theology of Atonement: Did Martyr Theology Shape Paul's Conception of Jesus's Death?* (Eugene, Or: Wipf and Stock, 2010); idem, *One New Man: The Cross and Racial Reconciliation in Pauline Theology* (Nashville: Broadman & Holman, 2010), chapter 3; idem, "Martyr Theology in Hellenistic Judaism and Paul's Conception of Jesus' Death in Romans 3:21-26," in *Christian Origins and Hellenistic Judaism: Literary and Social Contexts for the New Testament*, eds. Stanley E. Porter and Andrew W. Pitts (Leiden: Brill, Forthcoming); idem, "Violent Atonement in Romans: The Foundation of Paul's Soteriology," *JETS* 53 (2010): 579-99, esp. 588.
[45]See especially Travis' acknowledgement that Paul uses retributive language in Rom. 1:18-32 (*Christ and the Judgment of God,* 62).
[46]A point also made by Käsemann, *Romans*, 43-44.

The sins that Paul mentions in Romans 1:24-31 are not an exhaustive list, for Paul offers other vice lists in his letters that do not perfectly overlap with the vices here (e.g. Gal. 5:18-21). But the point remains for my thesis that the vices mentioned (and vices like these) are revelations of God's wrath against ungodliness in the present evil age.

For example, Paul states in Romans 1:24 that "God gave" the ungodly over "in the lusts of their hearts to impurity so that their bodies would be dishonored." He immediately thereafter states that "they exchanged God's truth for a lie and worshipped and served the creation rather than the creator" (Rom. 1:25). In Romans 1:26, Paul states again that "God gave" the ungodly over to "dishonorable passions," and he immediately thereafter says that both men and women began to practice unnatural sexual relations with one another, namely, homosexuality (Rom. 1:27). Finally, Paul states for a third time in the text that "God gave" the ungodly over to an unapproved mind to practice unlawful deeds (Rom. 1:28), and immediately thereafter he states that they practiced "unrighteousness," "evil," "covetousness," "envy," "murder," "deceit," "selfishness," and "meanness" and that they were "gossipers," "slanderers," "haters of God," "insulters," "arrogant," "prideful," "schemers of evil," "disobedient to parents," "foolish," "unfaithful," "without affection," and "unmerciful" (Rom. 1:29-31). Thus, God reveals his wrath in the current age upon those who suppress the truth by giving them over to immorality. Romans 1:32 also supports that sin manifests its power through sinful actions when Paul states that those who know God's righteous requirement demand death for those who practice unrighteousness, and yet they still both practice unrighteousness and approve of those who practice unrighteousness.

That sin manifests its dominating power through sinful actions is evident elsewhere in Romans. In Romans 2:1-3:8, Paul argues that God judges Jews and Gentiles in accordance with the same standard and that both groups apart from the work of the Spirit will be condemned before God at the eschatological judgment, for neither deeds, possession of the law, or lack thereof are sufficient to exonerate either group in the judgment. Paul, then, infers from Romans 2:1-3:8 in 3:9-20 that Jews and Gentiles (i.e. the entire world) stand condemned before God.[47] He first asks in Romans 3:9a if Jews have an advantage over Gentiles in terms of right standing before God since the latter group is not Jewish. He offers an emphatic answer in Romans 3:9b: "by no means" (οὐ πάντως)![48]

---

[47]So Dunn, *Romans*, 1:144-45; Moo, *Romans*, 196-210; Schreiner, *Romans*, 161. Against, however, Stowers, *A Rereading of Romans*, 176-93.

[48]Paul states earlier in Rom. 3:1-2 that Jews have an advantage over Gentiles. His statement in Rom. 3:9 does not contradict Rom. 3:1-2. Rom. 3:1-2 occurs in a context in which Paul lists the privileges that Jews have over Gentiles (cf. Rom. 2:17-18). Paul contends, however, that such ethnic and national privileges were not sufficient for a right standing before God (cf. Rom. 2:19-29). Yet, Jewish ethnic privileges grant them an advantage over the Gentiles in that "the oracles of God were believed" by the Jews and some Jews were in fact saved (Rom. 3:2). On the other hand, notwithstanding that

Humanity's Spiritual Plight

Paul gives the reason in Romans 3:9c for his answer in Romans 3:9b: "for we accuse both Jews and Greeks, all, to be under sin." The construction Ἰουδαίους τε καὶ Ἕλληνας includes everyone in the known world of Paul's time. This is supported by the phrases πᾶν στόμα, πᾶς κόσμος, and πᾶσα σάρξ in Romans 3:20. Πάντας in Romans 3:9 is in apposition to Ἰουδαίους τε καὶ Ἕλληνας, and it further defines the scope of Paul's indictment, because the latter phrase defines the meaning of the former. That Paul speaks of the universal condemnation of both Jews and Gentiles in Romans 2:1-3:20 is further evident by his statement in 3:19 that "every mouth would be made silent and that the entire world be answerable to God." "Every mouth" (πᾶν στόμα) and "the entire world" (πᾶς κόσμος) refer to both Jews and Gentiles. This point is further evident from the phrase πᾶσα σάρξ in Romans 3:20 and from the clause πάντες γὰρ ἥμαρτον καὶ ὑστεροῦνται τῆς δόξης θεοῦ ("for all have sinned and fallen short of the glory of God") in Romans 3:23. Therefore, Jews and Gentiles are under the power of sin, and they manifest their bondage to sin's power by God's judgment of them in this age in that he gives them over to their sinful desires.[49]

Romans 3:9-18 envisages this latter point. There Paul cites a catena[50] of Old Testament texts to support his argument of the universal condemnation that comes upon Jews and Gentiles because of the universal power of sin. Paul selects these verses about the wicked and applies them to Jews and Gentiles to illustrate the universal condemnation of humanity that results from the universal impact of sin (cf. Gen. 2-3).[51] That the universality of sin's dominating power manifests itself via sinful actions is apparent in Romans 3:10-18. After Paul states that no one is righteous and that no one seeks God (Rom. 3:10-11), he asserts that everyone has turned aside from following God and that everyone is debased (Rom. 3:12); no one pleases God (Rom. 3:12); their speech is evil (Rom. 3:13-14); they practice murder (Rom 3:15-16), and they are violent (Rom. 3:17). In other words, sin's reign over Jews and Gentiles manifests itself through their wicked and rebellious actions.

In addition, Jewish-Gentile conflict amongst the Roman Christians reveals sin's dominating power through sinful actions. In Romans 14:1, Paul

---

Jews have certain privileges; they are equally condemned before God because of their sin (cf. Rom. 3:9-18). In this sense, Jews will have no advantage over Gentiles in the judgment (Rom. 3:9).

[49]So Schreiner, *Romans*, 164.

[50]See Rom. 3:10-12 with Ps. 14:1-3; 53:1-3; Eccl. 7:20, Rom. 3:13 with Ps. 5:9; 140:3; Rom. 3:14 with Ps. 10:7; Rom. 3:15-17 with Isa. 59:7-8; Prov. 1:16, and Rom. 3:18 with Ps. 36:1.

[51]Dunn (*Romans*, 1:149) states that "it needs to be stressed that the point of the catena is not simply to demonstrate that scripture condemns all humankind, but more precisely to demonstrate that scriptures which had been read from the presupposition of a clear distinction between the righteous and the unrighteous (cf. Jub. 21:21-22) in fact condemned all humankind as soon as that clear distinction was undermined." More accurately, Cranfield, *Romans*, 1:191; Moo, *Romans*, 202, Schreiner, *Romans*, 164; Jewett, *Romans*, 259-60.

urges the Romans to receive "the one who is weak in the faith." That this command is given to a mixed group of Jews and Gentiles seems correct in light of Romans 14:2: "On the one hand, someone believes [that it is okay] to eat all things, but, on the other hand, the one who is weak eats vegetables" (brackets mine).[52] Romans 15:1-13 continues the discussion of the weak-strong brother. Romans 15:1 states that the strong brother ought to bear the burdens of the weak. Romans 15:7-9 appeals to the Romans to "receive one another" as Christ received them since Christ "became a minister of the circumcision for the truth of God, so that he would confirm the promises of the fathers and so that the Gentiles would glorify God for the sake of mercy." Paul specifically mentions Jews with the term περιτομῆς in 15:8 and Gentiles with ἔθνη in 15:9. Paul highlights the Gentiles in Romans 15:9-12. Furthermore, Paul's command "to receive one another" in Romans 15:7 is a call to Jews and Gentiles to accept one another since Paul gives this command in a context in which he speaks of Jesus becoming a servant for Jews and Gentiles. Thus, there appears to be a tension between two groups of people amongst the Roman Christians. One group consists of people with weak consciences, who believe that they should only eat certain types of foods and honor special days. The other group consists of people with strong consciences, who believe that they are free to eat anything without doing damage to their consciences and who deem it unnecessary to honor special days. The command to receive one another in Romans 15:7 assumes (if not the reality at least) the potential for division between these two groups over kosher food laws and special days since one group would abstain from certain foods but the other group would eat anything and since one group would honor special days and the other would not (1 Cor. 8-10).

Sin's dominating power through sinful actions is seen in 1 Corinthians. To say that the Corinthian congregation was divisive is an understatement (1 Cor. 1:11). The letter demonstrates that the Corinthians were full of "jealousy" and "selfish-ambition" (1 Cor. 12-14) and that they were divided over the apostles and Christ (1 Cor. 1:12-13).[53] Paul argues in 1 Corinthians 1:12-4:13 that the Corinthians should not be divided over men, because the apostles were simply servants of Christ. Paul also states that the Corinthians tolerated sexual immorality within the church (1 Cor. 5), that they were hostile toward one another, for they took one another to court (1 Cor. 6:1-11). Paul states that the Corinthians were formerly "fornicators" (1 Cor. 6:9), "idolaters" (1 Cor. 6:9), "adulterers" (1 Cor. 6:9), "homosexual perverts" (1 Cor. 6:9), "male sexual perverts" (1 Cor. 6:9), "thieves" (1 Cor. 6:10), "coveters" (1 Cor. 6:10), "drunkards" (1 Cor. 6:10), "revilers" (1 Cor. 6:10), and "swindlers" (1 Cor. 6:10), but God converted them from these things (1

---

[52]Contra the double-character of Romans, see A. Andrew Das, *Solving the Romans Debate* (Minneapolis: Fortress, 2007).

[53]David E. Garland (*1 Corinthians*, BECNT [Grand Rapids: Baker, 2003], 47-48) argues that the Corinthians were divided over allegiances, not necessarily over Paul, Christ, Peter, and Apollos.

Cor. 6:11, 20).

The Corinthians divided over food and especially over "meat offered to idols" (1 Cor. 8:1). Paul urges the Corinthians not to be desirers of evil things as Israel whom God struck down in the wilderness because of idolatry (1 Cor. 10:6-7), fornication (1 Cor. 10:8), testing the Lord (1 Cor. 10:8), and grumbling (1 Cor. 10:10). They were also divided over the manner by which they should celebrate the Lord's Supper (1 Cor. 11:17-21). The Corinthians did not celebrate the Lord's Supper when they gathered together as a church (1 Cor. 11:20). Instead, "each one takes ahead of time his own dinner when he eats" (1 Cor. 11:21). The well-to-do Corinthians, who possibly provided the food and drink for the meal, commenced to eat and drink before the have-nots arrived: "And, on the one hand, someone is hungry, but, on the other hand, someone is drinking freely" (1 Cor. 11:21b).[54]

Paul develops the latter point in 1 Corinthians 11:22 that they can eat and drink a common meal at home apart from the gathering together of the church. This latter statement clarifies that those who were eating and drinking in 1 Corinthians 11:21 were doing so to the exclusion of the have-nots, for Paul distinguishes between an ordinary meal at home where one might consume all of the food and drink all of the wine to the neglect of others and the Lord's Supper where the body of Christ feasts together on the body and blood of Jesus. Instead, the Corinthians' actions created a divisive setting at the Lord's Supper, for it is a meal that should unite the body of Christ instead of being a source of division. 1 Corinthians 12-15 further suggests that the Corinthians were also divided because of spiritual gifts (1 Cor. 12-14) and the resurrection of the dead (1 Cor. 15).

Sin's dominating power through sinful actions is seen in 2 Corinthians when Paul describes his hardships for the sake of the gospel. His opponents challenged his apostolic authority (2 Cor. 10:3, 7-8), and they attacked his personal appearance (2 Cor. 10:10). Paul was also imprisoned (2 Cor. 11:23; cf. Eph. 3:1; Phil. 1:13; Phlm. 1:1), beaten numerously (2 Cor. 11:23), in danger of death (2 Cor. 11:23), flogged (2 Cor. 11:24), and beaten with rods (2 Cor. 11:25). In Damascus, he was lowered in a basket from a window in order to escape the local authorities' plot against his life (2 Cor. 11:33).

Sin's dominating power through sinful actions is seen in Galatians. Paul contrasts in Galatians 5:16-26 the fruit of the Spirit and the works of the flesh. He commands the Galatians in 5:16 to walk by the Spirit and not to fulfill the "lust of the flesh." The term "flesh" (σάρξ) is an important Pauline term.[55] As I argued earlier, Paul uses this term differently throughout his letters,[56] but

---

[54]The verbs προλάμβανω in 1 Cor. 11:21 and ἐκδέξεσθε in 11:33 also support that some within the Corinthian congregation consumed their food and drink without leaving any for "the have-nots."

[55]See Dunn (*Theology*, 62-70) for Pauline uses of "flesh."

[56]Rom. 1:3; 2:28; 3:20; 4:1; 6:19; 7:5, 18, 25; 8:3-9, 12, 13; 9:3, 5, 8; 11:14; 13:14; 1 Cor. 1:26, 29; 5:5; 6:16; 7:28; 10:18; 15:39, 50; 2 Cor 1:17; 4:11; 5:16; 7:1, 5; 10:2-3; 11:18; 12:7; Gal. 1:16; 2:16, 20; 3:3; 4:13 14, 23, 29; 5:13, 16-17, 19, 24; 6:8, 12-13;

in Galatians 5:16 σάρξ in the phrase "lust of the flesh" and the occurrence in the corresponding phrase "works of the flesh" (Gal. 5:19) refer to sinful desires that manifest themselves by sinful actions.[57] Σάρξ in Galatians 5:16 would certainly include a reference to circumcision (Gal. 3:3; 5:13) and life under the law (Gal. 5:18; Rom. 6:14), but here it primarily refers to sin and to one's sinful nature.[58]

The preceding interpretation seems correct in light of Galatians 5:17 and 5:19. In Galatians 5:17, Paul provides a reason why the Galatians should walk by the Spirit and should not fulfill the lust of the flesh: "For the flesh desires contrary to the Spirit, and the Spirit [desires] contrary to the flesh, for these [i.e. flesh and Spirit] are opposed to one another" (brackets mine). In Galatians 5:19, Paul discusses the "works of the flesh," which I interpret to mean the works that flow from the flesh.[59] In Galatians 5:24, Paul states that those in Christ should "crucify the flesh with passions and desires." "Passions" and "desires" refer to sinful passions and desires since Paul has already contrasted walking in the Spirit with not fulfilling the lust of the flesh (Gal. 5:16) and since he asserts that flesh and Spirit are opposed to each other (Gal. 5:17) and that they produce different types of works (Gal. 5:19-26). Galatians 5:26 supports this interpretation, for it states that arrogance, irritation, and envy come from the flesh.

Paul follows his statement in Galatians 5:24 in 5:25 with a statement pertaining to living by the Spirit. Then, he states in Galatians 5:26 that Christians should not be known as "arrogant ones who irritate one another [and] who are jealous of one another" (brackets mine). Thus, in Galatians 5:24-26 Paul connects crucifying the flesh with sinful passions and desires, with living by the Spirit, and with an exhortation to Christians to be at peace with one another. The above interpretation of flesh is consistent with Paul's statement in Ephesians 2:3 that Jews and Gentiles prior to their faith in Christ lived by the lusts of their flesh "by doing the will of the flesh and of the mind" (Eph. 2:1-3; 4:17-24). Paul states that the result of one's living by the flesh was performing deeds of the flesh. Paul mentions in Galatians 5:19 that "enmities" (Gal. 5:19), "selfishness" (Gal. 5:20), "jealousy" (Gal. 5:20), "angers" (Gal. 5:20), "rivalry" (Gal. 5:20), "divisions" (Gal. 5:20), "factions" (Gal. 5:20), and

---

Eph. 2:3, 11, 14; 5:29, 31; 6:5, 12; Phil. 1:22, 24; 3:3 4; Col. 1:22, 24; 2:1, 5, 13, 18, 23; 3:22; 1 Tim. 3:16; Phlm. 1:16.

[57] As Bruce (*Galatians*, 240) states in his comments on Gal. 5:13, σάρξ is used here not simply of weak human nature nor yet of the life under bondage to the στοιχεῖα *["fundamental elements"]* as opposed to life in the Spirit; it denotes (as in vv 16f, 19, 24; 6:8) that self-regarding element in human nature which has been corrupted at the source, with its appetites and propensities, and which if unchecked produces the 'works of the flesh' listed in vv. 19f' (brackets mine).

[58] I think this is what Ernest De Witt Burton (*Galatians*, ICC, 2nd ed. [Edinburgh: T. & T. Clark, 1975], 292) meant when he asserted that σάρξ in Gal. 5 refers to "that element of man's nature which is opposed to goodness, and makes for evil."

[59] The above sense would understand the genitive τῆς σαρκός in the phrase τὰ ἔργα τῆς σαρκός as a subjective genitive/genitive of origin.

"envies" (Gal. 5:21) are works of the flesh.

Other statements scattered throughout the Pauline letters suggest that sin's power manifests itself through sinful actions. Paul urges the Ephesians not to live their current lives as Christians in the manner they formerly lived as Gentiles (i.e. non-Christians) in the futility of their mind (Eph. 4:17), because a Gentile manner of life is characterized by darkness, ignorance, and separation from eternal life from God (Eph. 4:18). He further states that Gentiles were spiritually insensitive and gave themselves over "to licentiousness for the working of all impurity by means of covetousness" (Eph. 4:19). Paul continues by exhorting the Ephesians to put off their former Gentile manner of life marked by sin and to put on the new manner of life marked by holiness and righteousness (Eph. 4:22-5:20).

While Paul was in prison on account of the gospel (Phil. 1:13), some were preaching the gospel with false motives "because of envy and selfish-ambition" (Phil. 1:15, 17) to "arouse affliction" in his chains (Phil. 1:17). In addition, according to Philippians 2, the power of sin manifested itself through sinful actions within the Philippian congregation. Paul suggests this because he both exhorts the Philippians to be humble toward one another and to serve one another by imitating Christ's example (Phil. 2:1-11) and because Paul commands two women (Euodia and Syntyche) to live in harmony with one another (Phil. 4:2). Similar to Ephesians, Paul addresses the Colossians' previous manner of life before their conversion (Col. 2:20-3:17), and he urges them to pursue God's will and to abstain from unrighteousness (Col. 3:2). The sorts of vices from which Paul demands the Colossians to abstain are "sexual immorality" (Col. 3:5), "impurity" (Col. 3:5), "evil desire" (Col. 3:5), and "covetousness" (Col. 3:5), "which is idolatry" (Col. 3:5). Paul affirms that the Colossians lived in compliance with the above vices before they were Christians, and then urges them to put away such vices by listing a similar set of sins that they should put away: "wrath" (Col. 3:8), "fury" (Col. 3:8), "evil" (Col. 3:8), "blasphemy" (Col. 3:8), "obscene speech" (Col. 3:8), and lying (Col. 3:9). Thus, according to Paul, sin is a power that dominates, and sin manifests its domination through sinful actions.

The *Nachwirgung* of Torah's Entrance into Salvation-History

Romans 2:1-3:20

Adam's transgression universally effected the entire creation. When the law entered into salvation-history, sin's effect upon the creation did not improve the spiritual predicament of Jews and Gentiles but made it worse. This point is evident in the unit of Romans 2:1-3:20.[60] The main argument of Romans 2:1-3:20 is in a diatribe fashion and it (along with the argument of 1:18-32) pertains

---

[60]For a rhetorical analysis of Rom 2:1-3:20, see Jewett, *Romans*, 195, 220-21, 241, 255-56.

to God's universal judgment of both Jews and Gentiles because of sin;[61] the issue is not the *nachwirgung* of Torah's entrance into salvation-history. But throughout Paul's argument of the universality of God's judgment of Jews and Gentiles because of sin, he addresses Torah's inability to deal with humanity's spiritual predicament.[62]

Romans 2:1-16

Romans 2:1-10 begins the argument by focusing on Jewish condemnation of Gentile vices.[63] The vices are those mentioned in Romans 1:24-31, which is supported by the διό that connects 2:1-10 with 1:18-32 (cf. Rom. 1:24; 4:22; 13:5; 15:7, 22; 1 Cor. 12:3; 2 Cor. 2:8; Gal. 4:31; Eph. 2:11; 1 Thess. 5:11).[64] Paul specifically highlights Gentile vices in 1:24-32, because these are precisely the types of immoralities for which Jews often indicted Gentiles (Wis. 11:1-16:1; Jub. 22:16-23; Sib. Or. 3.595-606) and because Romans 2:1 shifts its focus from the group who practices immorality and will receive God's judgment (Rom. 1:24-31) to another group that likewise will receive God's

---

[61]Against Jouette M. Bassler, "Divine Impartiality in Paul's Letter to the Romans," *NovT* 26 (1984): 43-58, who thinks the theme is divine impartiality and against Klyne R. Snodgrass, "Justification by Grace—to the Doers: The Place of Romans 2 in the Theology of Paul," *NTS* 32 (1986): 72-93, who thinks that the theme is the vindication of God. Kent L. Yinger rightly argues that Romans 1-4 functions to destroy distinction, privilege, or advantage in God's law-court based on racial or religious differences and that the chapters are Paul's defense of God's impartial judgment and salvation of a universal sinful world, but he emphasizes that Paul's indictment "is not against a world claiming 'we have sinned' that he is arguing, but against Jews or Jewish-Christians claiming that they will not be treated the same as the 'sinners' in the judgment of God. . ." (*Paul, Judaism, and Judgment According to Deeds*, SNTSMS 105 [Cambridge: Cambridge University Press, 1999], 152-53).

[62]On the diatribe in Romans, see Stanley K. Stowers, *The Diatribe and Paul's Letter to the Romans*, SBLDS 57 (Chico: Scholars Press, 1981). On the major point of 1:18-3:20, there appears to be general agreement. For example, see Nygren, *Romans*, 97-144; Cranfield, *Romans*, 1:104-199; Käsemann, *Romans*, 33; E.P. Sanders, *Paul, the Law, and the Jewish People* (Minneapolis: Fortress, 1983), 123; Dunn, *Romans*, 1:152-60; Moo, *Romans*, 90-210; Schreiner, *Romans*, 77-174; Richard H. Bell, *No One Seeks for God*, WUNT 106 (Tübingen: Mohr Siebeck, 1998), 1-20; Wright, "Romans," 428-64. However, Runar M. Thorsteinsson, *Paul's Interlocutor in Romans 2: Function and Identity in the Context of Ancient Epistolography*, ConBNT 40 (Stockholm: Almqvist & Wiksell, 2003), 165-88. He suggests that 1:18-2:29 is exclusively against Gentile believers.

[63]Käsemann, *Romans*, 54.

[64]So Nygren, *Romans*, 116; Jewett, *Romans*, 196; Chris VanLandingham, *Judgment and Justification in Early Judaism and the Apostle Paul* (Peabody, MA: Hendrickson, 2006), 217. Barrett (*Romans*, 43) understands the particle to have an argumentative force in 2:1, but only connects 2:1 with 1:32a since he understands 1:32b to be a parenthesis. Käsemann (*Romans*, 54) suggests that διό is a colorless particle in 2:1 and that the verse does not infer from the preceding argument in Rom. 1:18-32. He suggests that 2:1 is an out of place interpolation.

judgment since this latter group both condemns and practices similar immoralities as the first group mentioned in 1:18-32 (Rom. 2:1-3). However, Paul's indictment in 1:18-32 is offered against the Jews too because God impartially saves (Rom. 1:16) and judges Jews and Gentiles (Rom. 2:6-16) and because both groups will be without excuse when they stand before God's righteous judgment (Rom. 1:20; 2:1).[65] Romans 2:9-10 supports this point, for these verses confidently assert that Jews and Gentiles (not only Gentiles) will receive God's judgment if they disobey God (Rom. 2:10) and eternal life if they obey (Rom. 2:10; cf. 2:1-10), "because there is no partiality with God" (Rom. 2:11).[66]

To clarify, the vices mentioned in Romans 1:24-31 are an indictment of Gentiles, for these are precisely the sorts of sins for which Jews condemned Gentiles (Wis. 11:1-16:1; Jub. 22:16-23). A Jewish mindset was that if God weighed the sins of Jews and Gentiles on a scale, the latter's sins would outweigh the sins of the former group (4 Ezra 3:32-36). But Paul's indictment in 1:18-32 is radical because it (together with 2:1-3:20) places Jews and Gentiles on the same footing before God and because in the latter unit his indictment is especially against the Jews, for there is a connection between the vices and the indictment in Romans 1:18-32 and the vices and indictment in 2:1-3:20.[67] This connection is supported by the particle διὸ (Rom. 2:1) and elucidated by the ensuing argument of Romans 2:1b-3:20 that Jews and Gentiles are guilty before God, that they will be judged in accordance with their deeds, and that they will not be justified by the law in his presence.

However, the above analysis does not imply that Paul intended to convey in 1:18-3:20 that every single Jew without exception regularly committed these vices. For that matter, I neither imply that Paul's point is that the Gentiles on every occasion committed every sin in the vice list (cf. Rom. 2:14). Rather, my point here is that Paul starkly suggests that both Jews and Gentiles committed these types of sins (cf. Matt. 24; Mark 7:9-13, 21-22); the Gentiles were particularly known for such blatant violations of Torah (cf. 1 Cor. 5:1), and both groups are without exception guilty before God because neither group obeys Torah.[68] Paul's other vice lists scattered throughout his letters support my interpretation, for they do not perfectly harmonize with the

---

[65]Nygren, *Romans*, 118.

[66]For compelling arguments supporting the indictment of both Jews and Gentiles, see A. Andrew Das, *Paul, the Law, and the Covenant* (Peabody, MA: Hendrickson, 2001), 170-77.

[67]Although we disagree regarding the requirement of perfect obedience to the law in early Judaism and Paul, see Yinger for a similar point, *Judgment according to Deeds*, 159, 164, 164 n. 74, 165-69. See also Bell (*No One Seeks for God*, 137-41), who likewise suggests that Paul indicts Jews and Gentiles in 2:1-16 but that the Jew is not singled out in the indictment of 2:1-29 until 2:17.

[68]Against Heikki Räisänen's vicious and grotesque critique of Paul's argument in 1:18-3:20 (*Paul and the Law* [Philadelphia: Fortress, 1983], 97-101).

vice list given here.[69] The differences between the lists suggest that Paul mentions the types of vices that were pertinent to the particular audience. Thus, in order to defend my premise that Paul's indictment includes both Jews and Gentiles, to offer evidence that Jews and Gentiles regularly committed each of these individual sins is unnecessary. To the contrary, I simply need to provide examples where (1) Gentiles sinned in ways that Paul describes here, (2) that Jews sinned in ways that Paul describes here, and (3) that Jews judged Gentiles for committing the same or similar types of sins that they (Jews) committed. I provide such evidence below.

As I already noted above, certain Jewish literature indicts the Gentiles for similar sins as Paul's interlocutor in Romans 1:24-31 (Wis. 11:1-16:1; Jub. 22:16-23; cf. Ep. Arist. 142, 152-53; 1 Bar. 4:4; T. Nap. 3:3; 4:1-2). But Paul also independently offers a similar indictment of Gentiles elsewhere in his letters. Paul states that Gentile Christians were before their conversion "fornicators" (1 Cor. 6:9; Col 3:5; cf. Rom. 1:24, 26, 29), "idolaters" (1 Cor. 6:9; cf. Rom. 1:21-25, 30), "adulterers" (1 Cor. 6:9; cf. Rom. 1:29), "homosexual perverts" (1 Cor. 6:9; cf. Rom. 1:26-27), "male sexual perverts" (1 Cor. 6:9; cf. Rom. 1:26-27), "thieves" (1 Cor. 6:10; cf. Rom. 1:29), "coveters" (1 Cor. 6:10; cf. Rom. 1:29), "drunkards" (1 Cor. 6:10; cf. Rom. 1:29), "revilers" (1 Cor. 6:10; cf. Rom. 1:29-31), lewd children of darkness (Eph. 4:17-5:8), "swindlers" (1 Cor. 6:10; cf. Rom. 1:29-30), and were devoted to tenacious impurities and passions (Col. 3:5; cf. Rom. 1:26-31). Both the Jewish and the Pauline critiques of Gentiles fit with the evidence from the Greco-Roman world. According to their own literature, some Gentiles were polytheistic, belligerent, lived reckless immoral lives, and practiced all sorts of evil (cf. Eph. 4:17-20; 1 Thess. 4:1-6; 1 Pet. 4:1-4).[70]

In the Old Testament, Israel likewise practiced idolatry and all sorts of evil (cf. Exod. 32; Num. 25; 1 Kings-2 Chronicles). In fact, YHWH warns the nation not to associate with Gentiles because they would lead them away from serving their God (Deut. 6). In 1, 2, and 4 Maccabees, Israel suffers because the nation turned from serving YHWH faithfully in compliance with his law and followed the way of the Gentile ruler Antiochus Epiphanes IV (cf. 1 Macc. 1, 2 Macc. 7:32-38; 4 Mac. 6:28-29; 17:21-22). Jews indicted fellow Jews for teaching commandments that are opposed to God's just ordinances (T. Lev 14:4), such as stealing the Lord's offerings and eating them with whores (T. Lev 14:5-6), profanation of married women (T. Lev. 14:6), promiscuous relationships with whores and adulteresses (T. Lev 14:6), marriages to Gentile women (T. Lev 14:6), inflation of pride because of the priesthood (T. Lev

---

[69]See the vice lists in Rom. 1:24-31 with the vice lists in 1 Cor. 6:9-11; Gal. 5:19-21; Eph. 4:22-5:20; Col. 2:20-3:17.

[70]Gentile moral philosophers such as the Stoics would have likewise condemned the vices that Paul lists in Rom 1:24-31. For a bibliography of both primary and secondary literature on the similarities between the ethics of Seneca and Paul, see Peggy Vining, "Comparing Seneca's Ethics in Epistulae Morales to those of Paul in Romans," *Restoration Quarterly* (2005): 83-104.

14:7), and a derision of sacred things (T. Lev 14:8). In the New Testament, Jesus (Matt. 23) and Paul (1 Cor. 10:1-22) condemn the Jews for numerous activities that are contrary to the Torah. Thus, the Jew who knows God's righteous requirement and yet still both approves of those who disobey and likewise disobeys is guilty (Rom. 1:32), and the one who judges is guilty himself since he does the same things as the Gentile (Rom. 2:1).

That Romans 1:32 indicts the Jew and the Gentile becomes more evident in the ensuing argument of 2:1-29. Paul says that the one who judges is without excuse (Rom 2:1), because he does the "same things" (Rom. 2:1; cf. Wis. 15:8). Although Paul's indictment in Romans 1:32 emphasizes Gentiles and includes Jews (as argued above), Paul in Romans 2:1 primarily addresses his Jewish interlocutor because of the interjectory particle ὦ and the vocative ἄνθρωπε (Rom. 2:3; 9:20) and (perhaps more convincingly) because he has already expressed that salvation comes to the Jew first and to the Gentile second (Rom. 1:16). He, then, later expresses that judgment comes to the Jew first and to the Gentile second (Rom. 2:9-10).[71] The indictment against Jews is confirmed with the clause ἐν ᾧ γὰρ κρίνεις τὸν ἕτερον σεαυτὸν κατακρίνεις τὰ γὰρ αὐτὰ πράσσεις ὁ κρίνων.[72] Τὰ αὐτὰ in 2:1 likely refers to the vices mentioned in 1:29-31,[73] for τὰ αὐτὰ grammatically agrees with τοιαῦτα in 1:32 and in 2:2 and because the latter term is the antecedent of αὐτὰ in 1:32, just as τὰ αὐτὰ in 2:1 is the antecedent of τοιαῦτα in 2:2.

The verb οἴδαμεν introduces a statement that both Paul and his Jewish interlocutor could accept as truth (Rom. 3:19; 5:3; 7:14; 8:22, 28), which in this case is that God's judgment is according to the truth. Thus, the "we" in "we know" includes Paul but especially refers to Jews since his interlocutor at this point in the argument is Jewish and since God's divine judgment was a prominent idea in Jewish tradition (Isa. 13:6-16; 34:8; Dan. 7:9-11; Joel 2:1-2; Zeph. 1:14-2:3; 3:8; Mal. 4:1; Jub. 5:10-16; 1 En. 90:20-27).[74] Notwithstanding both that God revealed knowledge of himself to

---

[71] So Cranfield (*Romans*, 1:142), but he simply asserts the point. Against Barrett (*Romans*, 43) who objects that the one who judges is the Jew who practices the same things because Jews and moral Gentile philosophers possessed a real moral superiority. Barrett instead suggests that the sin addressed is the act of judgment. Against also Jewett (*Romans*, 197-218) who argues that Paul's interlocutor is the Roman congregational audience.

[72] Jewett (*Romans*, 197) points out that Paul's comments in 2:1b echo oral Jesus tradition recorded in Matt. 7:1-2: μὴ κρίνετε, ἵνα μὴ κριθῆτε ἐν ᾧ γὰρ κρίματι κρίνετε κριθήσεσθε. . .

[73] Dunn, *Romans*, 1:80; Schreiner, *Romans*, 108. Against Jewett (*Romans*, 198) who asserts that specificity has not yet been established at this juncture in the argument. Paul's "rhetorical purpose" is to visualize bigotry in objectionable terms to guarantee judgment from his hearers.

[74] Jewett (*Romans*, 198) argues that the construction οἴδαμεν ὅτι in Paul's letters refers to the audience of believers, not to a single conversation partner. He cites Rom. 3:19; 7:14; 8:22; 1 Cor. 8:1, and 2 Cor. 5:1 to support his argument. His evidence is compelling, but the construction in Rom. 2:2 and 3:19 seems especially to include both

Gentiles through creation, which they in turn suppressed (Rom. 1:18-23), and that the Gentiles instinctively perform the demands of the law although they do not possess the law (Rom. 2:14), Jews (not Gentiles) should have known precisely how they ought to honor God to the degree that he deserves, because they received Torah and because it set them apart from the Gentile nations (Exod. 20; Deut. 6-30; cf. Ep. Arist. 139, 142). More, they should have known from Torah that if they did not honor God to the degree that he deserves, then he would judge them "in accordance with the truth" (Rom. 2:2; 3:1; cf. Deut. 30:15-16).

"According to the truth" suggests that God's judgment is right/just since it is in accordance with the facts (i.e. all are guilty; cf. Rom. 1:18-32).[75] These facts are clearly set forth in Torah. Paul accentuates that Jews had the truth in Torah in Romans 2:20 when he states that they "have a form of the knowledge and of the truth in the law."[76] Further, the phrase "according to the truth" also recalls Paul's statement in Romans 1:18 and 1:25 that the ungodly suppress the truth about God,[77] and it anticipates his comments in Romans 2:8 that those who are disobedient with respect to the truth will be judged.

Other uses of ἀλήθεια ("truth") in Romans illuminate Paul's usage of κατὰ ἀλήθειαν in Romans 2:2. The phrase ἀλήθεια τοῦ θεοῦ occurs in Romans 3:7 and ἀληθείας τοῦ θεοῦ in Romans 15:8, and both refer to God's divine revelation, because Paul uses both phrases in these texts in contexts where he appeals to Old Testament revelation to support his argument (cf. Rom. 3:4, 10-19; 15:9-12). The phrases refer to judgment (ἀλήθεια τοῦ θεου in Rom. 3:7) and salvation (ἀληθείας τοῦ θεου in Rom. 15:8), and both concepts in both texts were revealed in the Jewish scriptures (either in Torah or in the prophets), for the former phrase occurs in an argument that defends God's right to judge Jews in accordance with what Torah has revealed (Rom. 2:17-3:8) and the latter phrase occurs in a context where Paul speaks of the fulfillment of God's promises of salvation for Jews and Gentiles through Jesus Christ (Rom. 15:8-12). Once more, Paul states in Romans 2:18 that the Jew "knows the will and tests the things which are excellent because he is taught from the law." Thus, "according to the truth" in Romans 2:2 may include the idea that God's judgment is predicated upon the truth that he has revealed about himself as creator through creation to Gentiles,[78] but it most likely emphasizes

---

Paul and his Jewish interlocutor since his central concern in 2:1-3:20 is to demonstrate that Jews and Gentiles are judged in accordance with the same standard and that both groups are guilty before God.
[75]Against Dunn, *Romans* 1:80. Appealing to several Jewish texts to support his interpretation (1QS 4:19-20; CD 20:30; 4 Ezra 7:34; 2 Apoc. Bar. 85.9), he thinks the phrase focuses on God's reliability. In his later comments of truth in Rom. 2:8 (*Romans*, 1:87), he suggests that truth refers to the knowledge of God as creator.
[76]Cranfield (*Romans*, 1:143) agrees that "according to the truth" means in accordance with the facts, but he does not connect the phrase with Torah.
[77]So Jewett, *Romans*, 199, but he simply defines truth "as the norm of judgment."
[78]Dunn, *Romans*, 1:80, 87.

Humanity's Spiritual Plight

his revelation to Jews through Torah (Rom. 1:18, 25; 2:8, 20; 3:7; 15:8). Paul's point is that just as God will judge Gentiles for suppressing the truth about himself revealed through creation (Rom. 1:18-32), so also God will judge Jews in accordance with the truth of Torah (Rom. 2:2). Paul will later argue that he is right to judge in this manner (Rom. 3:1-6), for obedience to Torah would protect Israel from God's wrath and not simply mere possession of Torah.[79]

Romans 2:3-16 develops 2:1-2. The main point in 2:3-16 is that Jews (along with the Gentiles) will be judged according to the same standard, because God is impartial.[80] Paul begins Romans 2:3 by asking those who judge (i.e. Jews) and commit the same sins whether they will escape God's judgment. Romans 2:3 could be sarcastic because Paul previously stated in 2:2 that "God's judgment is according to the truth," whereas now he asks his Jewish interlocutor whether he will escape God's judgment. He follows the question from Romans 2:3 with a subsequent question in Romans 2:4 pertaining to whether the one who judges despises God's goodness and patience because he is ignorant that God's goodness leads him to repentance and because Jews knew very well that those who disobey Torah would not escape his wrath (Deut. 30:16; Isa. 13:6-16; 34:8; Dan. 7:9-11; Joel 2:1-2; Zeph. 1:14-2:3; 3:8; Mal. 4:1; Jub. 5:10-16; Pss. Sol. 15:8; 1 En. 90:20-27). Verse 4 is a separate question from the one in 2:3, for the latter pertains to salvation and 2:4 to God's goodness. The particle ἤ connects verses 3-4, and it possibly heightens the question asked in 2:3, for the first question pertains to salvation and the second discusses how God's goodness leads the Jew to salvation. This answer is by repentance by means of his goodness and patience.

The phrase "abundance of his goodness and forbearance and patience" modifies τοῦ πλούτου ("of the richness"). Paul connects πλοῦτος in 2:4 with God's great act of salvation in Jesus Christ elsewhere in Romans (Rom. 9:23; 11:12, 33). In Romans 11, both πλοῦτος (Rom. 11:12) and χρηστότης ("goodness") (Rom. 11:22) appear in Paul's argument regarding Jewish exclusion and Gentile inclusion within God's salvation-historical promises to Israel. Romans 11:22 is the only other place in the letter where χρηστότης refers to God's goodness besides 2:4. In the former text, Paul discusses both the judgment of God (ἀποτομίαν θεοῦ) and the goodness of God (χρηστότης θεου) while arguing that some Jews have been cut off from God's promises of salvation because of their unbelief (Rom. 11:1-10), while some Gentiles have been grafted into these soteriological promises by faith (Rom. 11:11-24). Paul states that God's judgment comes against all (Jews and Gentiles) who fall away in unbelief (Rom. 11:22), but his goodness comes upon those who remain in his goodness or else they too will be cut off from his soteriological promises (Rom. 11:22). Romans 11:26 confirms that God's goodness refers to salvation,

---

[79] For this last point, see Nygren, *Romans*, 119-32.
[80] Jewett (*Romans*, 196-218) argues that 2:1-16 can be explained by "Paul's rhetorical goal of creating an argument that provides the premises for an ethic of mutual tolerance between the competitive house and tenement churches in Rome, which could enable them to participate with integrity in the Spanish mission."

because it assertss that when the Gentiles enter into God's promises of salvation, then "all Israel will be saved." In Pss. Sol. 18:1, the psalmist mentions God's χρηστότης and πλοῦτος in a text where Jews acknowledge God's goodness to them as a people, and they utter this prayer while they urge him to prepare them for the coming of their Messiah who will bring their salvation by crushing their enemies (Pss. Sol. 18:1-12; cf. Pss. Sol. 17).

"Forbearance" (ἀνοχῆς) and "patience" (μακροθυμία) are probably a hendiadys, for both terms overlap with one another. The former occurs in Romans only in Romans 2:4 and 3:26 (cf. 1 Macc. 12:25). As Romans 2:4, 3:26 focuses on God's judgment and salvation, but the latter focuses on God's judgment and salvation in the cross of Jesus because of his forbearance of previous committed sins during the Mosaic Covenant. Μακροθυμία occurs only once more in Romans in 9:22, and there (as in Rom. 2:4) Paul uses the term in the context of salvation and judgment. In Romans 9:22, Paul asks whether "God endured with much patience vessels of wrath, which have been prepared for destruction, so that he would even make known the riches of his glory upon the vessels of mercy, which he prepared for glory" (Rom. 9:22-23). That soteriology is in view in this text is confirmed by Paul's later statements that God has called both Jews and Gentiles to be vessels of mercy (Rom. 9:24-26) and that only a remnant of Israel will be saved regardless of their multiplicity (Rom. 9:27).

Similar to the above contexts, the question of Romans 2:4 appears in a soteriological context, for Paul asks whether the Jew will escape God's judgment and whether he is ignorant of the fact that God's goodness (τὸ χρηστὸν) will lead him to repentance (Rom. 2:3-4; cf. 2 Cor. 7:10; 2 Tim. 2:25). Τὸ χρηστὸν is a cognate of χρηστότης. Although τὸ χρηστὸν in Romans 2:4 is an adjective, it takes the force of a noun here ("goodness"), for it is the head term of the genitive θεοῦ. By τὸ χρηστὸν, Paul refers to God's patient forbearance to delay his judgment and to give sinners time to repent and be saved from his wrath because this term has this exact idea in the LXX (LXX Ps. 24:8; 33:9; 68:17; 85:5; 99:5; 105:1; 106:1; 108:21; 135:1; 144:9; Nah 1:7; 2 Macc. 1:24; Wis. 11:23; 15:1; Pss. Sol. 2:36; 2 Apoc. Bar. 21:20) and because τὸ χρηστὸν is the subject of an object clause, and the object clause is the object of an adverbial participle that modifies the main verbal clause. The main verbal clause pertains to despising God's goodness that leads to repentance. The main verb in the main verbal clause καταφρονεῖς implies that the Jewish interlocutor shows contempt against God's patience with regard to the judgment of Gentiles,[81] for the Jewish interlocutor takes the place of judge over the Gentiles when he judges them for their sins, but yet the Jewish interlocutor likewise violates Torah and unknowingly subjects himself to God's righteous judgment (Rom. 2:1-5). Hence, by judging the Gentiles in accordance with the standard of Torah instead of entrusting his judgment to God and by

---

[81] Against Jewett, *Romans*, 201, who thinks that the verse is not against the self-righteous Jew, but against the Roman congregational situation.

likewise violating Torah,[82] the Jew condemns himself and shows contempt toward God's kindness that he grants to both Jews and Gentiles, which is a season of time to repent before his eschatological judgment, because he (just as the Gentile) does not respond to God's kindness with repentance (cf. Wis. 11:23; 12:10; Sir. 5:4-7; Philo, *Leg. All.* 3.106).[83]

The above reading seems correct for at least three reasons. First, Paul states in Romans 2:1-3 that the Jewish interlocutor judges Gentiles for disobeying the "righteous requirement of God," but that the Jews are also guilty since they violate Torah too (Rom. 1:32-2:3). "Righteous requirement of God" (δικαίωμα τοῦ θεοῦ) refers to Torah, because the phrase refers to Torah in the LXX (LXX Num. 31:21; 36:13; Deut. 4:1, 5; 1 Macc. 2:21; 1 Bar. 2:12), because Paul uses a related phrase (δικαιώματα τοῦ νόμου) in Romans 2:26 to refer to obedience to stipulations in Torah (Rom. 2:17-12, 25, 27), and because the latter phrase occurs in Romans 8:1-4 to refer to Jesus' fulfillment of Torah for those who walk according to the Spirit. Second, Paul states that the Jewish interlocutor has a "hardened and unrepentant heart" (a critique against Israel [Exod. 33:3, 5; 34:9; Deut. 9:6, 13; 10:16; Jer. 4:4; Ezek. 3:7; Mark 10:5; Matt. 19:8]),[84] which results in final eschatological judgment even though the Jew possesses Torah, because the Jew does not obey Torah but only hears it (Rom. 2:5-3:20). Third, a parallel statement with Romans 2:4 occurs in Wisdom 14:30 where Jews indict the Gentiles for treating God with contempt in that they disobey Torah by worshipping idols, but the Jewish author confidently contends in Wisdom 15:1-2 that God is kind (χρηστοτής), true (ἀληθής), patient (μακρόθυμος), and merciful (ἐλεος) so that even if Israel sins (which the author says will not happen), Israel would still belong to God. Therefore, since Romans 2:1-3:20 speaks of the judgment of Jews and Gentiles in accordance with the same standard (i.e. Torah) in a way similar to other texts in a Jewish or Jewish-Christian tradition and since all of the genitives in Romans 2:4 occur in contexts of judgment, the statement "the richness of his goodness and forbearance and patience" refers to God's merciful patience in delaying his final judgment so that the disobedient Jewish interlocutor (and Gentile) would repent. Thus, the argument of Romans 2:1-4 can be summarized as follows: Paul introduces the idea that Torah condemns Jews along with Gentiles because they (Jews) violate Torah, judge the Gentiles for violating Torah, and show contempt toward his kindness that leads Jews (and Gentiles) to repentance, a kindness that he patiently displays in that he delays his judgment against all sinners to give them time to repent.

Romans 2:5-3:20 develops the argument that Torah condemns both Jews and Gentiles. In Romans 2:5, Paul answers questions pertaining to

---

[82] Against Sanders (*Paul*, 125) who downplays the point that Rom. 1:18-3:20 argues that no one obeys Torah.

[83] Similarly Cranfield (*Romans*, 1:144), but he short cuts the argument to defend his reading. Although he simply asserts his point without argumentation, similarly Wright, "Romans," 439.

[84] Cranfield, *Romans*, 1:144.

whether the Jew would escape God's judgment by stating "you" are storing up wrath for "yourself" in the day of wrath.[85] The terms "you" and "yourself" are singular. This suggests that Paul continues to address the Jewish interlocutor of Romans 2:1-4, i.e., the one who judges the Gentiles but does the same things as they. Stowers and (recently) Douglas Campbell argue that Romans 1:18-3:20 does not reflect Paul's own views, but that Paul's words are a case of "speech-in-character" whereby Paul's words reflect the mindset of another party. This other party is a person in the audience of the Romans whose behavior would reflect the vices in Romans 1:18-31, and Jews would have rightly thought that the Gentiles and they were judged in accordance with different standards. Contrary to this thesis, "you" who judge refers to Jews collectively (and not to Gentiles), for Paul singles out the Jew first in Romans 2:9-10 after he mentions God's wrath; Jewish condemnation is the focus of Romans 2:1-3:8, and (as I argued earlier) Jews were notorious for judging Gentiles on account of their immorality (cf. Wis. 11-15; Jub. 22:16-23). Thus, Paul's point is perhaps a shocking one for his Jewish interlocutor: Jews will be scorched with the heat of God's wrath along with the Gentiles because of their hardened and unrepentant heart, and their possession of Torah will not save them.

The phrase κατὰ τὴν σκληρότητα σοῦ καὶ ἀμετανόητον καρδίαν alludes to Israel's unbelief in the Old Testament, for σκληρότητης occurs in LXX Deuteronomy 9:27 in a context where Moses reminds Israel that YHWH did not destroy them in the wilderness when they committed idolatry (Exod. 32), and he states that YHWH showed mercy to Israel because he prayed to YHWH that he would remember the covenant he made with Abraham, Isaac, and Jacob and that he would not look upon "the hardness of this people and their impious acts and their sins" (cf. T. Gad. 5:7). Moses later urged Israel in Deuteronomy 10:16 to circumcise their hearts and not to stiffen their necks any longer.[86] In 1QS 4:11, a stiff neck and a hardened heart are listed with several vices that accompany the spirit of deceit,[87] and 1QS 4:12-14 continues that those who walk in the spirit of deception will be subject to the "wrath of the fury of God, eternal torment and endless disgrace together with shameful extinction in the fire of the dark regions" and that "the times of all their generations shall be spent in sorrowful mourning and in bitter misery and in calamities of darkness until they are destroyed without remnant or survivor."[88]

Thus, the phrase κατὰ τὴν σκληρότητα σοῦ καὶ ἀμετανόητον καρδίαν suggests that the Jews as a people in Paul's day (just as in the Old Testament) generally did not follow Torah to the degree that YHWH demanded

---

[85]For the idea of storing up heavenly rewards in Jewish thought, see Tob. 4:9-10; Pss. Sol. 9:3-5; 4 Ezra 6:5; 7:77; 8:33, 36; 2 Apoc. Bar. 14:12.

[86]For the danger of a hardened heart in Jewish thought, see Jer. 4:4; Ezek..3:7; Sir. 16:10; 1 En.16:3; T. Sim. 6:2; Philo, *Leg.* 1.305. References from Dunn, *Romans*, 1:83.

[87]Jewett, *Romans*, 202.

[88]Unless otherwise indicated, all translations of the Dead Sea Scrolls come from Geza Vermes (trans.), *The Complete Dead Sea Scrolls in English*, Revised Edition (London: Penguin, 2004).

Humanity's Spiritual Plight 63

and that they would consequently be judged for their disobedience in the day of wrath.[89] The day of wrath points to the great day of the Lord when God will righteously judge all unrighteousness (Rom. 2:5; cf. T. Levi. 3:2; 15:2; 1QS 5:12). This day is anticipated in the Old Testament (Joel 1:15; 2:1; 4:14; Obad. 1:15; Zeph. 1:14; Mal. 4:1; Isa. 13:6, 9; Ezek. 7:10). Paul states that it will be a great day of destruction and devastation (Rom. 2:5, 8, 9; cf. Zeph. 1:12-16, 18; Lam. 2:21-22), for his Jewish interlocutor is storing up wrath for a future day when God will judge (Rom. 2:5).[90] This day is especially reserved for those who reject the gospel and live in disobedience to the Lord (Eph. 2:3; 5:6; Col. 3:6; 1 Thess. 2:16; Rev. 14:10; 16:19; 20:1-15).

In this day of wrath, Paul states that God will give to each one in accordance with his works (Rom 2:6; cf. LXX Ps. 61:13; Prov. 24:12).[91] Those who obey Torah, whether Jews or Gentiles (Rom. 2:7, 10), will receive eternal life, but those who disobey, whether Jews or Gentiles, will receive God's wrath (Rom. 2:8-9),[92] "because there is no partiality with God" (Rom. 2:11). That is, Jews and Gentiles will be condemned in the judgment because God impartially judges both groups in accordance with the same standard, namely, whether they obey Torah.[93] Paul here challenges his Jewish interlocutor's eschatological perspective, for some pious Jews thought that God's righteous judgment would be in favor of his covenant people Israel (Jub. 5:16-19; Sib. Or. 3.702) and against the Gentiles (Jub. 22:16-23; Wis. 11-16).

Paul elaborates the impartiality of God's judgment in accordance with Torah in Romans 2:12-29 introduced by 2:11, which functions as a theme verse for the ensuing argument of 2:12-29.[94] Romans 2:12-14 begins this elaboration

---

[89]For an analysis of the vocabulary by which Paul describes God's wrath, see Jewett, *Romans*, 206-08.

[90]The concept of storing up occurs in Jewish literature with reference to good works safeguarded in heaven (2 Apoc. Bar. 14:12; 24:1) and to the divine storehouse of God's wrath (LXX Prov 16:27; Philo, *Leg.* 3.105-06). Jewett, *Romans*, 202 n. 96.

[91]Judgment according to deeds was a common theme in early Judaism (Job 34:11; Ps. 28:4; Jer. 17:10; 25:14; 32:19; 51:24; Ezek. 33:20; 1QS 10:16-18; 1QpHab 8:1-2; 2 Esdr [4 Ezra] 6:19; 7:17, 33-35; Sir. 16:12, 14; Pss. Sol. 2:16-18, 33-35; 9:4-5; 17:8-9; 2 Apoc. Bar 13:8; 44:4; 54:21; Jub. 5:13-19; 21:4; 33:18; T. Levi 3:2; 4:1-2; T. Gad 7:4-5; T. Ben. 10:7-9; 1 En. 1:7-9; T. Moses 12:10-11; Sib. Or. 4.183-85). Schreiner (*Romans*, 112 n. 1) pointed me to these above Jewish texts.

[92]Against Barrett, *Romans*, 46-47. For a different reading of the syntax, see T. Zahn, *Der Brief des Paulus an die Römer ausgelegt*, 3rd ed. (Leipzig: Deichert, 1925).

[93]Nygren (*Romans*, 120-22) thinks that Jews and Gentiles are judged in accordance with the same standard, but that the standard is whether they have done good or evil not whether they have obeyed Torah. Käsemann (*Romans*, 58-59) suggests that Paul's doctrine of judgment according to works in 2:6 refers to Christian works because of Paul's larger discussion of justification. Cranfield (*Romans*, 1:147, 152-53) expresses that the group who obeys in 2:7 and 2:10 and who is rewarded with eternal life are Christians and that Paul's comments apply to Old Testament believers as well.

[94]Sanders, *PPJ*, 489; Jouette Bassler, *Divine Impartiality: Paul and a Theological Axiom*, SBLDS 59 (Chico: Scholars Press, 1982), 137, 152. But she goes too far when she argues that divine impartiality is the central theme of the letter.

in 2:12-16 with a series of clauses introduced by γάρ. These clauses particularly stress the future judgment of the Jews who disobey Torah by highlighting the future judgment of Gentiles who have the work of Torah written on their hearts notwithstanding that they did not receive the written Torah. Paul first states that those who sinned without the law (Gentiles) will perish without law (Rom. 2:12a). Sinning "without law" or "lawlessly" (ἀνόμως) refers to the Gentiles who sinned against God although they did not possess the written law, because Romans 2:14 explicitly mentions that the Gentiles do not have the law, but they do the things in the law. Hence, the Gentiles will not be exonerated in the judgment based on the fact that God did not give them Torah, for they still sinned even without Torah (ὅσοι γὰρ ἀνόμως ἥμαρτον), and consequently they will be judged even though they never possessed Torah (ἀνόμως καὶ ἀπολοῦνται). The main verbal idea ἀνόμως καὶ ἀπολοῦνται does not mean that God will judge the Gentiles apart from the standard of Torah, but that he will judge them (and Jews) in accordance with the standard of Torah and that they will too perish along with Jews who received Torah and disobeyed it, even though the Gentiles did not receive Torah.[95] This seems right because he has already mentioned in Romans 2:6 that God will judge Jews and Gentiles in accordance with their works, because ἀπόλλυμι in 2:12 refers to God's eschatological destruction (Rom. 2:5-12, 16; 1 Cor. 1:18-19; 15:18; 2 Cor. 2:15; 4:3; 2 Thess. 2:10),[96] for it is the consequence of God's judgment of the Gentiles because of their sin (Rom. 2:6-12),[97] because he states that doing Torah justifies and not simply hearing Torah (Rom. 2:13), because he states that the Gentiles do some of the things that Torah prescribes although they do not possess Torah (Rom. 2:14), and because he states that they possess the work of Torah on their heart, which will either condemn or excuse them in the day of wrath when God judges (Rom. 2:15).

The second clause in Romans 2:12b is coordinate with the first clause, and both ground Romans 2:11. Romans 2:12b emphasizes that the Jew who sinned with the law (ὅσοι ἐν νόμῳ ἥμαρτον) will be condemned by the law (διὰ νόμου κριθήσονται) (cf. Rom. 3:20), "for the hearers of the law are not righteous ones before God, but the doers of the law will be justified" (Rom. 2:13; cf. 2 Apoc. Bar. 48:46-47). Romans 2:13 grounds 2:12, and 2:13 affirms that the Torah is the standard of judgment for Jews and Gentiles, a truth already affirmed in early Judaism (Pseudo-Philo 11.1-2). Romans 2:13 offers a reason why both Gentiles, who do not possess Torah and disobey God, and Jews, who possess Torah and disobey God, are both guilty in his law-court: viz., only

---

[95] Jewett (*Romans*, 210) makes the point that impartial judgment does not consider one's cultural or religious background.

[96] Jewett (*Romans*, 210) prefers the translation "death," but interprets the verse to refer to perishing.

[97] The verb ἀπόλλυμι occurs in many texts in the LXX as a warning against Israel of the consequence of their disobedience (Deut. 4:26; 8:19-20; 11:17; 28:20, 22, 24, 25, 52; 30:18). Also Dunn, *Romans*, 1:96.

Humanity's Spiritual Plight 65

those who obey Torah will be justified, not simply those who receive Torah as a badge of covenant membership.

The phrase οἱ ἀκροαταὶ νόμου is especially directed to the Jews (cf. Deut. 4:1, 5-6, 13-14; 30:11-14; 1 Macc. 2:67). The phrase recalls the Shema in Deuteronomy 5-6 and the ensuing chapters where Moses urges Israel to hear and obey the commandments of YHWH. Israel was a people who were proud of hearing Torah and of knowing from Torah what pleases the Lord (Jos. Ant. 5.107; 1 Bar. 4:34), whereas other Jewish texts assert that lawless men (possibly Gentiles) had not listened to God's word (Sib. Or. 3.70) and that the sinners are those who fail to hear Torah (Jos. Ant. 5.132).[98] Paul's statement in Romans 2:13 that doers and not the hearers of Torah are justified does not contradict Moses' words in the Shema regarding the importance of hearing Torah, for Moses urges Israel both to hear and to obey (Deut. 6:4-25). It was not enough for Moses that Israel heard Torah read from Sinai through Moses (Exodus-Deuteronomy) and received Torah from Moses; it did not satisfy Paul that Jews heard Torah read in synagogue on the Sabbath (Rom. 2:13),[99] and it was not enough that YHWH gave a written Torah to Israel to follow, a point with which even some within early Judaism would have strongly agreed (T. Jud. 13:1-5; 26:1; T. Iss. 5:1-2; T. Dan 5:1; T. As. 2:1-10; 6:1-5; T. Jos. 11:1).

Instead, according to *some* early Jewish texts, the only thing that would provide blessing for Israel in the land (Deut. 6) and eschatological exoneration in God's law-court (Rom. 2:13) was obedience to Torah (T. Jud. 13:1-5; 26:1; T. Iss. 5:1-2; T. Dan 5:1; T. As. 2:1-10; 6:1-5; T. Jos. 11:1).[100] This does not imply that early Jews believed that their obedience was apart from God's supernatural empowerment.[101] Rather, my point is that YHWH's expectation both in the Old Testament and maintained in some factions of early Judaism was that Jews must perfectly obey Torah to live long in the land and to merit the reward that Torah set forth for those who obeyed,[102] for Moses

---

[98] Jewett, *Romans*, 211-12.

[99] Dunn (*Romans*, 1:98, 104-05) stresses that Paul attacks the self-confidence of the Jew who regularly attends the synagogue, faithfully hears Torah read each Sabbath, and who consequently considers himself to be one of the righteous people of the covenant who is already assured of a positive verdict in the judgment in the here and now because he has membership within and has remained loyal to the covenant.

[100] Dunn (*Romans*, 1:98) seems to be against this point when he asserts that "Like his fellow Jews and the whole prophetic tradition, Paul is ready to insist that a doing of the law is necessary for final acquittal before God, but that doing is neither *synonymous with nor dependent upon maintaining a loyal membership of the covenant people*" (italics mine). For a helpful summary of Dunn's view of the law, see his "The New Perspective: whence, what and whither?" in *The New Perspective on Paul* (Grand Rapids: Eerdmans, 2008), 1-97, esp. 16.

[101] A point that A. Andrew Das persuasively argues regarding early Judaism ("Paul and Works of Obedience in Second Temple Judaism: Romans 4:4-5 as a 'New Perspective' Case Study," *CBQ* 71 [2009]: 795-812, esp. 797-801).

[102] I find Paul L. Owen's recent argument from Deuteronomy against perfect obedience (that Moses means that all of God's words are precious and therefore should not be

emphasizes that disobedience to one of YHWH's commands would result in judgment in the land (Deut. 28:15-68); certain segments of early Judaism placed confidence in their ability to obey God's laws in order to receive the reward of life (Sir. 11:26; 17:23; Tob. 1:3, 5-18; 4:5-11; 1 Bar. 4:1-2; Pss. Sol. 14:2-3, 10; 15:4, 16; Jub. 30:21-22; 4Q215a ii 2-7; 4 Ezra 6:7-9:25), and Paul states that God would give the appropriate reward to Jews and Gentiles in accordance with their works (Rom. 2:6-10, 13). The work of obedience results in eternal life (Rom. 2:7, 10), but the work of disobedience will result in condemnation (Rom. 2:8-9).[103]

Romans 2:13 affirms justification by works. Debate regarding the meaning of this verse has been fierce in New Testament scholarship.[104] Scholars have identified those who do the law in 2:13 as faithful Jews and moral Gentiles,[105] Gentiles who fulfill the law apart from the Christian community,[106] non-Christians who receive salvation by works through grace as they respond in obedience to the light that they have received,[107] non-Christians whose works bring faith that leads to salvation since faith is the missing middle term in Paul's argument,[108] a non-Christian's hypothetical justification that would be true if Christ had not come,[109] a general offer of eternal life to the non-Christian who does good works but no one can achieve it since sin prevents one from achieving the necessary obedience,[110] and Christians who, through their union with Christ, by the Spirit produce acceptable works to God

---

ignored and that one's intent to keep the law is the issue) to be unpersuasive ("The 'Works of the Law' in Romans and Galatians: A New Defense of the Subjective Genitive," *JBL* 126 [2007]: 560-61), for Deuteronomy and Paul appear to suggest more than simply one's intent to obey the law by their emphasis that all of Torah must be obeyed.

[103]Paul A. Rainbow argues that Paul holds to a double justification (an initial positive verdict in the present age, followed by sanctification in the present age, which results in a second positive verdict on the last day). See *The Way of Salvation: The Role of Christian Obedience in Justification* (Carlisle, UK: Paternoster, 2005), 107-198. Although I *strongly* disagree with his overall thesis (that works in the Old Testament, early Judaism, and in Paul determine election and final justification), VanLandingham rightly understands 2:6-11 to refer to a positive verdict in the judgment based on one's deeds. For this point, see *Judgment*, 218-24.

[104]For a helpful summary of the debate, see Dane C. Ortlund, "Justified by Faith, Judged according to Works: Another Look at a Pauline Paradox," *JETS* 52 (2009): 323-39.

[105]Chrysostom.

[106]Räisänen, *Paul and Law*, 105-07.

[107]Klyne Snodgrass, "Justification by Grace—to the doers: An Analysis of the Place of Romans in the Theology of Paul," *NTS* 32 (1986): 72-93; Jewett, *Romans*, 212.

[108]F. Godet, *Commentary on Romans*, trans. and ed. T.W. Chambers (Grand Rapids: Zondervan, 1956).

[109]Hans Leitzmann, *Die Briefe des Apostels Paulus I: Die vier Hauptbriefe*, HNT 3 (Tübingen: J.C.B. Mohr, 1910), 13.

[110]Murray, *Romans*, 1.78-79.

Humanity's Spiritual Plight 67

in the judgment and therefore will be justified.[111] Chris VanLandingham recently argues that δικαιωθήσονται in 2:13 refers only to moral righteousness in spite of the fact that the context is judicial, for he contends that a judicial tribunal could convene "for the purpose of a finding and not just a declaration" and because the context emphasizes "the moral state of a person as each appears before God."[112]

But it seems most likely that Paul's point in 2:13 is that those who perfectly obey all of the law are righteous before God, and they will therefore be justified in his law-court. The accent in the argument falls on exoneration from future judgment based on one's deeds.[113] This interpretation is envisaged when one takes seriously that 2:6-16 is a single unit that further develops Paul's discussion in 2:1-5. Romans 2:6 specifically begins with the relative pronoun ὅς, which introduces a clause that explains God's judgment according to deeds.[114] Romans 2:7-10 develops the theme of God's future judgment and

---

[111] Although the following scholars do not agree in every respect regarding their exegesis of 2:6-16; in favor of a Christian position, see Karl Barth, *A Shorter Commentary on Romans* (London: SCM Press 1959), 36-37; Cranfield, *Romans*, 1:154-55; Schreiner, *The Law and Fulfillment*, 179-204; idem, *Romans*, 119; Yinger, *Judgment According to Deeds*, 146-82, 283-91; N.T. Wright, "The Law in Romans 2," in *Paul and the Mosaic Law*, ed. James D.G. Dunn (Grand Rapids: Eerdmans, 2001), 131-150; Simon J. Gathercole, "A Law unto Themselves: The Gentiles in Romans 2:14-15," *JSNT* 85 (2002): 27-49; Rainbow, *The Way of Salvation*, 107-98; VanLandingham, *Judgment*, 228-32; Jewett, *Romans*, 212-13, esp. 213; Das, "Paul and Works of Obedience," 811; Francis Watson, *Paul, Judaism, and the Gentiles: Beyond the New Perspective* (Grand Rapids; Eerdmans, Revised Edition 2007), 210-16; and before 1983 Sanders (*PPJ*, 551-52). In his subsequent work on Paul (*Paul, the Law, and the Jewish People* [Minneapolis: Fortress, 1983], 126-32), Sanders changed his position and argued that Paul's concern in 2:12-29 is whether one is a good Jew.

[112] VanLandingham, *Judgment*, 226. For his analysis of the δικ-word group, see 242-332.

[113] Against Yinger, *Judgment According to Deeds*, 166-69. Rightly Moo, *Romans*, 147-48, esp. 148.

[114] Cosgrove argues that judgment according to works in 2:6 that results in final justification in 2:13 is different from the justification by works of law that Paul denies in 3:20. Cosgrove argues this based on both the preposition κατὰ in 2:6 in the statement ὃς ἀποδώσει ἑκάστῳ κατὰ τὰ ἔργα αὐτοῦ and the preposition ἐκ in 3:20 in the statement ἐξ ἔργων νόμου οὐ δικαιωθήσεται πᾶσα σὰρξ ἐνώπιον αὐτοῦ. The deeds that result in justification in 2:6-13 are the *evidential basis* upon which God will grant final justification, whereas the preposition ἐκ in the construction in 3:20 suggests that the law is not the *soteriological instrumentality* by which one will receive final justification. According to his view, judgment will mean justification for the believer. Cosgrove's analysis seems to identify the correct definition of the prepositions, but his argument fails because "by means" of works and "in accordance with works" essentially convey the point that works either do (2:13) or do not (3:20) contribute to final justification. In addition, his analysis does not solve the seemingly contradictory statements of justification by works in 2:13 and justification not by works in 3:20 as he assumes, for 2:13 states that the "doers of the law will be justified" and 3:20 that "not any flesh will

rewards according to deeds. To accentuate the severity of God's eschatological judgment against Jews and Gentiles, Paul states that God will give "affliction" and "distress." "Affliction" and "distress" appear together in contexts that highlight the devastation produced by one nation against another when it conquers another nation (LXX Deut. 28:53, 55, 57). Paul's language stresses that God will destroy the disobedient but will vindicate the obedient. In addition, justification in Romans 2:13 is certainly eschatological and forensic since Paul both refers to a future day of judgment in 2:5-13 and since he uses the future verbs κριθήσονται in 2:12b and δικαιωθήσονται in 2:13. Thus, God will destroy those who disobey him in this age on the last day but he will vindicate those who obey him.[115] Romans 2:11 provides the fundamental reason for God's judgment of Jews and Gentiles according to deeds: he shows no partiality.

Romans 2:12-16 elaborates the impartiality of God's judgment by arguing that Gentiles who sin without the law will perish without the law just as God condemns Jews through the law who sin with the law, because having the law does not justify, but doing the law justifies (Rom. 2:13-15).[116] Law here refers to Torah, because Paul earlier mentioned the "righteous requirement of God" (Rom. 1:32) and because he states that Gentiles did not receive the νόμος (Rom. 2:14) but do moral norms of Torah, whereas Jews received Torah and disobey it (Rom. 2:17-20; cf. LXX 1 Esdr. 8:12, 21; 9:39; Tob. 1:8; 6:13; 7:13).[117] To state the matter clearly, a point that should not be missed regarding 2:13 is this: *If either group (Jews or Gentiles) could genuinely reach the standard of obedience set forth in Torah, then both groups would receive its reward, namely, vindication in God's law-court.* However, since neither group does the law to the degree that it requires, neither group will be justified by the law in his law-court (Rom. 3:20).[118] Both Jews (who have the law but do not obey it) are condemned before God and Gentiles (who do not have the written law but have the work of the law written on their hearts) will be judged. Thus, Paul's argument focuses on the standard of judgment.[119] He neither refers to a

---

be justified by works of law in his presence." Paul still speaks of works' contribution to one's final justification (2:13) and works' inability to contribute to one's final justification (3:20). For his full argument, see Charles H. Cosgrove, "Justification in Paul: A Linguistic and Theological Reflection," *JBL* 106 (1987): 653-670, esp. 658-61. In agreement with Cosgrove, see Yinger, *Judgment According to Deeds*, 175.

[115] So Sanders (*PPJ*, 516-17), but he wrongly argues that justification in 2:13 excludes the concept of salvation, wrongly because judgment implies salvation (cf. Rom 1:16 with 1:17).

[116] For a recent article on Paul's use of νόμος in Romans, see Peter W. Gosnell, "Law in Romans: Regulation and Instruction," *NovT* 51 (2009): 252-71.

[117] Ibid.

[118] For a different reading of 2:13 and 3:20, see Cosgrove, "Justification," 653-670. However, as Bell (*No One Seeks for God*, 145-62) argues, "on reading 3:9-20 one must conclude that the pious Jews and pious Gentiles of Rom. 2:12-16 do not exist."

[119] Moo, *Romans*, 142.

Humanity's Spiritual Plight

hypothetical justification nor to a hypothetical obedience to Torah,[120] for Paul's argument in 2:1-13 is that Jews and Gentiles are both condemned by Torah because they do not obey Torah.[121]

Romans 2:14 offers a ground to the premises in 2:12-13. Romans 2:14 explains how God could hold the Gentiles to the same standard as the Jew in order to highlight Jewish condemnation. He states that "when the Gentiles, who do not have the law by nature, do the things in the law, these are a law to themselves although they do not have the [external demands of] the law" (brackets mine). The clause ἔθνη τὰ μὴ νόμον ἔχοντα φύσει refers to the Gentiles' identity whose "birthright lacked exposure to the Torah"[122] and not to the Gentiles' natural obedience to Torah, because Gentiles did not naturally do the law. Rather, they suppressed the truth revealed to them (Rom. 1:18-32). Furthermore, Paul states in 2:27 that Gentiles were uncircumcised by nature. Still, Romans 2:14 refers to some level of Gentile obedience to Torah even though he asserts that they do not possess the external demands of Torah, for Paul uses a verbal cognate (ποιῶσιν) of the noun (ποιηταὶ) in 2:14 to affirm Gentile obedience to Torah. He uses this cognate in Romans 2:13 to suggest that the doers of the law will receive justification. Thus, although the Gentiles do not possess Torah, they are a Torah against themselves (Rom. 2:14),[123] because they demonstrate that the work of Torah is nevertheless written on their hearts (Rom. 2:15; cf. Philo, *Abr*. 275-76).

In what way do these Gentiles demonstrate the work of Torah to be written on their hearts? Paul does not refer to the new covenant promise of Jeremiah 31:31-34 when YHWH would write his law on the hearts of his people (LXX Jer. 38:31-34),[124] for although there are striking parallels between the two texts, there are also striking differences. For example, both texts mention the law in context of the heart, but LXX Jeremiah 38:31-34 states that the law will be written on the hearts of God's people, whereas Romans 2:15 states that the "work of the law" is on the hearts of the Gentiles.[125] Unlike LXX 38:31-34, Paul in Romans 2:15 describes not a saving work of God whereby he writes his law on the hearts of his people through the power of the Spirit, but Paul asserts that Gentiles know and do some of the moral elements of Torah.[126] This fits with Paul's hearing-receiving versus doing antithesis in Romans 2:12-14. Hence, Paul is not talking about Gentile Christians in Romans 2:14-15 who fulfill Torah in the power of the Spirit.[127]

---

[120]Rightly VanLandingham, *Judgment*, 215-16.
[121]Similarly Sanders, *Paul*, 126, although he does not think 2:28-29 refers to Gentile Christians.
[122]Jewett, *Romans*, 214.
[123]Against Käsemann, *Romans*, 64.
[124]So Käsemann, 64; Schreiner, *Romans*, 122.
[125]So Schreiner, *Romans*, 122.
[126]Ibid.
[127]Against Cranfield, *Romans*, 1:158-59; Gathercole, "A Law unto Themselves," 27-49; Wright, "Romans," 441-42; VanLandingham, *Judgment*, 228-32.

On the contrary, Gathercole argues that Paul refers to Gentile Christians in 2:14-15.[128] To support his thesis, he offers strong arguments. First, in 2:14-15, Paul contrasts believing Gentiles with unbelieving Israel. Second, there is a logical connection between 2:13 and 2:14. Third, τὰ τοῦ νόμου is comprehensive and refers to "the fundamental knowledge of God that is lacking in the Jewish contemporaries of these Gentiles." Fourth, φύσει refers to what precedes in 2:13 instead of what follows. Fifth, the three witnesses (heart, conscience, and thoughts) defend these Gentiles in God's law-court.[129]

In spite of Gathercole's fresh insights and careful analysis, Romans 2:6-12 appears to speak against his thesis, for there Paul emphasizes that Jews and Gentiles will perish because neither group obeys Torah to the degree that it deserves. Moreover, we know from the argument of 1:18-31 that the ungodly suppress the truth (which includes ungodly Gentiles) that God has revealed about himself through creation instead of submit to it, and they perform unnatural vices. Gathercole suggests that the Gentiles in 1:18-31 are those outside of Christ, but those in 2:14-15 are those transformed by the Spirit and those whose heart and conscience will testify in their defense in the judgment.[130] Yet, in response to Gathercole, the condemnatory tone of which Paul speaks of the Gentiles in 2:7-12 and in 2:15 militates against his suggestion, for Paul's point seems to be in 2:13 that if in fact Jews and Gentiles reached the standard of obedience that Torah demands, they would in fact be justified in God's law-court. That this standard is unachievable does not become clear until Romans 3:20 when Paul states that no flesh will be justified by keeping Torah. However, in Romans 2:6-13, Paul sets forth a real promise of final justification for those who meet the demands of Torah.[131]

Jewett argues that the two objections to Romans 2:14 as a fulfillment of LXX Jeremiah 38:31-34 (MT and Eng. Jer. 31:31-34), that the eschatological fulfillment theme is absent and that Paul speaks of "work of law" instead of "works of law," are not convincing because the first objection is relevant only if the Gentiles in 2:14 are not Christians and because the second objection assumes that Paul argues against Jewish legalists.[132] However, Jewett neglects to consider additional arguments that tilt the scale in favor of the non-Christian interpretation in 2:14-15.

First, Paul's discussion in 2:14 focuses on the impartiality of God's judgment of Jews and Gentiles. Second, Paul speaks of the *condemnation* of those who have the work of the law written on their hearts in 2:15-16. Third,

---

[128]Gathercole, "A Law unto Themselves," 27-49.
[129]Ibid., 31-46.
[130]Ibid., 43, 45-46.
[131]Against Räisänen, *Paul*, 105-07; Murray, 1.78-79; Cranfield, *Romans*, 1:154-55; Sanders, *Paul*, 126-32; Snodgrass, "Justification by Grace," 72-93; Frank Thielman, *From Plight to Solution: A Jewish Framework for Understanding Paul's View of the Law in Galatians and Romans*, NovT Supp LXI (Leiden: Brill, 1989), 92-96; Schreiner, *The Law and Fulfillment*, 179-204; idem, *Romans*, 119; Jewett, *Romans*, 212-13.
[132]Jewett, *Romans*, 215.

the τὸ ἔργον τοῦ νόμου on the hearts of the Gentiles in 2:15 is another way of speaking about the τὰ τοῦ νόμου in 2:14 that the Gentiles obey, for 2:15 is a relative clause that further describes how the Gentiles are obedient to the things of the law and how they are a law against themselves in 2:14 even though they do not have the written Torah.[133] The work of the law, then, written on the hearts of the Gentile means that he, even without a written Torah, follows some of the precepts in the written Torah, because Gentiles obey certain moral norms of Torah.[134] This is supported by the subsequent language in the text that describes the coming judgment of those, Jews or Gentiles, who disobey Torah. In addition, Paul mentions the Gentiles' heart, conscience, and thoughts in 2:15. Heart refers to the center of the Gentiles' emotions by which they choose to make certain moral decisions that conform to and comply with some of the stipulations within Torah apart from possessing Torah, for Paul connects the concept of the work of the law written on their hearts with the witness of their conscience and with the concept of their thoughts either condemning or vindicating them in God's law-court when God will judge every man in accordance with the gospel through Jesus (Rom. 2:15-16),[135] and he mentions these things in a context wherein he discusses judgment in accordance with one's deeds (Rom. 2:5-14). Judgment in accordance with the gospel in 2:16 should be read in light of Paul's earlier statements in 2:6 that God will judge each person in accordance with one's works, for 2:6-16 is part of a singular argument regarding the impartiality of God's judgment.

Gentile moral sensibility to the written Torah is not unique to Paul, but this was already current in the Judaism that both preceded him and of which he was part prior to his faith in Christ. Philo speaks of Abraham (a Gentile) obeying the law without having the written commandments (*Abr.*, 275-76), and Jewish wisdom tradition affirms that the heavenly wisdom that those of good will sought could be found in the written Torah (1 Bar. 3:9-4:4).[136] Thus, Romans 2:14-15 adds to Paul's indictment of the Jew who hears but does not obey Torah by emphasizing the judgment of the Gentiles who do not possess Torah but nevertheless obey certain aspects of it.[137]

Fourth, Paul states that the Gentiles are a law "against themselves" in 2:14. The latter translation suggests that the work of the law of God written on their hearts is to their disadvantage. That ἑαυτοῖς in Romans 2:14 is a dative of

---

[133]Käsemann (*Romans*, 64) asserts this point rather than argues for it, but I credit him for this thought.

[134]He does not use the phrase "moral norms of Torah," but see also Bell, *No One Seeks for God*, 153-59.

[135]Against Cranfield, *Romans*, 1:158-63. For καρδία as the place from which moral decisions derive, see Rom. 1:21, 24; 2:5, 29; 5:5; 6:17; 8:27; 9:2; 10:1, 6, 8, 9, 10; 1 Cor. 4:5; 7:37; 14:25.

[136]James D.G. Dunn, *The Theology of Paul—the Apostle* (Grand Rapids: Eerdmans, 1998), 137 n. 50.

[137]Das (*Paul*, 181-82) emphasizes the point that in 2:12-16, the Jew who hears Torah but does not obey would be indicted.

disadvantage exegetically fits with the forensic and condemnatory context of 2:7-16, and it fits syntactically with Paul's only other use of this pronoun without a preposition in a forensic context in Romans. In Romans 13:2, Paul states that those who oppose the government "will receive judgment against themselves" (ἑαυτοῖς κρίμα λήμψονται) from the government. Fifth, Paul states that these Gentiles will be condemned by God in the Day of Judgment, for mere possession of Torah will not vindicate the Jew in God's eschatological judgment, and likewise the Gentiles' lack of possession of the written Torah will neither condemn them in God's eschatological judgment. Torah is not the inviolable private possession of the Jew, but rather it guarantees that no one will escape God's judgment.[138] Therefore, Paul's remarks in 2:13-15 are not in reference to Christians who obey Torah in the power of the Spirit. The argument that Jews and Gentiles are the Spirit empowered people of God does not emerge until 2:25-29 and 8:1-11.

With Romans 2:16, Paul adds another element of condemnation against the Jew (and at some level against the Gentile): viz., the gospel.[139] That is, the Jew who trusts in Torah and meets its demands and the Gentile who meets the demands of Torah, although he did not receive Torah, will be justified in God's law-court, but the Jew and Gentile who do not meet Torah's demands will be condemned in God's law-court (Rom. 2:15). Paul's gospel, which is God's gospel about Jesus, the Jewish Messiah (Rom. 1:1-5; Rom. 9:1-11:36), cooperates with Torah and with the Gentiles' conscience to add further condemnation to the Jew and the Gentile in God's law-court who does not meet the demands set forth in the Torah, because Paul's good news about Jesus, the Jewish Messiah, offers a way for the Jew and Gentile to circumvent God's eschatological judgment reserved for those who do not attain to the high standard of Torah. But the gospel pronounces judgment against those who fail to meet the demands of Torah outside of Christ (Rom. 1:16-17; 3:21-26).[140] However, the Jew who relies on Torah and does not fully obey and the Gentile who does not have Torah but obeys only some of its moral norms will not escape God's wrath because neither group meets the standard set forth in Torah. Thus, the Jew who judges the Gentile for violating Torah and yet likewise violates Torah will be subject to God's eschatological wrath in accordance with Torah along with the Gentiles, who do not have Torah, when God judges Jews and Gentiles in accordance with the gospel. Thus, the gospel along with the Torah will bear witness against both groups in God's

---

[138]Käsemann, *Romans*, 62.

[139]Regarding the complex nature of 2:16, see Jewett, *Romans*, 217-18.

[140]Against Barrett, *Romans*, 53-54. He thinks that "secret things of men" is the key phrase to determining the meaning of "my gospel." The former phrase refers to one's faith in God (cf. Rom 14:22). This faith is judgment, but it is likewise good news for sinners, for it provides the prospect of justification by faith. *Pace* also Jewett, *Romans*, 218.

Humanity's Spiritual Plight

eschatological law-court.[141]

Romans 2:17-29

Paul speaks further of the Jew's spiritual predicament in light of Torah's entrance into salvation-history in Romans 2:17-29. The entire passage indicts Jews.[142] Romans 2:17-20 introduces legitimate privileges that Jews received from YHWH, that made them distinct from Gentiles, and on which they relied.[143]

With a conditional statement,[144] Paul suggests that the Jew relies upon Torah and boasts in God (Rom. 2:17; cf. Exod. 24; Epistle of Aristeas; Pss. Sol. 17:1; 2 Apoc. Bar. 48:22-24),[145] that he knows the will of God and approves of the excellent things since he is taught by Torah (Rom. 2:18; cf. Deut. 6; 1 Bar. 4:4; Wis. 15:2-3),[146] that he persuades himself to be a teacher and a light of the spiritually blind (Rom. 2:19; cf. Isa. 42:6-7; 49:6; 1 En. 105:1; T. Levi 14:3-8; Wis. 18:4; Sir. 24:27; Sib. Or. 3.194-95; Jos. *Ag. Ap.* 2.291-95; Philo, *Abr.* 98; *Mos.* 1.149), a light for those in darkness (Rom. 2:19; cf. 1QS 1:9; 2:16; 3:13, 24-25; 1QM 1:1, 7, 11, 13-15),[147] an instructor of the foolish (Rom. 2:20; cf. 1QH 2:9; 1QS 3:13), and a teacher of infants (1QpHab 7:4-5), because they have the truth in Torah (Rom. 2:20; cf. Sir. 17:11; 45:5; 1 Bar. 3:36; 2 Apoc. Bar. 44:2-15).[148] The spiritually blind, the foolish, and the infants most certainly refer to Gentiles,[149] for this is a typical Jewish perception of them (cf. Wis. 11:1-16:1; Jub. 22:16-23; Isa 49:6) and this typical Jewish perception fits with Paul's earlier indictment of Gentiles in 1:18-31. In Romans 2:21-24, Paul indicts the Jew for failing to obey Torah. He accuses him of violating Torah while boasting in Torah (Rom. 2:21-23a), of dishonoring God through transgression of Torah (Rom 2:23b; cf. T. Levi 14:1-8), and consequently of provoking the Gentiles to blaspheme the God of Torah on account of Jewish disobedience to Torah (Rom. 2:24; cf. Isa. 52:5; Ezek. 36:20; T. Levi 14:1-8). His point here is not that every Jew or most Jews violate Torah and not even

---

[141]Against Dunn (*Romans,* 1:103; cf. 106-07) who emphasizes the point that the gospel replaces the law as the measure of judgment in Rom 2:16 instead of affirming that the law, conscience, and the gospel testify against both Jews and Gentiles in the eschaton.

[142]Contra Jewett, *Romans*, 219, whose heading of the section suggests that the text indicts Gentiles too. Rightly Bell, *No One Seeks for God,* 184-209.

[143]Dunn, *Romans*, 1:110; Wright, "Romans," 446. However, Wright ("Romans 2," 139-43) seems to downplay the point that Paul actually critiques the Jew for disobeying Torah.

[144]The unit is an anacoluthon. Jewett, *Romans*, 221 n. 16.

[145]On Jewish boasting in 2:17, see Bell, *No One Seeks for God*, 185-88.

[146]A point vividly expressed in 2 Macc. 1:3-4.

[147]DSS references in Jewett, *Romans*, 225.

[148]So Wright, "Romans," 446-47. For an example of Jewish confidence, see 1 Bar. 4:1-4.

[149]*Pace* Jewett, *Romans*, 225, who thinks that Paul's remarks refer to Jews and Gentiles since the Old Testament prophets often refer to disobedient Israelites as blind (Zeph. 1:17; Isa. 43:8; 56:10; 59:9-10).

that the Jews were legalistically trying to earn their salvation by keeping the law,[150] but that Jews as a people will not stand in privilege over the Gentiles in God's law-court based on their possession of Torah, because some Jews do in fact what Torah forbids (cf. Isa. 1; 1 Macc. 1; Matt. 23) while some Gentiles do what Torah commends (Rom. 2:15).[151]

In Romans 2:25-29, Paul directly takes up the question of the benefit of circumcision, one of the stipulations in Torah (Exod. 12:48; Lev. 12:3; Josh. 5:2) and one of the marks of covenant membership (Gen. 17:1-14; Jub. 15:1-34; Jud. 14:10; 1 Macc. 1:48, 60-61; 2:46; 2 Macc. 6:10; Jos. *Ant.* 13.257-58). By the profit of circumcision, Jewett argues that Paul means profit with regard to covenant membership and not with regard to salvation, because Jewish tradition expresses revulsion against those not circumcised (Jub. 15:26; 30:7-12; Add. Esth. C 14:15) and because circumcision was a distinct mark of covenant membership for the people of God (CD 16:4-6; Jos. *Ant.* 13.257, 318-19, 397; 20:139, 145; 1 Macc. 2:46).[152] Jewett is correct to emphasize the importance of circumcision for covenant membership, but he does not take seriously the point that Paul argues in Romans 2:25-26 that circumcision (an external sign of covenant membership) will profit the Jew *only* if he obeys Torah (Rom. 2:25; cf. LXX Deut. 30:16). Since Paul's discussion has focused on the final judgment in 2:4-16, the profit of circumcision must pertain to its value in God's eschatological law-court.[153] Furthermore, the obedience described must be perfect obedience to Torah, for LXX Deuteronomy 30:16 records that Moses urges Israel that if the nation hears "the commandments of the Lord," goes in "all his ways," and keeps "his righteous requirements," then the people would live and inherit the land. Since circumcision was one requirement of Torah, by obedience to Torah Paul means that if a Jew wants his circumcision to profit him soteriologically in God's eschatological law-court, then he must obey other stipulations in Torah in addition to circumcision (cf. Gal. 5:2-4).[154]

Moreover, since Paul has already accused both Gentiles and Jews of various vices in 1:27-31 and in 2:21-22 and indicted them for such vices (2:6-25), these sins represent some of the things that violate Torah, while circumcision represents one of the requirements of Torah. Furthermore, since Paul has already mentioned that the Jew knows the "righteous requirement of God" (δικαίωμα θεοῦ) in Romans 1:32 and in 2:26 that the Jew must keep the "righteous requirements of the law" (δικαιώματα τοῦ νόμου), both of which refer to specific stipulations in the Torah (LXX Num. 31:21; 36:13; Deut. 4:1, 5; 1 Macc. 2:21; 1 Bar. 2:12), since Paul argued in 2:6 that God will reward in the judgment in accordance with one's works and in 2:13 that only the doers of

---

[150] Rightly Das, *Paul*, 184.

[151] Dunn, *Romans*, 1:114.

[152] Jewett, *Romans*, 231-32.

[153] For a similar point, see rightly Bell, *No One Seeks for God*, 200.

[154] Against Barrett (*Romans*, 58) who states that for Paul, to do the law means to have faith. Rightly Schreiner, *Romans*, 138.

the law will be justified, and since YHWH expected Israel to obey perfectly all of his demands or else they would be judged (Lev. 18:4-5; 20:22; 25:18; Deut. 6-28; 30:16; 4 Ezra 6:7-9:25; 1QS 1.5-2.3), Paul refers to perfect obedience that will profit the Jew in his law-court *only* if he practices Torah (Rom. 2:25; cf. Sus. 1:22-23).[155] The οὖν in Romans 2:26 suggests that Paul infers from his premise in 2:25. In Romans 2:25, Paul states that circumcision profits the Jew *only* if he obeys Torah. Therefore, Paul concludes in Romans 2:26 if the uncircumcised (ἀκροβυστία), i.e., the Gentile (cf. Jud. 14:10; 1 Macc. 1:15), keeps Torah, his circumcision will be counted as circumcision.

By keeping Torah, Paul means perfect obedience, because of the same arguments put forth above to support perfect obedience in 2:25 and because he recalls in 2:26 the concept of justification by works in 2:13 (cf. 2:6) with the verb λογισθήσεται, which is a future passive just as δικαιωθήσεται in 2:13. Both verbs refer to God's pronouncement in his eschatological law-court,[156] for the entire argument of 2:1-29 focuses on God's standard of judgment in his law-court, and 2:27 specifically refers to a future judgment. Λογίζομαι with a passive force is a prominent word in Romans, and it occurs in soteriological contexts only with a passive force (Rom. 2:26; 4:3-6, 9, 10, 22, 23; 9:8; cf. Gal. 3:6; Jas 2:23). Paul argues that God counted (λογίζομαι) Abraham's faith as righteousness (Rom. 4:3-6, 9-11, 22, 23) and that God only counts some Jews (i.e. the elect Jews from within Israel) as his children (Rom. 9:6-8; esp. 9:8). Λογίζομαι means to reckon something to be true that was not previously true, for this is precisely how the verb is often used when it has a passive force in the LXX, and there this reckoning could be a positive (LXX Gen. 15:6; Num. 18:27, 30; Ps. 105:31; 17:28; Isa. 32:15; 1 Macc. 2:52) or a negative (LXX Lev. 7:18; 17:4; Isa. 29:17; 53:12; Wis. 7:9; 9:6) reckoning. In the case of Abraham, righteousness was reckoned to Abraham's credit because he believed God's word (Rom 4:1-25; cf. LXX Gen. 15:6). In the case of the Gentiles, circumcision (inclusion within the people of God) will be reckoned to them if they obey Torah (Rom. 2:26).

But how can the uncircumcised Gentile keep the Torah if he remains uncircumcised, for circumcision is one of the stipulations in Torah (Exod. 12:48; Lev. 12:3; Josh. 5:2) and one (thought to be the most important) mark of covenant membership (Gen. 17:1-14; Jub. 15:1-34; Jud. 14:10; 1 Macc. 2:26)? Just as justification by works in Romans 2:13, one might argue that Paul speaks here of a fictional or hypothetical fulfillment of Torah since a Gentile cannot both fulfill Torah and remain uncircumcised.[157] This interpretation is supported by the conditional clause introduced by ἐάν in 2:25.[158] However, since Paul has been arguing from 2:1 that Torah can only profit the Jew in the eschatological

---

[155]Against Dunn, *Romans*, 1:108-28, who emphasizes that Paul critiques the Jew because of his ethnic pride due to his perceived privileged status in the covenant community.
[156]Against Jewett, *Romans*, 233.
[157]Käsemann, *Romans*, 73; Thielman, *Plight*, 94-96.
[158]So Thielman, *Plight*, 96.

judgment if he obeys it and that God will reward in the judgment the one (Jew or Gentile) who obeys Torah, a hypothetical fulfillment of Torah must be rejected. It should also be rejected since neither a hypothetical view of judgment according to works nor a hypothetical view of final justification has a place in Romans 2:6-13. Rather, Paul seems to spiritualize what it means to be obedient to Torah in 2:26 by now speaking of an eschatological fulfillment of the new covenant promise of spiritual circumcision by faith in Christ (Deut. 10:16; 30:6; Jer. 31:31-34; Rom. 8:1-4; 9:30-10:13).[159]

Sanders argued approximately 28 years ago that Romans 2:26-29 does not refer to Gentile Christians.[160] To put it simply, Sanders defends this premise by arguing that (a) the "flesh" (2:28) and "spirit" (2:29) contrast is not between the spiritual power of the flesh and the Holy Spirit but between the physical body and the inner self (i.e., the heart), which (he suggests) is further strengthened by the occurrence of "heart" in 2:29 (cf. 2 Cor. 7:1).[161] That is, verses 28-29 refer to the person who obeys Torah, "the true Jew who does not make an external show, who may not be physically circumcised ('in the flesh'), but who is circumcised internally, in secret. . ."[162] (b) The true Jews are not the same group as in Philippians 3, who boasts in Jesus Christ, and they are not the same group in Romans 4 and Galatians 3, who have trusted in Jesus Christ, but the true Jew in Romans 2:28-29 is a non-Christian ethnic Jew.[163] (c) Paul's discussion in Romans 2 is an inner-Jewish debate as to whether right knowledge leads to right action.[164] (d) The unit of 1:18-2:29 is probably a synagogue sermon with no distinct Pauline imprint (except for 2:16), whose goal is to have his Jewish hearers become better Jews and not to have them become true children of Abraham by faith in Jesus.[165] (e) Paul's emphasis on the Jew doing the Jewish law in chapter 2 suggests that Paul is not speaking of Christians, but of Jews obeying Torah to attain salvation.[166] Nevertheless, in my view, 2:27-29 speaks of Gentile Christians because of the Old Testament promise of an eschatological spiritual circumcision of the heart of God's people (Jer. 31:31-34; Ezek. 36:22-37:28), because of early Judaism's reiteration of a future spiritual circumcision (Jub. 1:23; Odes Sol. 11:1-3), because of other contrasts in Paul between the old life under the law and new life in the Spirit (Rom. 7:6),[167] because of other Pauline statements about spiritual circumcision (2 Cor. 3:6; Phil 3:3; Col. 2:11-12), and most importantly because of Paul's ensuing argument in Romans 2:25-29. I elaborate each point in my exegesis

---

[159]Watson, *Paul, Judaism, and the Gentiles*, 214-15.
[160]Sanders, *Paul*, 126-32. Also Nygren, *Romans*, 133-35. But Nygren does not explain how the uncircumcised Gentile fulfills Torah.
[161]Sanders, *Paul*, 127.
[162]Ibid.
[163]Ibid.
[164]Ibid., 128.
[165]Ibid., 129.
[166]Sanders, 129-32. Against also Bell, *No One Seeks for God*, 194-200.
[167]For this specific point, see Wright, "Romans 2," 134-35.

Humanity's Spiritual Plight

below.

In texts in the Old Testament where both Israel and Judah are in exile because of their sin, YHWH promises a day when he will install a new covenant between himself and his people, a covenant wherein he would give the Spirit to his people as the sign of covenant membership and wherein he would write his law on their hearts instead of on stone tablets (Jer. 31:31-34; Ezek. 36:22-37:28; esp. 36:26-27; Deut. 30:6).[168] In Jubilees 1:22-25, the Jewish author states that YHWH informed Moses that he would circumcise Israel's stubborn heart and give the people a holy spirit so that they would not turn away from following him but would obey his commands. In 2 Corinthians 3:1-6, Paul informs the Corinthians that he does not need letters of commendation from men to them or from them to men to validate his ministry (2 Cor. 3:1), for the Corinthians are his letter (2 Cor. 3:2), which is read by all (2 Cor. 3:2b), written not with ink on tablets of stone but on their hearts by the Spirit (2 Cor. 3:3). God made Paul and his missionary companions ministers of this new covenant that is characterized not by Torah but by the Spirit (2 Cor. 3:6). In Colossians 2:11-12, Paul does not use the spiritual metaphor of circumcision of the heart, but he uses the same new covenant language already cited above when he says that the Colossians were circumcised with the circumcision of Christ when they were baptized into Christ.[169] This evidence in the Old Testament, early Judaism, and additional Pauline texts provide a helpful interpretive framework by which to read the argument of Romans 2:25-29. However, the above texts should not be read into Paul's argument in the latter unit so that they determine one's reading of Romans 2:25-29, but rather Romans 2:25-29 should be interpreted in light of the immediate argument in which the unit occurs.

In Romans 2:25, Paul states that if the Jew does not obey Torah, then his circumcision is viewed as lack of circumcision (sign of non-covenant membership). Paul does not mean in 2:25 that the Jew literally becomes uncircumcised if he fails to obey Torah, but he means that his physical circumcision is not enough to grant him covenant membership within the eschatological people of God, for a Jew who violated other portions of Torah (i.e. adultery, murder, etc. [cf. Rom. 2:21-23]) was still circumcised and still had the physical sign of covenant membership. Paul neither means in 2:26 that the Gentile who obeys Torah becomes physically circumcised when he states that his lack of circumcision is reckoned as circumcision if he obeys Torah, because Paul states that the Gentile who obeys Torah is still an uncircumcised Gentile since he asserts that "his uncircumcision will be reckoned as circumcision." As I argued earlier, λογισθήσεται means to reckon something

---

[168]For the argument that Paul's negative critique of Israel and his pessimistic view of Torah were the result of his "drastic recasting of eschatological expectation bound up with acceptance with Jesus as Messiah along with a decidedly apocalyptic cast of thought," see Brendan Byrne, "The Problem of Νόμος and the Relationship with Judaism in Romans," *CBQ* 62 (2000): 294-309.

[169]Sanders (*PPJ,* 431) dismisses evidence from Colossians as anti-Pauline.

to be true that was not previously true (cf. LXX Gen. 15:6; Num. 18:27, 30; Ps. 105:31; 17:28; Isa. 32:15; 1 Macc. 2:52), and circumcision was a sign of covenant membership for the people of God in the Old Testament (Gen. 17:1-14; Jub. 15:1-34; Jud. 14:10; 1 Macc. 2:26). Thus, the primary issue in 2:25-26 is not physical circumcision, but covenant membership/status in the eschatological law-court.[170] This interpretation is vindicated by Romans 2:26-29.

In Romans 2:26, Paul states that the uncircumcised Gentile condemns the circumcised Jew "as a transgressor of the law through the writing and circumcision because the [uncircumcised Gentile] fulfills the law" (brackets mine). Paul cannot literally mean that an uncircumcised Gentile condemns a circumcised Jew as a transgressor of Torah because the uncircumcised Gentile cannot literally or even hypothetically obey Torah, for an uncircumcised Gentile is guilty of breaking Torah by virtue of being uncircumcised (cf. Eph. 2:11-12). Rather, the Gentile condemns the Jew as a violator of Torah because Jews have not perfectly obeyed Torah, but the Gentile in 2:27 fulfills Torah. It is exegetically significant that Paul does not say here that the Gentile condemns the Jew because the former obeys Torah, but rather because he "fulfills" it (τελοῦσα).[171]

How have these particular Gentiles fulfilled Torah in contrast to the Gentiles in Romans 1:18-31? The Gentiles in 2:27 fulfill Torah because they have received the new covenant promise of the Spirit (Jer. 31:31-34 [LXX Jer. 38:31-34]; Ezek. 36-37; Joel 2), which is fulfilled in Jesus Christ and which one receives when he unites himself to Christ by faith and obeys the gospel (Rom. 8:1-4).[172] Romans 2:28-29 supports this when Paul stresses that Jewishness (i.e. covenant membership) is not marked merely by external commands and physical circumcision as demanded by Torah (Rom. 2:28-29), but by the internal (spiritual) work of the Spirit (Rom. 2:29; cf. Jer. 31:31-34; Ezek. 36-37; Joel 2), and this internal, spiritual circumcision results in God's approval in the judgment. This interpretation seems likely because Romans 4:1-25 argues that God counted Abraham (an uncircumcised Gentile) righteous by his faith before he received the covenant sign of circumcision, and God included him within the people of God by faith before he received the covenantal sign of circumcision.

That Paul means that these Gentiles fulfill Torah because they unite themselves to Jesus by faith and that they thereby receive the new covenant promise of the Spirit, which is fulfilled in him, is further supported by Romans 8:1-4. In Romans 8:1-4, Paul states that Torah does not condemn those in

---

[170]Similarly Wright, "Romans 2," 138-39, 147. Gathercole ("A Law unto Themselves," 35) is rightly hesitant to use covenant status language in the sense that Wright uses it, but he acknowledges that such language appears in Rom. 2.

[171]Against Jewett, *Romans*, 234, who interprets τελέω in 2:27 as a rough equivalent of φυλάσσω in 2:26. Against also Schreiner, *Romans*, 140.

[172]Against Moo, *Romans*, 169-71. He thinks Paul anticipates his discussion about Christians in Romans 8, but that 2:26-29 does not refer to Gentile Christians.

Humanity's Spiritual Plight

Christ Jesus (as opposed to those in Adam), "for the law of the Spirit of life in Christ Jesus has freed you from the law of sin and death since God did what the law was incapable of doing in that he sent his son in the likeness of sinful flesh and he condemned sin in [Jesus'] flesh, so that the righteous requirement of the law would be fulfilled in us who walk not according to the flesh, but according to the Spirit" (brackets mine). This paragraph is significant in Paul's argument for many reasons, but one is that it reveals a connection with the argument of Romans 2:25-29 and with the new covenant promises of the Spirit in the Old Testament. Paul mentions νόμος (Rom. 8:2-3; cf. 2:25-29), δικαίωμα νομοῦ (Rom. 8:4; cf. 1:32; 2:26), fulfillment language (πληρωθῇ) (Rom. 8:4; cf. 2:27), and the Spirit in both texts (Rom. 2:29; 7:6; 8:4).

Another connection with Romans 2:25-29 and with the new covenant promises of the Spirit in the Old Testament occurs in the argument of Romans 9-11. After expressing that Israel has a zeal for God but not in accordance with knowledge since the nation is ignorant with respect to God's righteousness by faith in Jesus (Rom. 9:30-10:3), Paul states that the "goal/end" (τέλος—a nominal cognate of τελοῦσα in 2:27) "of the law is Christ resulting in righteousness for everyone who believes" (Rom. 10:3). In Romans 10:5-13, Paul continues the argument that he began in 9:30 by pitting Israel's unsuccessful pursuit of righteousness in Torah because of the nation's disobedience against the Gentiles' successful pursuit of righteousness by faith in Jesus Christ (Rom. 9:30-10:13). Paul cites a portion of LXX Joel 2:32 (a text that prophesies about the new covenant promise of the Spirit for all the nations who call upon the name of the Lord) in Romans 10:13 when he states that everyone who calls on the Lord will be saved. He states in Romans 10:8-9 that this Lord is Jesus Christ. In Romans 10:14-11:36, Paul continues the discussion of Jewish unbelief, Gentile salvation, and the future salvation of Israel. Thus, it seems most likely that Romans 2:25-29 refers to a spiritual obedience to Torah that finds its fulfillment in Jesus Christ and those who have united themselves to him by faith and who thereby receive the gift of the Spirit. By arguing in this way, Paul highlights the condemnation of Jews (Torah insiders) outside of Christ now that Torah has entered salvation-history by accentuating that Gentiles (Torah outsiders) have in fact fulfilled Torah by receiving the Spirit by faith in Jesus.

Romans 3:1-8

Romans 3:1-8 considers whether the Jew has an advantage over Gentiles (Rom. 3:1). On the one hand, Paul states that Jews have a real advantage over Gentiles in that they were given the oracles of God (Rom. 3:2). The phrase "oracles of God" (τὰ λόγια τοῦ θεοῦ) could simply refer to God's words (LXX Num. 24:4, 16; Ps. 11:7; 17:31; 104:19; 106:11; 118:11; Isa. 28:13). However, in Romans 3:2, the phrase most likely refers to God's words as revealed to Israel in Torah,¹⁷³ which makes the phrase synonymous with δικαίωμα τοῦ θεοῦ (Rom. 1:32), τὰ τοῦ νόμου (Rom. 2:14), and τὰ δικαιώματα τοῦ νόμου (Rom. 2:26). The latter interpretation seems right because 3:1-8 infers a conclusion from the preceding argument of 2:1-29, which has focused on the universality of God's judgment in accordance with the standard of Torah, because God's τὰ λόγια occurs in LXX Deuteronomy 33:9-10 as a nominal hendiadys with τὴν διαθήκην σου (LXX Deut. 33:9) and in a parallel statement with δικαίωμα and νόμος (LXX Deut. 33:10), both of which likewise function as a nominal hendiadys, and because Israel received direct and special revelation of YHWH's will through Moses in Torah (Rom. 2:17-20; cf. Deut. 4:6-8).¹⁷⁴

In the latter text, Moses gave Israel a final word before his death and asserted that YHWH gave the nation his law (LXX Deut. 33:4), that some guarded the oracles and kept the covenant (LXX Deut. 33:9), and that Israel was taught the ordinances and the law (LXX Deut. 33:10).¹⁷⁵ Acts 7:38 supports the above reading of τὰ λόγια τοῦ θεοῦ, for Stephen states there that Moses received oracles in the wilderness from angels to give to Israel (cf. Gal. 3:19). The phrase τὰ λόγια τοῦ θεου also includes promises from God regarding salvation (cf. Rom. 9:1-11:36).¹⁷⁶

But Paul's answer raises the question as to whether God's faithfulness to Israel is nullified on account of the faithlessness of some Jews (Rom. 3:3; cf. chapters 9-11). Τὴν πίστιν θεοῦ most certainly refers to God's covenantal faithfulness to Israel,¹⁷⁷ because Paul's entire argument since 2:1 has been that the Jew's mere possession of Torah will not vindicate him in God's law-court and the Gentile's lack of the written Torah will not necessarily condemn him in God's law-court and because 3:4 refers to God's truthfulness and vindication when accused in his law-court. The argument of 2:1-3:3 would raise the question as to whether God is just to condemn Jews in his law-court and to vindicate Gentiles and specifically whether he has forsaken his promises to provide salvation for Israel. The question in 3:3 anticipates Paul's detailed argument in Romans 9-11 where he provides a *tour de force* in defense of

---

¹⁷³Against Dunn (*Romans*, 1:130-31) who takes the phrase to include both Torah and the prophets and against Jewett (*Romans*, 244, 247) who interprets the phrase to refer to God's promise concerning Messiah.

¹⁷⁴For the above latter point, see Owen, "The 'Works of the Law' in Romans and Galatians," 556.

¹⁷⁵Against Barrett, *Romans*, 62, who takes the phrase to refer to the Old Testament.

¹⁷⁶Schreiner, *Romans*, 149.

¹⁷⁷So Barrett, *Romans*, 63. Also Wright, "Romans," 453, but he wrongly defines δικαιοσύνη θεοῦ as "God's covenantal faithfulness." In agreement with Dunn (*Romans*, 1:134-35), I see a strong covenantal flavor within θεοῦ δικαιοσύνην in 3:5 since Paul parallels this phrase with God's faithfulness and Jewish unfaithfulness in 3:3. Still, the presence of covenantal language in 3:5b-8 *does not* support the premise that θεοῦ δικαιοσύνην should be translated as God's covenantal faithfulness, for Paul also surrounds θεοῦ δικαιοσύνην with forensic, law-court language in 3:4 and in 3:5b-8 and with justification language in 2:13 and in 3:20.

Humanity's Spiritual Plight

God's faithfulness to Israel in spite of the fact that many Jews reject Jesus as the Jewish Messiah, to whom God's oracles pointed (Rom. 10:4). His answer in Romans 3:4 (as in Rom. 9-11) regarding God's unfaithfulness is an emphatic μὴ γένοιτο. He asserts that God is true and mankind is a liar so that God's words vindicate him (God) and he (God) will conquer when he (God) is accused of unrighteousness in the judgment (cf. LXX Ps. 115:2; 50:6; CD 20; 1QH 7, 9, 14).[178] Thus, Jewish disobedience to Torah and God's judgment of the Jew because of disobedience does not nullify his faithfulness to his people (Rom. 3:3; cf. 9:1-11:36), for he is right to judge Gentiles and even Jews for their unrighteousness or else he would not be able to judge the world for its unrighteousness, because both Jews and Gentiles are guilty of disobedience (Rom. 3:4-8; cf. Pss. Sol. 8:1-34; 9:1-11).

Romans 3:9-20

Romans 3:9-20 concludes the unit of 2:1-3:20 by emphasizing Torah's universal condemnation of Jews and Gentiles.[179] In 3:10-18, Paul recalls the condemnation of Gentiles in 1:18-31 and extends condemnation to the Jews by arguing that they and Gentiles are guilty before God.[180] In light of his stark indictment of Jews in 2:1-3:8, Paul asks in 3:9 if the Jews have an advantage over Gentiles in God's eschatological judgment.[181] He responds with a sharp no and then offers a reason: "because we have already charged in advance both Jews and Greeks, all, to be under sin" (Rom. 3:9).[182] Paul charged both groups to be under the power of sin in the previous argument of Romans 1:18-3:8.[183]

To bolster the charge of Torah's universal condemnation of Jews and Gentiles, he cites in Romans 3:10-18a a catena of Old Testament texts that refer to wicked God-haters in their contexts (cf. CD 5:13-17; 4 Ezra 7:22-24),[184] but Paul applies them to both Gentiles and (especially to) Jews to highlight the universal condemnation of both groups. Although, after the catena, Paul refers to Torah in 3:19, this catena of texts is not from passages from Torah, but from other parts of the Jewish scriptures. Paul broadens the indictment of Jews and

---

[178]DSS references in Sanders, *PPJ*, 305-12.
[179]Dunn, *Romans*, 1:145.
[180]Jewett, *Romans*, 260-61.
[181]For the different ways to translate 3:9a, see Barrett, *Romans*, 66-68 and Jewett, *Romans*, 256-58. See also Bell (*No One Seeks for God*, 211-13) who creatively argues that Paul's question in 3:9 pertains to whether he will circumvent God's judgment in response to the charge in 3:8 that Paul was antinomian. For the relationship between 3:1 and 3:9 and the latter's meaning, see rightly Schreiner, *Romans*, 163-64.
[182]Against Dunn's translation (*Romans*, 1:146-47). Bell (*No One Seeks for God*, 213-14) insightfully argues that Paul's point in 3:9b is that every single person without exception is under the power of sin.
[183]Similarly Dunn, *Romans*, 1:148; Wright, "Romans," 457; Moo, *Romans*, 203; Schreiner, *Romans*, 164. Against Räisänen, *Paul & the Law*, 98-99; Watson, *Paul, Judaism, and the Gentiles*, 223. Watson argues that Paul *only* refers back to his comments in Rom 3:4 and not to his earlier comments in Rom. 1-2.
[184]For the specific texts cited, see Schreiner, *Romans*, 165.

Gentiles by appealing to other parts of the Jewish scriptures that speak of the condemnation of the wicked,[185] and he subsequently in 3:19 again refers to the Torah. His usage of Torah in 3:19 makes the point that the entire body of the Jewish scriptures pronounces universal judgment upon those who disobey God, even upon the Jews who possessed the Jewish scriptures, for the wicked ones listed in the catalogue of breaches in 3:10-18 are wicked precisely because they violate Torah.

Finally, Paul concludes the argument of 1:18-3:20 with 3:19-20. Based on his argument that Gentiles (and Jews) are guilty of suppressing the truth about God and of disobeying his righteous requirement (1:18-32), that God judges Jews and Gentiles in accordance with the same standard (2:1-29), his universal condemnation of Jews and Gentiles (3:1-18), his solution to the spiritual plight of both Jews and Gentiles (3:21-4:25), and based on his fuller exposition of how Torah is rightly fulfilled in the people of God (Jews and Gentiles) who possess the Spirit by faith in Jesus (8:4; 9:1-11:36), Paul seems to confirm in 3:19-20 that Torah speaks to those in the realm of Torah. Although Torah was especially given to the Jews, all Jews and Gentiles who have not received the new covenant promise of the Spirit are in the realm of Torah,[186] which means that the entire world (Jews and Gentiles) will be without excuse and accountable to God in the judgment (Rom. 3:19).[187] Thus, Paul can say that "no flesh will be justified in his presence by works of law, for knowledge of sin comes through the law" (Rom. 3:20; cf. LXX Ps. 142:2; 2 Apoc. Bar. 51:3).[188]

The meaning of justification in Romans 3:20 and the phrase ἐξ ἔργων νόμου ("by works of law") are debated.[189] The verb δικαιωθήσεται in 3:20 is

---

[185] See Rom. 3:10-12 with Ps. 14:1-3; 53:1-3; Eccl. 7:20, Rom. 3:13 with Ps. 5:9; 140:3; Rom. 3:14 with Ps. 10:7; Rom. 3:15-17 with Isa. 59:7-8; Prov. 1:16, and Rom. 3:18 with Ps. 36:1.

[186] Regarding the above analysis of 3:19, against Käsemann, *Romans*, 87-88; Barrett, *Romans*, 70; Dunn, *Romans*, 1:152; Wright, "Romans," 459; Moo, *Romans*, 205-06; Schreiner, *Romans*, 168.

[187] Dunn (*Romans*, 1:152) sees a reference to God's judgment of the entire creation with his use of "entire world," not just his judgment of Jews and Gentiles. But the phrases "every mouth" (3:19) and "all flesh" (3:19) together with "the entire world" (3:19) seem to emphasize in this text God's judgment against Jews and Gentiles, for these groups have been the subject of 1:18-3:18.

[188] Jewett (*Romans*, 265-66) argues that not "any flesh" refers to circumcised flesh and is a specific attack against the Judaizers, because Paul alters the original word from LXX Ps. 142:2b from "every one who lives" to "any flesh," which fits Paul's earlier discussion of circumcision in 2:28.

[189] Although I disagree with his analysis of Paul's theology of justification at several points, see Douglas A. Campbell, *The Deliverance of God: An Apocalyptic Rereading of Paul* (Grand Rapids: Eerdmans, 2009) for a recent survey of the debate. For a recent survey of ἐξ ἔργων νόμου and the law in Paul, see Stephen Westerholm, *Perspectives Old and New on Paul: The "Lutheran" Paul and His Critics* (Grand Rapids: Eerdmans, 2004).

Humanity's Spiritual Plight 83

forensic, and it is a relational term (cf. 2:13).[190] Paul means that God will not exonerate Jews or Gentiles in his law-court based on works of law, because this verb is connected to the phrase "in his presence" in 3:20;[191] the verb concludes the argument of Romans 1:18-3:20 that Gentiles will not be condemned in God's law-court for lack of possession of Torah and Jews will neither be exonerated in God's law-court for mere possession of Torah (1:18-3:20); Paul uses this verb in Romans 5:9 to argue that justification in the present age guarantees future salvation from God's wrath in the judgment for those who believe, and reconciliation through Jesus' death in Romans 5:10 is closely connected to justification by Jesus' blood in 5:9. In addition, Paul mentions justification in Romans 3:24 with the participle δικαιούμενοι in conjunction with the nominal cognate δικαιοσύνη in 3:21-22 (cf. 1:17), and he connects the participle in 3:24 with the sinfulness of humanity in Romans 3:23 and with the phrase "redemption in Christ Jesus" in Romans 3:24. Since Jesus' blood is the foundational reason why Jews and Gentiles can partake of the revelation of God's righteousness through faith according to 3:21-26 (cf. Rom. 5:8-10), δικαιοσύνη θεου in 3:21-22 (cf. 1:17) and δικαιούμενοι in 3:24 refer to God's saving righteousness whereby he exonerates sinners in his law-court. This point is further supported because Paul connects the preceding δικ-words in Romans with the salvation that comes through the gospel by faith in Jesus (1:16-17; 3:21-5:1; 9:30-10:21), because he connects justification with "in the presence of God" (3:20), and because δικαιοσύνη θεου occurs in a text in which Paul emphasizes that faith is the means through which one receives salvation through the gospel (cf. 1:16-17; 3:21-5:1; 9:30-10:21).

Wright is one of the many current challengers of the above reading of

---

[190]See the following texts for different uses of δικαιοσύνη in the biblical (e.g. δικαιοσύνη: LXX Gen. 18:19; 19:19; 20:5; 20:13; 21:23; 24:27; 24:49; Exod. 15:13; 34:7; Lev. 19:15; Deut. 9:4-6; 33:19; 33:21; Josh. 24:14; Jud. 5:11; 1 Kgs 2:10; 12:7; 26:23; 2 Kgs 8:15; 22:21, 25; 1 Chr. 18:14; 29:17; 2 Chr. 6:23; 9:8; Ps. 4:2, 6; 5:9; 7:9, 18; 9:5, 9; 10:7; 14:2; 16:1, 15; 17:21, 25; Matt. 3:15; Acts 10:35; 17:31; 24:25; Rom. 6:16; 8:10; 2 Cor. 6:7; 9:9-10; 11:15; Eph. 4:24; 5:9; 6:14; Phil. 1:11; 3:6; 1 Tim. 6:11; 2 Tim. 2:22; 3:16; 4:8; Titus 3:5; Heb. 1:9; 5:13; ; 7:2; 11:7, 33; 12;11; Jas 3:18; 1 Pet. 2:24; 3:14; 2 Pet. 1:1; 2:5, 21; 3:13; 1 John 2:29; 3:7, 10; Rev. 19:11; 22:1) and extrabiblical literature (Tob. 1:3; 2:14; 4:5-7; 12:8-9; 13:6; 14:6, 11; 1 Macc. 14:35; 4 Macc. 1:4, 6; 1:18; 2:6; 5:24; Wis. 1:1, 15; 2:11; 5:6, 18; 8:7; 9:3; 12:16; 14:7; Sir. 16:22; 26:28; 44:10; 45:26; Pss. Sol. 1:2; 2:15; 8:6, 24, 25, 26; 9:2-5; 14:2; 17:23, 37; 1 Bar. 1:15; 2:6, 18; 4:13; 5:2, 4, 9). However, the verb δικαιόω primarily has a forensic meaning in the LXX (e.g. LXX Gen. 38:26; 44:16; Exod. 23:7; Deut. 25:1; 1 Kgs 8:32; Isa. 1:7; 5:23; 43:9) and in the extrabiblical literature (e.g. Sir. 1:22; 7:3; 9:12; 10:29; 13:22; 23:11; 26:29; 31:5; 42:2; Pss. Sol. 8:26). When salvation, faith, and judgment are in view in the New Testament, the verb *always* carries a forensic meaning (Matt. 12:37; Acts 13:38-39), especially in Paul (Rom. 2:13; 3:4, 20, 24, 26, 28, 30; 4:2, 5; 5:1, 9; 8:30, 33; 1 Cor. 4:4; 6:11; Gal. 2:16-17; 3:8, 11, 24; 5:4; Titus 3:7; Jas 2:21, 25). The only exception is possibly Rom. 6:7.

[191]Against VanLandingham, *Judgment*, 277-90.

δικαιοσύνη θεου and δικαιόω.[192] A few of the important features of Wright's view are the faithfulness of Jesus as the Messiah and the themes of covenant, exile, law-court, and eschatology. According to him, πίστεως᾽ Ἰησοῦ Χριστοῦ in Romans 3:22 (cf. Gal. 2:16) should be translated as "faithfulness of Christ" (subjective genitive) instead of "faith in Christ" (objective genitive).[193] Thus, says Wright, Paul is not saying that one can be justified by "faith in Christ," but that God fulfills his promises with regard to the covenant by the faithfulness of Christ for those who believe in Jesus as Messiah, so that God's faithfulness/righteousness to the covenant is demonstrated through the faithfulness of Jesus. However, the context of Romans 3 best supports the translation "faith in Christ" in 3:22 since Paul's argument focuses on how the individual personally receives and participates in God's saving righteousness.[194] The emphasis on "faith in Christ" as the means to receiving God's saving righteousness also highlights the forensic element of this righteousness since Paul has argued in 1:18-3:20 that (1) Jews and Gentiles stand condemned in God's law-court because of sin (2:1-16) and (2) in 3:21-4:25 that they can be "justified" by faith on the basis of Jesus' blood. (3) In 4:1-25, he uses Abraham as the example *par excellence* that God's righteousness comes to the believer by faith (4:1-25; cf. Gal. 2:16-3:9).[195]

---

[192]For a few examples from Wright's works, see N.T. Wright, *The Climax of the Covenant: Christ and the Law in Pauline Theology* (Minneapolis: Fortress, 1991); idem, *What Saint Paul Really Said: Was Paul of Tarsus the Real Founder of Christianity?* (Grand Rapids: Eerdmans, 1997); idem, "4QMMT and Paul: Justification, 'Works,' and Eschatology," in *History and Exegesis: New Testament Essays in Honor of Dr. E. Earle Ellis for His 80th Birthday*, ed. Aang-Won (Aaron) Son (New York and London: T&T Clark, 2006), 104-132; idem, *Justification: God's Plan & Paul's Vision* (Downers Grove, IL: InterVarsity Press, 2009).

[193]Also Hays, *The Faith of Jesus Christ*, 119-62. See especially 156-60 where Hays specifically discusses Rom 3:21-26. For recent discussion of the debate, see Michael F. Bird and Preston M. Sprinkle (eds.), *The Pistis Christou Debate* (Peabody, MA: Hendrickson, 2009).

[194]Seifrid ("Romans," 618) argues that πίστεως ᾽ Ἰησοῦ Χριστου ("faith in/of Jesus Christ") is a genitive of source. Seifrid presupposes the "objective sense" since "it is in any case in Paul's larger usage of faith." But, Seifrid says, that Paul's idea is larger than faith in Christ. Instead, "the faith of Jesus Christ (3:22) is the faith given through Jesus Christ." Paul does not, however, describe "a pattern of obedience in which we participate, but rather the source of faith: God gives us faith as a gift through the crucified and risen Christ and [through] the gospel that proclaims him" (brackets mine).

[195]Paul's discussion of Abraham supports that Paul's emphasis in 3:21-26 is that one can be made right with God by faith in Jesus as opposed to by obeying Torah (3:20). Regarding Paul's citation of Gen 15:6 in Romans 4, with the exception of Paul's usage of δὲ instead of καὶ, his citation of Gen 15:6 in Rom. 4:3 exactly follows LXX Gen. 15:6: καὶ ἐπίστευσεν ᾽Αβρααμ τῷ θεῷ καὶ ἐλογίσθη αὐτῷ εἰς δικαιοσύνην ("and Abraham *believed God* and it was *reckoned to him as righteousness*."). Paul's citation is: ἐπίστευσεν δὲ ἐπίστευσεν ᾽Αβρααμ τῷ θεῷ καὶ ἐλογίσθη αὐτῷ εἰς δικαιοσύνην ("and Abraham believed God and it was reckoned to him as righteousness."). With the clause ἐλογίσθη αὐτῷ εἰς δικαιοσύνην ("it was reckoned to

Humanity's Spiritual Plight 85

Regarding the meaning of ἐξ ἔργων νόμου,[196] Dunn argues that these "works of law" are actual deeds that the Jew does and that "acceptance by God is not dependent on that doing."[197] The phrase cannot refer to the catalogue of breaches of the law in 2:21-24, referred to also in 2:25, 27, or to Israel's unfaithful wickedness in 3:10-18, because failure to comply to the law could never be described as "works of the law" (i.e. as doing what the law demands).[198] Paul's critique in 3:20 rather attacks Israel's boast in the privileges mentioned in 2:17-20, 23, and he attacks their presumption that those privileges make Jews better off than Gentiles.[199] Contrary to Dunn, Paul likely refers in 3:20 to the Jews' attempt at perfect obedience to the demands of Torah, which (if achieved) would merit eschatological exoneration in God's law-court because of the following reasons.[200] First, obedience to Torah means

---

him as righteousness. . ."), the translators of LXX Gen. 15:6 depart from the wording in the MT to emphasize that God counted Abraham's faith "in him" as the basis for his right-standing before God. MT Gen. 15:6 reads as follows: ויחשבה לו צדקה והאמן ביהוה ("and he [Abraham]) believed in God and he [God] reckoned it to him [Abraham], namely, righteousness.").

[196]As scholars know well, 4QMMT is the only extant place in Jewish literature where a similar Hebrew phrase occurs. For recent interaction with 4QMMT, see Albert L.A. Hogeterp, "4QMMT and Paradigms of Second Temple Jewish Nomism," *Dead Sea Discoveries* 15 (2008): 359-79. Jacqueline C.R. de Roo recently argues that "works of the law" refer to inspired deeds of obedience to Torah and serve as a means of atonement in the DSS, but in Paul "works of law" are the works of Abraham that do not function as a means of atonement. Accordingly, Paul's reaction against "works of law" is a reaction against Abraham as a redeemer figure. Thus, the phrase in Paul is absolutely negative since justification comes by faith in Jesus Christ apart from works of law. This thesis proposes an alternative to both the Old and New Perspectives of Paul. See her *Works of the Law at Qumran and in Paul*, NTM 13 (Sheffield: Sheffield Phoenix Press, 2007).

[197]James D.G. Dunn, *The New Perspective on Paul*, Revised edition (Grand Rapids: Eerdmans, 2008), 44-45, 45 n. 178.

[198]Ibid., 45.

[199]In response to one of Mark A. Seifrid's criticisms of the New Perspective ("Unrighteousness by Faith: Apostolic Proclamation in Romans 1:18-3:20," in *Justification and Variegated Nomism: The Paradoxes of Paul*, eds. D.A. Carson, et al., WUNT 2.140 [Tübingen: Mohr Siebeck, 2004], 106-45), Dunn (*New Perspective*, 45-46, n. 180) asserts that Seifrid misunderstands the New Perspective since he critiques it for focusing on ethnocentrism or Jewish privilege. Dunn responds by noting that his position is *not* that Paul critiques the Jews for boasting in *privilege* but for their *presumption* that they believed that their privileges afforded them. In my reading of Dunn, he seems to affirm that Paul attacks both Jewish privilege and Jewish presumption of the benefits of those privileges. For example, see his *New Perspective*, 46.

[200]Against Sanders, *PPJ*, 33-428; Dunn, *Theology*, 354-58; idem, *Romans*, 1:153-55; Wright, "Romans," 460-61; Jewett, *Romans*, 266; Owen, "The 'Works of the Law' in Romans and Galatians," 553-577. Dunn's view of ἐξ ἔργων νόμου is particularly important because of its influence. He defines ἐξ ἔργων νόμου as "what the law requires, the 'deeds', which the law makes obligatory," and he suggests that these works

perfect obedience in the preceding argument of 2:1-3:19.[201] Second, God expected Israel to obey perfectly the demands of Torah to live in the land (Deut 30:15-16), and third (as Gathercole has convincingly shown) there appears to be a merit theology in certain factions of early Judaism to which Paul could have been responding (e.g. Sir. 11:26; 17:23; 35:19; 1QS; CD 3:14-16; 4Q257 2i 3-6; 2 Apoc. Bar. 51).[202]

Paul's denial that one could stand on his own terms before God in the judgment was not novel with him, but this idea was also denied by some within early Judaism (1QH 9:14-16).[203] However, as we have already seen above, there was *a* strong Jewish perspective that Jews would be exonerated in God's law-court because they were distinctively Jewish and because they yielded obedience to Torah.[204] This perspective is evident by their trust in Torah, by their emphasis on circumcision and proselytizing, by their disdain for Gentiles, and by their optimistic view of their ability to keep Torah to the fullest (Gen. 17:1-14; Exod. 24; Isa. 42:6-7; 49:6; Ep. Arist. 139, 142; Jub. 14:10; 15:1-34;

---

specifically refer to Israel's response to God's grace that he showed in making them his people (*Theology*, 355). He describes the law as marking out Israel's set apartness, and he contends that the boundary markers of circumcision, Sabbath-keeping, and purity laws particularly set Israel apart from the nations, not that the phrase ἐξ ἔργων νόμου only refers to these three boundary markers (*Theology*, 355-56), a point which he recently reemphasizes ("The New Perspective on Paul," 23-28) on account of the critical reaction of opposing scholars to his earlier publications on works of law. Depending on the Hebrew equivalent of the phrase in 4QMMT, Wright ("Romans," 460) defines the phrase as "the sign, in the present, of that membership in Israel, God's covenant people, which will be vindicated in the future when the long-awaited 'righteousness of God' is finally unveiled in action," but he agrees with Dunn that the Sabbath, the food laws, and circumcision were the big three that demarcated Israel from the nations ("Romans," 461). Jewett (*Romans*, 266) asserts that law in 3:20 refers not only to the Jewish law, but to law as an identity marker in any culture. Owen ("The 'Works of the Law' in Romans and Galatians," 556-57) argues that the emphasis in the phrase "by works of law" is not on a human's failure to obey fully Torah (though this point is implied), but on Torah's inability to effect in people a righteousness that would exonerate in God's law-court because of the gripping power of sin. Since Paul's concern in 3:20 is what has the law accomplished for whose who received it, Owen argues that Paul's point in 3:20 is on the effectiveness of God's words in Torah and not how many works a person must keep to be justified by God. However, he overlooks and underestimates the impact of the argument of 2:1-3:20 as a whole on one's reading of ἐξ ἔργων νόμου, for the entire section together emphasizes that God judges Jews and Gentiles in accordance with whether they obey Torah.

[201] Against Dunn, *Romans*, 1:154-55.

[202] For a discussion of the relevant Jewish texts, see Simon J. Gathercole, *Where is Boasting? Early Jewish Soteriology and Paul's Response in Romans 1-5* (Grand Rapids: Eerdmans, 2002). Contra Sanders, *PPJ*, 33-428. See also Bell's (*No One Seeks for God*, 224-35) incisive critique of Dunn.

[203] For a similar point, see Das, "Paul and Works of Obedience," 798-801.

[204] This perspective is affirmed by some modern Jewish interpreters of Paul. For example, Pamela Eisenbaum, *Paul Was not a Christian* (New York: HarperCollins, 2009).

22:15-23; Tobit; Wis. 18:4; Sir. 24:27; 1 Bar. 4:4; Sib. Or. 3.195; Jos., *Ag. Ap.* 2.293; Philo, *Abr.* 98; *Mos.* 1.149; 1QH 2:9; 1QS 3:13). But, with his words in Romans 3:19-20, Paul crushes any hope that either a Jew (a Torah insider) or a Gentile (a Torah outsider) could meet the standards set forth in Torah. Romans 3:20 does not contradict 2:13.[205] Although a real promise of final justification awaits the one who obeys Torah (Rom. 2:6, 13), absolutely *no one* will be vindicated in God's law-court by Torah because Torah simply reveals that one has broken specific commands of God (cf. Rom. 4:15; 5:13-14; 7:7-23).[206] Torah does not provide salvation. Hence, Paul denies that Torah will grant final vindication in God's law-court,[207] for he states that "no flesh will be justified" (future passive) "in his presence by works of law, for through the law comes the knowledge of sin" (Rom. 3:20). Thus, Romans 2:1-3:20 suggests that Torah's entrance into salvation-history makes the spiritual predicament of Jews and Gentiles worse than before it entered, for it reveals specific commands of God that humanity in turn disobeys; it gives Jews and Gentiles a knowledge of their sin, and it places Jews and Gentiles under God's just condemnation in God's eschatological law-court (cf. Rom. 4:15; 5:14; 7:1-25).

Romans 7

Romans 7 supports that Torah's entrance into salvation-history makes humanity's spiritual predicament worse. Romans 7 is one of the most debated chapters in the letter.[208] The role of Torah in salvation-history is the fundamental issue in Romans 7, not anthropology.[209] The two primary arguments in the chapter suggest this. First, as I discussed earlier, Paul uses an analogy from marriage to illustrate the power of Torah over one's life until death before faith in Christ (Rom. 7:1-6). Second, Paul states that the law holds

---

[205]Contra Sanders, *PPJ*, 125.

[206]Dunn (*Romans*, 1:155-56) takes the phrase "a knowledge of sin through the law" to refer to the "typical Jewish attitude which saw the law as the means and measure of life within the covenant (as in Sir. 45:5; Pss. Sol. 14:2) and as a bulwark and hedge against the sinfulness of the Gentiles (as in Ep. Arist. 139, 142)." In contrast, Paul argues, says Dunn, that Torah was not given to elicit a sense of distinctiveness and security for the Jew, but to make the Jew to whom Torah was addressed aware that he was still in need of God's grace even as a member of God's covenant, just as the Gentile sinner is in need of God's grace.

[207]Similarly Cranfield, *Romans*, 1:198.

[208]Similarly Moo, *Romans*, 409; Schreiner *Romans*, 343. For a detailed exegesis, see Cranfield, *Romans*, 1:331-70, Dunn, *Romans*, 1:269-300; Moo, *Romans*, 409-67; Schreiner, *Romans*, 345-94; Jewett, *Romans*, 428-73.

[209]Dunn, *Romans*, 1:377; Moo, *Romans*, 409; Schreiner, *Romans*, 343; 364. Emma Wasserman's thesis offers a contrary reading ("The Death of the Soul in Romans 7: Revisiting Paul's Anthropology in Light of Hellenistic Moral Psychology," *JBL* 126 [2007]: 793-816; idem "Paul among the Philosophers: The Case of Sin in Romans 6-8," *JSNT* 30.4 [2008], 387-415). Although the text is not about anthropology, Rainbow (*The Way of Salvation*, 148) duly notes that a correct understanding of Romans 7 is critical to Pauline anthropology.

people in bondage to sin (Rom. 7:7-25). Furthermore, Romans 7 is a continuation of the argument in Romans 5:12-6:23 regarding eternal death in Adam, eternal life in Christ, and freedom from sin because of the thematic connections between the current and the latter section.[210] Paul argues in 5:12-6:23 that Adam's disobedience produced slaves to sin resulting in death, but Christ's obedience produces slaves of righteousness resulting in eternal life and that Torah's entrance into salvation history exacerbated sin's power (Rom. 5:20). Then, in Romans 7, Paul argues that since the power of sin uses Torah, the spiritual predicament of the Jew in Adam under Torah apart from Christ becomes worse.

In Romans 7:1, Paul specifically addresses Jews with the words to those "who know the law." In light of his argument in Romans 2:1-3:20, especially his comments that Jews have no advantage in the judgment over Gentiles even though the former received the oracles of God (Romans 3:1-9; cf. 2:17-3:9), the statement "those who know the law" in Romans 7:1 most certainly refers to the Jews. Paul has already argued that Torah's entrance into salvation-history did not make the *nachwirkung* of Adam's transgression better, but worse for those under Torah, for Torah demands obedience (Rom. 2:1-29) and sin reigned from Adam until Moses (i.e., before Torah) even over those who did not sin in the same way as Adam (Rom. 5:13-14). Moreover, when the Torah entered into salvation-history, the power of sin simply increased (Rom. 5:20). Torah makes the Jewish (and to some degree the Gentile) spiritual predicament worse than it was before the Torah entered into salvation-history, for sin is more defiant because it is now reckoned as a transgression against a revealed command of God in Torah (Rom. 4:15; 5:13; Gen. 2:17). Romans 7, therefore, serves to elaborate the spiritual plight of the Jew in Adam under Torah and outside of Christ, a plight that exists because of Torah's ability to stimulate sin and because of its inability to disarm sin's power (cf. Rom. 8:1-2).

Romans 7:7-25 develops the motif of 7:5.[211] After discussing that the presence of the law increased the power of sin (Rom. 7:7-9), Paul states that "I died" and that the commandment that was supposed to result in life produced "death in me" (7:10). The identity of the ἐγώ and of the "in me" statements in Romans 7:7-25 are still the subject of scholarly debate.[212] At least three views exist.

First, ἐγώ refers to Adam and his experience with God's commandment in the Garden of Eden.[213] Second, ἐγώ refers to Israel's

---

[210]Schreiner (*Romans*, 343) thinks Rom. 7 points back to 5:20 and explains why the Mosaic Law's presence stimulates sin.
[211]So Schreiner, *Romans*, 344. Against Moo, *Romans*, 424), who suggests that the main line of development flows from 7:6b to chapter 8.
[212]See Jewett, *Romans*, 440-73.
[213]Käsemann, *Romans*, 196; Dunn, *Romans*, 1:381.

Humanity's Spiritual Plight

experience with YHWH's commandment on Sinai.[214] Third, ἐγώ is an autobiographical reference either to Paul's pre-Christian[215] or Christian experience.[216] The third option at first glance best represents the context of Romans 7:7-25 since Paul conveys an agonizing, personal tone in the text. But all three positions express some truth, and each grasps the context of the argument, because Paul's discussion of the law in Romans 7 flows from his discussion of Jewish inability to keep the law (Rom. 2:1-3:20), because of his discussion of the universal impact of Adam's transgression (Rom. 5:12-21), and because of the statement in Romans 7:5 that the law stimulated sin when "we" were in the flesh.[217] However, in my view, ἐγώ specifically represents Paul the Jew (and all Jews) in Adam and under Torah apart from faith in Christ.[218] This interpretation seems right because of the connection with Romans 5:12-6:23, where Paul discusses the disobedience of Adam and the obedience of Jesus (Rom. 5:12, 14-21), where he states that Torah's entrance into salvation-history made humanity's spiritual predicament worse (Rom. 5:13), and where he forcefully argues that believers should no longer be slaves to the power of sin since they died to sin's power when they died with Christ (Rom. 6:1-23), and because Paul asks in Romans 7:24 who would deliver him from his miserable predicament. He states confidently in Romans 7:25 that Jesus will, and he boldly confirms this point in Romans 8:1: "there is no condemnation for those in Christ Jesus" since God disabled Torah's power in salvation-history in Jesus' cross and resurrection (Rom. 8:2-11). Thus, Romans 7 emphasizes that sin uses the law to increase the Jew's spiritual predicament.[219]

The ἐντολή in Romans 7:8-9 likely refers to a specific stipulation within the Torah, for Paul uses the broader term νόμος in Romans 7:1-10 to refer to the Torah and he uses ἐντολη in Romans 7:8 to refer to a specific commandment ("you shall not lust") that occurs in the νόμος. Death as a result of Torah's entrance into salvation-history in Romans 7:10 must refer to the condemnation that the Torah brought with it when it entered into salvation-

---

[214] Moo, *Romans*, 427. Moo, in fact, thinks that a combination of both an autobiographical reference and a reference to Israel best explains Paul's use of ἐγώ in Rom. 7:7-25.
[215] W.G. Kümmel, *Römer 7 und das Bild des Menschen im Neuen Testament* (Munich: Kaiser Verlag, 1974), 85-87. Recently Jewett (*Romans*, 443) affirms a pre-Christian view of "I."
[216] So Schreiner, *Romans*, 359. Schreiner (*Romans*, 364-65) admits that views 1 and 2 have viability and thus he appears to agree that all 3 positions could accurately capture Paul's intent in Romans 7.
[217] Similarly Thielman, *Theology*, 363-64.
[218] Hae-Kyung Chang argues the point that the "I" represents the situation of Jews and Judaizing Christians who seek justification and holiness in Torah and that Paul probably looks back on his life as a Pharisee ("The Christian Life in a Dialectical Tension? Romans 7:7-25 Reconsidered," *NovT* 49 [2009]: 257-280, esp. 272-80).
[219] For a discussion and interaction with the different readings of Romans 7, see Schreiner, *Romans*, 379-90.

history and when a specific commandment in the Torah was broken, for Paul states in Romans 7:9 that he was alive before the Torah came, but that after the commandment came sin sprang to life and that he died due to the commandment (Rom. 7:10).[220] In addition, Paul uses θάνατος as a metonym for judgment. He states that violators of God's righteous requirement are "worthy of death" (Rom. 1:32), "death spread through sin" (Rom. 5:12), "death reigned through Adam's transgression" (Rom. 5:14, 17; 1 Cor. 15:21), slavery to sin "results in death" (Rom. 6:16, 21), "the wages of sin is death" (Rom 6:23), those under the power of Torah "bear fruit to death" (Rom. 7:5), "the commandment results in death" (Rom. 7:10, 13, 24; 8:2), life under Torah leads to death (Rom. 8:6), death is an enemy (1 Cor. 15:26), death will be defeated (1 Cor. 15:54-55), "the sting of death is sin and the power of sin is the law" (1 Cor. 15:56), the ministry of the Torah was a ministry of death and judgment (2 Cor. 3:7-8), and death results from sin in contrast to life that results from the Spirit and the resurrection (2 Cor. 3:7-10; 4:12; 7:10). Thus, by death in Romans 7:9, Paul means condemnation/judgment. This point is further supported by Paul's words in Romans 8:1 that no condemnation exists for those in Christ Jesus and both by God's words to Adam in Genesis 2:17 and to Israel in the Old Testament: viz., if they disobeyed his commandments, they would be judged by death or by some other means (Gen. 2:17; Exod. 32-34; Lev. 16:2; Num. 25; Deut. 9, 27).

The γάρ in Romans 7:11 provides the reason for death/judgment in Romans 7:10: sin took opportunity through the commandment, deceived, and killed (i.e. judged) through the commandment. Thus, Paul can say that the Torah is "holy," and the commandment is "holy," "just," and "good" (Rom. 7:12), because it rightly pronounces condemnation against those over whom Torah has jurisdiction on account of the power of sin. Based on the preceding statement in Romans 7:12 that the "law is holy, and the commandment is holy, righteous, and good," Paul argues here that the good law and the holy commandment were not the fundamental source of the death/judgment of the Jew in Adam under Torah (Rom. 7:13). Rather, sin was the fundamental source of death/judgment, for sin "worked death through the good, so that sin would produce a sinner according to surpassing greatness through the commandment" (Rom. 7:13). The "good" that sin used to produce death is the law and the commandment (i.e. Torah), for Paul states in Romans 7:12 that "the law is holy, and the commandment is holy and righteous and good." Romans 7:13, therefore, affirms that the *nachwirgung* of Adam's transgression was so devastating that sin even used YHWH's Torah to increase its power and to bring about judgment upon those under sin's power and under Torah's jurisdiction (1 Cor. 15:56; 2 Cor. 3:7-10).

Romans 7:14a grounds Paul's initial question and answer in Romans

---

[220]Against L. Ann Jervis, "The Commandment which is for Life (Romans 7:10): Sin's Use of the Obedience of Faith," *JSNT* 27 (2004): 193-216, who creatively argues that the commandment to which Paul refers in Rom. 7:9-12 is the commandment inherent to new life in Christ: namely, obedience.

7:13 pertaining to whether the Torah was the source of Paul's condemnation. Paul's answer suggests that the problem is not with Torah but with sin, under whose bondage he (the Jew in Adam under Torah apart from Christ) has been sold. This latter statement is one reason that reading Paul's argument exclusively as his reflection on his Christian experience is fundamentally incorrect, for he would never assert that a Christian (and more importantly that he while a Christian) has been sold under the power of sin. Rather, he arduously argues elsewhere that believers are free from sin's tyranny by the power of the Spirit because they have died with Christ (Rom. 6:1-8:39; 2 Cor. 3:7-10; Gal. 3-5). Romans 7:15a should be interpreted parallel to 7:14, and 7:15a functions as a ground to the initial question and answer in 7:13: "Therefore, did the good produce death in me? May it never be (7:13a)... For we know that the law is spiritual, but I am fleshly, and I have been sold under sin (7:14), for I do not know what I am doing" (Rom. 7:15a).

The γὰρ in Romans 7:15b further explains the preceding statement introduced by γὰρ in Romans 7:15a, and Romans 7:15b too grounds the initial question and answer in Romans 7:13a. Romans 7:16-20 further develops the argument regarding the condemnation that comes through sin's use of the law. Paul states that sin uses the law to provoke one to do the opposite of what he wants to do (Rom. 7:15-20). Interpreters who think that Paul's words in Romans 7:15-20 express the Christian's internal struggle with sin need to keep in mind that Paul is still commenting here on the spiritual predicament of the Jew in Adam under Torah apart from Christ, for he calls himself "fleshly" (σάρκινος), a term that means belonging to this world (Rom. 15:27; 1 Cor. 3:3; 9:11; 2 Cor. 1:12; 10:4; 1 Pet. 2:11), and he states that he is "sold under the power of sin" (Rom. 3:9; Gal. 3:22). In Paul, those who are under the power of sin are likewise under both the powers of the world and under the law (Gal. 4:3, 5), and they are under God's judgment (Rom. 3:9; 3:10-12, 22; 8:1-4), for they are outside of Christ (Rom. 4:15; 9:30-10:13) and under a curse (Gal. 3:10). Paul, thus, has not launched into a (what would be an unrelated) discussion of the Christian's struggle with sin. Instead, he is still talking about the spiritual predicament of the Jew in Adam under Torah apart from Christ.

Romans 7:15-20 connects with the argument of Romans 7:13-14, especially 7:14, because of the conjunctions γὰρ (Rom. 7:15, 18, 19), δὲ (Rom. 7:16-18), and ἀλλὰ (Rom. 7:17, 20). In Romans 7:13, Paul states that Torah was not the source of death, but sin, because the Torah is spiritual, but Jews in Adam under Torah apart from Christ are fleshly because they are sold under sin's power (Rom. 7:14). In Romans 7:15-20, Paul explains 7:14. He uses a series of relative clauses (Rom. 7:15-16, 19-20) to do so. The relative pronoun that he uses throughout does not have the same antecedent in each clause. The first relative pronoun in Romans 7:15 simply takes the force of a demonstrative, for it does not point to a specific grammatical antecedent. The conceptual antecedent is the inability of the Jew in Adam under Torah apart from Christ to achieve life through obedience to the Torah because of sin in spite of the fact that the desire to obey the Torah is present. This interpretation seems likely for the following reasons.

First, Paul has already asserted in Romans 7:1 that the audience of Romans 7 is "those who know the law." As I argued earlier, this group is likely the Jewish audience of Romans because the Jews received the oracles of God in Torah (Rom. 3:1; Gal. 3:19-20). Second, by using an analogy from marriage, Paul discusses the bondage under which a Jew in Adam under Torah apart from Christ finds himself because of the entrance of the law into salvation-history (Rom. 7:2-3). He states that Jews, just as the woman whose husband died to the law, died to the law when they united themselves to Jesus Christ, who was raised from the dead, so that they now bear fruit to God (Rom. 7:4). But when they were in the flesh (i.e. outside of Christ), sin worked in them through the law to bring about their death (Rom. 7:5). The phrase "in the flesh" refers to the status of the Jew in Adam under Torah apart from Christ, because of the γὰρ in Romans 7:5 that grounds Romans 7:4, because of the imperfect verb ἦμεν in 7:5 that points to Jews' previous life outside of Christ and contrasts the readers' previous situation in Adam under Torah with their current situation in Christ, because the Torah has been the subject of discussion in Romans 7:1-4, because Paul states that sinful passions worked in "our" members through the law resulting in death (Rom. 7:5), and because Paul states that in Christ "we have been severed from the law" so that we serve God by the power of the Spirit not in the oldness of the letter (Rom. 7:6).[221]

Third, Paul states in Romans 7:7 that the Torah is not sin, but rather he would not know sin apart from Torah, because the Torah reveals specific commands. Fourth, Paul states that sin used Torah to stimulate sin and to bring about death/judgment (Rom. 7:8-11), while the Torah simultaneously remained holy, just, and good (Rom. 7:12). Fifth, Paul clarifies that the Torah was not the source of death/judgment but sin introduced judgment/death and used Torah to stimulate sin (Rom. 7:13). Sixth, Paul grounds Romans 7:13 in 7:14 by stating that the law is spiritual, but the Jew in Adam under Torah apart from Christ is fleshly because he is sold under the power of sin. Seventh, in Romans 7:15-16, 19-20, Paul uses several relative clauses to elaborate his point. The relative clauses focus both on one's desire to do Torah and on an inability to do Torah even though one delights in it, because sin's power is simply too strong for the Jew in Adam under Torah apart from Christ to be overcome by his desire for the good (Rom. 7:15-24). Instead, the Jew in Adam under Torah apart from Christ needs Jesus Christ to deliver him from sin's power stimulated by Torah (Rom. 7:24-25; 8:1-11). I further defend this interpretation below via my exegesis of Rom. 7:15-25.

Paul states in Romans 7:15 in the first relative clause that he does not know the things that he practices. Paul cannot mean here that he (the Christian Jew) does not have knowledge of the spiritual predicament of the Jew now that the Torah has entered into salvation-history, for Paul's entire argument thus far gives the impression that he is fully aware that sin uses Torah to stimulate sin

---

[221]Γράμμα in Rom. 7:6 is used six of its seven times in Paul to refer to the Mosaic covenant/the Old Testament scriptures (Rom. 2:27, 29; 7:6; 2 Cor. 3:6, 7; 2 Tim. 3:15).

and to actuate death (Rom. 7:5, 7-12, 21-23), that the Jew under Torah needs Christ to deliver him from its power (Rom. 7:24-25; 8:1-11), that Torah is not the source of sin (Rom. 7:7-13), and that Torah is fundamentally good (Rom. 7:12-13). Furthermore, Paul is neither saying that he (the Christian Jew) is unaware of Torah's role in the current spiritual predicament of the Jew in Adam under Torah apart from Christ, for he states that he is writing to "those who know the law" (Rom. 7:1); he explains the situation of the Jew in Adam under Torah apart from Christ in the argument of Romans 7:7-25; he states that he knows sin because of Torah (Rom. 7:7), and he articulates that the fundamental reason for the current spiritual predicament of the Jew under Torah is due to Adam's transgression (Rom. 5:12-7:25), which is further supported by his statement that he knows (οἶδα instead of γινώσκω) that nothing good dwells in his flesh (Rom. 7:18).

Instead, by "know" in 7:15, Paul means that he as a Jew in Adam under Torah apart from Christ (and all Jews in Adam under Torah apart from Christ) fundamentally did not grasp the negative role the Torah played in their spiritual predicament when it entered into salvation-history. For example, they pursued God's righteousness via Torah instead of by faith in Jesus Christ, and they failed to attain to that righteousness (Rom. 9:30-33).[222] Paul persecuted Christians before his conversion in obedience to Torah as a means of attaining the righteousness in Torah (Phil. 3:8-9), but sin was simultaneously using Torah to bring about Paul's death apart from faith in Christ (Acts 8-9; Rom. 7:7). Thus, "the thing that I do not know" refers to the failure of the Jew in Adam under Torah apart from Christ to grasp that Torah's entrance into salvation-history makes the Jew's spiritual predicament worse than before Torah came. This interpretation of Romans 7:15 takes serious the normal meaning of γινώσκω in the letter as "to understand/grasp" (Rom. 1:21; 2:18; 3:17; 6:6; 7:1, 7, 15; 10:19; 11:34).

Paul grounds 7:15a in 7:15b by stating that he does the thing that he does not desire. In 7:15b-21, the focus turns from "knowing" and "doing" Torah to "desiring" and "doing" Torah (contra Rom. 7:15a). Thus, the Jew in Adam under Torah apart from Christ does not grasp what he does, which is supported when he does the opposite of what he desires and which is in fact what he hates: namely, the opposite of Torah (Rom. 7:15b). Both doing the opposite of what the Jew desires and doing what the Jew hates refer to disobedience to Torah and to sin's use of Torah to make the spiritual predicament of the Jew in Adam under Torah apart from Christ worse than it was before Torah came, for Paul states that the Torah is good in 7:16 and that sin is working "in me" in 7:17. Some evidence in early Judaism suggests that at least some Jews expressed that they were spiritually privileged because they received Torah (cf. Rom. 2:1-3:9; Epistle of Aristeas) and that Torah's entrance into salvation history gave them a special privilege over Gentiles in God's salvation-historical plan (Rom. 2:17-3:20). However, Paul argues the very

---

[222]For a similar point, see Das, *Paul*, 226-27.

opposite.

Paul states in Romans 7:16 that if the Jew in Adam under Torah apart from Christ does the opposite of what he desires (i.e. the opposite of what the law demands), then the law is good. In other words, since the law is not sin but reveals sin (Rom. 7:7), since sin uses the law to stimulate sin (Rom. 7:8-11), and since the law is holy and the very opposite of sin, therefore, the law is good and is not the fundamental reason why the Jew in Adam under Torah apart from Christ disobeys Torah. Rather, the reason is sin. This is Paul's point in Romans 7:17 with the emphatic "but now I am no longer doing it, but sin which dwells in me."[223] Paul here does not circumvent or abdicate personal responsibility unless he is an incoherent thinker,[224] for he has already argued that both Jews and Gentiles are guilty before God and responsible for their sin (Rom. 1:18-3:20, 23; 5:12-21). Paul means that the Jew in Adam under Torah apart from Christ disobeys Torah because of the "sin which dwells" in him. Thus, the accent should be placed on the spiritual predicament of the Jew in Adam under Torah apart from Christ due to the power of sin, which Paul has already argued uses the Torah to stimulate more sin (Rom. 7:7-13).[225] That sin should be understood in Romans 7:17 as a power that dominates is likely since Paul argues in Romans 6 that sin reigns over those outside of Christ and since he states here that sin dwells in him in Romans 7:17.

This reading of Romans 7:17 is supported by 7:18. The γάρ in Romans 7:18 grounds 7:17. The proposition of 7:17 (that the power of sin in the Jew in Adam under Torah apart from Christ causes him to do the opposite of what he desires) is grounded in the fact that nothing good dwells "in my flesh." The phrase ἐν τῇ σαρκί μου in Romans 7:18 refers to the Jew in Adam under Torah apart from Christ, because the phrase takes this meaning in Romans 7:5. The absence of the possessive pronoun in Romans 7:5 does not impede this interpretation, for the possessive in Romans 7:18 is expected since Paul uses the singular first personal pronoun ἐγώ both explicitly (Rom. 7:9-10, 14) and implicitly in a verb (Rom. 7:7, 15-23) throughout the argument of Romans 7:7-23 and since he consistently uses ἐμοί or μοι (Rom. 7:8, 10, 13, 17, 21) throughout the argument of Romans 7:7-21. The issue in Romans 7:18 is that the Jew in Adam under Torah apart from Christ has nothing good in him because the power of sin dwells within him (Rom. 7:17). This depravity is envisaged by the fact that the power of sin in the Jew in Adam under Torah apart from Christ conquers the desire to do good (i.e. to obey Torah) and instead produces evil (i.e. disobedience) (Rom. 7:19). Paul reiterates in Romans 7:20 the proposition of 7:17: the Jew in Adam under Torah apart from Christ disobeys Torah in spite of a desire to obey, because of the indwelling power of sin.

---

[223] For other emphatic uses of "but now" (νυνί δέ) in Romans, see Rom. 3:21; 6:22; 7:6; 15:23.
[224] For such a critique of Paul, see Räisänen, *Paul*; Sanders, *Paul*.
[225] Against Sanders, *Paul*, 72; Räisänen, *Paul*, 18-23; Das, *Paul*, 227, who see Paul indicting both Jews and Gentiles.

In Romans 7:21, Paul concludes that with respect to the law, sin is present in the Jew in Adam under Torah apart from Christ along with the desire to do the good. Paul explains this statement in Romans 7:22-23. In Romans 7:22, he states that sin is present in him who desires good, "because" he delights in the law of God in the "inner man," but the law of sin fights against "the law of" his "mind" and holds him captive "to the law of sin, which is in" his members (Rom. 7:23). By delighting in the law, Paul means that the Jew in Adam under Torah apart from Christ desires to do what the law says. This seems right because Romans 7:22 grounds 7:21, which (7:21) provides an inference from 7:15-20. The latter unit emphasizes that although the Jew in Adam under Torah apart from Christ desires to obey the Torah, this desire is not sufficient to fulfill the desire's goal of obedience because of sin's power.

The "inner man" (τὸν ἔσω ἄνθρωπον) in Romans 7:22 refers to the whole person and specifically to the Jew's inward desire to obey Torah,[226] for Paul previously mentions the desire to obey Torah (Rom. 7:15-21) and he uses the phrase "law of my mind" in Romans 7:23 to refer to one's desire. Paul concludes the argument of Romans 7 in 7:25b after he states that Jesus will deliver him (Rom. 7:25a) and that the ἐγώ serves both God's law in his mind (i.e. the inner man/desire) and the principle of sin in the flesh.[227] The above interpretation of the "inner man" is supported by its only other occurrence in the Pauline corpus in Ephesians 3:16. Paul states in Ephesians 3:16-17 that he prays for the Ephesians to be strengthened with power through the Spirit in the "inner man" and that Christ would dwell through faith in their hearts. Then, in Ephesians 3:19, he states that he wants the Ephesians "to know" the surpassing greatness of "the knowledge" of the love of Christ. Thus, we see in Ephesians 3:16-19 that the "inner man" is connected to the heart and knowledge, and that it has the ability to respond to truth through the work of the Spirit by faith in Christ.

In Romans 7:22, Paul contrasts the belief of the Jew in Adam under Torah apart from Christ that Torah is fundamentally good and his desire to do Torah with the inability to do what Torah demands. Thus, Romans 7:24 requests who will deliver the Jew in Adam under Torah from the judgment that Torah brings upon him. Romans 7:25a states that Jesus will. Then, Romans 7:25b contrasts the desire of the Jew in Adam under Torah to do Torah with the inability of the Jew in Adam under Torah to do what the law demands. Therefore, Paul's point in Romans 7:15-25 is that when Torah entered into salvation-history, it made the spiritual predicament of the Jew (and Gentiles too) in Adam under Torah worse than before there was a Torah, for sin used Torah to stimulate sin and to produce condemnation (cf. Rom. 5:20-6:23; 2 Cor. 3:6). This reading of Romans 7 explains Paul's earlier statement in Romans 7:8 that he "was formerly living apart from the law, but that sin came to life after the commandment came;" it explains Paul's statements in Romans 5:12-21 regarding the transgression of Adam that produced death prior to the

---

[226] Against Wasserman, "Death," 813.
[227] Against translating νόμος as principle in Rom. 7, see Das, *Paul*, 228-33.

giving of the Torah; it fits with Paul's comments in Romans 7:10-11 that sin used the law to produce death through the commandment, and it illuminates Paul's statement in Romans 7:21 that "evil is present in me."

Galatians 3-4
Galatians 3-4 supports that Torah's entrance into salvation-history makes humanity's spiritual predicament worse. Galatians 3:15-25 is part of a unit where Paul explains who are legitimate children of Abraham (Gal. 3:1-5:1). But within the argument of Galatians 3:15-25, Paul mentions the role of Torah in salvation-history in light of his promises to Abraham. Paul begins by stating that no one adds to or nullifies a covenant that has been ratified (Gal. 3:15). In Galatians 3:16a, he asserts that the promises were given to Abraham and his seed. These promises refer to God's promises to Abraham regarding land, seed, and universal blessing (Gen. 12:1-3, 7; 13:14-16; 17:2-8; 24:7). In Galatians 3:16b, Paul interprets these promises to find their fulfillment in Jesus, for he interprets Jesus to be Abraham's descendant whom God promised.

In Galatians 3:17, Paul specifically turns his attention to Torah. His concern is that the Torah's entrance into salvation-history did not nullify God's promises to Abraham, for the promises were given to Abraham years before the Torah came (Gal. 3:17), so that the inheritance that God promised Abraham is not fulfilled through Torah (Gal. 3:18), but Torah was decreed through angels by the hand of a mediator "because of transgressions" until Abraham's promised seed would come (Gal. 3:19). Galatians 3:21 further affirms that the law is not contrary to God's promises to Abraham, because the law does not fulfill the promise (Gal. 3:21), but the scripture (at least Torah) declared all things a prisoner under sin's power so that the promise would be given (not by law but) by faith in Jesus Christ for those who believe (Gal. 3:22). Galatians 3:23 forcefully highlights that Torah's entrance into salvation-history made humanity's spiritual predicament worse. But, Paul says, before faith in Christ entered into salvation-history after Torah had already entered after sin, "we were being guarded [as prisoners] because we were kept in prison with respect to the faith which was about to be revealed" (Gal. 3:23) (brackets mine). The spiritual predicament is obvious from the bondage language in the text. He views Torah as a guard and those under its jurisdiction as prisoners (Gal. 3:23), and he speaks of the Torah later as a guardian who rules over those under it until an appointed time (Gal. 3:24-4:7). He further speaks of the bondage of Torah in Galatians 4:21-5:1 when he argues that the Gentile Christians are placing themselves under bondage by aspiring to subject themselves under Torah and that Christ freed them from Torah's bondage.

Jewish and Gentile Slavery to Sin's Power

Spiritual Bondage before Faith in Christ
Paul argues that Jews and Gentiles were slaves to the power of sin before their faith in Christ. In Romans 6, Jew and Gentile slavery to the power of sin is

observable.[228] As noted earlier, Paul's argument in Romans 6 arises from a potential inference that his interlocutor would make from his argument in Romans 5:12-21. In the latter unit, Paul argues that Adam's disobedience introduced sin and death into the world upon everyone, but Jesus' obedience introduced liberation from Adam's transgression for everyone (Rom. 5:12-19). In Romans 5:20-21, Paul discusses the role of the law in salvation-history in light of Adam's sin and Jesus' obedience. He states that the "law entered so that transgression would increase" (Rom. 5:20). That is, the law entered into salvation-history to make the spiritual predicament worse for those under the law. However, when the power of sin increased through the entrance of the law, the power of grace increased more through Jesus Christ and conquered the power of sin, so that just as sin reigned by means of death, "so also grace reigned through righteousness resulting in eternal life through Jesus Christ, our Lord" (Rom. 5:20b-21). Thus, one might infer that since the increase of sin's power galvanizes the power of grace, then one should continue to be subdued under sin's power so that the power of grace would continue to increase (Rom. 6:1).

Paul argues against this inference by stating that believers died to the power of sin (Rom. 6:1). This death to sin was visualized when believers were baptized into the death of Christ through water-baptism so that they would live in new resurrection-life (Rom. 6:2-5).[229] In Romans 6:6-7, the spiritual bondage of Jews and Gentiles before faith in Christ is emphasized. In Romans 6:6, Paul speaks of "our old man." He states that "our old man was crucified together with Christ." The "old man" refers to the believer's former identity in Adam before faith in Christ because the "therefore" in Romans 6:1 connects the current argument in 6:1-23 with the previous argument in 5:12-21 and because Paul describes Adam in the latter text as the one man who introduced sin and death into the world and Jesus as the man who brought grace and eternal life. Sin and death entered the world through "one man," and the entrance of sin and death into the world consequently results in the universal condemnation of "all men" (Rom. 5:12-21). The one man, Jesus Christ, brought grace and a gift to many (Rom. 5:15-21), but the man who sinned introduced the universal reign of sin and death to the many (Rom. 5:15-21). Then, in Romans 6:1-5, Paul states that "we" died to sin because "we" were baptized into Jesus' death and "we" were raised to live in new resurrection-life in contrast to the former identity that "we" had in Adam.

Paul's use of the phrase "old man" in contrast to the "new man" in Ephesians 4:22 and Colossians 3:9 further supports that the "old man" in Romans 6:6 refers to the believer's identity in Adam before faith in Christ. He

---

[228]For a recent investigation of slavery metaphors in Paul, see John Byron, *Slavery Metaphors in Early Judaism and Pauline Christianity*, WUNT 162 (Tübingen: Mohr Siebeck, 2003).

[229]For a detailed investigation of baptism in Romans 6 and its background, see Søren Agersnap, *Baptism and the New Life: A Study of Romans 6:1-14* (Aarhus: Aarhus University Press, 1999).

urges the Ephesians to put on the "new man" and to put aside the "old man" by giving them several exhortations throughout the letter. He grounds these exhortations in the great work of God through Jesus Christ. He begins Ephesians by praising God for the great spiritual blessings that they have in Jesus (Eph. 1:3-14); he prays that they would better understand these spiritual blessings that God has bestowed upon them (Eph. 1:15-22; 3:14-19); he expresses that they were once dead in trespasses and sins until God saved them by his grace through faith and seated them in the heavenly places with Jesus Christ (Eph. 2:1-10); he encourages them to remember that they were formerly alienated from God's salvation-historical promises to the Jewish people before they came to faith in Jesus since they were Gentiles, but in Christ Jesus God has incorporated them into both the family and people of God with other believing Jews and Gentiles (Eph. 2:11-22). Finally, he urges them to live in a manner that is consistent with their new life in Jesus Christ (Eph. 4:1-6:20). He commands them to live no longer as they did as Gentiles "in the futility of their mind when they were darkened in ignorance" (Eph. 4:17). Paul similarly states in Romans 7:23, a verse whose unit possibly points back to Romans 5:12-21, that the mind of the Jew in Adam under Torah apart from Christ was captive to the power of sin. In Ephesians 4:18, he states that the Ephesians were also formerly separated from eternal life from God because of their ignorance and hardened heart, whose spiritual ignorance enabled them to give themselves over to practice all forms of impurity (Eph. 4:19), whereas in Romans 5:17 he asserts that those who received grace and the gift of righteousness will reign in life through Jesus Christ.

Paul furthermore urges the Ephesians to put off the "old man," which he describes as "corruptible corresponding to the lusts of deception," to renew their mind, and to put on the "new man" who was created in accordance with God in righteousness and holiness of the truth (Eph. 4:22-24). That the "old man" in this text refers to the believer's identity in Adam before faith in Christ seems to be a plausible reading, for Paul associates the "old man" with the Ephesians' "former conduct" (Eph. 4:21); he suggests that this "old man" enabled them to pursue an immoral lifestyle marked by ungodliness instead of being marked by the Spirit (Eph. 4:18-20), and he contrasts the "old man" with the "new man" and associates the latter with Jesus Christ (Eph. 4:20-21, 24). Unlike the "old man," the "new man" was created for righteousness and holiness (Eph. 4:24). Similarly, in Romans 5:12-21, Paul speaks of Adam as the one who brought sin, transgression, and death into the world and as the one whose sin resulted in universal condemnation for all, whereas Jesus introduced life and righteousness into the world for all who believe and as the one whose obedience resulted in the gift of righteousness and eternal life for all who believe.

As Ephesians 4:22-24, in a similar text in Colossians 3:9, Paul urges Gentile Christians to put off the old man and to put on the new man, because they died with Christ. The Colossian Christians were evidently in potential danger of being duped by false teaching (Col. 2:4, 8; 3:16-19). Paul reminds them that they had received Christ and had benefited from his redemptive work, for God through Christ placed them into the kingdom of his son whom he loves (Col. 1:3-4, 13-14), and Paul thanks God for the Colossians' steadfast faith in Christ (Col. 1:3-4; 2:5). He, then, urges them to live in accordance with the new man since they received Christ (Col. 2:6-4:1). Just as in Romans 6:2-4, Paul asserts that they died with Christ in water-baptism and was raised to walk in a new resurrection-life when they were previously dead in trespasses and sins, for God made them alive with Christ (Col. 2:12-13). Paul further urges that since they have died with Christ (Col. 3:1, 3), they should pursue obedience, because their lives were in fact hidden in Christ (Col. 3:3).

Paul restates the positive command from Colossians 3:1-4, to set their mind on the things above, in Colossians 3:5-17 by telling the Colossians how to set their mind on the things above. He states that they should put to death earthly things such as "sexual sin," "impurity," "sinful passion," "evil desire," and "covetousness" (Col. 3:5). He further notes that they should put aside "wrath," "fury," "blasphemy" and "obscene speech" (Col. 3:9), and he contends that they should not lie to one another," because they "put off the old man with its deeds and they put on the new man" (Col. 3:9-10). The new man is associated with Jesus Christ and is marked by holiness (Col. 3:1-10, 12-17), and this new man is the Colossians' current identity in Christ (Col. 3:1). The old man represents who they were before they died with Christ and before they were hidden in him (Col. 2:12; 3:1-4), for the old man is characterized by disobedience and sin. That this old man was the Colossians' identity in Adam before faith in Christ is certain because Paul here, as in Romans 6, speaks of dying to the old man in Christian baptism and he contrasts the old man with new life in Jesus Christ. Based on this contrast, he urges the Colossians (as the Ephesians) to live in a way consistent with the new man, just as he does in Romans 6:1-23 after he finishes discussing the universal impact of Adam's transgression and the digression of humanity's spiritual predicament after Torah's entrance into salvation-history (Rom. 5:12-21). The parallels between the "old man" and Adam and the "new man" and Christ in Romans 5:12-21, Ephesians 4:24, and Colossians 3:9 support my interpretation of the "old man" in Romans 6. Identity in Adam/old man is characterized by sin and disobedience (Rom. 5:12, 14, 15, 16, 17, 18, 19; Eph. 4:17-19; Col. 3:5-9a), and identity in Jesus/new man is characterized by obedience, righteousness, and eternal life (Rom. 5:15-21; Eph. 4:24; Col. 2:12-13, 20; 3:1-4). Thus, when Paul affirms that "our old man" was crucified with Christ in Romans 6:6, he refers to the old identity in Adam before faith in Christ since the first man (Adam) was the old man and the one who brought about humanity's curse, but the new man, Jesus, reverses the curse (cf. Rom. 5:14) and incorporates those who believe into a new community of the redeemed through faith in his death and resurrection (Rom. 6:9).

Paul's argument in Romans 6 further elucidates the above premise that Jews and Gentiles are in bondage to sin. When he asserts that the old man was crucified, he simply means that the old man died with Christ, because he has already argued in Romans 6:2-4 that Christians died with Christ (Rom. 6:2), were baptized into his death (Rom. 6:3), and were buried with him through baptism (Rom. 6:4) and because crucifixion was a popular mode of execution/death in the ancient world.[230] Paul states the purpose of the old man's death with two different clauses: "so that the body of sin would be abolished and so that we would no longer serve sin" (Rom. 6:6b). The second clause should be interpreted as epexegetical to the first, because the first clause (ἵνα καταργηθῇ τὸ σῶμα τῆς ἁμαρτίας) conveys purpose with a ἵνα, because the second clause (τοῦ μηκέτι δουλεύειν ἡμᾶς τῇ ἁμαρτίᾳ) conveys purpose with an articular infinitive of purpose (τοῦ δουλεύειν), and because both clauses adverbially modify συνεσταυρώθη. To say that the old man was crucified is another way of saying that "we died to sin," for the latter is the very point that Paul defends in Romans 6:1-23 (namely, we died to sin [Rom. 6:1-11]; therefore, we should no longer be slaves to the power of sin [Rom. 6:12-23]).

But what does Paul mean by "body" of sin in Romans 6:6? The meaning of σῶμα (and other Pauline anthropological terms) in the Pauline writings is a tired discussion in New Testament scholarship.[231] As I argued above, in Romans 6:6, σῶμα refers to the old man/old identity in Adam before faith in Christ. It certainly has a physical element to it and refers to the whole person in this context since Paul speaks of the crucifixion of the old man and the abolishment of the sinful body along side of resurrection and eternal life (Rom. 6:2-10; 7:24; 8:10-11, 13, 23) and since Paul exhorts the Romans that they should not "present their members to be weapons of unrighteousness to sin but to present *themselves* to God as alive from the dead and their members as weapons of righteousness to God" (Rom. 6:12).

However, σῶμα in Romans 6:6 is especially used as a synonym for σάρξ. In this regard, it carries a completely negative tone. For example, Paul speaks of the "sinful body" (Rom. 6:6), the "mortal body" (Rom. 6:12), and being "in the flesh" (Rom. 6:5; 7:18, 25) while making the argument that one should not continue to be subdued to the power of sin (Rom. 6:1, 15). He accentuates that σῶμα is a negative term in 6:6 by stating that one should not be a slave to sin (Rom. 6:6, 16-18, 20-23), that one should not let sin rule over his mortal body (Rom. 6:12-13), and that one should not walk according to the flesh (Rom. 8:1-11).

The phrase "body of sin" (τὸ σῶμα τῆς ἁμαρτίας) is used in Romans 6:6 as a reference to the old man/previous identity in Adam for three reasons. First, Paul has not yet abandoned the discussion regarding the *nachwirkung* of Adam's transgression from Romans 5:12-21. Second, Adam's transgression introduced a universal curse of sin and death upon the entire creation (Rom. 5:12). Third, Paul continues to discuss in 6:6 and in the following verses that believers in Christ have died to the power of sin since they died with Christ (Rom. 6:6-11). For example, Paul states that the "old man

---

[230] See Matt. 27:32-44; Mark 15:21-32; Luke 23:26-43; John 19:17-27; Philo, *Against Flaccus*; 6.36-39; 10.75; Seutonius, *Domitian* 11; Jos. *Wars* 2.14.9; *Ant.* 6.5.3.302-304.
[231] For example, see Jewett's history of research in the 1970s in *Anthropological Terms*.

was crucified" (Rom. 6:6a), the "body of sin would be abolished" (Rom. 6:6b), and "if we died with Christ" (Rom 6:8), "we will live with Christ" (Rom. 6:8), just as Christ died and was raised (Rom. 6:9-10). Thus, "body of sin" refers to the old man/previous identity in Adam, and the abolishment of the "body of sin" means that the power of sin and the old man have been destroyed.[232]

Liberation from Bondage

Paul's argument as to why Christians should not continue in the power of sin continues with an explanation in Romans 6:7. After Paul states that the old man was crucified in order to destroy sin (Rom. 6:6), he offers a reason: "for the one who died to sin has been liberated from sin" (Rom. 6:7). The one who died to sin could refer to Jesus, for Paul states in Romans 6:10 that "Jesus died to sin once and for all" (Rom. 6:10). However, "the one who died" most likely refers to the believer who has died to sin by becoming united to Christ, for Romans 6:2 states that "we died to sin;" Romans 6:3 states that "we were baptized into his death;" Romans 6:4 states that "we were buried with him through baptism;" Romans 6:5 states that "we have become united in the likeness of Jesus' death;" Romans 6:6 states that "our" old man was crucified and abolished; Romans 6:8 states that "we died with Christ" and "we" will live with him, and Romans 6:11 commands believers to consider themselves to be dead to sin.

In addition, the verb translated above as "has been liberated" is δεδικαίωται. This is an important soteriological term for Paul (along with the other words from the δικ-word group).[233] With the possible exception of Romans 6:7, every occurrence of δικαιόω in Romans is forensic and refers to God's verdict whereby he declares sinners in his law-court to be in the right based on their faith and union with Jesus Christ (Rom. 3:21-5:1, 9). In Romans 6:7, Paul most certainly has liberation in mind because he attaches the phrase "from sin" to the verb, which suggests separation, and he uses the same phrase with ἐλευθερωθέντες ("having been freed") in Romans 6:18. As a result, the accent in 6:7 should not be placed on God's forensic act whereby he makes one right with himself on the basis of faith in Christ, as the argument goes in Romans 3:21-5:1, but rather Paul focuses on the reason that the one who has died with Christ has crucified and abolished the old man and no longer serves sin (Rom. 6:6): viz., when the believer receives the gift of righteousness (Rom. 5:17-22) and dies with Christ (Rom. 6:1-7), he is liberated from sin's tyranny (Rom. 6:7). Consequently, he will certainly live in new resurrection-life (Rom. 6:8-11). This interpretation is sustained by the reason that Paul offers as to why the Romans should not let sin reign over their lives (Rom. 6:12-13): "because sin will not rule over you, for you are not under law but under grace" (Rom.

---

[232]For καταργέω as destruction, see Luke 13:37; Rom. 3:3, 31; 4:14; 7:2, 6; 1 Cor. 1:28; 2:6; 6:13; 1 Cor. 13:8, 10, 11; 15:24, 26; 2 Cor. 3:7, 11, 13, 14; Gal. 3:17; 5:4, 11; Eph. 2:15; 2 Thess. 2:8; 2 Tim. 1:10; Heb. 2:14.
[233]For this word-group, see Rom. 2:13; 3:20, 24, 26, 28, 30; 4:2, 5:1, 9; 8:30, 33; Gal. 2:16-17; 3:8, 11, 24; 5:4; Titus 3:7.

6:14). That is, the power of sin no longer rules as a lawless tyrant over those who have died with Christ, because his death has liberated them from the *nachwirgung* of both Adam's sin and from the *nachwirgung* of Torah's entrance into salvation-history because of Adam's sin.

That the one who has died with Christ has been set free from sin's lordship is further envisaged in Romans 6:15-23. The "therefore" in 6:15 connects 6:15-23 with the argument of 6:1-14. Romans 6:15-23 basically restates the argument that he began in Romans 6:1, because, although he introduces 6:15 with a different grammatical construction (τί οὖν ἁμαρτήσωμεν) from the construction in 6:1 (τί οὖν ἐροῦμεν ἐπιμένωμεν τῇ ἁμαρτίᾳ), he takes up the same question: namely, since the believer has been liberated from sin's power, which includes his liberation from sin's use of Torah to worsen the spiritual predicament of him while he was under Torah, does it follow then that a believer should sin because he is not under law but under grace (Rom. 6:15; cf. 6:1)? Paul's answer in both 6:1 and in 6:15 is an emphatic NO! Paul develops his answer more precisely in Romans 6:16-23.

Paul picks up the language of slavery and liberation from Romans 6:6-7 and uses it throughout Romans 6:16-23. He states that one is either a slave to whatever he presents himself, either a slave of sin resulting in death or a slave of obedience resulting in righteousness (Rom. 6:16).[234] He thanks God that although the Roman Christians "were slaves of sin" before their faith in Christ, they believed the gospel (Rom. 6:17), and they were made slaves to righteousness because they were freed from sin when they believed the gospel (Rom. 6:18). He states that the Romans were slaves to impurity and lawlessness prior to their faith in Christ and urges them to present themselves to be slaves of righteousness now that they have faith in Christ (Rom. 6:19). He states that they were free with respect to righteousness when they were slaves of sin (Rom. 6:20).

As I argued earlier, death in the argument of Romans 5-8 is often a metonym for God's judgment, for Adam's sin brought the universal curse of sin and death (Rom. 5:12) and Paul contrasts death resulting from slavery to sin with eternal life resulting from slavery to God (Rom. 6:21-22). He affirms that the Romans were liberated from sin and arrested by the power of righteousness, the end of which is eternal life (Rom. 6:22). Paul concludes the argument by providing a reason in Romans 6:23 for his statement in 6:22: "for the wages of sin are death, but the gift of God is eternal life by means of Christ Jesus, our Lord." The lordship of sin compensates its subjects with death (=judgment), but God's gift through the Lord Jesus Christ grants the gift of eternal life to all who are found in him.

Paul speaks of liberation from bondage elsewhere in his letters. He insists that before faith in Christ, Christians were both enslaved under and

---

[234] Paul's remarks in Rom. 6:16 echo Jesus' words in the gospels that one cannot serve two masters (Matt. 6:24; Luke 16:13). I credit Agersnap (*Baptism and the New Life*, 241) for pointing out this connection to me.

served the demonic forces of the world (Gal. 4:3, 9; Col. 2:8, 20).[235] In Galatians, the phrase τὰ στοῖχεια τοῦ κόσμου is equated with subjection under the Torah, for Paul states that the Galatians were formerly under the τὰ στοῖχεια τοῦ κόσμου before their faith in Christ and he questions the reason they want to return to these weak and poor elements, to which they desired to be "slaves again and again" (Gal. 4:9). In addition, he contends that if these Gentile Christians received circumcision that they would be under obligation to keep the entire law (Gal. 5:3). Yet, Paul also says elsewhere that the Galatians turned from the gospel (Gal. 1:6) and were attempting to place themselves under Torah to become part of the people of God rather than to continue to trust in the gospel (Gal. 2:11-5:14). By doing so, the Galatians were placing themselves under Torah's power and under bondage (Gal. 3:23; 4:5, 21; cf. Rom. 6:14) just as when they were under the τὰ στοῖχεια τοῦ κόσμου. Although Torah came from God through angels by the hand of a mediator, although Torah is not contrary to the promises of God (Gal. 3:15-21), and although Torah is not equivalent to the τὰ στοῖχεια τοῦ κόσμου, Paul views bondage under Torah the same as bondage under the τὰ στοῖχεια τοῦ κόσμου, for he considers both to be sources of bondage under sin (Gal. 3:21-22).[236] Paul, therefore, urges the Galatians to embrace the freedom that they received in Jesus when they received the gospel and not to subject themselves again to a yoke of slavery by placing themselves under Torah's bondage (Gal. 5:1).

Conclusion

Paul argues that because of sin's ability to use Torah to exacerbate the spiritual predicament of those under its jurisdiction, Jews and Gentiles are incapable of responding to God's great work of salvation in Jesus Christ. For Paul, their ability to respond to the gospel has been destroyed by sin's power, introduced by Adam's transgression. When Torah entered into salvation-history, the human predicament became worse. Instead of liberating humanity from sin's power, Torah placed humanity in spiritual bondage. Jews and Gentiles are under the bondage of Torah and faced with both God's present and eschatological wrath if they do not perfectly obey it (Rom. 2:1-3:20); they are dead in trespasses and sins (Eph. 2:1, 5; Col. 2:13); they gladly and freely choose to walk contrary to the gospel in accordance with the forces of evil (Eph. 2:2), and they gladly pursue the lusts of their flesh and exercise the flesh's will instead of God's (Eph. 2:3). Although God has revealed universal knowledge about himself through creation, Jews and Gentiles pervert this knowledge and instead turn on themselves to worship the creation rather than the creator, which leads to their radical rebellion against God (Rom. 1:18-32). God has revealed his righteous requirements to Israel in Torah, but the Jew

---

[235] So Clinton E. Arnold, "Returning to the Domain of the Powers: Stoicheia as Evil Spirits in Galatians 4:3, 9," *NovT* 38 (1996): 55-76.
[236] Ibid.

defiantly violated his commands (see Rom. 2-3, 7), and sin used the Torah to stimulate sin and to condemn both the Jews who have the external Torah and the Gentiles who have God's law written on their hearts (Rom. 2:12-3:20, 23; 5:14; 7:1-25). Therefore, Paul deems Jews and Gentiles to be under the power of sin as a result of Adam's transgression and that such power both condemns and destroys their ability to respond by faith to God's great act of salvation in Jesus Christ.

Chapter 3

Divine and Human Agency in Paul's Soteriology

Introduction

This chapter discusses the role of both the divine and human agents in Paul's soteriology. I argue that in Paul's soteriology, divine agency surrounds human agency. The human agent has an important role in Paul, but divine agency is the cause of human agency, and the latter is consequent to and the result of the former in Paul's soteriology. The chapter endeavors to support this thesis by arguing that Paul's soteriology has strong roots in early Jewish soteriology and that in both many early Jewish traditions and in the Pauline corpus, only those who are part of the believing community receive God's soteriological benefits *only* because the divine agent takes the initiative and works both to accomplish salvation for the human agent and to enable the human agent to receive God's promises that result in salvation. I argue these points by an analysis of selected early Jewish and Pauline texts.

Divine and Human Agency in the Hebrew Bible

Since one of the goals of this chapter is to argue that Paul's soteriology (and particularly the role of divine and human agency in his soteriology) has strong roots in early Judaism, the most logical place to begin the investigation is with a discussion of divine and human agency in early Jewish literature. Although my investigation of the sources will only provide a survey on account of the wealth of examples in the literature,[1] it will hopefully (as John Barclay has aptly stated) provide reasons by which to 'un-think' many of our Western and contemporary assumptions about divine and human agency, and the investigation will hopefully thereby help readers to interpret Paul's

---

[1]This chapter also resists the enticing temptation to interact with and cite much of the commentary on the secondary literature. Rather, I mainly interact with primary literature. I cite secondary literature only when I deem it helpful in shedding an insightful ray of light on the primary texts or when I borrow exact quotations or ideas from the secondary literature to express my ideas or to support my arguments. Thus, discussions of the date of the primary literature and other extraneous exegetical and theological discussions are ignored here. I encourage the reader to read specialized works on the Jewish literature to see specialized discussions extraneous to my thesis in this chapter.

understanding of agency in his 1st century Greco-Roman and Jewish context.[2] In addition, the Judaism of which Paul was part prior to his conversion to Christianity and the Judaism that was contemporary with his missionary movement was deeply devoted to Israel's scriptural traditions. Such devotion is expressed in much of the early Jewish literature, written both prior to and after Paul, and this literature interprets, revises, and expands the traditions in the Hebrew Bible. Thus, I begin this chapter with an analysis of selected texts in the Hebrew Bible that could shed light on Paul's conception of divine and human agency, and I follow this discussion with an analysis and discussion of selected texts from the apocrypha, pseudepigrapha, Dead Sea Scrolls, and Philo.[3] I conclude the chapter with discussions of texts in Paul.

DIVINE AND HUMAN AGENCY IN THE TORAH

Examples of divine and human agency in the Hebrew Bible are plentiful. To preserve space, I want to offer only examples from Exodus, Jeremiah, and Ezekiel. Examples from these texts will provide support for the premise that divine agency surrounds human agency and that the latter is consequent to and the result of divine agency as agency pertains to Jewish soteriology.[4]

Exodus 3:1-15:21: YHWH's Deliverance and Pharaoh's Destruction

Exodus is about YHWH's deliverance of Israel from Egyptian slavery and the establishment of his covenant with them at Sinai. Pharaoh's disobedience to YHWH reveals both the divine agent's and the human agent's role in YHWH's salvation of Israel. Moses pleaded with Pharaoh to release Israel from slavery. Each time, however, Pharaoh defied YHWH by refusing to listen to his command given to him through Moses and Aaron. YHWH tells Moses early in the Exodus narrative that he (YHWH) has seen the affliction of his people and that he (YHWH) would come down and deliver his people from the hand of the Egyptians (Exod. 3:7-9). YHWH immediately thereafter informs Moses that he would send him to Pharaoh to lead his people out of Egypt (Exod. 3:10), and YHWH promises Moses that when he goes to Pharaoh, he would be with Moses and that Israel's deliverance from Egyptian slavery would be a sign of his presence with Moses (Exod. 3:11).

The divine agent (YHWH) affirms at the beginning of the narrative that he would act on behalf of his people, Israel, and deliver them from Egyptian slavery, but that he (the divine agent) would use Moses and Aaron (human agents) as means by which he would bring about Israel's deliverance

---

[2] John M.G. Barclay, "Divine and Human Agency in Paul," in *Divine and Human Agency in Paul and His Cultural Enviornment*, LNTS 335 (London: T&T Clark, 2006), 4.

[3] I investigate the relevant texts in the Hebrew Bible in the order given in the Masoretic text. All translations of ancient texts are mine unless otherwise indicated.

[4] By soteriology here, I mean both Israel's physical and spiritual salvation. Although the two types of salvation are not the same in biblical literature, they are often closely connected in the Hebrew Bible (cf. Joshua).

(Exod. 3-4). Although the human agent's secondary role in Israel's salvation from Egypt is crucial to the narrative and to Israel's liberation, his role is consequent to and the result of the divine agent's initial action to accomplish such salvation. That is, without the divine agent's initial action on behalf of his people, the human agent's secondary action would not have been able to accomplish Israel's deliverance. Of course, the divine agent does not need the human agent, but he chooses to use him to accomplish his purposes for his people. On the contrary, the human agent absolutely needs the divine agent to act first so that the human agent could in fact obey the divine agent's command (cf. Exod. 3:10-22). For example, YHWH makes it clear to Moses that Pharaoh would not obey Moses' command "but by a strong hand" and that he (YHWH) would accomplish salvation and deliverance on behalf of his people with his strong hand when he states that "I" will bring Israel from the afflictions of the Egyptians (Exod. 3:17); "I" will stretch forth "my" hand; "I" will strike Egypt with all of "my" miracles in their midst (Exod. 3:20), and "I" will grant favor to this people (Exod. 3:21). As a result of YHWH's strong hand, Pharaoh let Israel go, but *only after* YHWH acted on behalf of his people (Exod. 3:20).

As the dialogue between YHWH and Moses continues, the latter begins to lose sight of the divine agent's role in accomplishing salvation on behalf of his people. Moses asks YHWH what he would do if the people refused to listen to him or if they should say that YHWH had not really spoken to him (Exod. 4:1). YHWH responds by essentially stating that he would give signs that attest to his revelation of himself to Moses. When Moses' staff converts into a snake only to return to being a staff when seized by the tail at YHWH's command (Exod. 4:2-5), when Moses' hand was stricken with leprosy only to regain health again after YHWH's command to place it back within his bosom (Exod. 4:6-7), and when Moses struck the Nile with the plague of blood after YHWH's command (Exod. 4:9), these events served to assure Moses that YHWH would be with him and that the divine agent would initiate and actuate the salvation of his people through Moses and Aaron (human agents). The roles of both the divine and the human agent in Israel's salvation are further apparent when YHWH promises to use Aaron as Moses' mouthpiece in response to Moses' complaint that he could not address Pharaoh due to his inability to speak (Exod. 4:10-17).

After YHWH convinces Moses that he would be with him throughout his mission to deliver his people from Egyptian slavery and after he commands Moses to show Pharaoh all the wonders that he had given within Moses' power, YHWH informs Moses that "I will harden his heart so that he will not send forth my people" (MT Exod. 4:20-21). The result of YHWH's hardening of Pharaoh's heart was his refusal to heed to YHWH's command to let his people go (Exod. 4:22-23). The rest of the narrative about Pharaoh develops the motif of YHWH's command to Pharaoh to let his people go, YHWH's hardening of Pharaoh's heart, Pharaoh's hardening of his own heart, Pharaoh's refusal to obey YHWH as a result of this hardening, and YHWH's judgment of Pharaoh and the Egyptians through supernatural-natural disasters (Exod. 5:1-14:30).

YHWH uses Moses and Aaron in the narrative as secondary agents through whom he delivered his people (Exod. 3-14), but the author makes it especially clear that YHWH is the primary reason that Israel would be delivered from Egyptian slavery (cf. Exod. 3:7-8). Moreover, Pharaoh hardened his own heart on multiple occasions (MT Exod. 8:15; 8:28; NASB 8:32), but the narrative suggests that YHWH's initial promise to harden Pharaoh's heart so that he would disobey YHWH's command (MT Exod. 4:20-21) and YHWH's final promise in the narrative that he would harden Pharaoh's heart so that he would disobey YHWH's command (MT Exod. 14:8) surround the internal statements between the sections of Exodus 4:20-21 and 14:8 regarding Pharaoh's hardening of his own heart (cf. Exod. 7:13-14, 22; 8:19; 9:7, 12, 35; 10:1, 20, 27; 11:10; 14:8). Thus, this literary arrangement seems to suggest that Pharaoh's hardening of his own heart and his refusal to obey YHWH are both the result of and consequent to YHWH's initial hardening of Pharaoh's heart. The Song of Praise that resounds from Israel in Exodus 15 after the destruction of Pharaoh and his army supports this interpretation. Throughout the song, Israel never attributes the nation's salvation to Moses but exclusively to YHWH. The song acknowledges that YHWH destroyed Pharaoh and his army while likewise affirming that Pharaoh chose to pursue Israel's destruction without mentioning YHWH's hardening of Pharaoh's heart (Exod. 15:9). However, the narrative affirms that Pharaoh's choice to pursue Israel's destruction had its origin in YHWH's action since the former is embedded between statements that affirm YHWH's salvation of Israel and his judgment of Pharaoh (Exod. 15:1-8, 10-20).

DIVINE AND HUMAN AGENCY IN THE PROPHETS
My examples of divine and human agency in the prophets will come from Jeremiah and Ezekiel. Both Jeremiah and Ezekiel offer promises of judgment because of the nation's sin and future restoration because of YHWH's faithfulness, and both emphasize that the human agent's salvation is consequent to and the result of the divine agent's work on behalf of the human agent.

Jeremiah 30-31, Ezekiel 11, 36-37: The New Covenant Promise in Jeremiah and Ezekiel
Jeremiah 30-31 are perhaps the signature chapters in Jeremiah wherein the author communicates both the divine and the human agents' role in Israel's salvation. YHWH proclaims through Jeremiah to the exiles that "behold days are coming when I will restore the captivity of my people Israel and Judah, and I will cause them to be restored to the land that I gave to their fathers so that they will inherit it" (Jer. 30:3). Israel's inheritance of the land (a divine blessing) is consequent to and the result of YHWH's work of deliverance. The divine agent is again emphasized in Jeremiah 30:8 when YHWH exclaims that he would remove the yoke from Israel's neck placed upon it by foreign nations. As a result of YHWH's work of deliverance, YHWH proclaims that Israel and Judah (human agents) would then serve YHWH their God and David their king "whom I will establish for them" (Jer. 30:9). The rest of the oracle in Jeremiah

Divine and Human Agency 109

30:10-31:40 develops both the ideas that YHWH will save and restore his people and that his people (Israel and Judah) would consequently serve YHWH in response to YHWH's judgment and salvation. YHWH states that he would save Israel and Judah (Jer. 30:10), that he would be with them (Jer. 30:11), that he would destroy other nations and spare them (Jer. 30:11), that he would chasten them (Jer. 30:11), that he has used other nations to destroy them (Jer. 30:15), that those who plundered them would be plundered by him (Jer. 30:16), and he states again that he would restore his people (Jer. 30:17-23).

In Jeremiah 31, YHWH's promises of future restoration and salvation for his people continue. YHWH affirms that he would be God to all of the clans of Israel and they would be a people to him (Jer. 31:1, 23). He expresses that he has loved Israel with an everlasting love (Jer. 31:3). He promises to rebuild Israel and Judah (Jer. 31:4-6) and to bring them from exile (Jer. 31:8-9). He declares that he will ransom Israel from captivity (Jer. 31:11). As a result of YHWH's redemption, Israel will shout with joy and she will be radiant over the goodness of YHWH (Jer. 31:12-14), and she will repent of her sins against YHWH (Jer. 31:19, 21). Then, in Jeremiah 31:31-34, YHWH promises more than mere physical restoration. He promises to make a new covenant with his people, a covenant unlike the Mosaic covenant that Israel and Judah broke by their disobedience to the external commands and a covenant that thereby forced them into exile (Jer. 31:31-32). Instead, this covenant will be one in which YHWH puts his Torah within them and writes his commands on the hearts of his people and enables them to obey such commands (Jer. 31:33). The result will be that each one within this new covenant will know the Lord; their sins will be forgiven, and again they will know YHWH (Jer. 31:34). The consequence of human knowledge of YHWH and forgiveness of sins is YHWH's initiatory act of putting his covenant within his people.

Similar to Jeremiah, Ezekiel offers promises of judgment because of the nation's sin and future restoration because of YHWH's faithfulness.[5] In Ezekiel 11, YHWH gives Ezekiel a word for Israel. He expresses that he has sent Israel into exile (Ezek. 11:16) and that he would restore the nation by putting a new spirit within it and by transforming its heart of stone (=the heart of disobedience) and by converting it into a heart of flesh (=a heart of obedience) (Ezek. 11:17-19). The consequence of YHWH's action on behalf of Israel would be "that they would walk in my statutes and my judgments they would keep and do them" with the result that "they would be to me a people and I would be to them God" (Ezek. 11:20). But YHWH promises to destroy those whose hearts go after false gods (Ezek. 11:21).

The theme of divine and human agency in Israel's restoration appears again throughout Ezekiel 36-37. YHWH promises Israel that he would once again turn to his people in the face of the nations to restore them and their land.

---

[5]For a discussion of agency in Ezekiel, see P. Boyce, *Divine Initiative and Human Response in Ezekiel* (Sheffield: JSOT Press, 1989).

He also promises that the land would no longer devour his people but would be fruitful for them (Ezek. 36:1-15). YHWH declares that he would act on behalf of Israel for the sake of his name, which Israel profaned so that the nations would know that he is YHWH (Ezek. 36:22-23). YHWH, then, explains that he would gather Israel from all of the nations (Ezek. 36:24), that he would sprinkle Israel with clean water in order to cleanse her spiritual filthiness (Ezek. 36:25), and that he would put within Israel a new and clean heart and a new spirit (Ezek. 36:26-27). In Ezekiel 36:27, YHWH specifically states that he would put his Spirit within Israel and cause them to obey his statutes, and the result of YHWH's work on behalf of Israel would result in their living in the land that YHWH promised to their forefathers, and YHWH would be their God and they would be his people (Ezek. 36:28). YHWH's divine initiative on behalf of Israel would also result in their salvation from their sin and salvation from YHWH's judgment of them by means of cursing their land (Ezek. 36:29-38).

In Ezekiel 37, YHWH gives to Ezekiel another vision whereby he explains to him how he would accomplish the promises of Ezekiel 36. To state the point simply, YHWH promises to create life within Israel so that she would obey his word, and he promises to reunite Israel and Judah into one kingdom and to bring them into their land (instead of being scattered in foreign nations via exile) and to place her under the rule of the Messiah (David's son) instead of under the rule of foreign nations (Ezek. 37:1-28). Thus, just as in Jeremiah 30-31, Ezekiel 11 and 36-37 suggest that human agency is consequent to and the result of YHWH's divine agency. That is, the people of Israel would obey YHWH's commands and experience his salvation only *when* and *after* YHWH would place his Spirit within them to enable them to obey.

Divine and Human Agency in Early Judaism

Similar to the Hebrew Bible, several early Jewish texts address the issue of divine and human agency and support that the human agent's decisions with respect to salvation are consequent to and the result of the divine agent. This section of the chapter is not exhaustive. Rather, it provides selected examples from early Jewish texts that predate, were contemporaneous with, or post-date the composition of Paul's writings.

DIVINE AND HUMAN AGENCY IN THE APOCRYPHA[6]
1 Esdras (2nd Century BCE)
1 Esdras basically offers a recapitulation of Ezra with a few novel alterations. Regarding divine and human agency, 1 Esdras speaks of the latter as consequent to and the result of divine agency. 1 Esdras expresses that the Lord

---

[6]Unless otherwise indicated, I discuss the apocryphal texts in the order given in the 2006 edition of the Rahlfs-Hanhart Septuaginta, and the textual references are from this edition.

Divine and Human Agency

aroused the spirit of King Cyrus to release the Jews from exile; he released the Jews from exile (2:1-11), and the Lord did not forsake his people even when they were in exile, but he brought favor upon them in the presence of the Persians and enabled them to rebuild Jerusalem (8:77-78). Zerubbabel praised God because victory and wisdom came to God's people from God's hand and because God gave the Jews rest from their enemies and forgiveness, which he demonstrated by releasing the Jews from exile to return to Jerusalem to rebuild the city and its temple (4:58-60); the Lord relieved Israel of its sins and left a seed (8:84); Ezra praised God because he put the desire into the heart of the king to be favorable toward Israel and because God granted Ezra favor before the king and his friends (8:25-27), but Artaxerxes speaks of Jews who *chose* to go up to Jerusalem from exile to rebuild the city (8:10). The Jews received favor from God and were released from exile (6:5), and King Cyrus granted permission to the Jews to return to Jerusalem to rebuild the city and its temple (6:23-34). Nebuchadnezzar deported the Jews to exile (5:7; 6:15) and Jerusalem's calamities happened because of their sins and evil (8:83), but the Lord gave Israel over to Nebuchadnezzar to be deported into exile because of the nation's sin (6:15).

2 Esdras (2nd-3rd Centuries CE)[7]

2 Esdras 1-2 is a Christian prophecy and apocalypse about God's rejection of Israel and its replacement by the church. 2 Esdras 3-14 is a Jewish apocalypse that focuses on conditions that arise from the destruction of Jerusalem in 70 CE. 2 Esdras 15-16 is a Christian prophecy and apocalypse that seeks to confirm Christians who suffered persecution.

That human agency is consequent to and the result of divine agency appears true in 2 Esdras. 2 Esdras states that God brought Israel out of bondage (1:7). The Lord destroyed other nations for Israel's sake (1:10-23). The sovereign God created the world by his word (3:3-4; 6:38-53). Rebellious Israel sinned against God (1:4-7). The righteous can endure difficult circumstances while they hope for relief (7:18). Those who disregard the Lord's law will perish, for they disobey the Lord's instructions regarding what they should do to live and avoid punishment (7:19-24) and Israel disobeys Torah (7:22-24, 71-73). God takes the kingdom away from Israel and gives it to another people, and God commands his people to obey him to participate in the resurrection (2:10-32), but the Lord did not remove Israel's evil heart from within them after they came out of Egypt, so that his law might produce fruit in them (3:20). Instead, those after David had an evil heart, and the Lord handed them over to foreign nations (3:27). All humanity has sinned and has an internal evil spirit,

---

[7]The textual traditions of 2 Esdras are dated as follows: 2nd Century CE [chapters 1-2=5 Ezra]; late 1st Century CE [chapters 3-14=4 Ezra], and 3rd Century CE [chapters 15-16=6 Ezra). All textual citations and translations of 2 Esdras are from the NRSV, which relies upon the Latin and other versions, since 2 Esdras in Rahlfs-Hanhart is the canonical Ezra. All of the dates for the early Jewish texts are both standard and approximate dates.

which results in their judgment (7:45-61). Ezra had a treasure of works stored up with the Most High God that would protect him from his judgment at the resurrection (7:77). God saves only a few who obey him (7:45-61), but God ordained in his law that the righteous would inherit God's blessings and that the ungodly would perish (7:17, 79-80, 105). God grants (physical) life and takes it when he pleases (5:4; 8:7-17), but Moses commanded Israel to choose life so that they would live in the land (7:129). God created and chose Israel for his own glory and handed the nation over to be destroyed by other nations who hated his law (5:21-30). God determined the end of the world before he created it (6:1-6). Fruit results in eternal life for those who bear it. But Ezra asked the Lord to "give us a seed so that fruit may be produced, by which every mortal who bears the likeness of a human being may be able to live" (8:6). The righteous will receive their reward from the Lord in accordance with their deeds that they lay up with the Lord (8:33), but the unrighteous chose to disobey the Lord's ways (8:56-58; 9:26-36). Based on the author(s) earlier statements that the Lord did not remove the evil heart from his people so that they would obey (3:20), one can infer that those who do evil deeds do so because the Lord did not enable them to obey his law, and those who obey do so because of the Lord's enablement.

LXX Esther (BCE 2nd Century-1st Century)
LXX Esther differs from the MT of Esther. The translator(s) of LXX Esther added material to fill certain theological lacuna (e.g. they inserted God's name in the text) (2:20; 4:8; 6:1, 13). LXX Esther explicitly suggests that the God of the Jews is the author of their salvation. The figure of Esther in the additions in the LXX is presented as a Romantic heroine just as Judith in the book ascribed to her name.

Mordecai saw in a vision that some were plotting to kill the king. The Lord revealed this vision to Mordecai, and he made known the plot to the king after he overheard the conspirators discussing their plan (1:1a-1r). Mordecai commanded Esther to tell the king, her husband, about Haman's plot against the Jews. He urged her to pray first (presumably to ask for help) and to proceed thereafter to speak to the king to incite him to provide salvation for the Jews (4:8). Mordecai then prayed to God because he remembered all the works of the Lord on behalf of his people (4:17-a-z). His prayer expresses that God is the king of all things. Everything is in his power. No one can oppose God when he desires to save Israel, because God is the creator of the heaven and the earth (4:17b-c). He is Lord of all things, and no one can oppose his lordship (4:17d). Mordecai urged the Lord to spare his people from the destruction of Haman (4:17f).

Immediately after Mordecai prayed, Queen Esther began to pray. She acknowledged that the Lord was her king, and she summoned him for his help, for God alone was her helper (4:17l-z). She confessed that he is the God whom she learned delivered her ancestors from Egypt and that they sinned against him and currently lived in exile. She urged God to give her a rhythmical word for the king's ear and to change the king's heart toward hatred of those who want to harm the Jews that would result in both the destruction of Haman and of those who conspire with him against the Jews (4:17s). After Esther finished praying, she adorned herself with beauty and entered into the king's court. When the king first saw her, he became furious since her visit was unsolicited. But the king's appearance of anger was appeased, because "God changed the spirit of the king to gentleness" to the point that the king jumped from his throne and consoled Esther to calm her fear (5:1e). In spite of Haman's plot to kill Mordecai (5:9-14), God intervened in that he "turned sleep from the king during that night;" he read the records, noticed that Mordecai helped spare the king's life, and asked whether a special honor was bestowed upon Mordecai, to which the king's servants responded by saying: none (6:1-3). At dinner, Esther exposed Haman's plot against the Jews, and Artaxerxes killed Haman, promoted Mordecai, and spared the Jews (8:1-10:3k). Mordecai proclaimed that *God* saved his people and destroyed the wicked plot of Haman (10:3f-k). He used human agents (Esther, Mordecai, etc.) to bring about their salvation, but the human agents' role was consequent to and the result of the divine agent's initial action.

Judith (BCE 135-100)
The book of Judith is an historical Romance that tells the story of a beautiful Jewish heroine named Judith. She was a widow who alone would fight for Israel against the Assyrians to defend the Jewish nation because of the cowardice of the Jewish men. The story records that Judith defeated the Assyrian leader by seducing him without dishonoring YHWH's law and by chopping off his head while he slept.

Divine and human agency is very much part of the story of Judith. Nebuchadnezzar initiated a war against Arphaxad and summoned other nations to fight with him, but they refused since they did not fear him. He fought against him and defeated Arphaxad (1:1-16).[8] Nebuchadnezzar summoned his general to lead soldiers against the other nations who refused to fight with him against Arphaxad, and he pronounced that he would destroy these other nations (2:1-13). Holofernes (Nebuchadnezzar's top general) led the military charge against the disobedient nations, and he and his fellow soldiers slaughtered the nations and plundered their properties. Those who remained greatly feared Nebuchadnezzar (2:14-3:9).

When the Jews in Judea heard of Holofernes' actions, they were alarmed. The high priest wrote the Jews in the towns around Judea to be on guard lest Judea would be invaded, and they incited the Lord to protect them (4:1-12). The Lord heard their prayers as they fasted, prayed, and offered sacrifices to him (4:13-15), and God promised to defend Israel *only* if the nation obeyed his commands (5:21). Holofernes threatened Achior (who suggested that the Jews' God was too strong for the Assyrians) that the

---

[8]The book of Judith wrongly states that Nebuchadnezzar was the king of Assyria. This obvious historical blunder is one reason that the book should be understood as a Romance and not an historical narrative.

Assyrians would destroy the Israelites (6:1-10), and the Israelites again prayed that God would protect them from the Assyrians (6:17-21).

Judith confronted Israel's leaders for their cowardice and exhorted them to hope in the Lord, for she firmly believed that God could and would save his people if he wanted to do so (8:11-17). Judith plotted against the Assyrians, and Uzziah acknowledged that her action was in compliance with God's action. That is, Judith would exercise a deceptive plot against the Assyrians, and the Lord would exercise his will via Judith's duplicity (8:32-35). Judith demonstrates that human action is consequent to and the result of divine agency via her prayer before she executed her plot against the Assyrians.

As Judith prayed, she acknowledged that God did the "former things, these things, and the things to come" (9:5-6). She continued by saying that "the things that you intended have come to pass" and "what you desired is present and said 'behold: we exist.'" Judith continued this line of discourse in her prayer by affirming that "all [God's] ways are prepared, and [his] judgment is with foreknowledge" (9:5-6) (brackets mine). Her prayer acknowledged that, on the one hand, the Assyrians were prideful because of their military force (9:7), but, on the other hand, that God is the God who crushes wars (9:7). Judith, then, petitioned God to "overthrow their strength by means of his power" and to "shatter their strength by means of [his] wrath" (9:8) (brackets). Judith continued by asking God to "look at their arrogance," to send his "wrath against their heads," and to "give" into her hands "strength which she intended in advance" (9:9). She prayed that God would "strike the slave by means of [her] lips of deception because of the one who rules" and to strike "the one who rules because of the one who serves him" (9:10). She prayed that God would "strike their majesty by means of the hand of a female" (9:10), because he protects and helps the weak and desperate, not the strong, and because he is the savior of the hopeless (9:11). She prayed that God would use her "word of deception as their wound and bruise" against those who plotted to hurt God's people and their land (9:13). Finally, Judith prayed that the Lord would grant Israel knowledge that he alone is the God and protector of Israel (9:14).

When Judith planned to carry out her deceptive plot against the Assyrians, the elders blessed her with the prayer that "God would give" her grace to fulfill "her pursuits" for Israel's exaltation (10:8-9). Judith lied to the Assyrians about her motives for coming to the Assyrian camp. When asked what was her ethnic origin and from where she had come, Judith responded by saying she was a Jew but that she was fleeing from the Jews since they would be devoured by the Assyrians. Judith lied about her loyalty to the Assyrians (10:11-16; 11:5-23; 12:10-13:3). Judith informed Holofernes that she would not run out of supplies of food and drink until the Lord should complete that which he desired to complete by means of her hand (12:4). However, Judith prayed that God (the divine agent) would execute her plan to destroy the Assyrians for the exaltation of Israel when she was in Holofernes' bedchamber after he became "overflowing with wine" (13:3). After this prayer, Judith prayed again that God would give her strength to carry out her plot. Judith, then, dismembered the drunken Holofernes' head with his own sword, placed it in a

Divine and Human Agency 115

bag, and gave it to her maid (13:4-8). When Judith and her maid returned to her fellow Hebrews with the severed head, she proclaimed that ". . .God, our God, is still with us to make power in Israel and strength against the enemies just as he did today" (13:11). Judith urged her fellow Jews to praise God who did not withdraw his mercy from his people but who destroyed their enemies by means of her hand. Judith immediately thereafter further states that "the Lord struck him by means of the hand of a woman" and that her face deceived Holofernes resulting in his destruction (13:14-16).

After the people heard Judith's report, they worshipped God and confessed that "he scorned" their enemies. Then, Uzziah remarked that God is praised because "he guided" Judith to wound the head of the ruler of Israel's enemies, and Judith's praise would never cease from remembrance of her people due to God's power (13:17). Israel defeated the Assyrians, and the elders of Jerusalem witnessed the things that the Lord had done for Israel. The high priest blessed Judith by calling her the glory of Israel because she defeated the Assyrians (15:1-10), but the text makes clear that the Lord defeated the Assyrians (14:10). In fact, Judith praised God for his deliverance of her from the nation's enemies (16:1-5). She acknowledged that the Lord "crushed wars" and "delivered" her from those who were pursuing her (16:2). The Assyrians boasted that they would destroy Israel (16:3-4), but "the Lord almighty rejected them by the hand of a woman" (16:5).

Tobit (BCE 250-175)[9]

Tobit is about the righteous deeds of a devout Jew named Tobit and that he was not to blame for Israel's exile, although he too lived in exile with the nation. Tobit exhorts his son, Tobias, to continue in his (Tobit's) righteous deeds. The book emphasizes that almsgiving and righteous deeds atone for sin. The book also speaks to the issue of divine and human agency.

Tobit (a righteous Jew) prayed and acknowledged that the Lord sent Israel into exile (BA 3:1-6). The Lord sent an angel to heal Tobit when he became blind and to provide his son, Tobias, Sarah as a wife (BA 3:16). Sarah was prepared for Tobias before the foundation of the world by God. That God did the preparation seems right because Raphael (the angel sent from God) insisted that Tobias and Sarah should pray in their bridal chamber that the Lord would be merciful to them and grant them safety (BA 6:18). After Raguel agreed to give his daughter to Tobias as a wife, he explained to him that her previous seven husbands had died in the act of sexual relations with her, but that the Lord would work on behalf of Tobias and Sarah to spare Tobias (S 7:11). When Raphael and Tobias returned to the latter's blind father, Tobias applied eye salve on his father's eyes precisely as commanded by Raphael, but Tobit ascribed the healing to God. He praised God for afflicting him and for showing him mercy (BA 11:7-15). God was merciful to Tobit (BA 11:17), but

---

[9]In my discussion of Tobit, I work from two textual traditions: the S tradition and the BA tradition. I cite the appropriate abbreviations beside of the textual references to identify the specific textual tradition from which I am working.

he used an angel and his son to showcase his mercy (BA 3:16). Raphael urged Tobias and Tobit to worship God *because* of what God had done for them. Raphael did not take credit for the miracle, *but* he affirmed that God used him to heal Tobit and to provide a wife for his son. Raphael further stated that while he was with Tobit and Tobias, he came to them not "by his own grace but by means of the will of our God" (BA 12:6-18), and Tobit praised God for his judgment and salvation of his people (BA 13:1-17).

1 Maccabees (BCE 100)
1 Maccabees records a history of the Maccabean revolt, the Hasmonean dynasty, and the rise of the high priestly office in early Judaism. Divine and human agency with regard to Israel's physical salvation also arises in the narrative of 1 Maccabees.

Antiochus Epiphanes IV (henceforth, Antiochus) conquered Egypt and Jerusalem, and he especially commanded the Jews to forsake their laws, honor the laws of the Greeks, to worship their gods, or else they would die. In essence, Antiochus commanded the Jews to stop being Jewish. Some Jews heeded Antiochus' commands, but other Jews who were zealous for God's Torah, led by Mattathias and after his death by his son, Judas Maccabeus, fought against Antiochus and his army (1:16-62). When Judas Maccabeus and his fellow warriors noticed the size of the Syrian army when it invaded Judea, some of them feared that the army was too large to conquer in battle. Judas, however, reminded his fellow Jewish warriors that victory in battle would not happen based on the size of one's army but based on "strength from heaven" and that "God would crush" the Syrian army through Judas and his smaller army (3:16-22). Judas and his army eventually defeated the Syrian army in battle, and the nations feared him (3:23-25).

On another occasion, Antiochus sent forces to Emmaus against Judas' outnumbered army. The latter had insufficient weapons and armor with which to fight. When they saw that the Gentile camp was strong, Judas' army feared. Still, he urged them not to fear and reminded them that God would redeem and save Israel, just as he had saved their ancestors from Pharaoh. Thus, Judas exhorted his army to pray and ask God for help against the Gentiles (4:10-11), and the text also expresses that Judas and his army crushed the Gentile army and praised the God of heaven after their victory (4:12-25).

When Judas saw the strength of another cavalry of soldiers sent to destroy him and his army, he prayed that the God who crushed David's enemies through David would crush Israel's current enemies. Judas asked the Lord to grant their enemies a heart of cowardice and to melt their strength. He asked the Lord to shaken their enemies by means of their crushing and to overtake them "by means of the sword of those who love you" (4:30-33, esp. 4:33). Judas and his army fought and overtook Lysias' army of 5,000 soldiers (4:34). After the Jews thought that they would fall to the sword of Nicanor and his army, they prayed that God would take vengeance upon them and that God would cause them to fall by their sword. Likewise, Judas prayed that God would "crush" their camp and judge Nicanor on account of his wickedness

Divine and Human Agency

against Israel (7:37-42). As a result, the Jews outflanked their enemies and crushed them in battle. Therefore, God saved Israel through Judas and his army.

2 Maccabees (BCE 130)

2 Maccabees is an abridgment of Jason of Cyrene's five-volume work about the Maccabean revolt (2:23-42). 2 Maccabees especially highlights the selective events from Jewish history from the reign of Nicanor, King Seleucus IV, and the reign of Onias III as high priest until the defeat of the Seleucid king at the hands of Judas Maccabeus in BCE 161. But the book likewise speaks to both the divine agent's and the human agent's role in salvation.

Early in the narrative, the author states that God saved the Jews from Antiochus and that he expelled from the city those who joined themselves together in battle array in Jerusalem (1:11-12; 2:17-18). The author(s) also points out that the priests struck down Antiochus and his men and cut off their heads, for God handed over those who acted impiously (1:16-17). The Jews prayed to the "all powerful" Lord to protect them from Heliodorus (one of the king's men), and God sent an angel to attack him (3:22-28). Heliodorus' friends begged Onias (the high priest) to ask "the exalted one" to grant life to him. As Onias offered atonement for Heliodorus, angels appeared and warned him that he should be grateful to Onias since he was the means by which the Lord preserved his life. The angels proclaimed that Heliodorus had been flogged from heaven and spoke of the "magnificent strength of God" (3:31-34), and Heliodorus made known the mighty acts of Israel's supreme and powerful God who destroys those who do evil (3:35-39). Andronicus killed Onias; Antiochus killed Andronicus, and the narrator immediately thereafter states that the Lord killed Andronicus (4:35-38).

Divine and human agency is further seen in the description of Israel's suffering and Antiochus' death. God's anger burned against Israel's sins against him, and he demonstrated his wrath to them by using Antiochus to judge them (5:17-26; 6:1-11). The redactor of 2 Maccabees offers a theological explanation of Israel's suffering: viz., God brought this upon the nation because of his love for Israel (6:12-17). Antiochus tortured and killed the Jews, but God would raise them up to everlasting life at the resurrection (7:9). Regarding the martyrdom of the mother's seven sons, the author states that the Lord gives and takes away. He created the mother's seven children, chose to take them away through martyrdom, and would give them back to her again at the resurrection (7:23). The Lord used Judas and his army to strike Antiochus with a fatal blow (8:36; 9:5; 10:1; 12:11), and Judas and his army prayed to the sovereign God who destroyed the walls in Jericho through Joshua and who shattered Israel's enemies (12:15, 28). God aroused the anger of Antiochus Eupator against Menelaus, and the former killed the latter (13:4). Judas asked God for help to conquer his enemies, and Judas conquered the enemies of Israel because the Lord protected him (13:9-17; 14:34; 15:7-8, 21, 25-36). Israel's salvation was consequent to God's actions on behalf of the nation.

3 Maccabees (BCE 100)

3 Maccabees records that Ptolemy IV became angry with the Jews due to their refusal to let him enter the temple. Yet, God delivered Israel from his hands. The author places the accent in 3 Maccabees on divine agency. Human agency appears only as consequent to and the result of divine agency.

When Ptolemy IV (henceforth, Ptolemy) expressed that he wanted to enter the Jews' temple, the priests called upon the supreme God to help them keep him from doing this (1:16). They offered their prayer to the God who always defended them against their enemies (1:27). Simon, the high priest, especially prayed that God, who destroyed those who opposed him in ages past, would defend his people once again against the insolent nations (2:1-23). God heard his prayer, for the sovereign God aided the Jews from heaven to escape Ptolemy's judgment on earth by causing his generals to run out of paper and ink so that they could not take a census of the Jews in Egypt to kill them (4:20-21). The Jews prayed that God would avert the king's evil plot against Israel. The Lord heard their prayer and caused a deep sleep to fall upon the king to frustrate the king's plan. The Lord caused the king to forget a second time his plot (5:7-9, 11-13, 25-30, 35, 51). Eleazar, a wise sage, asked the Lord to protect Israel from the destruction of the Egyptians while he and his fellow Jews were about to be trampled by wild elephants due to the hatred of Ptolemy against the Jews. The Lord heard Israel's prayer a third time and protected them from their enemies by sending two angels from heaven to confuse the Egyptian forces and their animals so that they would release the Jews from their chains (6:1-29, 32, 36, 39; 7:6, 9-23). God's action on behalf of Israel preceded their victory over Ptolemy.

4 Maccabees (2nd Century BCE-2nd Century CE)

4 Maccabees focuses on the singular thesis that religious reasoning has mastery over the sinful passions. The author of 4 Maccabees reveals this with different examples from the Old Testament where God's people chose to act in compliance with their knowledge of what was right (1:1-2:18), but he especially supports this thesis by using the Maccabean martyrs as primary examples (6:1-17:22).

Regarding divine and human agency, faithful Jews prayed that God would protect them from Apollonius and his military by not allowing them to enter into the temple treasury to pilfer the funds. God answered this prayer by sending angels on horseback to preclude him from entering the temple even as he was walking up the steps (4:8-14). Eleazar proved the author's thesis that divine reason is master over the passions in that he refused to yield to the king's demand to eat unlawful foods. Instead, Eleazar obeyed Torah's prescription for food. The author, then, commends Eleazar for his mastery over the passions. The author does not seem to credit God for giving Eleazar (or any other faithful Jew) the ability to obey Torah and to master the passions. But he credits their wisdom for their ability to obey (6:1-7:23). The author credits the philosophy and the reason of the seven sons and their mother for their ability to endure the tyrant, Antiochus, and obey God's law (8:15-13:1). The seven sons

Divine and Human Agency

promised Antiochus that he would experience God's wrath (9:9). The mother of the seven sons loved godliness more than the prospect of salvation from the Tyrant's judgment, because godliness would save her for eternal life in accordance with God (15:3), and the first son martyred suggested that their faithful obedience to God in the face of suffering would result in their final salvation and the salvation of the nation (9:24). However, Eleazar suggested earlier in the narrative that God would atone for the nation's sin by means of his blood (6:28-29), and the narrator concludes the discussion about the martyrs' deaths by affirming that their deaths served as a propitiation for the nation's sin, that their deaths purified Israel, and that their deaths saved the nation from God's wrath (17:21-22). Thus, one can infer that Israel's salvation is consequent to and the result of God's divine action: He offered the martyrs in death to atone for the nation's sin (17:21-22).

Prayer of Manasseh (1st Century CE)
The prayer of Manasseh is a prayer of confession placed upon the lips of the evil king Manasseh. The prayer confirms that human agency is consequent to and the result of divine agency.

Manasseh prays that God is the sovereign and almighty one who has appointed repentance and forgiveness of sins for sinners (1:1-13). As he prays for God to forgive him for his voluminous sins, he declares that God would demonstrate his goodness "in me" by saving "me" according to his great mercy although he was unworthy (1:14). God's goodness that he would demonstrate "in" him and the salvation that he would provide for him results in Manasseh's praise of God (1:15). Here, as elsewhere, the penitent's prayer includes a confession that God must act on behalf of the sinner so that he would be forgiven and respond to God with praise (1:1-15).

Wisdom of Solomon (BCE 100-50 CE)
Wisdom of Solomon is a collection of wisdom sayings ascribed to King Solomon. As with both canonical and extracanonical Jewish wisdom literature, the sayings emphasize the fear of the Lord and obedience to Torah as the expression of true wisdom. The priority of divine agency over human agency arises to the surface in the Wisdom of Solomon.

Solomon commands the reader to love righteousness and to seek the Lord with a sincere heart, because the Lord is found by those who do not test him and reveals himself to those who trust him (1:1-2) and because "unjust thoughts separate [people] from God" (brackets mine) (1:3). A holy and disciplined person will flee deceit and abandon foolish thoughts and disdain unrighteousness (1:5), and those who fear the Lord must fear ungodliness (1:11-12). Those who trust the Lord will understand truth, and the faithful ones will serve the Lord in love, because "grace and mercy [are] in his elect ones" [brackets mine]. A holy and righteous spirit (i.e. a godly human) will flee from deceit (1:5). God observes the heart and the inmost feelings of the wicked (1:7). Such language establishes the point that grace and mercy are divine gifts from God that reside within the elect and presumably enable them to pursue wisdom.

In 4:15, the author states that God takes the elect from the world early to keep them safe from evil, because his mercy and grace are "in/with his elect." The Lord protects the righteous with his right hand and he shields them by means of strength. The Lord's protection of the righteous is a means by which they will receive a beautiful crown from him for their godliness (5:16).

The author further gives insight into divine and human agency when he discusses Solomon's request for wisdom. Solomon prays that God would grant him the ability to speak with sound judgment and affirms that he received wisdom from God to do so (7:15). God gave knowledge to Solomon of reality (7:17-22). Wisdom is an extension of God's power and breath (7:25-26), but Solomon possessed wisdom because God gave it to him (8:21-9:18). Solomon, thus, asked the Lord to give him wisdom. Solomon confesses that for him to know that wisdom comes from God was a divine grace (8:21). Wisdom knows God's works since it has always been present with him. She knows what is right according to his commandments. Since wisdom comes from God and no one has access to it unless God grants it to him or her and since Solomon urges his readers to obey God's commands and pursue wisdom, it follows that God gives the human agent the ability to do what is commanded. This point is further supported when Solomon says that wisdom will guide him in all things and provide salvation (9:9).

The divine and human role in salvation is especially evident throughout other texts in the Wisdom of Solomon. The author pronounces that God is sovereign (12:12-18). God grants his people repentance for their sins (12:19). The potter (God) created good vessels and bad vessels and determined the function of each vessel (15:7), but the bad vessels (ungodly humans) created idols and worshipped them and failed to see the folly in such worship (15:18-19). God saved his people when they turned to him (16:2, 7; 18:1-8; 19:1-5, 22).

Sirach (BCE 180)[10]

The Wisdom of Jesus Ben Sirach (Sirach) is the translation of Sirach's grandson, who translated from Hebrew into Greek his grandfather's words of exhortations to his fellow Jews in the Diaspora. The work essentially promotes Judaism and urges its readers to fear the Lord and pursue wisdom in Torah. As with other Jewish wisdom traditions, the fear of the Lord is wisdom, and wisdom can be found in Torah. Divine and human agency is also a strong theme in the book.

All wisdom comes from God; he created her before all other things, and he gives wisdom to all who love him (1:1-10). Yet, Sirach commands those

---

[10] I rely upon the Greek textual tradition of Sirach and not the Hebrew tradition. For an interaction with the relevant texts in the Hebrew tradition that pertain to divine and human agency, see Jason Maston, *Divine and Human Agency in Second Temple Judaism and Paul: A Comparison of Sirach, Hodayot, and Romans 7-8*, WUNT 297 (Tübingen: Mohr Siebeck, 2010), 22-74.

Divine and Human Agency

who desire wisdom to keep God's commandments, for fearing God is the beginning of wisdom (1:14), the crown of wisdom (1:18), and the root of wisdom (1:20). Sirach commands his audience not to neglect fearing God (1:28; 2:15-18) and to set its heart right and serve the Lord faithfully regardless of what befalls the nation (2:1-10), for the Lord is compassionate and merciful, and he forgives sins and saves his people in the time of affliction (2:11). But the Lord loves those who love wisdom (4:14). The audience is commanded to reflect upon the Lord's commandments, and Sirach promises that God would establish the heart of the one who reflects upon the Lord's commandments and that he would grant him wisdom (6:37), but God will judge in accordance with one's works (11:26; 16:11-14; 35:22-26). Human's pride was the beginning of sin and the beginning of human pride was to forsake the Lord. Thus, the Lord responded by bringing judgment upon those who forsook him. God did not create arrogance and human anger (10:12-18), and the offspring that is worthy of honor is the offspring that fears the Lord, but the offspring that is worthy of dishonor is the offspring that transgresses the commandments (10:19-24). Sirach exhorts its readers not to blame their sin and disobedience on the Lord, for he hates sin and created humans with the ability to choose good or evil (15:11-20). He exclaims that if the righteous should desire, they would keep the commandments so that they would do faith with good pleasure." God has placed before each person a choice for life and death (15:16-17), "because the Lord's wisdom is great, and his strength is with power, and he sees all things. And his eyes are upon those who fear him, and he will know man's every work. He does not command to anyone to be ungodly, and he does not give praise to anyone to sin" (15:19-20).

Jason Maston thinks that Ben Sira's own view (in contrast to the two-ways paradigm considered earlier in Sirach) is most clearly laid out in Sir 15:11-20. He contends that although Ben Sira acknowledges a two-ways paradigm current in 1st century Judaism, he, however, emphasizes the primacy of the human agent in salvation. He suggests that when Ben Sira affirms the primacy of divine agency prior to Sirach 15, he is simply acknowledging a view that was current in 1st century Judaism and that this acknowledgment does not represent Ben Sira's own view. Maston offers a careful discussion of the relevant texts in Sirach. He argues that Ben Sira's comments on the role of life through Torah observance, the Wisdom Tradition and Torah in Sirach, the creator, his commandments, obedience, fear of God and faith, and atonement and sin support that Ben Sira's emphasis is on human agency.[11]

In my view, however, Sirach also offers statements that emphasize the role of the divine agent, and such statements seem to represent his own view of agency and not simply representative of alternative theologies in early Judaism.[12] He states that good and bad come from the Lord (11:14, 21-28). Sir 22:27-23:6 is a strong early Jewish example where human agency appears to be consequent to and the result of divine agency. Sirach petitions the Lord not to

---

[11] See Maston, *Divine and Human Agency*, 27-34.
[12] Ibid., 22-26.

abandon him to sin (23:1). Then, he asks who would protect him "so that my ignorance would not be multiplied and so that my sins would not increase and would fall in the presence of my enemy and my enemy rejoice" (23:2-3)? He answers this question immediately by again asking the Lord not to give him a "lifting up of the eyes" (23:4) and by asking the Lord to "turn desire from me" (23:5). He concludes his prayer by asking the Lord "let not [sexual] desire and sexual intercourse overtake me and do not give me over to a shameless life" (23:6) (brackets mine). This text suggests that in spite of the fact that Sirach states on more than one occasion that the wise ones should fear God and that God created humans with the ability to choose right or wrong with the result that no one can blame him for any individual decision (15:11-20), unless God (the divine agent) enables the human agent, the latter could not and would not obey the commands to stay free from sin, because Sirach asks the Lord to keep desire from him (23:4-6).[13] Additionally, he later states that God fashioned human beings into what he wanted them to be, as a potter fashions clay (33:7-13). This latter point is affirmed when he states: "Just as the potter's glass is in his hands—all its ways are in accordance with his pleasure—in the same way men are in the hand of the one who made them so that he gives to them in accordance with his judgment" (33:13b; cf. 42:15-50:24).

In addition, the contingency of human agency on divine agency seems evident when one considers other statements scattered through Sirach. He states that God created wisdom (24:1-17). Wisdom summons everybody to come to her and to obey her so that he would not sin (24:19-22). Those who seek God will be filled with wisdom (32:14-24). Humans should fear the Lord and love him (34:14-20), and they should pray that God would guide their paths (37:15).[14] If the Lord wills, the one who desires wisdom will be filled with a spirit of understanding (39:6-11).[15] Joshua was a savior of God's elect and he avenged the enemies of God's people (46:1). The Lord gave Caleb strength to obtain the inheritance, so that Israel would see that to follow the Lord is good

---

[13] Against Maston, *Divine and Human Agency*, 50. He contends that Ben Sira's prayer focuses on actual obedience and not on a change of character or disposition. My position above suggests that the two are inseparable in Ben Sira's prayer, so that the human agent's request to obey is achievable if and when the Lord acts to take away his evil proclivities toward sin.

[14] For the point that the themes of the fear of the Lord and keeping the commandments speak to the priority of divine agency in Ben Sira, see Eckhard J. Schnabel, *Law and Wisdom from Ben Sira to Paul*, WUNT 2/16 (Tübingen: Mohr Siebeck, 1985), 45. Similarly Don B. Garlington, '*The Obedience of Faith:' A Pauline Phrase in Historical Context*, WUNT 2/38 (Tübingen: Mohr Siebeck, 1991), 20, 23, 27. Contra Maston, *Divine and Human Agency*, 50-53.

[15] Sirach also states that God created physicians (38:1) and medicines from the earth (38:4-6). He heals by using physicians (38:7-8), but Sirach exhorts its audience to ask the Lord for healing when sickness falls upon them (38:9); repent of sin (38:10); offer sacrifices to the Lord (38:11), and see a physician (38:12a), "for even him the Lord created" (38:12b), and "let not a physician turn from you, for there is even a need for him" (38:12c).

Divine and Human Agency 123

(46:9-10). The Lord raised up Solomon upon David's throne. Solomon sinned, but the Lord did not remove his mercy from his chosen people who love him (47:12-22). He promises that the Lord rescues those who wait for him (51:13-30). Thus, although Sirach says much about human agency (as Maston has demonstrated), such statements ought perhaps to be understood in light of his other comments about divine agency.

Psalms of Solomon (BCE 1st Century)[16]

The 18 Psalms of Solomon are a Jewish response to the capture of Jerusalem by the Romans in the first century BCE. They too contain the theme of divine and human agency.

The psalmist confesses that he is full of righteousness and that the Lord will hear his prayer on account of his righteousness (Pss. Sol. 1:3), and he praises God for his ability to repay sinners and to show mercy to the righteous (Pss. Sol. 2:33-35). The psalmist claims that the righteous (pious Jews) obey God and that their confidence comes from God (Pss. Sol. 3:1-8). On the one hand, God judged Israel through the Gentiles because of the nation's sin in accordance with their evil deeds, but, on the other hand, the psalmist asks the Lord to repay the Gentiles for their treatment of Israel (Pss. Sol. 2:1-37). Those who fear the Lord in innocence are blessed. The Lord will deliver them from treacherous and sinful men, and he will deliver his people from stumbling into sin and judgment, because God is a "great judge and a strong Lord in righteousness;" the psalmist concludes the psalm with a prayer that God's mercy would continue to be upon his people (Pss. Sol. 4:23-25). In light of the judgment that comes to those who disobey and sin (Pss. Sol. 4:23-25), the bestowment of God's mercy, for which the psalmist prays, could be understood as divine enablement to obey his commands to escape judgment because of sin. This is supported by other prayers throughout the psalms. The psalmist asks the Lord not to make his hands heavy upon his people, so that they would not sin because of necessity. He continues: "and if you should not turn us, we will not flee [from you], but will come to you" (Pss. Sol. 5:6-7) (brackets mine). The psalmist prays for divine enablement to flee to the Lord.

God's people followed the ways of the Gentiles and disobeyed his Law and dishonored his temple (Pss. Sol. 8:1-13). Consequently, God brought a spirit of deception upon them. He gave them a cup of strong wine for drunkenness. He brought destruction upon Jerusalem via a foreigner from the ends of the earth, and the people received him with pomp and laud. This foreigner captured Jerusalem because God led him with security by means of their deception. Israel sinned (human agency); God gave Israel a spirit of stupidity so that they would continue in sin (divine and human agency); God led a foreigner into Jerusalem to capture the city (divine agency) because of their sin (human agency), and Israel welcomed him into their city (human

---

[16] I have included Psalms of Solomon here and not under my discussion of the Pseudepigraphal literature because the Psalms occur in Rahlfs-Hanhart's critical edition of the LXX.

agency) due to their God-given stupor (divine agency) (Pss. Sol. 8:14-34). The psalmist confesses that "our works are in the choice and authority of our soul to do righteousness and unrighteousness in the works of our hands," but the psalmist immediately follows this statement with "and in your righteousness you oversee the sons of men" (Pss. Sol. 9:4). The one who performs righteousness stores up (eternal) life for himself with the Lord (emphasis mine), but the one who performs unrighteousness, he, is guilty of a soul in destruction. The reason for the preceding assertions according to the psalmist is because of divine agency: "because the judgments [of the Lord] [are] in righteousness with respect to the man and [his] house" (brackets mine). God grants either life or destruction to the two groups because they store up either righteousness or destruction for themselves.

Human agency is not altogether described above as consequent to and the result of divine agency, but divine agency seems to respond to the decisions of the human agent (Pss. Sol. 9:5). That is, the divine agent grants either life or destruction in response to the human agent's performance. However, the preceding statements that seem to give priority to human agency could assume the prerequisite of divine agency over human agency since the psalms continue with statements that affirm the priority of divine agency. For example, the psalmist's soul was distant from the Lord for a season until the Lord received him by means of his mercy forever (Pss. Sol. 16:3). The Lord nudged the psalmist from his spiritual drowsiness. This resulted in the psalmist's praise of him. The Lord's salvation also serves as the basis upon which the psalmist asks the Lord to keep him safe from sin (Pss. Sol. 16:1-11), and the psalmist would endure poverty only if the Lord would strengthen his soul (Pss. Sol. 16:12-15).

1 Baruch (BCE 164)

1 Baruch is composed in three parts. Baruch 1:1-14 focuses on Israel's second exile during the reign of King Jehoiachim (BCE 609-598). Baruch was amongst those first exiles. When he learned that Jerusalem had been destroyed, Baruch read his book to the king and the people. This provoked repentance and mourning. Baruch 1:15-3:8 focuses on a communal confession of sin. The second part of the book (3:9-4:4) focuses on wisdom. The last portion (4:5-5:9) consoles the exiles about Jerusalem. The text seeks to encourage the Jewish community that lived through Antiochus' plundering of Jerusalem. Baruch's message is that God will not abandon his people or his city. The priority of divine over human agency is evident in 1 Baruch.

Baruch emphasizes that God judged Israel via the other nations because of her sin (1:1-2:10). Baruch informs the people that God brought Israel out of Egypt (2:11-26) and gave them a law through Moses to be followed in order to remain in God's favor (2:27-35). Since everyone who disobeys Torah would die and everyone who obeys would live, Baruch appeals to Israel to obey Torah. Instead, they disobeyed, and Torah is personified as weeping for Israel who betrayed her and her God. God, therefore, gave Israel over to a foreign nation because of Israel's failure to obey Torah (4:1-29). Baruch comforts the people by reminding them that God would deliver them

Divine and Human Agency

from their enemies if they would obey Torah (4:30-5:9). These words of comfort to Israel should be interpreted in light of Baruch's earlier statements in 3:1-8 about the priority of divine agency in the human agent's ability to obey the divine agent's commands and be saved from judgment. Baruch asked the Lord to work on behalf of Israel and to forgive them of their sins. Baruch confessed that he and his people would praise the Almighty Lord (3:6), "because you are our God, the Lord, and we will praise you, Lord" (3:6). Then, Baruch states a further reason why they would praise God: "because for this reason, you gave your fear 'in our heart' so that we would call upon your name" (3:7). Once Baruch states that God put his fear inside of their hearts, he expresses that the people of God could therefore obey God because of his work within them: "we will praise you in our captivity, because we will turn from our heart every unrighteous deed of our forefathers who sinned against you" (3:7).

History of Susanna (2nd Century BCE)
The message of Susanna is God is the sovereign protector of Susanna.[17] The story of Susanna is short, only consisting of one chapter. 1:42-64 is pertinent to the priority of divine agency over agency.

Susanna was falsely accused of promiscuity by the elders of the people. These elders were evil and reported such lies about Susanna because they were mad that she would not sin against her God by having sex with them. Unfortunately, however, the people believed the lies of the elders and sentenced Susanna to death for her sin with an alleged young man. Susanna asked the Lord for deliverance. He heard her prayer and aroused the holy spirit of Daniel (1:44-46). Another textual tradition records that an angel aroused Daniel's spirit (Th. 1:44-46). So, Daniel testified on behalf of Susanna attesting to her innocence. But the point that both traditions make is that Daniel's response to help/save Susanna from judgment on earth was consequent to and the result of the divine agent's work. After Daniel examined the two elders on behalf of the people, he proved the two elders to be liars and sentenced them to death. Afterwards, the people praised the God who saves (divine agency) those who hope (human agency) in him.[18]

---

[17] When I refer to the Theodotian text, I place a Th. before the citations.

[18] For other divine and human agency texts in the apocrypha that feature Daniel, see Th. Dan. 3:24-90 (2nd Century BCE: The Prayer of Azariah and the Song of the Three Jews). The Prayer of Azariah and the Song of the Three Jews appear in the middle of the story about Daniel's three friends. God judged Israel by sending them into exile because of their sins. The angel of the Lord protected Daniel's three friends from the flames by quenching it. Daniel's three friends ascribed praise to God because he quenched the flame through the angel from heaven (Th. 3:24-90). The story of Bel and the Dragon appears as chapter 14 in the Greek version of Daniel. The story teaches that Daniel's God is the true God and idol worship is foolish. An angel of the Lord appeared to Habakkuk and told him to take food to Daniel (Th. 1:35). The angel of the Lord guided Habakkuk by the top of his head to Babylon since Habakkuk claimed that he had never

DIVINE AND HUMAN AGENCY IN THE PSEUDEPIGRAPHA[19]
The Apocalyptic Writings
1 Enoch (2nd Century BCE-1st Century CE)

The first place to begin the discussion of divine and human agency in the pseudepigraphal literature is with a discussion of the apocalyptic writings. 1 Enoch is a composite work that is a Jewish apocalypse. Divine and human agency appears throughout the first half of the work. The author(s) states that God will judge the world and save his elect, and he will grant peace to all of the righteous (1 En. 1:1-9). Everything functions in the way in which God has ordered it (1 En. 5:2), and the elect will complete the number of their days given to them by God (5:9), for the Lord has both made and has authority over everything (1 En. 9:5; cf. 2 Apoc. En. 33:1-8). God has given the righteous grace and would cause the righteous to dwell before him, but the unrepentant will suffer judgment in his presence (1 En. 45:6; 50:4-5; cf. 2 Apoc. En. 2:2-4). So, by way of inference, the righteous, to whom God grants mercy to dwell before him, repent, and the unrepentant, to whom God does not grant mercy, choose not to repent. Those who repent do so because God enables them.

4 Ezra (1st Century CE)

4 Ezra is a continuation of 1 Ezra, but it includes an apocalypse and a Christian introduction. The book is largely a Jewish response to the Jerusalem crisis of 70 CE. Regarding divine and human agency, 4 Ezra states that God chose Abraham, loved him, and revealed to him the end of times (4 Ezra 3:13-14), but the Lord did not take the evil heart away from Israel so that Torah would bear fruit in them (4 Ezra 3:20). 4 Ezra further expresses that the heart is evil (4 Ezra 4:4), and he questions why the sovereign Lord handed over Israel, his vineyard, to be trampled by the ungodly nations (4 Ezra 5:22-30). Although God elected Israel through Abraham, he did not enable the nation as a whole to obey Torah and yet expected them to obey and judged them when they disobeyed. 4 Ezra states that God has organized the world to work a certain way (4 Ezra 5:49); God planned all things before the foundation of the world (4 Ezra 6:1-6), but God also commanded Israel to obey him so that the nation would live (4 Ezra 7:21). Such life pertains to eternal life, because 4 Ezra later speaks of the eternal torment of those who disobey God's law (4 Ezra 7:61, 72-74).

4 Ezra pronounces that all humans are sinners (including Israel) (4 Ezra 7:68), but those who perfectly keep God's law will inherit eternal life (4 Ezra 7:90-99). Everyone (human agency) will bear his own righteousness or

---

been there. Once he arrived at Daniel's dungeon, Habakkuk commanded him to eat the dinner that "God sent to you" (Th. 1:37). Daniel responded by saying to God that he remembered him and did not forsake (divine agency) "those who love him" (human agency) (Th. 1:38).

[19] Unless otherwise indicated, translations and textual references of all Pseudepigraphal literature will be from James H. Charlesworth (ed.), *The Old Testament Pseudepigrapha*, 2 vols. (New York: Double Day, 1983 & 1985), and I discuss this literature in the order given in volumes 1 and 2.

unrighteousness in the day of judgment (4 Ezra 7:102-105), but Ezra blames Adam for the fall (not God), and both Adam and humanity will suffer the consequences of Adam's transgressions (4 Ezra 7:116-118). Humans engage in a contest in this life (known as obedience to Torah). If they succeed, they will receive the reward of eternal life promised by Moses and the prophets, who likewise commanded the people to choose life by exhorting them to obey Torah. This life, promised to those who obey, is the resurrection, because Ezra contrasts this age with the age to come in the resurrection and because he contrasts it with the salvation of the righteous and the damnation of the wicked (4 Ezra 7:125-131). The key point, though, is that eternal life is within the grasp of the human agent if he obeys the divine commands. However, Ezra makes it clear that not everyone will obey God's commands and thereby receive eternal life, for God gives mercy and grace *only* to those who repent (4 Ezra 7:132-140). The Lord did not intend that men should be destroyed, but they defiled the Lord's name and became ungrateful to him who gave them life (4 Ezra 8:59-60; cf. 8:4-36). Nevertheless, Ezra states that God destined a multitude of the world for destruction (4 Ezra 10:10). Since 4 Ezra speaks often of resurrection, eternal life, and judgment (4 Ezra 7:102-140), destruction in 4 Ezra 10:10 likely refers to final destruction in the Day of Judgment, and God will deliver from this destruction those whom he enables to obey Torah.

2 (Syriac Apocalypse of) Baruch (2nd Century CE)
Similar to 4 Ezra, 2 (Syriac Apocalypse of) Baruch is a response to the fall of Jerusalem to the Romans in 70 CE. The book consists of letters, laments, prayers, questions, answers, and apocalypses that pertain to this crisis. Divine and human agency emerges throughout the book. God used foreign nations to judge Zion (2 Apoc. Bar. 13:9). After Adam sinned, God appointed a number of people to live and to die (2 Apoc. Bar. 23:4). Living and dying appear to refer to spiritual life and death, for Baruch begins with discussing Adam's transgressions and concludes with comments about life and death. God will protect those from judgment who obey his law (2 Apoc. Bar. 32:1; cf. 54:5, 21-22), and God enlightens those who conduct themselves with understanding (2 Apoc. Bar. 38:1-2). By the latter statement, Baruch means that God enlightens those who obey his law, for Baruch follows his statements with the words that God's law is life, and his wisdom is the right way. He further says thereafter that he has always obeyed God's law and never departed from it (2 Apoc. Bar. 38:1-2). Thus, God enlightens, says Baruch, with understanding those who seek to understand and obey his law, but Baruch expresses in his prayer that God willed Israel to enter into the world and that Israel lives not of its own will, for the nation had no control over its birth or death (2 Apoc. Bar. 48:15-16). Rather, Baruch asks God to impart his saving mercy to his people, Israel, because they are his elect who possess his law (2 Apoc. Bar. 48:18-24). With this statement, Baruch suggests that Israel would not stumble if the nation keeps God's law, but the nation would not be able to keep his law unless God imparts his mercy to enable them to keep it.

The Apocalypse of Abraham (1st-2nd Century CE)
The Apocalypse of Abraham is about God's election of Israel and his covenant with them. The book states that God predestined a generation to be born through Abraham, and he promised to be with Abraham and with this generation to be born through him (2 Apoc. Abr. 10:17). God ordained everything that exists, and he ordained some for judgment and some for blessing (2 Apoc. Abr. 22:1-5). God granted Abraham understanding because he was pleasing in God's sight (2 Apoc. Abr. 23:1-4). One can infer that Abraham was pleasing in God's sight precisely because God predestined him (2 Apoc. Abr. 10:17; 22:1-5) and enabled him to be (2 Apoc. Abr. 23:1-4), for the pleasure of Abraham before God is consequent to and the result of God's divine initiative. In addition, Abraham pleased God because he appointed him to receive a soteriological blessing and to escape judgment for which he ordained some (2 Apoc. Abr. 22:1-5).

Expansions of the "Old Testament" and Legends
The Letter of Aristeas (3rd Century BCE-1st Century CE)
The Letter of Aristeas is an important source for understanding the Septuagint. It attests to the process by which the Torah was translated into Greek by 72 elders and that these elders were sent to Alexandria for this purpose. The author, Aristeas, wrote to his brother, Philocrates, about this mission. The book also speaks to the priority of divine agency over human agency.

The author states from the outset of the book that God appointed the Jews their law and prospered the king's kingdom, and the Jews worshipped the overseer and creator of all (Ep. Arist. 1:15-16). The Jews prayed that God would dispose the king's mind to release the Jews from captivity. The author parenthetically states that mankind is God's creation and is changed and converted by him. The author, then, states that prayer was offered to God with the hope that he would answer this request (Ep. Arist. 1:17), because although men make decisions to do certain things, "God, the Lord of all, directs their acts and intentions" (Ep. Arist. 1:18). The king grants Aristeas' request and releases several Jews from exile (Ep. Arist. 1:19), because God answered Aristeas' prayer and compelled the king to release the Jews (Ep. Arist. 1:20). Eleazar responds to a letter written to him from the king to express his hope that the king's desire to release the Jews and to translate the Law would come about and that God, the ruler of all, would preserve his kingdom in peace and glory (Ep. Arist. 1:35), for nothing is hidden from God and all things that come to pass are manifest to God (Ep. Arist. 1:32). God upholds the things that he commands by his divine providence, who is the supreme God and upholder (of all) (Ep. Arist. 1:57; [emphasis Charlesworth, 2:23]).

The priority of divine agency over human agency is seen further in the narrative sections of the Letter of Aristeas. The king asked his guests at a party a series of questions pertaining to war (Ep. Arist. 1:87-202). Each person responds by appealing to the need to trust in God's sovereignty over military matters. The king asked one of the guests a question pertaining to the supreme blessing of life. The guest replied by saying "to know that God is Lord over all,

Divine and Human Agency

and that we ourselves do not direct our plans in the finest of actions, but God brings to completion the affairs of all men and guides (them) with his sovereign power" (Ep. Arist. 1:195) (emphasis Charlesworth, 2:25). When the king asked the guest how one could transmit the same attitude to his descendants, the guest's answer was "by continued prayer to God that he may receive good designs for what is to be done, and by exhorting his descendants not to be dazzled by fame or riches—the bestower of these things is God himself, and men do not have excess of anything through their own merits" (Ep. Arist. 1:196). When the king asked yet another question pertaining to courage (Ep. Arist. 1:199-200), a guest answered if the king's intentions were honorable everything would be brought to pass advantageously for him by God. Aristeas states that the king asserted that each guest made God the basis of their argument to the king (Ep. Arist. 1:200). A philosopher in the room agreed and said "Yes, indeed, O King, for since the whole universe is governed by providence, and on the correct assumption that man is a creature of God, it follows that all power and beauty of argument has its origin in God" (Ep. Arist. 1:200). Another guest said that "God guides all men in mercy" (Ep. Arist. 1:208; cf. 1:216, 224) and that it is a gift of God for one to do good works and not to be a doer of evil works (Ep. Arist. 1:231). When asked about the highest form of glory, the tenth guest responded: "Honoring God" is the highest honor with purity of heart, for "everything is ordained by God and ordered according to his will" (Ep. Arist. 1:234).

Aristeas states that wisdom comes from God, and self-control cannot be received unless God grants it (Ep. Arist. 1:236-238). One must pray that God would bestow blessings (Ep. Arist. 1:242). God directs men toward good deliberations in everything (Ep. Arist. 1:243). God gives prosperity to some and takes it away from others (Ep. Arist. 1:244). God will direct the king's mind (Ep. Arist. 1:246). One's prayer that a child will have some discretion comes to pass only by means of God's power (Ep. Arist. 1:248). One of the king's guests suggested that the purpose of speaking was to persuade the hearer by pointing out his errors, but he acknowledged that persuasion would only come "through the activity of God" (Ep. Arist. 1:266). God controls all reputation and directs it where he wishes (Ep. Arist. 1:266). God bestows blessings upon people as he wills (Ep. Arist. 1:271-72). God grants to humans to have a pure mind (Ep. Arist. 1:292). Other guests likewise provided the king with insights that urged him to recognize that human agency is dependent upon divine agency (Ep. Arist. 1:197).

Jubilees (2nd century BCE)
The book of Jubilees gives an account of information revealed to Moses at Sinai (Exod. 24:18). Chapter 1 records that God describes to Moses that Israel will apostatize but that the nation would eventually receive God's restoration. Chapters 2-50 record a long revelation to Moses given by an angel from the presence of God. The angel recounts for Moses the primeval history of humanity and God's people and the subsequent history of God's people until the time of Moses. The book also addresses divine and human agency.

God commands Moses to write the words that he will cause Moses to understand (1:7) and that he would cause Israel to enter into the land that he swore to their fathers (1:7). God tells Moses that he would send witnesses to his people to call them to repent, but the people would reject those witnesses by persecuting them. They would also disobey God's law. Their disobedience would result in God's discipline of his people. He would hide his face from them; he would give them over to foreign nations to be devoured; and he would remove them from the land and scatter them throughout the nations (1:7-11). Consequently, Israel would forget the ways of the Lord (1:12-14). God tells Moses that Israel would repent after their rebellion and that he would restore them. He would gather them from amongst the nations, and they will seek him, and the Lord would transplant them as a righteous plant. They would be a blessing and not a curse. The Lord would not alienate himself from them due to their repentance (1:15-18). After Moses heard God's words, he fell upon his face and began to pray, asking the Lord not to abandon his people to walk in the error of their heart and not to deliver them into the hands of their enemies (the Gentiles). He urged that God's mercy would be upon his people and that he would create for them an upright spirit. He further asked the Lord to "create a pure heart and a holy spirit for them" and not to let them be snared by their sin (1:19-22). The Lord answered Moses, stating that Israel would rebel against him unless he (the Lord) should take the initiative and work in them so that they would obey. He states that he would "cut of the foreskin of their heart and the foreskin of the heart of their descendants. And I shall create for them a holy spirit, and I shall purify them so that they will not turn away from following me from that day and forever" (1:23). The result of God's work in his people would be that they would "cleave to me and to all of my commandments. And they will do my commandments" (1:24). Then, they will be called sons of the living God (1:22-25).

God ordained the judgments of those who disobey him and mercy for those who obey him (5:17-19), and God saved Noah and his family from the flood because of his great mercy. Noah states that God placed his mercy upon his soul. When he received word that the demons were deceiving and killing his children, he asked God to pour out his grace upon his sons by not allowing the demons to rule over them (10:4). Likewise, Abraham prayed to God at a young age that he would save him from worshipping idols and straying away from God as his people had done (11:16-17), and Abraham asked God, the creator, to save him from evil spirits and not to let the evil spirits rule over his heart. He finally asked that God would not allow him to walk in the error of his heart (12:19-21). God answered Abraham's prayer for divine help to obey, for Abraham reveals that he no longer worshipped idols when he appeals to his father to avoid idolatry (12:2-5).

Jubilees appears to suggest that God's election of Jacob and forgiveness of sins are based upon God's foresight of their actions and human obedience (15:29-33; 21:21-26; 22:10-12; 24:10-13), but these statements of election and forgiveness should be viewed in light of Jubilees' statements about divine agency. For example, Abraham asked God to show his mercy and peace

Divine and Human Agency

to him and to his son's descendants "so that they might become an elect people for you and an inheritance from all of the nations of the earth from henceforth and for all the days of the generations of the earth forever" (22:9). The latter suggests that God's mercy was a prerequisite to the election of Abraham and his descendants. This point is further supported when Abraham subsequently called Jacob to himself and blessed him. He asked God to strengthen and bless Jacob to do his righteousness before him, and he prayed that God would elect Jacob and his seed "so that you would become a people for him who always belong to his inheritance according to his will" (22:10). Although election is connected to obedience in 2:10, God's election is consequent to and the result of God's mercy, for Abraham prayed that God would elect Jacob so that Israel would be a people for him (22:10).

Joseph and Aseneth (1st Century BCE-2nd Century CE)
Joseph and Aseneth is a romance about Joseph and his Gentile wife (Aseneth). She is a beautiful 18 year old virgin. She refuses to be married to Egyptian men, but instead prefers to remain single and to worship idols. When Joseph visits her father, she falls in love with him, only to be refused by Joseph (a God-fearing man). But Joseph prays for her conversion. Aseneth shatters her idols, fasts, repents of her idolatry, and converts to Israel's religion. This is confirmed by the chief angel who appears to Aseneth to inform her of her conversion. The angel promises Aseneth (amongst many things) that Joseph would marry her, and he eventually does. Joseph prays that God would convert Aseneth. The priority divine agency over human agency is apparent in the rest of the story. After Joseph's prayer, Aseneth went to her room and repented of her infatuation with idols and destroyed them. Aseneth's actions suggest that Joseph's God converted her for the following reasons. Later in the story, God is called the father of repentance (8:9-15:11). The angel changed Aseneth's name to City of Refuge after/because her conversion to Joseph's religion, and the author states that God would dwell in her City of Refuge (19:5, 9). Aseneth's family is described as praising God, who gives life to the dead, when they saw her beauty and when they saw Joseph sitting beside of her (20:7), and Aseneth prays that God would make her alive (27:10).

Life of Adam and Eve (1st Century CE)
The Life of Adam and Eve is a deathbed Jewish reflection of the lives Adam and Eve after they were expelled from Paradise.[20] The tradition sheds light on divine and human agency. Adam recounts to Seth his prayer after God threatened to kill him after he disobeyed his command and instead obeyed Eve. Adam prays that God would "convert my soul," that God would "cast me not from your presence, whom you formed from the clay of the earth," and that God would not "withhold [his] grace from him whom you nurtured" (Vita 27:1-

---

[20]There are two traditions (Latin and Greek) of the Life of Adam and Eve cited here. The following abbreviations will be used to distinguish between them: Latin (=Vita) and Greek (=ApMos.).

3) (brackets mine). Adam's prayer suggests that the human agent's experience of grace is absolutely consequent to and the result of the divine agent's action on behalf of the human agent. After Adam sinned and the Lord began to drive him out of Paradise, Adam begged the Lord to allow him to eat from the tree of life so that he would eat before he was cast out. But the Lord told Adam that he could not partake of the tree, but that he would raise him up again at the resurrection and give him eternal life if he would keep himself from evil (ApMos 28:3-4). God promised to raise Adam from the dead at the resurrection when Michael brought his body before him into the third heaven (ApMos 41:3).

Pseudo-Philo (1st Century CE)

Pseudo-Philo is an imaginative retelling of a selection of the Old Testament story from Adam to David. It includes both biblical material and revisionist history of biblical accounts, and it speaks to divine and human agency.

God expresses that because he is pleased with Amram's plan, he would act on behalf of his people and that he would kindle a lamp that would abide in him. The context suggests that the lamp is the law, for God states in 9:9 that "I will kindle for him my lamp that will abide in him, and I will show him my covenant that no one has seen. And will reveal to him my Law and statutes and judgments, and I will burn an eternal light for him" (9:7-8). Moses prays before his death that God's mercy would be upon his chosen race because he has loved them. Moses expresses that without God's mercy, Israel would not be established in his law since everybody sins (19:8-9). As Joshua prays for the people, he confesses that the Lord has done everything for Israel that he promised and that "God has established every word of his Law that he spoke at Horeb," but he quickly utters that Israel's blessings from God are dependent upon their obedience to him (21:9). In 21:10, Joshua, then, prays that God would grant to his people a heart that would abide in his law and not forsake the Lord's ways, and the Lord promises Joshua that he would take care of the people whom he has chosen (23:1-14). Deborah prays that the Holy Spirit's grace would awaken *in* Israel praise for the works of the Lord (32:14).[21]

---

[21]Other texts in the pseudepigraphal literature shed a little light on divine and human agency in early Judaism. For example, in T. Reuben 4:1, Reuben exhorts his children to live with integrity before God and with fear of God until he gives them the woman whom he wills for them. He states this in context of appealing to his children to avoid sexual promiscuity. In T. Zebulon 1:4-5, Zebulon states that he was not aware of any sin that he committed with the exception of his sin against Joseph, which he confesses that he committed ignorantly. In T. Joseph 9:2, Joseph states that God loves self-control. In T. Joseph 11:1, Joseph states that "everyone who obeys the law of the Lord will be loved by him." This statement suggests that God's love is a consequence of human obedience. In T. Job 5:1, Job states that he will endure Satan's wrath. In T. Job 7:13, Job tells Satan that he will endure anything that he inflicts upon him. In T. Job 19:4-20:3, the Lord used Satan to inflict Job with suffering. In the Mart. Isa 1:13, Hezekiah wanted to kill his son, Manasseh, after Isaiah prophesied that Manasseh would martyr Isaiah, but Isaiah informs Hezekiah that the Beloved one had made the thought of his heart to

DIVINE AND HUMAN AGENCY IN THE DEAD SEA SCROLLS (200 BCE-70 CE)[22]

1QS

1QS was likely written for the teachers in the community. It contains extracts from liturgical ceremonies, tractates on the spirits of truth and falsehood, statutes about the initiation within the community and with its communal life, instructions about organization, discipline, religious duties of the Master, and penal codes. Regarding divine and human agency, the scroll places a premium on the former.

The scroll begins with instructions for the Master. It states that the Master must teach the community to seek God with a whole heart and soul, to do good and right in God's presence as he commanded Moses and the prophets, and to command them to love everything that God loves and to hate everything that he hates. They must teach the community to abstain from evil and to hold fast to the good and to practice righteousness and to follow no longer a sinful heart and lustful eyes committing evil. The consequence of obeying the Master's instructions would be entrance into the Community, but such obedience must be perfect (1QS I.1-25). However, the scroll also expresses that God has bestowed mercy upon those within the Community from everlasting to everlasting and that the priests will bless those who walk perfectly in accordance with God's law. The priests will bless them by saying: 'May he bless you with all good and preserve you from all evil! May he lighten your heart with life-giving wisdom and grant you eternal knowledge! May he raise his merciful face towards you for everlasting bliss'" (1QS II.1-4)! This prayer

---

kill his son ineffective. In Mart. Isa 2:1-6, the author states that Sammael (a chief archangel according to Jewish tradition) dwelt "in Manasseh" and "clung closely to him." The result of this was that Manasseh abandoned the Lord's service, and he served Satan, his angels, and his powers. He turned his whole house from serving the Lord toward the service of Beliar. In Mart. Isa 3:11-12, the author states that Beliar dwelt *within* Manasseh and moved him to believe Belkira's lies against Isaiah and he consequently seized Isaiah. In Mart. Isa 5:1-2, Beliar dwelt *in* the heart of Manasseh, which resulted in Manasseh's sawing Isaiah in half. In Mart. Isa 5:14-16, Beliar is given credit for sawing Isaiah in half, but the author states that he performed this deed through Belkira and through Manasseh due to the fact that Sammael was angry with Isaiah. In Mart. Isa 11:41, Sammael Satan sawed Isaiah in half "by the hand of Manasseh" because of the visions that Isaiah saw. In LivPro 10:6, God raised a widow's son from the dead through Elijah. In LivPro 21:7, God raised a son from the dead after Elijah prayed. In JanJam 25a, the Lord sent angels to lead Jannes to Hades. In HistRec 1:1-5, Zosimus asked God to show him where the sons of Jonadab were placed during the days of Jeremiah. God answers his prayer by using angels to reveal to him their location. In LT. Orp 43, the author states that God rules over everything according to an order. In Fragment 2 of the Fragments of Aristobulus, the author emphasizes God's comprehensive sovereignty over all things.

[22] Unless otherwise indicated, all references to, translations of, and versification of the Dead Sea Scrolls come from *The Complete Dead Sea Scrolls*, trans. and rev. by Geza Vermes (New York: Penguin, 2004), and I discuss the scrolls in the order listed in this volume.

expresses that the divine and the human agents are in tension with one another. On the one hand, those who want access within the Community must perfectly obey the precepts of the Master. But, on the other hand, the scroll reveals that God must preserve and protect from evil those who want to obey perfectly the precepts and he must lighten their hearts, otherwise they will not meet the demands of the divine agent.[23]

Furthermore, the scroll states that God would accept those who atone their sins by perfectly obeying the precepts of God (1QS III.7-10), but the Master must instruct the Community in accordance with the spirit that they possess. God ordained and designed everything to carry out its purpose (even the obedience of those within the Community). God created man to govern the world and has given for him two spirits in which to walk: a spirit of truth or a spirit of injustice (1QS III.16-20). The God of Israel and his angel of truth will relieve all the sons of light, for God created both the spirits of light and darkness and he loves the former and hates the latter (1QS III.11-IV.1).[24]

1QM (The War Scroll)
1QM discusses the war between God's elect in the community and the nations. 1QM XII.11-5 states that God has established the elect for himself and that he has engraved for them the favors of his blessings and his covenant of peace. The scroll further states that God will raise up his elect by the thousands to be victorious in battle against their enemies and that the elect on earth, the angels, and the holy ones will triumph with the elect of heaven against their enemies. 1QM XIII.8-11 states that God has decreed a destiny of light for his people, Israel, so that they would walk according to the truth, and he has appointed the Prince of light (probably the Messiah) to come to the aid of his people. But the scroll also affirms that God has likewise appointed Belial (the angel of malevolence) for the pit. Consequently, Belial's rule is in darkness; he proposes to bring about wickedness and iniquity, and all of the angels in his company walk in darkness. 1QM XIV.7-10 expresses that the God of mercies fulfills his covenant with his people by destroying the wicked in battle. He bestows his wonderful favors on the remnant, and he does not cause his people to stray from his covenant. Rather, he has driven the wicked from his people, and he preserves the soul of the redeemed in the midst of wickedness. The scroll continues by acknowledging that God has cut down the wicked and exalted the righteous.

---

[23]For predestination and free will in the Dead Sea Scrolls, see Philip S. Alexander, "Predestination and Free Will in the Theology of the Dead Sea Scrolls," in *Divine and Human Agency in Paul and His Cultural Environment*, LNTS 335, eds. John M.G. Barclay and Simon J. Gathercole (London: T&T Clark, 2006), 27-49.

[24]For a discussion of predestination and free-will in 1QS, see Philip S. Alexander, "Predestination and Free Will in the Theology of the Dead Sea Scrolls," in *Divine and Human Agency in Paul and His Cultural Environment*, LNTS 335, eds. John M.G. Barclay and Simon J. Gathercole (London: T&T Clark, 2006), 27-49.

1QH (Thanksgiving Hymns or Hodayot)

1QH derives its name from the many places wherein it expresses thanksgiving to God.[25] This scroll provides the most elaborate material of divine and human agency in the available DSS. In 1QH Hymn 2, the composer(s)[26] of the hymn confesses that God has given to him the spirits of obedience so that he can recount the righteous deeds of the Lord. He confesses that he has wallowed in sin, and he therefore implores God's mercy. He requests that the Lord would redeem his servant, for he knows that God establishes the path of the righteous and hedges him in his care so that he would not sin against God. The composer continues by acknowledging that God purifies the hearts of his people and asks that he would preserve him so that he would not sin against him. He also asks God to strengthen his servant to resist evil spirits so that he would walk in all that God loves and despise everything that the Lord hates. The composer expresses that his heart is a heart of flesh and implies with this statement that he needs God's Spirit to enable him to obey God's commands.

The hymn further confesses that one becomes righteous only by God's goodness (1QH Hymn 3 V.17). God gives understanding to the heart of his servant so that he would understand all things and resist wickedness and so that he would bless those who love God's will and hate those who despise it (1QH Hymn 4 VI). The hymn expresses that God instructs his servant and has determined the lot of every spirit whether a good or a bad lot, and each lot accomplishes his task for which God appointed (VI.10). The composer additionally states that God has drawn him near to give him understanding (VI.12). God has granted him a spirit of knowledge, which results in his ability to choose truth and to hate iniquity (VI.25).

The hymn continues by expressing that the composer(s) has freely loved God with all of his heart. The hymnist expresses that he has freely loved God with all of his heart and soul, that he purified himself, and has clung to his laws (VII.10-11). But he contends that he has freely loved God due to the understanding that comes from God (VII.11). Such understanding has enlightened him to know that righteousness does not reside with man, that man is not a master of his own way, and that mortals cannot direct their paths, for every inclination of every spirit is in God's hand and that God established the destiny of every spirit before he created it and no one can alter that particular destiny (VII.11-14). The composer suggests that God alone has created the just womb and that he established from the womb that the just would walk in accordance with God's covenant; he expresses that God expresses his mercy to the just, grants salvation, and provides unfailing peace for the just, and he exclaims that God will "raise up his glory from among flesh," which likely refers to the resurrection of the righteous due to the hymn's previous remarks about eternal salvation and unfailing peace (VII.15-16). The hymn purports that loving God, loving truth, and hating evil are consequences of God's mercy and

---

[25]For a recent discussion of divine and human agency in the Hodayot and for background issues, see Maston, *Divine and Human Agency*, 75-123.
[26]Henceforth composer.

grace that enable the composer to understand. On the other hand, the hymn expresses that God created the wicked for wrath, and that he determined from the womb that the wicked would experience a day of massacre, for they walk in the way which is not good. That is, they despised God's covenant; their souls have hated the truth; they have not delighted in God's commandments, and they have loved what God hates (VII.17-18). Thus, says the composer, God has ordained for them great judgment in the presence of the entire creation so that they would serve as an eternal sign of God's power (VII.18-20). The wicked are created by God to disobey, and they gladly disobey. God has chosen the righteous to serve him (VII.20-25).

In 1QH Hymn 5 VIII, the hymnist states that because he knows the works of the Lord for the righteous and the wicked, he will confess his transgressions to the Lord (VIII.1). He continues that he will hold fast the truth of the covenant and serve the Lord with the wholeness of heart (VIII.2-4), for he knows that God had blessed him with his mercy to obey (VIII.5-9; cf. IX-X). Because the Lord has marked the spirit of the just, the hymnist utters that he will keep his hands clean in accordance with God's will, for man can be righteous only through the aid of the Lord (VIII.10-12). Thus, he implores God to grant him favor, because God has created him for his will and because he has no purpose apart from God's will. All that he conspires flows from God's desire for him (1QH Hymn 19 XVIII). The hymnist confesses that he knows the Lord because he has given to him his Spirit and because he has opened mercies to him (1QH Hymn 23 XX.10-15).[27] Thus, human agency is consequent to and the result of divine agency in the Hodayot.

---

[27] In manuscripts from cave 4, the scrolls address divine and human agency. 4Q181 is a fragmentary scroll that speaks of the destinies of the damned and the righteous. Regarding the righteous, the scroll states that God caused some of the sons of the world to draw near (him) in accordance with his mercies, goodness, and glory, so that they would be counted with him in the community of the righteous to obtain eternal life. In 4Q267, fr. I; 268, God decreed an age of wrath for those who do not know him and good will for those who search his commandments and walk in perfection of way. The latter suggests that the human agent either obeys or disobeys God apart from any interference of the divine agent. However, the fragment states that "he revealed hidden things to their eyes, and opened their ears so that they might hear deep (secrets) and understand all future things before they befall them." The fragment concludes by urging those who know righteousness to hear. See also the Apocryphal Psalms (11QPs[a]=11Q5, 4Q88). These Psalms either focus on God's election of David or provide a Midrashic account of the poetic activities of David. In Syriac Psalm iii=Psalm 155 XXIV.9, the hymnist asks the Lord to cause him to understand his law and to teach him his judgments. In addition to the preceding texts, other DSS express that human agency is consequent to and the result of divine agency. In The Words of the Heavenly Lights (4Q504-6), this scroll consists of three fragmentary manuscripts from Cave 4. The scroll is a collection of prayers for the days of the week. 4Q504-6 II.10-15 expresses that Israel has sinned against God, but God has placed his law within the hearts of those who repented. The scroll additionally expresses confidence that God will save his people from sinning against him and that he would make them understand his testimonies. 4Q504 V.15 states that God poured out his Holy Spirit upon his people, Israel, and gave them blessings so

Philo (20 BCE-50 CE)[28]

Philo was a Jewish-Hellenistic philosopher and a contemporary of Paul. In Philo, God is the gracious giver of all. He demonstrates this in part by his creation of all things (*Deus* 108; *Mut.* 46; *Leg.* 3.166; *Conf.* 182; *Migr.* 30; *Spec.* 4.187; *Ebr.* 105-10; *Her.* 102-11; *Somn.* 2.75-78). He contends that grace is never merited by the recipient, but God deems worthy the recipients of grace in that he chooses to endow them with his grace apart from anything that they do to attain it, for virtue is a gift from God (*Deus* 109; *Mut.* 51-53; *Cher.* 98-101; *Sacr.* 124; *Spec.* 1.43; *Sac.* 52-58; *Leg.* 3.137). Humans are the agents through whom God acts (*Ebr.* 105-10; cf. *Leg.* 1.82 where praise of God is ascribed as an act of God). God aids human choice (*Virtues* 100-200). Even Philo's discussion of the ascent of the soul depends on God's grace (*Abr.* 79-80; *Leg.* 3.219; *Sacr* 42; *Mig.* 26-35; *Fug.* 166-76).

Divine and Human Agency in Paul

With the above Jewish background in mind, the context is now set for a discussion of divine and human agency in the Pauline corpus. When Paul addresses (either directly or indirectly) divine and human agency, his discussion comfortably fits with many of his Jewish contemporaries' comments within Second Temple Judaism. The investigation below, however, seeks to demonstrate that Paul (unlike his Jewish contemporaries) soteriologically redefines divine agency as God's action in Christ on behalf of those whom he chose to be in Christ, and those whom God chose to be in Christ consist of both Jews and Gentiles and not only Jews, unlike God's election in early Jewish literature. In this section of the monograph, I specifically argue that just as with many of his Jewish contemporaries (represented in the literature surveyed above), in Paul's soteriology, divine agency surrounds human agency. That is, divine agency is the cause of human agency, and the latter is consequent to and the result of the former in Paul's soteriology. In order to keep the discussion of

---

that they would seek him in their distress. 4Q504 VI.5-10 states that God has sent enemies against Israel and strengthened her heart so that the nation would recount his mighty deeds to everlasting generations. 4Q393 (The Confession Ritual) is a group of fragmentary remains of communal confession of sins. 4Q393 I.5 asks God to create in his people a new spirit and to forgive sinners of their sins. 4Q393 II.4 asks God not to forsake his people and not to let them walk in the stubbornness of their hearts. This petition implies that unless God takes the initiative and works within the hearts of his people, they would continue to live in disobedience to God. 4Q393 II.5-10 suggests that God has caused his people to stand and asks God not to forsake his people and not to let them walk in the stubbornness of their own heart. 4Q521 (A Messianic Apocalypse) suggests that God will revive the dead and bring good news to the poor (4Q521 II.11).

[28]My discussion of divine and human agency in Philo strongly relies upon the work of John Barclay's essay "By the Grace of God I am What I am: Grace and Agency in Philo and Paul," in *Divine and Human Agency in Paul and His Cultural Environment,* LNTS 335, eds. John M.G. Barclay and Simon J. Gathercole (London: T&T Clark, 2006), 140-57.

the relevant Pauline texts that support my thesis in Paul's first century Jewish and Greco-Roman context and for simplification, I discuss the key texts as they appear in his letters in canonical order and not in order of composition, and I discuss the relevant themes related to divine and human agency in these letters as they emerge from the individual message of each letter. It is my hope that this approach will keep me from forcing Paul to say what I want him to say about divine and human agency, but enable me instead to allow his voice to be heard.[29]

DIVINE AND HUMAN AGENCY IN ROMANS

The priority of divine agency over human agency in Paul's soteriology is most apparent in Paul's letter to the Romans. The basic message of the letter is the gospel. Paul wrote to the Romans to expound to them his apostolic gospel so that they would support his mission to Spain (Rom. 1:1-7, 15-17; 15:22-33). But as he expounds his gospel, he emphasizes God's work of salvation in Christ *in* and *on behalf of* Jews and Gentiles (human agents).

Romans 1:1-7: Paul's Apostolic Calling and God's Divine Grace through Christ

The first place in Romans where Paul begins to elucidate the concept of the priority of divine agency over human agency in his soteriology is in his salutation in Romans 1:1-7. He states that he is a "slave of Christ Jesus, a called apostle who has been separated to the gospel of God" (Rom. 1:1). At first, the word "slave" seems to counter Paul's apostolic status since the term is often used in both extrabiblical (cf. 1 Esdr. 4:26; Jud. 3:4; 5:11; 6:10; Sus. 1:7) and in biblical literature to refer to slaves (LXX Lev. 25:44; 26:13; Matt. 8:9; Phlm. 1:16). Here, however, in Romans 1:1 "slave" is used metaphorically, because Paul connects the term with "of Christ Jesus." Regarding the phrase, "slave of Christ," some have suggested that the background is the Old Testament prophets where the phrase "servant of YHWH" often appears (Amos 3:7; Jer. 7:25; Dan. 9:6; cf. LXX Josh. 24:30; Jud. 2:8; 4 Kgs 9:7; 10:33; 18:12; Ps. 35:1; Ps. 133:1; Jonah 1:9).[30] Others suggest that Paul uses this phrase later in Romans 15:15-20 to describe his ministry in priestly rather than in prophetic

---

[29]The above statements by no means intend to imply naively that my method allows for a "purely objective" investigation of Paul, for the evidence that I offer in this section is my subjective interpretation of Paul based on how I understand the objective evidence in the Pauline texts. I readily acknowledge that what I deem to be objective is subjective in that "my" interpretation of objective evidence in Paul is "my" interpretation of what I deem to be objective evidence in Paul. Rather, my point is that a book-by-book investigation of the relevant Pauline texts in their own historical context (in my judgment) better preserves the appropriate context within which Paul's statements about divine and human agency should be interpreted than a topic by topic approach. The latter approach could border on systematic theology in that it could impose un-Pauline categories onto the Pauline texts, and the devastating result would be that Paul's voice would be eclipsed by arbitrary and perfunctory un-Pauline categories.

[30]So Thomas R. Schreiner, *Romans*, BECNT (Grand Rapids: Baker, 1998), 32.

Divine and Human Agency 139

terms.[31] Rather, Paul employs the title "slave," because he was writing to a Greco-Roman context in which slaves of Caesar were very prominent figures in Greco-Roman society.[32] The slaves spoke on behalf of Caesar and thus were given full military support. Thus, Paul uses the phrase "slave of Christ" to demonstrate that he has the proper credentials to write the letter as an agent of Jesus Christ.[33] Moreover, Paul aspires to demonstrate here that he is the property of Jesus Christ and that Jesus is master and Lord over his life and that his gospel (the gospel of God, which is about Jesus [Rom. 1:2-3]) was preached by the prophets in the Old Testament scriptures (Rom. 1:2). The rest of Romans 1:1 elaborates that Paul was a slave of Christ Jesus because of God's action *in* him *through* Christ.

In Romans 1:1, Paul states that he is a "called apostle" (cf. Gal. 2:15-16). The phrase "called apostle" further explains the noun Paul. Paul was not only a slave of Jesus, the Messiah, but he was also a "called apostle." Paul uses the adjective "called" three times in Romans 1:1-7. In Romans 1:1, it refers to his apostleship and conversion since the two cannot be separated (Acts 9; Gal. 1:15). In Romans 1:6, it refers to the Romans' conversion to Jesus. In Romans 1:7, it refers to the Romans' Christian status as the called of Jesus Christ: "called saints." The term occurs elsewhere in Romans. In Romans 8:28, the term also refers to those whom God effectually calls to saving faith. In each occurrence of the term in Romans, God is the subject of the call, and humans are the recipients of the calling, and the human's response to the call is subsequent to God's call. That is, God initiates the call, and humans receive it. Thus, "called" in Romans 1:1 specifically refers to God's supernatural calling by which he summons and places one into a particular office, because the call offered effects change in the recipients (cf. Rom. 8:28, 30; 9:7, 12, 24, 25, 26; 1 Cor. 1:9).

The term "apostle" is a cognate of the verb "to send." The latter occurs as a technical term in Paul for those whom God has commissioned to preach the gospel only twice (Rom. 10:15; 1 Cor. 1:17). When the verb is used in a technical sense, it specifically refers to the act of preaching the message about Jesus by those whom God has appointed and commissioned. The noun apostle that Paul uses in Romans 1:1 is a technical term that refers to the person uniquely called and sent by God to proclaim the message of Jesus, the Messiah. That this is Paul's use is supported by the phrase "separated to the Gospel." "Apostle" certainly includes the 12 (Luke 6:13; 9:10; Acts 1:26), but the term is not limited to the 12 (Luke 11:49; Rom. 1:1; Acts 14:12—Barnabas' apostleship is connected with Paul's, 2 Cor. 8:23). Paul was an apostle

---

[31]So Robert K. Jewett, *Romans*, Hermeneia (Minneapolis: Fortress, 2007), 100.
[32]Ibid.
[33]For a discussion of slavery in Paul's Greco-Roman context, see David J. Williams, *Paul's Metaphors: Their Context and Character* (Peabody, MA: Hendrickson, 1999), 111; J. Albert Harrill, "Paul and Slavery," in *Paul in the Greco-Roman World: A Handbook*, ed. J. Paul Sampley (Harrodsburg, PA: Trinity Press International, 2003), 575-607, esp. 576.

appointed by God for a unique mission: viz., the gospel of God (cf. Acts 2:42; 4:33).

Paul further states in Romans 1:1 that he has been "separated to the gospel of God." The verb "to separate" occurs 9 times in the New Testament (Matt. 25:32; Luke 6:22; Acts 13:2; 19:9; Rom. 1:1; 2 Cor. 6:17; Gal. 1:15; 2:12). Each time it conveys the idea of separation or withdrawal, either from people (Matt. 25:32; Luke 6:22; Acts 19:9; 2 Cor. 6:17; Gal. 2:12) or to the mission of the gospel (Rom. 1:1; Gal. 1:15; Acts 13:2). The verb also conveys the idea of separation in the LXX (cf. Gen. 2:10; 10:5). Paul's use is similar to the use in Acts 13:2 where Luke records that the Holy Spirit told the church to set apart Barnabas and Saul for missionary endeavors, and God set apart Paul for "the gospel of God" (Rom. 1:1). The latter phrase modifies the participle phrase "having been separated," and the phrase "for the gospel of God" likely conveys purpose, for Paul appears to be stating the purpose for which he was set apart to the gospel of God (cf. Rom. 1:5, 1:7; 1:16, 24, 26; 3:7).

Gospel is an important Pauline term. It occurs in pagan literature to refer to the Emperor cult when the birth of an heir to the throne was announced.[34] This announcement of the good news was the new era.[35] A form of this noun occurs only once in the LXX in 2 Kgs 4:10 (MT 2 Sam. 4:10). There it refers to the good report that the messenger thought he was giving to David regarding Saul's death until David seized the one who gave this report and killed him. The term "gospel" (εὐαγγέλιον) occurs approximately 57 times in Paul's letters (1 Cor. 4:15; 9:12; 9:14), 9 times in Romans (Rom. 1:1, 9, 16; 2:16; 10:16; 11:28; 15:16, 19; 16:25). But the verbal cognate of εὐαγγέλιον (εὐαγγελίζω) occurs approximately 20 times in the LXX, whereas it occurs only three times in Romans, but 16 other times outside of Romans (1 Cor. 1:17; 9:16, 18). In the LXX, the verb refers to the announcement about the death of Saul (LXX 1 Kgs 31:9), an announcement that God has delivered David from his enemies (2 Kgs 18:19), an announcement of good news to the king (LXX 2 Kgs 18:26, 31), a proclamation of good things (LXX 3 Kgs 1:42), and an announcement of bad news (LXX Jer. 20:15).

Closer parallels to Paul's use in Romans are places in the LXX where the verb is used to refer to the announcement of the good news of Israel's salvation. For example, in LXX Psalm 95 (MT Ps. 96), the psalmist praises the Lord for his judging acts. He proclaims that he is a glorious God who will come in judgment against the nations. But in LXX Psalm 95:2 (MT Ps. 96:2), before the psalmist describes that the Lord will come in judgment against the nations, the psalmist exhorts the people of God to praise the Lord and to announce (εὐαγγελίζω) his salvation. In light of LXX Psalm 95:10 (MT 96:10), the announcement of the Lord's salvation is an announcement that the Lord currently reigns as king. In Psalms of Solomon 11, the psalmist praises God for

---

[34]C.E.B. Cranfield, *Romans 1-8*, ICC (Edinburgh: T&T Clark, 1975), 1:55.
[35]U. Becker, "Gospel," in *Dictionary of New Testament Theology*, ed. Colin Brown (Grand Rapids: Zondervan, 1986), 2:104-114.

his faithfulness, petitions the Lord to keep being faithful, and exhorts Israel to be holy. In Psalms Solomon 11:1, the psalmist urges the people to announce in Jerusalem with the voice of one who "announces good news" (εὐαγγελιζομένου) that "God has been merciful to Israel by means of watching over them."

Similarly, LXX Joel 3:5 connects God's salvation with the announcement (εὐαγγελίζω) of his salvation (i.e. good news). Before he gives a promise of salvation, Joel warns that God will come in judgment (LXX Joel 2:1-17). Then, Joel announces the Lord's promise of salvation for his people (LXX Joel 2:18-3:2), which includes the promise of his Spirit. Immediately thereafter, Joel announces that God will come in judgment (LXX Joel 3:3-4), but everyone who calls out to the Lord for salvation will be saved (LXX Joel 3:5), just as the Lord has promised, and Joel states that the one who is saved and those who announce (εὐαγγελιζομένου) this salvation will be survivors in Jerusalem and Zion. LXX Nahum is a pronouncement of judgment against Nineveh. The book begins with the prophet's announcement of the Lord's judgment (LXX Neh. 1:1-6), but he also has mercy on those who seek their refuge in him (LXX Nah. 1:7). Before the prophet again promises Israel that the Lord will destroy his adversaries (LXX Nah. 1:8-14; 2:1-3:19), in LXX Nah. 2:1, the author urges the people to see that upon the mountains (above the destruction that will fall upon Nineveh and all of the Lord's adversaries) stands the feet of the one who proclaims good news (εὐαγγελιζομένου). This good news is the salvation of Judah from the Lord's judgment that is reserved for Nineveh and all of his enemies in light of the prophet's message about God's imminent judgment.

Especially relevant for Paul's use is the verb's occurrence in LXX Isaiah. In LXX Isaiah 40:9; 52:7; 60:6; and 61:1 the verb refers to the announcement of Israel's salvation. In LXX Isa 40:9, Israel is exhorted to get on a high mountain to announce this salvation (cf. LXX Nah. 2:1). In LXX Isaiah 52:7, YHWH himself announces Israel's salvation to Israel and to the nations. Paul appeals to this text in Romans 10:15 during his discussion of his desire for Israel to be saved (Rom. 10:1-13). In LXX and MT Isaiah 52:7, YHWH himself announces the good news of Israel's salvation and that he reigns over her. His message of salvation stands in authority over those upon whom he's bringing destruction. Thus, the bearer of this good news (YHWH or another spokesperson) is described as beautiful because he brings a message of salvation in the midst of judgment, and this message of salvation is able to deliver from destruction those who hear and believe. In LXX Isaiah 60:6, the nations announce Israel's salvation, and in LXX Isa 61:1, the Lord has anointed someone to preach (εὐαγγελίζω) the good news of salvation (cf. Luke 4:18-19). This proclamation comes to Israel as the prophet pronounces her judgment in exile.

With the announcement of exile and judgment, the Lord gives good news of salvation. These occurrences speak to the priority of divine agency in salvation. In each of these examples where εὐαγγελίζω is connected with the announcement of YHWH's mercy or salvation, YHWH himself is present in the proclamation, so that the heralds of the message are not simply proclaiming what YHWH will do, but they are proclaiming YHWH himself. When the gospel of YHWH is announced, YHWH himself is present in the announcement in order to accomplish both the salvation and the judgment that the announcement brings (cf. 1 Cor. 1:18; 2 Cor. 2:15-16). The verb refers to the act of announcing the message of salvation, and the verb and noun in Paul essentially carry the same force and convey the same idea. The only difference of course is that one is a verb and the other a noun. Each time in Paul's letters the noun "gospel" refers to the good report/announcement about Jesus: he is the crucified and resurrected Lord and Messiah who brings salvation (Rom. 1:1, 9; 10:8-16; 15:19; cf. 2 Cor. 2:12).[36] Thus, if the preceding Old Testament concept of gospel is Paul's background behind his gospel, which seems likely in light of Romans 1:2-4, and if Paul uses the noun "gospel" and the verb "to preach the good news" (Rom. 10:15-16) in a context where he possibly conflates LXX Nahum 2:1 and Isaiah 52:7 to discuss faith in the report/message about Jesus, then he emphasizes in Romans 10 that the gospel is God's message of salvation for those who hear. As we will see later in Romans, whenever and wherever this gospel is proclaimed, "this gospel has power. (1) It creates faith (Rom. 1:16; Phil. 1:27), effects salvation and eternal life (Rom. 1:16; 1 Cor. 15:1-2—verb and noun together), and judgment (Rom. 2:16)."[37] (2) Furthermore, when this gospel is proclaimed, it reveals God's righteousness (Rom. 1:17; 3:21-22), and (3) it fulfills hope in God (Col. 1:5, 23).[38] Thus, Paul's emphasis in Romans 1:1 is on God's supernatural work of Paul's apostleship in Paul. That is, Paul's focus is the priority of divine agency both over his apostolic call and in the salvation of sinners. This calling to apostleship would include his calling to conversion.[39] Romans 1:1, then, emphasizes the

---

[36]Similarly Becker, "Gospel," 113.
[37]Ibid.
[38]Ibid., 111.
[39]Paul's remarks in Rom. 1:1 are also reminiscent of the prophetic call to office in the Old Testament (cf. Isa. 49:1; Jer. 1:5). Since God called Paul and set him apart for his apostolic ministry, his apostolic calling was similar to the Old Testament prophets but superior, for his apostolic ministry to which God called him focused on preaching the fulfillment of God's universal plan of salvation in Jesus, the Messiah, which was not clearly seen by the prophets. That Paul's apostolic calling, commission, and message were superior to the prophets is confirmed by the fact that Paul proclaimed the very gospel that the prophets and the prophetic scriptures only promised (cf. Rom. 1:2; 16:26). The purpose of Paul's apostolic ministry was to proclaim God's divine message of salvation through Jesus, the Messiah. It was to proclaim the good news from God about his son regarding the salvation of Israel and the nations. The phrase "gospel of God" also occurs in Rom. 15:16. In the latter text, Paul connects the gospel of God with being a minister of Jesus Christ, just as he connects the phrase with being a slave and an apostle of Christ in Rom 1:1 (cf. 2 Cor. 11:7; 1 Thess. 2:2, 8-9). Paul also refers to the gospel as the gospel of God's son in Rom. 1:9, the gospel of Christ in Rom. 15:19 (cf. 2 Cor. 2:12; 9:13; 10:14; Phil. 1:27; 1 Thess. 3:2), the gospel of our Lord Jesus (2 Thess.

Divine and Human Agency

priority of divine agency over human agency and that human agency is consequent to and the result of divine agency in Paul's soteriology. This point is further elaborated in Romans 1:2-7.

Romans 1:2-6 is a theologically complex parenthesis, but this is necessary since Paul wrote Romans to a church that he did not establish and which he did not personally know prior to writing the letter. Regarding divine and human agency, Paul states in Romans 1:5 that he *received* his gracious apostleship for the obedience of faith amongst the Gentiles through Jesus Christ. Since God was the initiator of Paul's divine call to be an apostle of and his separation for the gospel of God, then it follows that Paul *received* his apostleship from God. Paul's apostleship from God focused on the proclamation about Jesus as the Jewish Messiah from the seed of David, who was installed as the Messiah at his resurrection from the dead (Rom. 1:2-4). His apostleship served to provoke faithful obedience amongst the Gentiles, but the divine agent was the initiator of that faith, for Paul states that in Romans 1:6-7 that the Romans (Jews and Gentiles) were the "called ones of Jesus Christ" (Rom. 1:6), "beloved ones of God" (Rom. 1:7), and "called saints" (Rom. 1:7), and he prays that grace and peace *from* God and Jesus Christ would be upon the Romans.[40]

Romans 1:16-17: Paul's Gospel as God's Power for Salvation for Believing Jews and Gentiles

Paul's further remarks about the gospel speak to the priority of divine agency over human agency in his soteriology. Many scholars have rightly suggested that Romans 1:16-17 contains the thesis of the letter since the verses summarize much of the content of Romans: viz., God's righteousness, justification, and salvation.[41] Furthermore, there is a connection between Romans 1:16-17 and 1:8-15. The connection is evident by the word "for" in 1:16-17. In 1:16-17, Paul states the reason that he is eager to preach the gospel in Rome: "for he is not ashamed of the gospel for it is the power of God resulting in salvation for all who believe, for the Jew first and also for the Greek, for in it the righteousness of God is revealed from faith to faith, just as it has been written: the righteous one will live by faith."

1:8), his gospel in Rom. 2:16 and Rom. 16:25 (2 Tim. 2:8), the gospel of salvation (Eph. 1:13), the gospel of peace (Eph. 6:15), and the gospel of the glory of God (2 Tim. 1:8). In Rom. 1:1, the phrase could be a genitive of possession (the Gospel belonging to God). It could be a genitive of content (the gospel about God). His gospel was divinely given to him by God; God commissioned him to preach the gospel, and his gospel is about Jesus, the Messiah (cf. Rom. 1:2-9; 15:19).

[40]For similar benedictions in Paul, see 1 Cor. 1:3; 2 Cor. 1:2; Gal. 1:3; Eph. 1:2; Phil. 1:2; Col. 1:2; 1 Thess. 1:1; 2 Thess. 1:2; 1 Tim. 1:2; 2 Tim. 1:2; Titus 1:4. For the background of grace in Paul, see J. Harrison, *Paul's Language of Grace in Its Graeco-Roman Context*, WUNT 2.172 (Tübingen: Mohr Siebeck, 2003).

[41]For example, see Jewett, *Romans*, 135.

The statements that are especially pertinent to my thesis are the gospel is "God's power resulting in salvation for everyone who believes" (Rom. 1:16), and "God's righteousness is revealed by faith" (Rom. 1:17).[42] In Romans 1:16-17, Paul includes statements of human agency ("those who believe" [1:16] and "by faith" [1:17]) along with statements of divine agency ("God's power" [1:16] and "God's righteousness" [1:17]). God's power and God's righteousness are parallel statements, and both refer to salvation, for Paul contends that the gospel is God's power "resulting in salvation for everyone who believes" (Rom. 1:16) and that "God's righteousness" is revealed in the gospel "by faith" (Rom. 1:17).[43] The noun faith in Romans 1:17 is another way to express believing in Romans 1:16, for believing and faith together communicate the means by which God's salvation is applied to Jews and Gentiles: viz., trust in Jesus as the Jewish Messiah (cf. Rom. 10:8-13). This is supported by the fact that Paul begins 1:16 by expressing that he is not ashamed of the gospel to express why he states in Romans 1:15 why he was eager to preach the gospel in Rome. As argued above, this gospel is the proclamation of the crucified Jesus as the Jewish Messiah risen from the dead (Rom. 1:1-7), and God grants salvation to anyone, Jew or Gentile, who believes in Jesus as the crucified and resurrected Jewish Messiah. But the faith/believing of Jews and Gentiles in Jesus is consequent to and the result of God's action in Jesus Christ, for God's power is revealed through God's gospel (cf. Rom. 1:1, 16), and God's righteousness is revealed through God's gospel (Rom. 1:17). Thus, the action of God in Christ, revealed through the power of the gospel and proclaimed beforehand in the scriptures (Rom. 1:1-2), precedes and creates the faith in those who believe.

---

[42]In current Pauline scholarship, many interpreters of Paul wrongly strip Paul of individualistic concerns in his soteriological framework by overemphasizing the importance of corporate salvation in his letters. For a discussion of these scholars and for a lucid rebuttal of their arguments, see Gary W. Burnett, *Paul & the Salvation of the Individual* (Leiden: Brill, 2011). He aptly argues that in the Hellenistic world, in which Paul lived and ministered, there was a lively sense of the individual self in persons in the urban centers, whereby individualistic behavior was not unknown and where individuals were not simply determined by their culture and the group of which they were part. The importance of the individual is a feature of Paul's letter to the Romans. Burnett investigates Rom. 1:16-17; 3:21-26, and 7:7-25 to support that Paul is concerned with the individual's salvation and not *only* with questions pertaining to the collective nature of the identity of the people of God.

[43]It is well known in New Testament scholarship that the meaning of the "righteousness of God" in Paul is debated. For recent discussions, see Thomas R. Schreiner, "Justification: The Saving Righteousness of God in Christ," *JETS* 54 (2011): 19-34; Frank Thielman, "God's Righteousness as God's Fairness in Romans 1:17: An Ancient Perspective on a Significant Phrase," *JETS* 54 (2011): 35-48; N.T. Wright, "Justification: Yesterday, Today, and Forever," *JETS* 54 (2011): 49-63. See also my discussion of the phrase in chapter 2.

Romans 1:18-3:20: God's Wrath and Human Disobedience

Romans 1:18-3:20 focuses on God's universal judgment of Jews and Gentiles due to their failure to honor him to the degree that he demands. This unit also speaks to the priority of divine agency over human agency. In Romans 1:18, Paul states that God's wrath currently resides upon all ungodliness of all mankind, because the ungodly fail to honor and glorify God to the degree that he demands (Rom. 1:18-23). Instead, they worship the creation. The result is that God gives the ungodly over to commit the desires of their own hearts (Rom. 1:24, 26, 28).

The important point for my thesis is that Romans 1:18 begins with the revelation of God's (the divine agent's) wrath from heaven upon those who suppress (human agents) the truth, and Romans 1:19-32 continues with a discussion of why God's wrath is revealed from heaven and how it is revealed. As to why, Paul states that Jews and Gentiles failed to allow God's revelation of himself through creation to push them to exclusive worship of him (Rom. 1:19-23). As to how, God gave Jews and Gentiles over to commit the perverse desires of their own hearts (Rom. 1:24-32). Although God revealed himself to be powerful through creation to Jews and Gentiles (Rom. 1:19-20), he did not give them the power to embrace the knowledge about him revealed through creation (Rom. 1:21-23). Yet, he gave them over to continue in disobedience against him when they refused to embrace the knowledge of him revealed through creation (Rom. 1:24-32).

A similar point regarding divine and human agency emerges from Romans 2:1-3:20, but the focus is on God's future day of wrath. That is, those who disobey God and fail to honor him to the degree that he demands (regardless of whether they are Jewish or Gentile) will not escape God's final day of wrath because he will judge Jews and Gentiles in accordance with the same standard: viz., whether they obeyed Torah. However, God expects Jews and Gentiles to obey him perfectly if they seek to obtain eternal life by their obedience (Rom. 2:1-16), but he does not give all Jews and Gentiles the ability to obey Torah to the fullest (Rom. 2:17-3:19), so that neither group can attain justification/salvation by their obedience to Torah (Rom. 3:20).

Romans 3:21-4:25: God's Righteousness, Justification by Faith, and Jesus' Blood

The priority of divine agency over human agency in Paul's soteriology is apparent in Paul's discussion of justification in Romans 3:21-4:25. As many scholars have stated throughout the history of interpretation of Romans 3:21-26,[44] this passage is likely the central section of the letter, and virtually everything in the text is debated. Without commenting on every detail in the text, I will simply state that in my view, Romans 3:21-26 teaches that God's righteousness comes to those who have faith in Jesus, for God offered Jesus in death to deal with sin on account of his righteousness so that he would be the

---

[44]See critical commentaries of Romans.

justifier of Jews and Gentiles. Although Paul certainly mentions the human agent's role in attaining God's righteousness in Romans 3:21-26 (namely, by faith), the emphasis in the text is on divine agency. Paul states that no human agent can be justified by his works (Rom. 3:20), but God has manifested his righteousness apart from the human agent's works (3:21-22); God has offered Jesus to die for the sins of the human agents to justify them and to put an end to his wrath against them since his righteousness demanded it (Rom. 3:24-26), because God is the patient, just justifier (Rom. 3:26). Paul emphasizes the priority of divine agency over human agency by accentuating that God acted in history to manifest his saving righteousness to Jews and Gentiles by offering Jesus to die for their sins.

Paul continues discussing the universality of God's justification for Jews and Gentiles in Jesus in Romans 3:27-31 by contending that the God who justifies by faith is the God of both Jews and Gentiles. Paul recalls here the theme of impartiality from Romans 2:16-29. He infers that no one (Jew or Gentile) has the right to boast in himself before God, because God justifies both Jews and Gentiles by faith. "Boasting" in Romans 3:27 occurs as a positive term (LXX 1 Chr. 29:13—boasting in God's name; Sir. 31:10—boasting in the righteousness of a rich man; Rom. 15:17; 1 Cor. 15:31—boasting in Christ; 2 Cor. 1:12—boasting in one's conscience; 2 Cor. 7:4, 14; boasting in others) and as a negative term (Jas 4:16—boasting in one's arrogance). In Romans 3:27, the term is negative, for Paul states that boasting was "shut out." The latter verb is only used twice in the New Testament (here and Gal. 4:17). In Galatians 4:17, the term is used negatively to refer to the reason why the opponents were seeking to make the Gentile Christians in Galatia receive circumcision: namely, because they desired to shut them out of the faith.[45]

The sort of boasting to which Paul refers is nothing less than Jewish national pride (not Jewish legalism as traditionally defined) because of the privileges that God bestowed upon Israel as a people. This position is supported by Paul's earlier argument in Romans 2:1-29 (esp. Rom. 2:12-29) where Paul argues that Jewish privileges (e.g. circumcision, reception of Torah) will not vindicate them in God's law-court, but only their obedience to the law will provide eschatological exoneration. A connection between 3:27 and 2:17-29 is especially evident by virtue of the verb "to boast" (καυχάομαι) in Romans 2:17 and in 2:23, which is a cognate of the noun for boasting in 3:27 (καύχησις). In 2:17, Paul states that the Jews boast in God, and in 2:23 he indicts them for boasting in Torah, which probably means that they place

---

[45]The other Pauline noun for boasting (καύχημα) only occurs in Rom. in 4:2 where Paul argues that Abraham was justified by faith before he was circumcised and before there was a Torah so that he does not have "a boasting against God" since he believed God and God reckoned his faith to him as righteousness" (Rom. 4:3) (cf. other uses of καύχημα in 1 Cor. 5:7; 9:15-16; 2 Cor. 1:14; 5:12; 9:3; Gal. 6:4; Phil. 1:26; 2:16; Heb. 3:6). For the theme of boasting in Paul, see Simon J. Gathercole, *Where is Boasting: Romans 1-5 and Early Jewish Soteriology* (Grand Rapids: Eerdmans, 2002).

Divine and Human Agency   147

confidence in their Jewish heritage, their reception of Torah from Sinai, and in their ability to keep it, for he critiques them later in 2:25-26 for disobedience to Torah. Jewish boasting in Torah possibly also includes their false perception of themselves that they actually do what Torah says, for Paul acknowledges that they are circumcised in 2:25-26, that they only heard Torah but did not obey it (Rom. 2:25), and that only some Jews (not all) were disobedient to God's oracles (Rom. 3:1). The sort of boasting to which Paul could be referring can be found in his comments about his confidence in his Jewish heritage before his conversion (Phil. 3:5-6), but perhaps this sort of boasting is best illustrated in Tobit. Although the lexical words that Paul uses for boasting do not occur in Tobit, the concept of boasting is woven throughout the book.

    The book begins by Tobit's assertion that he has walked in the ways of truth and righteousness all of his life (Tob. 1:3). He notes that he practiced charitable acts on behalf of his fellow Jews (Tob. 1:3). He acknowledges that he is in exile along with his fellow Jews, but that it was not due to his disobedience to Torah since he alone (unlike his fellow Jews) went to Jerusalem to offer sacrifices in obedience to Torah (Tob. 1:5-7). He also boasts in the fact that he faithfully gave money to the orphans and widows and to Gentile converts to Judaism in accordance with Torah (Tob. 1:8). Tobit further acknowledges that all of his kinsmen ate unclean Gentile food when they were in exile, but he refused to eat such food because he remembered God with all of his heart (Tob. 1:11-12). He continues to boast in the many acts of charity that he performed for his fellow Jews (Tob. 1:16). When he falsely accuses his wife of stealing, she in turn questions him about his good deeds of charity (Tob. 2:11-14), and consequently he begins to weep and to petition his God, not because of a repentant heart, but because his wife questioned his righteousness (Tob. 3:1-6). At first, this may appear to be an incorrect reading of Tobit's prayer since he confesses and acknowledges sin (Tob. 3:2-6a). However, he urges God to take his life because he thinks that his wife falsely accused him of unrighteousness (Tob. 3:6b-c). Thus, what seems to grieve Tobit most is not the reality that he is a sinner but that his wife accused him to be what he thinks he is not: namely, unrighteous. Tobit later urges his son to follow Torah all the days of his life so that he would receive a payment from God (Tob. 4:5-14). This sort of boasting places the priority on the human agent's role attaining eschatological vindication. But, according to Paul in Romans 3:27-31, boasting in one's deeds has no place in the lives of those who have been justified because of the priority of the divine agent's role in their justification. That is, God is the justifier of Jews and Gentiles without partiality (Rom. 3:20-31).

    Paul further elaborates the priority of divine agency over human agency in Romans 4:1-25. Paul states in this text that Abraham believed God and his faith was counted to him as righteousness, just as David speaks about the blessedness of the man against whom the Lord does not count sin (4:7-8), and those who believe in the God who raised Jesus from the dead (4:24-25). The "therefore" in 4:1 signals a connection with 3:20-31. The inference probably goes as far back as 3:20, for justification by faith apart from works is prominent in the entire unit of 3:20-31. This interpretation is bolstered by the appearance of the same vocabulary and concepts in 4:1-25 as in 3:20-31 (e.g. δικαιοσύνη [3:21-22, 25-26; 4:3, 5, 6, 9, 11, 13, 22, 25], δικαιόω [3:20, 24, 26, 28, 30; 4:2, 5; cf. 4:25], πίστις [3:21-22, 25-31; 4:5, 9, 11-12, 14, 16, 19, 20], νόμος [3:21, 27, 28, 31; 4:13-14], and ἔργον [3:20, 27-28; 4:2, 6]). Paul develops the argument of justification by faith apart from Torah with the example of Abraham. He asks what "Abraham, our father according to the flesh, found" (4:1). This verse could also be translated: "therefore, we will say that Abraham, our forefather, found what according to the flesh?" Either way, the point of Paul's question seems to be how Abraham was justified, because Paul grounds ("for") his comments in verse 2 with a proposition that affirms that if he were justified by works, he would have a ground for boasting. Paul affirms that Abraham does not have a reason to boast with God (4:2). Paul explains why Abraham does not have a ground for boasting in 4:3: "Abraham believed God and it was reckoned to him as righteousness." Paul cites Genesis 15:6 in Romans 4:3. Abraham is a very prominent figure in Jewish literature (e.g. Jub. 12; 17:15-18; 1 Macc. 2:52; Odes of Sol. 7:35; Sir. 44:19). He is upheld by Jews in certain Jewish literature as the ideal Jew. For example, Jubilees 12:1-14 records that Abraham pleaded with his father that they should abandon paganism and worship the true God of heaven, and it describes a scene where Abraham burns the idols in his house. Jubilees 12:19 suggests that Abraham chose to do God's will, and Genesis 12 states that God appeared to Abraham and chose him.

As I argued in chapter 2, with the exception of two words, his citation of Genesis 15:6 in Romans 4:3 exactly follows LXX Genesis 15:6 ("and Abraham believed God and it was reckoned to him as righteousness."). The context of Genesis 15:6 is when God promises Abraham that he would give him an heir from his own body. After persuading him, God convinced Abraham that he would fulfill his word to him, and Abraham believed God and God counted his belief in his word in his favor as righteousness. The ground of Abraham's righteousness was *his faith* in God's word, but the emphasis in the Abrahamic narrative in Paul's argument is God's work *in, through*, and *for* Abraham (cf. Gen. 12-50).

My above interpretation is supported by Paul's comments in Romans 4:4-8. Paul states that the wage of a worker is not reckoned to his favor in accordance with grace but in accordance with a debt (Rom. 4:4). But, on the other hand, "his faith is reckoned as righteousness for the one who does not work but to the one who believes in the one who justifies the ungodly" (Rom. 4:5). In Romans 4:4-5, Paul pits working and receiving against believing and receiving. To bolster the point that God gives righteousness by faith apart from works, Paul appeals to David in 4:6-8. Abraham is a good example because he was justified by faith before circumcision and before Torah entered salvation-history (cf. Gen. 15:6 with Gen. 17:1-9). But David illustrates more precisely that one is justified by faith apart from the works of Torah, for David lived under Torah.

Paul links Abraham and David with the comparative adverb "just as" (καθάπερ). He states that righteousness comes by faith apart from works in the case of Abraham, "just as" David even says "with respect to the blessedness of the man to whom God reckons righteousness apart from works." With the exception of deleting the first three words of verse 1 and the last seven words of verse 2, Paul's citation of Psalm 32:1-2 is a direct quote from the LXX (Ps. 31:1-2).[46] In Psalm 32 (LXX Ps. 31), David attests to the blessedness of the man whom God forgives of his sins and who trusts in YHWH. The two verses that Paul quotes focus specifically on God's work of forgiving sins, which is supported by the statements of forgiving lawless deeds and covering sins (Rom. 4:7). But Romans 4:8 takes forgiveness of sins to another level in that this verse asserts that "a man is blessed whose sin the Lord should by no means consider/reckon." With Paul's appeal to LXX Psalm 31:1-2 (MT & Eng. Ps. 32:1-2), he defines more precisely what it means for a man to whom God reckons righteousness to be blessed, and he expresses another element of what it means for one to be reckoned with righteousness.

This reckoning of righteousness apart from works to the one who has faith includes the forgiveness of sins. This means that the Lord does not take into account the sinner's sins, for God has given him a status of righteousness (Rom. 4:6) by virtue of forgiving his sins (Rom. 4:7-8). This forgiveness comes not by works (Rom. 4:3-6, 9) but by faith (Rom. 4:3-6, 9). Justification by faith and not by works is precisely what Paul emphasizes in 4:9-25, and it is precisely the way LXX Psalm 31 (MT and Eng. Ps. 32) ends (see Eng. Ps. 32:10-11). The latter text states that those "who trust in YHWH will be surrounded with loving kindness" (Eng. Ps. 32:10), and it appeals to the righteous ones to rejoice. The priority of divine agency over human agency is seen in both Psalm 32 and Paul's use of this text, because the righteous ones are the ones whose sins *the Lord has forgiven* and whose sin that *he has not taken into account* (cf. Eng. Ps. 32:10; Rom. 4:7-8).

The same point regarding divine agency is evident in Romans 4:9-12. In 4:9, Paul infers ("therefore") from his previous statements in 4:1-8: "therefore, is this blessing upon the circumcision or even upon the uncircumcision?" He returns to Abraham in 4:9b since he is the chief of all patriarchs and since the promises were originally given to him and to his seed. He answers in 4:9b: "for we say: faith was reckoned to Abraham as righteousness." But, then, he asks in 4:10: "therefore, how was it reckoned? Was it reckoned to the one who was in circumcision or in uncircumcision" (4:10)? He answers: "not in circumcision but in uncircumcision" (4:10b). Paul here is still talking about Abraham, and 4:11 elucidates the person of Abraham. Paul's point about Abraham is simply that God reckoned righteousness to Abraham before his circumcision. Righteousness was counted in Abraham's

---

[46]See MT Ps. 32:1-2 and LXX Ps. 31:1-2 and compare with Paul's citation.

favor in Genesis 15:1-6, but he was not circumcised until Genesis 17.

In Romans 4:11, Paul explains the purpose of Abraham's circumcision: "And he received a sign of circumcision to be the seal of the in uncircumcision-faith." Paul states that circumcision was not the means by which righteousness was counted to Abraham's favor and it was not the means by which God entered into a covenant with Abraham, but it was the sign that God had entered into a covenant with Abraham. This is precisely what Genesis 17:1-14 says. Paul attaches three purpose clauses to 4:11a in 4:11b-12: "so that he is the father of all who believe through uncircumcision, so that righteousness would be reckoned to them, and so that he would be the father of the circumcision for those not only from circumcision but also for those who walk in the footsteps of the uncircumcision-faith of our father, Abraham." The three clauses affirm that Abraham received circumcision to be a sign of God's covenant that (1) Abraham would be a father of all who have faith in God; (2) righteousness would be reckoned to them (i.e. all who believe), and (3) Abraham would be the father of all who have faith. Points one and three are essentially the same, and they surround point two, which makes it the middle clause within an *inclusio*. Paul offers here an exegesis of Genesis 15:6 and 17:1-14 by conflating the two texts into a singular argument regarding faith as the means by which God justifies.

Paul's statements in Romans 4 are an antithesis to his comments in Romans 3:19-20. In the former text, Jews and Gentiles are children of Abraham by faith, and they have righteousness reckoned to them by faith. In the latter verses, Torah shuts up both Jews and Gentiles in sin, makes both groups accountable to God, and condemns both groups in God's law-court. A point that should not be missed regarding the priority of divine agency over human agency is that in 3:19-20, Torah imprisons and condemns those who do not have faith, but in 4:1-12, Paul makes the point that God justifies and reckons as righteous those who have faith. Divine and human agencies come together in this text, but the human agent receives from God and does not earn God's free gift of justification and forgiveness of sins. This same point is further demonstrated in 4:13-25.

In 4:13, 25, Paul continues the argument regarding the importance of faith as the means by which God will vindicate sinners in his law-court, but he highlights in these verses that God fulfills his promises to Abraham through faith. The latter unit connects with 4:1-12 because Paul begins 4:13 with a "for." Thus, 4:13-25 provides a reason for the premise argued in 4:1-12. Romans 4:13 states: "for the promise is not through Torah to Abraham or to his seed, so that he is an heir to God's promises of the world, but through the righteousness of faith." To point out the connection between 4:1-12 and 4:13-25, I must briefly summarize the verses: God reckoned righteousness to Abraham's credit because of his faith not his works (David even attests to righteousness by faith apart from works in that he speaks of God forgiving the sins of those who confess and hope in him in Psalm 32; the righteous ones are the ones whom God has forgiven, not the ones who have kept his law), and all (Jews or Gentiles) who have faith in God receive this righteousness from God and become children of Abraham (4:1-12), because God's promise to Abraham in Genesis 12, 15, 17 was neither given nor fulfilled based on either his or his seed's ability to obey Torah (since there was no Torah when God initially gave the promise and entered into a covenant with him), but God fulfilled his promise to Abraham through faith.

The promise given to Abraham was land, seed, and universal blessing (Gen. 12, 15, 17), and Paul states that the promise came to Abraham through the righteousness of faith. The phrase "righteousness of faith" continues Paul's argument in 3:21-4:12 regarding justification. He speaks of the manifestation of righteousness to those who have faith in Jesus (3:21-22). He states that all are justified (passive verb) freely by God's grace through Jesus' blood by faith (3:24-25). He states that God justifies Jews and Gentiles by faith (3:27-30). He states that Abraham was justified (passive verb) by faith and that righteousness was counted to him by faith (4:1-6, 9, 11). Now, in 4:13, he states that God's promise to Abraham came to fulfillment through the righteousness that flows from faith, not through Torah. Thus, Paul uses righteousness and justification language synonymously throughout Romans 3-4, and he states that God grants both to those who have faith, not by their keeping of Torah. This collocation suggests that when Paul speaks of righteousness by faith and justification by faith apart from works, he speaks of God's act of vindication of those who have faith in his law-court. That is, the divine agent justifies the human agent who has faith.

Paul explains this point further in 4:14 when he explains 4:13 with another clause that begins with "for": "for if those from law are heirs [of the promise to Abraham], then faith has become deprived of any meaning and the promise has been destroyed" (brackets). Those from law refer to the Jews, but specifically to those who receive Torah and those who pursue its demands, for Paul does not simply critique the Jews for possessing Torah, but rather because they do not do in total what it says. He mentions that they are circumcised (a stipulation in Torah) in 2:25-26 along side of his comments that they do not do Torah, and he speaks of justification/righteousness coming to Jews and Gentiles by faith apart from Torah and apart from works of Torah (3:20-22, 24, 28; 4:1-5). He wants to accentuate the point that if God's promise to Abraham was based on obeying Torah (i.e. based on human agency), then faith is void and the promise is no longer a promise. In other words, Paul pits faith and promise (God's action) against works (human action) to argue that if the promise is fulfilled through works (human action), then faith (divine action) is superfluous and the promise has been broken.

Paul explains his reasoning in 4:15: "for the law produces wrath. . ." The promise is abolished if the means by which it is achieved is through human obedience to Torah, for the Torah brings judgment. In 4:15, Paul recalls his statement in 3:20 when he states that "not any flesh will be justified in his presence by works of law, for through the law comes the knowledge of sin," and he anticipates his assertion in 5:13-14, that Torah's entrance into salvation history made the problem of sin worse not better, and he anticipates his larger exposition in Romans 7 regarding Torah's condemnation of the Jew in Adam under Torah apart from Christ. The point in 4:15 is simply that Torah brings judgment, and this interpretation is supported by Paul's argument in 2:1-3:20 and 7:1-25. Thus, the human agent's attempt to keep Torah results in a failure to receive the fulfillment of the divine agent's soteriological promises. In both Romans 2-3 and Romans 7, Paul states that Torah condemns those over whom it has jurisdiction because no one meets the demands set forth in Torah to the degree that God expects (e.g. 3:9-20). Furthermore, the above interpretation (that Torah brings judgment upon the human agent apart from the divine agent's intervention) is supported by 4:15: "there is neither transgression where there is not Torah." Paul cannot mean here that sin is absent when there is no Torah, for Jewish tradition expressly states that God destroyed the universe because of sin (Gen. 6) when in fact there was no Torah to break. Thus, his point must be that when there is no Torah, transgression is absent. Consequently, the human agent is incapable of receiving salvation and eschatological exoneration in God's law-court unless the divine agent acts on behalf of him in Christ. Yes, those of faith become heirs of the divine agent's promises, just as Abraham (4:16-20, 24), but the divine agent likewise takes the initiative and credits righteousness to the human agent in Jesus whom he handed over because of the transgressions of the human agents and because he raised him for their justification (4:25). Both Jesus' death and resurrection for the transgressions of those who have faith were the divine agent's initiatory action of salvation in history on behalf of the human agents apart from their actions. Thus, human agency is consequent to and the result of God's divine action for Jews and Gentiles *in* Jesus.

Romans 5:1-11: God's Grace and the Spirit *through* and Salvation *by* Christ
In Romans 5:1, Paul begins a new section that continues throughout 8:39. Many scholars agree that the entire section focuses on hope.[47] In 5:1, Paul speaks of God's justification of those who have faith with a verb in the passive voice (δικαιωθέντες, "having been justified by faith"). Since God justifies according to 3:21-4:25, the passive voice suggests that justification is something *received from* the divine agent and *not earned by* the human agent. He further states in 5:1 that this justification results in peace with God, and both justification and peace with God come to the justified ones "through our Lord Jesus Christ." That is, justification and peace with God are gifts bestowed upon human agents by the divine agent's action through Christ. Paul continues this point in 5:2. Here he states that God grants access to grace to the human agent through Jesus. He affirms that humans stand in grace, but this reality exists only because he grants them access into this grace through Christ. Although humans boast in hope, they boast in the hope of *God's* glory (Rom. 5:2). In addition, although they boast in suffering because they know the positive outcome of their afflictions (Rom. 5:3-4), God's promise of hope and

---

[47]For a list of scholars, see Jarvis J. Williams, *One New Man: The Cross and Racial Reconciliation in Pauline Theology* (Nashville: Broadman & Holman, 2010), 80 n. 79.

Divine and Human Agency

his gift of love work in the human agents through the power of the Spirit the ability to boast in hope and to boast in afflictions (Rom. 5:3-5).

The priority of divine agency over human agency is further evident in Romans 5:6-11. Paul states that Jesus (divine agent) died for the ungodly (human agents), and his death saves the ungodly from God's wrath and reconciles them to God. He states that Jesus died for sinners in Romans 5:6-7. He explains this statement in Romans 5:8: "but God demonstrated his own love toward us: namely, while we were sinners, Christ died for us."[48] God demonstrates his love toward "us" (human agents), but the accent in the text is on *God's action* in demonstrating his love for the ungodly *through* Jesus' death, for Paul states that Jesus died *for sinners* in Romans 5:6-8. In 5:6, Paul states that Christ died "for the weak." In 5:7, he states that someone would scarcely die "for a righteous person" and that someone would perhaps die "for a good person." In 5:8, Paul states that Christ died "for us."[49] In 5:9, Paul connects Jesus' death mentioned in 5:8 with salvation: "Therefore, how much more we will be saved through him from wrath, because we were justified by his blood." Jesus' death for sinners was the basis of this salvation in 5:8-10, and the human agent's salvation is consequent to and the result of God's action *in* and *through* Jesus on behalf of human agents. Romans 5:9-11 envisages this point.

Paul states that because those who have faith have been justified by Jesus' blood, "they will be saved from God's wrath" (Rom. 5:9). In 5:10, he states that "if while we were enemies, we were reconciled to God through the death of his son, how much more we will be saved by his life because we have been reconciled" (Rom. 5:10). In 5:11, Paul states that "we boast in God through our Lord Jesus Christ, through whom we have now received reconciliation" (Rom. 5:11).[50] In 5:9-11, Paul makes some salient points about

---

[48] For a discussion of the Christ died for-formula, see Martin Hengel, *The Atonement: A Study of the Origins of the Doctrine in the New Testament* (trans. John Bowden; London: SCM, 1981), 47-55; Cilliers Breytenbach, "Christus starb für uns: Zur Tradition und paulinischen Rezeption der sogennanten Sterbeformeln," *NTS* 49 (2003): 447-75.

[49] Otfried Hofius ("The Fourth Servant Song in the New Testament Letters," in *The Suffering Servant: Isaiah 53 in Jewish and Christian Sources*, trans. Daniel P. Bailey, eds. Bernd Janowski and Peter Stuhlmacher [Grand Rapids: Eerdmans, 2004], 172-83) has suggested that Paul understood Jesus' death as "inclusive place-taking" rather than as substitution. That is, Jesus "takes the place of sinners in such a way that he does not displace them (as in the substitutionary model) but rather he encompasses them as persons and affects them in their very being." For further explanation of Hofius' view, see Daniel P. Bailey, "Concepts of Stellvertretung in the Interpretation of Isaiah 53," in *Jesus and the Suffering-Servant: Isaiah 53 and Christian Origins*, eds. W. H. Bellinger and W.R. Farmer (Harrisburg, PA, 1998), 223-50.

[50] For reconciliation in Paul, see Ralph Martin, *Reconciliation: A Study of Paul's Theology* (Atlanta: John Knox, 1981); Cilliers Breytenbach, *Versöhnung: Eine Studie zur paulinischen Soteriologie*, WMANT 60 (Neukirchener-Vluyn: Neukirchener Verlag 1989).

the priority of divine agency over human agency in his soteriology. First, God will save from his wrath those whom he justifies by Jesus' blood (Rom. 5:9). Second, God will save those whom he reconciled by Jesus' death because of both Jesus' death and resurrection (Rom. 5:10). Third, God's reconciliation of those for whom Jesus died is a gift received from God through Jesus (Rom. 5:11). Thus, this section accentuates that the divine agent grants the Spirit to believers, salvation from God's wrath, justification in the present age and in God's law-court, and reconciliation for the ungodly *through* Jesus.

Romans 5:12-21: Adam's Curse to All Versus Jesus' Righteousness to All
That human agency is consequent to and the result of divine agency in Paul's soteriology is evident in 5:12-21. In Paul's view, Adam's transgression (a human agent) brought death to all men regardless of their choice, but Jesus' righteous obedience brought life to all men. The death to all through the one man (Adam) and the life to all through the one man (Jesus) should not be viewed the same. That is, Adam's transgression universally affected the lives of everyone without exception. This is supported (Paul argues) by the reign of death and sin over everyone without exception between the times of Adam and Moses (Rom. 5:14; cf. 1:18-3:20). The preceding point is further supported when Paul states that "all" (without distinction and without exception) "have sinned and have fallen short of the glory of God" (Rom. 3:23; cf. 1:18-3:20). In addition, Paul states that the transgression through the one man results in condemnation (Rom. 5:16), but the gift through the one man, Jesus Christ, results in justification. Everyone without exception experiences judgment because of the one man's transgression. This judgment is envisaged by the fact that everyone dies. Thus, the condemnation of the one man is limitless. However, the justification of the one man that comes to all is limited to those who believe, for the judgment of the one man results in death reigning over everyone, whereas the life of the one man results in a victorious reign over death for everyone who receives the gift of righteousness (Rom. 5:17). The priority of divine agency over human agency in Paul's soteriology is evident here in his mentioning of both judgment and salvation. Death came to all due to one man's disobedience of the divine command, and God gave Adam and Eve the ability to choose contrary to what God commanded (cf. Gen. 2:17).

Likewise, salvation comes to all "who receive the gift of grace and the gift of righteousness," and this group will reign through the one man, Jesus Christ (5:17). That Paul says grace is a *received* gift through Jesus suggests that the human agent's reception of the gift of grace is consequent to and the result of the divine agent's action in Christ. The divine agent offers Jesus to reverse Adam's curse and to satisfy his justice by dying for sin and extending his righteousness to those who believe (cf. Rom. 3:21-26; 5:12-21) due to the human agent's inability to respond in obedience to God's commands to the degree that he demands (Rom. 1:18-3:20). When the human agent receives the gift of righteousness as a gift from God, he is, therefore, justified and receives the status of righteous (Rom. 3:21-5:19).

Divine and Human Agency 155

Romans 6:1-23: Not under God's Law, but under God's Grace
That human agency is consequent to and the result of divine agency in Paul's soteriology seems to be further supported by Paul's discussion of law and grace in Romans 6. He begins the chapter by inferring from 5:20-21 in 6:1 that God's grace does not warrant individuals to practice sin. Instead, those who have died to sin's power should no longer subject themselves to sin's power since they have died to sin when they were baptized into Jesus' death, so that they would be raised to spiritual life just as he was raised to physical and spiritual life (Rom. 6:2-4). Furthermore, those who were baptized into Jesus' death likewise have died to sin (Rom. 6:5-7), which no longer rules over them (Rom. 6:8-11). Paul certainly emphasizes human agency in 6:1-11 when he uses the active verbs "we died" (6:1, 8); "we should walk" (6:4); "we have become partakers" (6:5); "we will be partakers" (6:5); "we no longer serve sin" (6:6); "we believe" (6:8); "we will live" (6:8), and "you consider" (6:11).

Yet, the human agent's actions are grounded in the divine agent's actions in this text, for Paul uses passive verbs to describe the human agent's active participation in God's work of salvation in Jesus. He states that "we were baptized into Christ Jesus" (6:3); "we were baptized into his death" (6:3); "we were buried with him through baptism into death" (6:4); "our old man was crucified" (6:6), and "the body of sin would be abolished" (6:6). Of course, the voice of the verbs alone does not determine that the divine agent is the doer of the action that the human agent receives, but since 4:24 states that Abraham believed in the God who raises the dead and since 6:4 speaks of Christ being raised from the dead through the strength of the Father in a context where Paul emphasizes God's work of salvation through Christ to conquer the power of sin and death (5:12-6:23), a plausible reading of Romans 6 is that God was the divine agent behind the Romans' baptism into Christ and that this baptism points to their resurrection life in Christ.

As a result of the divine agent's work through Christ on behalf of those who were buried with Christ (6:1-10), Paul commands the Romans not to be ruled by the power of sin and instead to die to it by presenting their members as weapons of righteousness (6:11-13). Paul's reason for the preceding commands is God's grace (6:14). That is, the Romans were under the lordship of grace because they died with Christ in baptism (6:1-3), and they participated in God's divine grace because God acted on their behalf to offer Jesus as a gift to the many so that through Jesus they would receive the gift of righteousness (cf. 5:12-21, esp. 5:17). In 6:15-17, Paul again speaks of the obedience of the human agent. But he expresses that the human agent can obey the gospel because the divine agent has graciously given eternal life to the human agent, freed the human agent from sin's power, and made him a slave of righteousness (6:18, 22-23), whereas the human agent was a slave to unrighteousness prior to God's action on behalf of the human agent (6:19-20).

Romans 7:1-8:39: Death to the Law, Death because of the Law, and Life *in* Christ

In Romans 7-8, Paul continues to discuss the effects of Adam's sin upon those under the power of Torah and not under the power of grace. By using an example from marriage, Paul argues that Torah holds in bondage everyone under its jurisdiction until death (7:1-3). In his discussion of the freedom that comes when one dies to Torah, Paul argues that the Romans "were put to death with respect to the law through the body of Christ," so that they would be united to Christ, who was raised from the dead, and so that they would bear fruit to God (7:4). Just as in 6:1-23, Paul speaks in Romans 7 of dying with Christ and living in obedience to God (Rom. 7:4), and he speaks of the death and resurrection of Jesus (Rom. 7:4). The passive statement "we were put to death" in Rom 6:4 provides the basis under which the Romans were able to accomplish the action "we would bear fruit to God" (Rom. 7:4). Namely, they bore fruit to God because they were put to death with respect to Torah by their death with Christ. This point is confirmed by 7:5 when Paul states that "when we were in the flesh," "we" bore fruit resulting in death (Rom. 7:5).

"In the flesh" refers to the time when Paul and the Romans were under Torah's jurisdiction prior to their faith in Jesus, for the entire discussion of 7:1-25 focuses on Torah's power to produce death and its inability to produce life within those who are under its jurisdiction because of sin and the deliverance that comes through Jesus to those under Torah's jurisdiction. Romans 7:6 expresses both the role of the divine agent and of the human agent by stating that "we were severed from the law because we died to what we were being held so that we would serve in the newness of the Spirit and not in the oldness of the letter" (Rom. 7:6). Severance from Torah and service in the Spirit came to the Jewish audience (and to the Romans) because of death to the law, but 7:6 is the result of God's work of putting to death those under Torah so that they would live to God (Rom. 7:4), for 7:6 is an inference from 7:4-5. Thus, God's action of metaphorically putting to death those under Torah to Torah was the impetus behind and the basis upon which they would live to God. As Maston states, "Paul contends that under the law the human has no agency, but in Christ the human becomes an agent."[51]

The argument of 7:7-25 continues to shed light on this latter point. Paul begins the section by discussing the relationship between the law and sin. He states that the "I" would not have known sin except through the law (Rom. 7:7) and that sin took the opportunity to provoke the "I" to sin in that it produced in the "I" all covetousness (Rom. 7:8). Prior to the entrance of Torah into salvation-history, the "I" was living (or so he thought) in an eschatological sense apart from Torah (Rom. 7:9).[52] However, once the "I" and Torah met, sin came to life in the "I" (Rom. 7:9), and the Torah that was supposed to result in life for the "I" actually produced death in him (Rom. 7:10), for sin took the opportunity to deceive the "I" by using Torah and killed the "I" via the Torah

---

[51] Maston, *Divine and Human Agency*, 126-74, esp. 126.
[52] Rightly Maston, *Divine and Human Agency*, 137.

Divine and Human Agency

(Rom. 7:11). Paul continues this line of argumentation in 7:13-23. The verses that are especially important for my thesis are 7:15-23. There Paul speaks of the human agent's inability to act in obedience to the divine agent's Torah. He states that the "I" does not know what he is doing (Rom. 7:15), that the "I" does what he does not desire (Rom. 7:16, 19-20), and that sin is working in the "I" (Rom. 7:17). He also states that nothing good dwells in the flesh of the "I" (Rom. 7:18), for the desire to obey the Torah is present in him but the ability to obey is not since sin/evil dwell in the "I" (Rom. 7:18-21). The "I" delights in the law of God in his inner man (Rom. 7:22), but he gives priority to the law of sin and death that rage war within his body (Rom. 7:23). Paul asks in 7:24 who would deliver the "I" from his miserable state.

In 7:25-8:11, Paul answers that God (the divine agent) through Jesus Christ, the Lord of the "I," would deliver the "I" from the condemnation actuated by sin's use of Torah and that this deliverance would impart to the "I" (and to all who are in Christ) the Spirit of liberation. In 7:25, Paul thanks God that he has provided through the Lord Jesus Christ deliverance for the "I" from sin's bondage to Torah. In 8:1, Paul expresses that there is no condemnation for those "in Christ Jesus." The latter phrase suggests that deliverance from sin's bondage to Torah does not come until God acts through Christ to unite the "I" (and those underneath Torah's bondage [Rom. 7:1-6]) to Christ. The divine agent's work on behalf of the human agent in Christ, therefore, emancipates the human agent from slavery to Torah exacerbated by sin's use of Torah. In 8:2, Paul confirms this point.

Paul grounds 8:1 (that condemnation no longer exists for those in Christ Jesus) in 8:2-7 with a discussion of the Spirit. In 8:2, he states that "the law of the Spirit of life in Christ Jesus has freed you from the law of sin and of death." As I have argued elsewhere,[53] the phrase "law of the Spirit of life in Christ Jesus" refers to the principle of the Spirit instead of to Torah, for Torah was characterized by life only if obeyed; it was otherwise characterized by death. Torah was not characterized by life in the Spirit (Lev. 18:5; Jer. 31:31-34; Ezek. 36-37; Rom. 7:1-25, esp. 7:10, 24; 2 Cor. 3:6-18). In addition, Paul specifically states in 8:2 that this law is "in Christ Jesus" and that this law liberates from the "law of sin and death." As Paul argues in Romans 7 (Rom. 7:10, 24), Torah brings death. Romans 8:1 reiterates the new covenant language of Jeremiah 31:31-33 and Ezekiel 36-37, to which Paul alludes in Romans 2:28-29 but develops more fully in Romans 8:1-11:36 when he speaks both of God's work of salvation on behalf of and his impartation of the Spirit to Jews and Gentiles through Christ by faith.

In Romans 8:3, Paul provides the reason for God's work of liberation from Torah's bondage by the Spirit in Christ versus liberation from Torah's bondage through Torah: "for God did what the law was incapable of doing, because it was weak through the flesh, in that he sent his own son in the likeness of sinful flesh as a sin-offering, and he condemned sin in [Jesus'] flesh" (brackets mine). Torah was incapable of delivering those under its

---

[53] Williams, *One New Man*, 51.

jurisdiction from the power of sin and the human agent was incapable of achieving the life promised in Torah if obeyed (cf. Deut. 30:15-20) since sin used Torah to worsen the latter's effect upon those under its jurisdiction (Rom. 5:12-21, esp. 5:12-14, 20-21; 7:1-25). But Jesus (Paul says), on the other hand, was able to dismantle Torah's hold on those under its jurisdiction for those on behalf of whom he died and *only* on behalf of those for whom he died, for his death "fulfilled the righteous requirement of the law in us who walk not in accordance with the flesh but in accordance with the Spirit" (Rom. 8:4). Those who walk in accordance with the Spirit are believers who obey the gospel, because Paul emphasizes walking in the Spirit, living in the Spirit, and the Spirit dwelling in believers versus walking in the flesh, enmity with God, disobedience to Torah, and death because of sin (Rom. 8:4-11) and because he speaks of adopted children, who are joint heirs and who have the Spirit, as putting to death the deeds of the flesh (Rom. 8:12-17).[54] Thus, everyone for whom Jesus died as a sin-offering puts to death the deeds of the flesh and fulfills Torah by their Christian obedience, which they achieve by the power of the Spirit, for Paul states that Jesus' death for those in Christ Jesus fulfilled Torah in them who walk in accordance with the Spirit (i.e. in those who have faith in Jesus as the Jewish Messiah).[55] In addition, Paul makes the point that God, who raised Jesus from the dead, will give future resurrection life through the Spirit to all who receive the Spirit by faith (Rom. 8:11). Hence, human agents are condemned by Torah in Paul's view unless the divine agent works on their behalf in Christ by the Spirit, and the divine agent only works on behalf of those for whom Jesus died, which is attested to by the fact that they are the only ones who receive God's Spirit of liberation from Torah's spiritual bondage and by the fact that they are the only ones who are liberated from Torah's condemnation.

That human agency is consequent to and the result of divine agency in Paul's soteriology and that the divine agent applies the soteriological benefits, achieved by Jesus' death, only to those who are part of the believing community is apparent in the rest of Paul's argument in Romans 8:18-39. Romans 8:18 connects with 8:17 because of the "for" in 8:18 and because of the presence of the theme of suffering in 8:17-18. The divine agent's work in the believer and the human agent's agreement with the divine agent are apparent from Paul's words in 8:18 that "the sufferings of the current time are not comparable to the glory which is about to be *revealed in us*." To state Paul's words another way, God will reveal glory in/to his children. Romans

---

[54]Maston (*Divine and Human Agency*, 160-61) is correct to see a connection between Paul's comments that the Spirit enables the human agent to obey God and the words of Ezekiel 11 and 36-37 and the Hodayot regarding the Spirit's work within his people. However, he downplays the importance of Jer. 31:31-34 in Paul's thought in Rom. 8:5-11.

[55]So also recently Kevin W. McFadden, "The Fulfillment of the Law's Dikaiōma: Another Look at Romans 8:1-4," *JETS* 52 (2009): 483-97. For a discussion of the different readings of Rom. 8:1-4, see McFadden.

Divine and Human Agency

8:19 supports this reading since it states that the creation awaits the *"revelation of the sons of God,"* and he continues that the creation will be freed from its slavery (Rom. 8:22), which will include the "freedom of the glory of the children of God" (Rom. 8:22), that "we await the redemption of our bodies" (Rom. 8:23), that "we were saved in hope" (Rom. 8:24), that "the Spirit helps us in our weakness" so that "we" know what "we" should pray (Rom. 8:26), that the Spirit prays for God's children and searches their hearts (Rom. 8:26-27), that God works all things together for the good to those who love God because of his work of foreknowledge, predestination, calling, justification, and glorification in their lives (Rom. 8:28-30), that no one is against "us" if God is "for us" (Rom 8:31), that God gave up his son "for us all" and will freely give "us" all things (Rom. 8:32), that no one will bring a charge against God's elect (Rom 8:33-34), that no one can separate "us" from God's love in Christ (Rom. 8:35-36), and that in Christ "we" are more than conquerors over everything through the God who loved "us" in Christ (Rom. 8:31-39).

Romans 8:28-30: Foreknowledge, Predestination, Calling, Justification, and Glorification

The priority of divine agency over human agency appears in Romans 8:29-30. These verses provide a reason for Paul's assertion in 8:28 that "all things work together for the good to those who love God to those who are called in accordance with his purpose." Furthermore, since 8:30 begins with the relative pronoun "whom," whose antecedent is "those" in the statement "those who love God," 8:28-30 belongs together as one syntactical unit. Thus, the "because" in 8:29 is implied in 8:30, which makes 8:29-30 function as the ground to 8:28. To state the matter simply: Paul asserts in 8:28 that all things work together for the good for those who love God, i.e., for Christians, then in 8:29-30 he provides five reasons why: (1) God foreknows (Rom. 8:29); (2) God predestines to be conformed to the image of his son (Rom. 8:29); (3) God calls (Rom. 8:30); (4) God justifies (Rom. 8:30), and (5) God glorifies a people (Rom. 8:30). Below I interpret each of the preceding statements in 8:29-30 in consecutive order.

Romans 8:29: God's Foreknowledge

As with election, God's foreknowledge is debated because God's election/predestination and foreknowledge often occur side-by-side in the New Testament, which is clearly the case here. Regarding foreknowledge, Paul could mean that God foresaw who would believe and he therefore chose this group to believe based on the decision that he foresaw them to make. Thus, according to this reading, God's choice to save some is based on his foresight that some would choose him first. This concept of foreknowledge does occur in the New Testament in a couple of contexts where one makes a decision based on information known in advance of that decision, so that the information foreknown actually helps one to make the appropriate choice. For example, in Acts 26:5, the Pharisees foreknew Paul before he came to Jerusalem after his conversion. In 2 Peter 3:17, Peter gives his audience information about the false teachers in advance so that they can respond to them in the appropriate way with their foreknown knowledge when the false teachers seek to deceive them.

But, in my view, the above reading of foreknowledge in Romans 8:29 does not take seriously the force with which Paul discusses God's sovereignty in both the immediate and the remote context of Romans, and it does not take seriously the Old Testament and Second Temple Jewish roots underneath Paul's view of God's foreknowledge. When the concept of foreknowledge is applied to God's election of a people for his redemptive purposes, it does not refer to God's choice based on foreseen actions. Rather, God's foreknowledge refers precisely to his predetermined decision to set his covenantal love upon a people for his glory, and this choice is based on nothing that he foresaw in humans. Instead, the decision was based on his will to set his love on an elect people for his glory. This understanding of foreknowledge is supported by texts in the Old Testament, in early Judaism, and in the New Testament. Because of limited space, a few texts must suffice.

> Deuteronomy 7:6-8: The Lord did not set his love on you nor <u>choose</u> you because you were more in number than any of the peoples, for you were the fewest of all peoples, but because the <u>Lord loved</u> you and kept the oath which he swore to your forefathers, the Lord brought you out by a mighty hand and redeemed you from the house of slavery, from the hand of Pharaoh king of Egypt (NASB).[56]

> Judith 9:1-14: Then Judith prostrated herself, put ashes on her head, and uncovered the sackcloth she was wearing. At the very time when the evening incense was being offered in the house of God in Jerusalem, Judith cried out to the Lord with a loud voice, and said, O Lord God of my ancestor Simeon, to whom you gave a sword to take revenge on those strangers who had torn off a virgin's clothing to defile her, and exposed her thighs to put her to shame, and polluted her womb to disgrace her; for you said, It shall not be done-yet they did it; so you gave up their rulers to be killed, and their bed, which was ashamed of the deceit they had practiced, was stained with blood, and you struck down slaves along with princes, and princes on their thrones. You gave up their wives for booty and their daughters to captivity, and all their booty to be divided among your beloved children who burned with zeal for you and abhorred the pollution of their blood and called on you for help. O God, my God, hear me also, a widow. "For you have done these things and those that went before and those that followed. You have designed the things that are now, and those that are to come. What you had in mind has happened; the things you decided on presented themselves and said, Here we are!

---

[56]See also Gen. 18:19 where God knew/chose Abraham, Amos 3:2 where God sets his covenantal love on/has known Israel, and Jer. 1:5 that says before Jeremiah was in the womb, God knew him.

Divine and Human Agency 161

> For all your ways are <u>prepared in advance</u> and your judgment is with <u>foreknowledge</u>. Here now are the Assyrians, a greatly increased force, priding themselves in their horses and riders, boasting in the strength of their foot soldiers, and trusting in shield and spear, in bow and sling. They do not know that you are the Lord who crushes wars; the Lord is your name. Break their strength by your might, and bring down their power in your anger; for they intend to defile your sanctuary, and to pollute the tabernacle where your glorious name resides, and to break off the horns of your altar with the sword. Look at their pride, and send your wrath upon their heads. Give to me, a widow, the strong hand to do what I plan. By the deceit of my lips strike down the slave with the prince and the prince with his servant; crush their arrogance by the hand of a woman. For your strength does not depend on numbers, nor your might on the powerful. But you are the God of the lowly, helper of the oppressed, upholder of the weak, protector of the forsaken, savior of those without hope. Please, please, God of my father, God of the heritage of Israel, Lord of heaven and earth, Creator of the waters, King of all your creation, hear my prayer! Make my deceitful words bring wound and bruise on those who have planned cruel things against your covenant, and against your sacred house, and against Mount Zion, and against the house your children possess. Let your whole nation and every tribe know and understand that you are God, the God of all power and might, and that there is no other who protects the people of Israel but you alone! (NRSV).[57]

> Acts 2:23: . . .this man, handed over to you according to the definite plan and <u>foreknowledge of God</u>, you crucified and killed by the hands of those outside the law (NRSV).

The above texts shine a ray of light on Paul's use of foreknowledge in Romans 8:29. However, the most helpful examples for Paul's use are from the text of Romans.

Foreknowledge in 8:29 does not mean foresight for the following reasons. First, the immediate and remote context of 8:28-30 is strongly God-centered. That is, God's action for God's purposes is emphasized. In 8:3, Paul states that *God* condemns sin. In 8:11, *God* raised Jesus from the dead and resurrects those who believe in Jesus. In 8:29, *God* calls. In 8:29, *God* predestines. In 8:30, *God* calls. In 8:30, 33, *God* justifies. In 8:30, *God* glorifies. In 8:31, *God* is for "us." In 8:32, *God* did not spare his son but offered him for "us." In 9:11-13, *God* loved Jacob and hated Esau so that his electing purpose would stand apart from their works. In 9:17, *God* raised up Pharaoh to destroy him. In 9:22-24, *God* created vessels of wrath and vessels of destruction. In 9:24-25, *God* calls Jews and Gentiles to be vessels of mercy. In

---

[57]See also 1QS 3:18-25; 11; 1QH 15:13-19; cf. 14:11 1QM; CD; 1QpHab 1:11; 1QSa 1:5-7.

11:1-24, *God* hardens some Jews so that they would not be saved and includes Gentiles within his saving promises. In 11:33-36, Paul praises *God* for his incomprehensible ways. Second, Paul uses foreknowledge and predestination together (Rom. 8:30). At first, this might seem to suggest that foreknowledge and predestination are two distinct divine prerogatives in Paul's soteriology. However, since Paul mentions predestination and election elsewhere in Romans (e.g. Rom. 9:10-24) and in his letters (e.g. Eph. 1:3-14) without mentioning foreknowledge, the two concepts are *not synonymous* but *are closely related*, so that one implies the other. This is exactly what Deuteronomy 7:6-8 suggests when it speaks of God's covenantal love for and choice of Israel. Thus, Paul can speak of God's election of Jacob and Esau without using the word foreknowledge (Rom. 9:11-12), and he can speak of his foreknowledge of Israel (Rom. 11:2) without using the word predestination because the two concepts are closely related. Third, Paul states that God foreknew Israel. With this statement, Paul cannot mean that God foresaw that Israel would choose to be his chosen nation and that God in anticipation of Israel's choice selected Israel first, because (a) to my knowledge there is absolutely no evidence in the Hebrew Bible that gives even the slightest impression that God foresaw something good in Israel that moved him to choose them (cf. Deut. 7:6-8) and (b) because not every Israelite whom God foreknew remained faithful to YHWH, and (c) not every Israelite was a member of the spiritual Israel that followed YHWH.[58] Therefore, when Paul speaks of God's foreknowledge in Romans 8:29, he refers to God's covenantal love that he chose to set upon an elect group of people, and his foreknowledge was apart from any foreseen decision of the group upon whom he placed his covenantal love.[59]

Romans 8:29: Predestination in Conformity with Christ's Image

The verb "to predestine" (προορίζω) in 8:29 occurs elsewhere in the New Testament.[60] Every occurrence refers to God's predetermined choice to do something apart from the actions offered by a human and apart from foreseen faith. Because of the weight of evidence in the New Testament, predestine as Paul mentions it in 8:30 likely means that God made a predetermined choice to save some humans apart from any merit foreseen or earned by those whom he chose. The preceding interpretation is supported by Paul's statement that God

---

[58]For example, see the Jews in the wilderness (see Numbers) and also the renegade Jews in 1 Maccabees who apostatized from their Jewish faith. See also Romans 9-11.

[59]Although he states that foreknowledge in Rom. 8:28 refers to the human's response to God's initiative, Leander Keck obscures the meaning of foreknowledge in this text when he calls it God's "prevenient grace." For example, see Leander Keck, *Romans*, ANTC (Nashville: Abingdon, 2005), 217.

[60]Acts 4:28—refers to God's determining the choices of Herod, Pilate, and the Gentiles so that they would do precisely what he wanted with regard to Jesus' death; Rom. 8:29—refers to God's predestination of some to be saved; 1 Cor. 2:7—refers to God's predestination of his divine wisdom; Eph. 1:5, 11—refers to God's predestination of some to be saved in accordance with God's good pleasure.

Divine and Human Agency

predestined some humans to be conformed to the image of Jesus (Rom. 8:29). In other words, the divine action of predestination results in the human agent's conformity into Jesus' image, and the latter is consequent to and the result of the former's action. In 12:1-2, Paul urges Christians not to be conformed to the present evil age, but to be transformed by the renewing of the mind. In 8:29, he states that God predestined some humans to be conformed into the image of his son. Quite simply, this means that God predestined a people to be converted. What is conversion? It is at least spiritual transformation by faith in Jesus Christ that results in a changed life (cf. Rom. 12:1-15:12). Paul's use of the adjective συμμόρφους ("to be conformed/to share in the likeness of") confirms this point. The only other occurrence of this term in the New Testament is in Philippians 3:21 where Paul remarks that Christians await Jesus' return from heaven (Phil. 3:20), and when he returns "he will transform our humble body to be conformed to the body of his glory. . ." (Phil. 3:21).

Romans 8:29: The First-Born among Many Brothers

Paul's next statements in 8:29 support the above understanding of predestination and the priority of divine agency in his soteriology. He states that God predestined some into Jesus' image "so that he would be the first-born amongst many brothers." The "he" in the preceding verse refers to Jesus, not to God, for the adjective first-born primarily applies to Jesus in the New Testament (Luke 2:7; Col. 1:15, 18; Heb. 1:6; Rev. 1:5).[61] The term, however, occurs approximately 60 times in the LXX. There it refers to the first-born child (LXX Gen. 27:19) or to the first-born of one's flock (e.g. LXX Gen. 4:3). The first-born is special by virtue of being the first to be born (LXX Exod. 13:2), and the first-born experiences or at least expects to experience (e.g. LXX Gen. 27:19) certain privileges. In other words, he is the priority since he is superior to all of the others by virtue of being the first to be born to his parents (LXX Exod. 6:14). Paul expresses in Romans 8:29 that Jesus is to be chief priority amongst those whom God has chosen to be conformed into his image. He is to be valued and treasured above all others, for he is privileged as God's first-born (and only) son. Thus, God's act of predestination of some human agents was for the purpose of conforming them into Jesus' image so that they would give Jesus preeminence over everything in their lives.

Romans 8:30: Calling, Justification, and Glorification

In 8:30, Paul continues: "whom he predestined, these he also called." The verb for calling here (καλέω) is a cognate of the adjective "called ones" (κλητοῖς) in 8:28. Neither the adjective in 8:28 nor the verb in 8:30 refers to a general, audible, or external call, although the verb can be used this way in some contexts (cf. Matt. 4:21; 20:28). Rather, in 8:30, the verb refers to God's effectual calling of unbelievers to faith in Jesus Christ, and this call creates spiritual life within the human agents who experience it. I offer 14 arguments to

---

[61]The only two exceptions are Heb. 11:28; 12:23.

defend this interpretation. (1) Romans 8:28 states that God calls those who love him in accordance with his purpose, and 8:29-30 suggest that the purpose is conformity into the image of Jesus Christ. Thus, those who receive this call are likewise conformed into the image of Christ. (2) Paul states that the called ones are justified in 8:30. (3) Paul states that the called ones are glorified in 8:30. Justification refers to God's eschatological verdict in his law-court that has invaded the present age, and glorification refers to the full and final realization of that verdict, for which all Christians and the entire creation currently long and about which they and it groan (cf. Rom. 8:18-25). (4) Paul states elsewhere that this calling created life when and where there was no life (Rom. 4:17). (5) Paul states that God's calling makes one a child of God (Rom. 9:7, 12, 24-29). (6) Paul states that God's calling grants one entrance into fellowship with Jesus (1 Cor. 1:9). (7) God's calling is equivalent with conversion (1 Cor. 7:17-24; Gal. 1:15). (8) Paul states that God's calling results in freedom for the recipients of the call (Gal. 5:13). (9) Paul states that God's calling demands that the called live a changed life (Eph. 4:1; 1 Thess. 4:7). (10) Paul states that believers are called to hope (Eph 4:4). (11) God's calling grants entrance into his kingdom (1 Thess. 2:12). (12) God's calling enables the recipients to obtain the glory of the Lord Jesus Christ (2 Thess. 2:14). (13) Paul states that believers were called to eternal life (1 Tim 6:12). (14) God's calling is connected to salvation (2 Tim. 1:9). Therefore, God's calling is effectual (i.e. it creates spiritual life within those who receive the call), and it is the prerequisite to the human agent's experience of justification by faith and glorification on the last day.

Romans 9-11: God's Faithfulness to and Election of Some Jews and Gentiles

The major premise of Romans 9-11 is that God has not forsaken his promises to Israel (cf. Rom. 9:6; 11:1-2).[62] Yet, the priority of divine agency over human agency in Paul's soteriology emerges from the unit.

Romans 9:6-18: God's Electing Mercy, the Patriarchs, and Pharaoh

Paul begins the section by agonizing over Israel's unbelief in Jesus as the Jewish Messiah (Rom. 9:1-5). In Romans 9:6-11:32, a discussion of divine and human agency develops in defense of the faithfulness of God. He states that a Jewish rejection of Jesus as the Jewish Messiah does not support that God has forsaken his promises to Israel, although God has fulfilled his promises of salvation to Israel in Jesus and although unbelieving Jews fall short of his soteriological promises in Jesus, because not every Jew is a child of Abraham/of God (Rom. 9:1-8).

In Paul's view, God has always operated in salvation-history with a principle of election (Rom. 9:1-18). Paul suggests that God has neither promised to choose all Jews to be his people nor that all Jews would be his

---

[62] Against Jouette M. Bassler, *Divine Impartiality: Paul and a Theological Axiom*, SBL Dissertaion 59 (Chico: Scholars Press, 1982), 160-62.

Divine and Human Agency

spiritual offspring (Rom. 9:6).[63] To support this premise, Paul gives examples from the Old Testament patriarchs. God promised to give Abraham a child (Rom. 9:7-9; cf. Gen. 21:12; 18:10, 14). This promised child was Isaac and not Ishmael so that God's purpose of election would stand with Isaac (Rom. 9:10-12). Paul states that God likewise promised to give Isaac a child through whom he would fulfill his promises to Abraham, and this child was Jacob and not Esau (Rom. 9:13; cf. Mal. 1:2-3). In Romans 9:14-15, he states that God was not unrighteous to make this choice, because God has always chosen to give his free grace and mercy to whomever he desires irrespective of human effort (cf. Exod. 33:19).

In 9:16, Paul concludes his previous argument regarding God's sovereign choice to grant mercy to some and to withhold it from others in order to sustain the point that God has not forsaken his promises to Israel (Rom. 9:6-15). In 9:16, Paul concludes that God imparts his saving mercy to some and withholds it from others based on his will and not based on one's works or human effort. In 9:17, Paul grounds the premise of 9:16 with a statement about Pharaoh. He quotes Exodus 9:17 to make his point and conflates both the MT and LXX traditions, but he alters the wording in his citation from both the MT and the LXX to accentuate God's sovereignty over the deeds of Pharaoh. Whereas MT Exodus 9:16 translates as "But, on account of this, I have caused you to stand: so that I would cause you to see my strength and so that I would declare my name in all of the earth" and whereas LXX Exodus 9:16 translates as "and on account of this reason you were allowed to survive: so that I would demonstrate my strength in you and so that my name would be declared in all of the earth," Paul actually states in 9:17: "For the scripture says with respect to Pharaoh: that for this very reason I raised you up: so that I would demonstrate in you my power and so that my name would be proclaimed in all the earth."

Paul's alterations of both the MT and the LXX traditions are subtle, but very precise. The basic structure and meaning of each tradition are the same. Each tradition emphasizes that God had a purpose for Pharaoh and used him to that end, and each tradition accentuates that God's dealings with Pharaoh served to proclaim his power in all of the earth. However, with the additions of the intensive phrase εἰς αὐτὸ τοῦτο ("for this very reason") instead of the LXX's ἕνεκεν τούτου ("for this reason") and ἐξήγειράς σε ("I raised you up") instead of the MT's העמדתיך ("I caused you to stand"), which would normally translate in Greek as ἵστημι (e.g. LXX Gen. 47:7; Lev. 14:11; Num. 4:16; Judg. 16:25), and instead of the LXX's διετηρήθης ("your were allowed to survive"), Paul emphasizes the divine agent's role in extending mercy to some and withholding mercy from Pharaoh.

Ben Witherington maintains that the issue in 9:18 is not Pharaoh's destruction when Paul speaks of God's hardening of him but Pharaoh's limited

---

[63]For a detailed and recent discussion of Paul's use of the Old Testament in Rom 9:1-9, see Brian J. Abasciano, *Paul's Use of the Old Testament in Romans 9:1-9: An Intertextual and Theological Exegesis*, JSNTSup/LNTS 301 (London: T&T Clark, 2005).

duration, for Paul's purpose (says Witherington) is to deal with Israel's fate and not Pharaoh's.[64] Yet, on the contrary, Witherington seems to be misguided since Paul primarily credits God for Pharaoh's disobedience and destruction and since Paul concludes 9:18 by stating that God imparts mercy to whomever he desires and hardens (i.e. withholds mercy from) whomever he desires and in 9:19 when Paul anticipates a question of personal responsibility.[65] That is, if Pharaoh disobeyed God and if to disobey was the precise reason that God created Pharaoh (cf. Rom. 9:16-17), then "why does God still find fault [with Pharaoh]" (Rom. 9:20) (brackets mine)? Paul responds by simply stating that humans should not question God's will (Rom. 9:19), and he continues that God chooses to show his power by creating some for destruction and by creating some for salvation and that this is his divine prerogative as the creator (Rom. 9:20-29). Paul does not circumvent attributing personal responsibility to Pharaoh, for Paul has already made clear in Romans 1-8, as he will again in 9:30-11:36, that God imparts wrath to those who reject the gospel (or in the case of Pharaoh who reject his word). Still, Paul places the accent in 9:6-29 on the divine agent's control of the destiny of the human agent as a means by which to explain to his interlocutor that God has not forsaken his promises to Israel.

Romans 9:22-23: Vessels of Mercy and Vessels of Wrath
In Romans 9:22-23, Paul makes strong statements about divine agency. Here he develops his comments from 9:20-21 regarding the potter's prerogative to shape his clay for the potter's desires.[66] Paul states that God was willing to demonstrate his wrath and to make know his power to the vessels of mercy by destroying the vessels of wrath, whom he prepared for destruction (Rom. 9:22). The words "willing," "to demonstrate," and "power" in 9:22 reveal a connection with Paul's comments about God's mercy and hardening in 9:17-18.[67] Such connections suggest that Paul continues in 9:22-23 to answer the question whether God is unrighteous to give his mercy to some and to harden others. In 9:17-18 and 9:19-23, Pharaoh serves as a prototypical example for Paul that God's hardening of some is not unrighteous. He states that God has in fact "prepared some for destruction" (Rom. 9:22).

The statement translated as "prepared" in the clause "prepared for destruction" is the participle κατηρτισμένα, and it describes the phrase

---

[64]Ben Witherington, III and Darlene Hyatt, *Paul's Letter to the Romans: A Socio-Rhetorical Commentary* (Grand Rapids: Eerdmans, 2004), 256.
[65]For a detailed and recent discussion of Paul's use of the Old Testament in Rom 9:10-18, see Brian J. Abasciano, *Paul's Use of the Old Testament in Romans 9:10-18: An Intertextual Exegesis*, LNTS 317 (London: T&T Clark, 2010).
[66]The potter-clay metaphor was popularly used in Jewish literature to emphasize God's sovereign power. For examples, see Isa. 29:16-17; 45:9-11; 64:8; Jer. 18; Ps. 2:9; Job 2:9; 38:14; Sir. 27:5; 33:13; 38:29-30; Wis. 15:7; T. Nap. 2:2, 4; 1QS 11:22; 1QH 1:21.
[67]For these connections, compare the Greek text of Rom. 9:17-18 with 9:22.

"vessels of wrath."⁶⁸ Some have contended that this participle should be rendered as a middle voice ("prepared themselves") instead of as a passive ("were prepared") to preclude God from actively creating some to destroy them and instead to place total responsibility of the hardening and destruction upon the human agents.⁶⁹ Nevertheless, since the righteousness of God is in question in this text and since God is the subject of the main verbal clause in Romans 9:22, κατηρτισμένα should be understood as a passive, and it conveys the point that God created some vessels specifically "for [eternal] destruction" (brackets mine). Although many would challenge this reading,⁷⁰ it appears most likely from the text. For example, first, Paul juxtaposes God's mercy and compassion to some (Rom. 9:15-16; cf. Exod. 32-34) with his destruction of others (Rom. 9:17) in 9:15-17, with his wrath and hardening of others in 9:17-18, with his creation of vessels of honor and vessels of dishonor in 9:21, and with his demonstration of his wrath upon vessels of destruction and demonstration of mercy upon vessels of mercy and glory in 9:22-23. Second, ὀργή ("wrath") in Romans most often refers to God's present (Rom. 1:18) or eschatological wrath reserved for those who reject the gospel (Rom. 2:5, 8; 3:5; 4:15; 5:9). Third, the phrase "vessels of wrath, the statement "were prepared," the phrase "for destruction," which often refers to eschatological destruction in

---

⁶⁸For "vessel" or "object" as the appropriate translation of σκεῦος, see 1 Esdr. 2:10; Jud. 4:3; 1 Macc. 4:49; Sir 45:8; 50:9; Pss. Sol. 17:23; Ep. Jer. 1:17.

⁶⁹For example, John Stott, *The Message of Romans: God's Good News for the World*, TBST (Downers Grove, IL: InterVarsity Press, 1994), 272-73; Leon Morris, *Romans*, PNTC (Grand Rapids: Eerdmans, 1991), 368; Joseph Fitzmyer, *Romans*, ABC (New York: Doubleday, 1992), 569; Witherington, *Romans*, 258.

⁷⁰For example, A.T. Hanson, "Vessels of Wrath or Instruments of Wrath? Romans 9:22-2, *JTS* 32 (1981): 443-44; idem, *The Wrath of the Lamb* (London: SPK, 1957), 90-110. Hanson prefers to translate "vessels of wrath" as "instruments of wrath." He argues that Paul's point is that God creates instruments through whom he demonstrates his wrath, not that God creates vessels to be the objects of his wrath. Contra also Pelagius, *Pelagius' Commentary on St. Paul's Epistle to the Romans*, ed. and trans. Theodore De Bruyn (Oxford: Clarendon Press, 1993), 22; Phillip Melancthon, *Commentary on Romans*, ed. and trans. Fred Kramer (St. Louis: Concordia, 1992), 191-92; Dunn, *Romans*, 2:559; Roger T. Forster and V. Paul Marston, *God's Strategy in Human History* (Wheaton: Tyndale House, 1974), 80-84. Many interpret Romans 9 to refer only to the corporate salvation of nations. For examples, see H.H. Rowley, *The Biblical Doctrine of Election*, 2ⁿᵈ ed. (London: Lutterworth, 1950), 40-42; Cranfield, *Romans*, 2:492; W.W. Campbell, "The Freedom and Faithfulness of God in Relation to Israel," *JSNT* 13 (1981): 27-45; Mary Ann Getty, "Paul and the Salvation of Israel: A Perspective on Romans 9-11," *CBQ* 50 (1988): 456-69; Bruce W. Longenecker, "Different Answers to Different Issues: Israel, the Gentiles, and Salvation History in Romans 9-11," *JSNT* 35-37 (1989): 95-123; Keck, *Romans*, 238. For a summary and critique of an exclusively corporate reading of Romans 9, see Thomas R. Schreiner, "Does Romans 9 teach Individual Election unto Salvation?" in *Still Sovereign: Contemporary Perspectives on Election, Foreknowledge, and Grace*, eds. Thomas R. Schreiner and Bruce A. Ware (Grand Rapids: Baker, 2000), 89-106.

Paul,[71] and the argument of 9:6b-11:32 suggest that God creates the vessels for the purpose of destroying them.

Witherington is convinced that Paul does not speak of (as he says) "some notion of double predestination" in 9:22-23 when he comments on the "vessels of wrath" and "vessels of mercy." He argues this based on the possible middle voice of the participle κατηρτισμένα and based on the verb "to prepare beforehand" to describe the "vessels of mercy."[72] He suggests that Paul's description of the "vessels of mercy" as "prepared for glory" with a different verb from the one used to describe the vessels of wrath supports that Paul addresses the sanctification of the vessels of mercy: namely, just as Romans 8 has communicated, "God did always plan for believers to be conformed to the image of his Son, and during their Christian lives, throughout the process of being set right and being sanctified, they have been prepared for such glorious destiny."[73] He, thus, concludes that Paul alludes to sanctification in 9:23 and that sanctification has a "pre-temporal plan behind it."[74] Nevertheless, Paul's own language in the text speaks against Witherington's view. Paul begins Romans 9-11 by lamenting the lack of the salvation of fellow Jews (Rom. 9:1-5; 10:1). In addition, the purpose clause in 9:23 ("so that he would even make know the riches of his glory upon the vessels of mercy") establishes that God creates one group for eternal destruction (i.e. vessels of wrath) and another for eternal salvation (i.e. vessels of mercy),[75] for Paul's discussion of both groups is in conjunction with his discussion of God's right to extend mercy to some and to withhold it from others (Rom. 9:14-18) and in conjunction with his comments that God has the right as the creator to create from the same lump two different vessels for two different purposes (Rom. 9:19-21). In addition, Paul also contends in 9:23 that God is still righteous even though he does this, for it suggests that God does not arbitrarily create vessels of wrath for destruction without an intended purpose. Instead, he creates vessels of wrath and patiently endures them, giving them time to repent (cf. Exod. 3-15), so that he would manifest his saving mercy upon the vessels of mercy when he destroys the vessels of wrath when they refuse to repent (cf. Exod. 34:6-7, 29). Paul's point seems to be here that just as Israel praised YHWH in Exodus 15 in light of the backdrop of his destruction of Pharaoh and his army, so also vessels of honor will praise and honor God in light of the backdrop of the eternal destruction of the vessels of wrath, whom God prepared to display his glory through their destruction.[76]

---

[71]See Phil. 1:28; 3:19; 2 Thess. 2:3; 1 Tim. 6:9; cf. verbal cognate: 1 Cor. 1:18-19; 8:11; 10:9-10; 15:18; 2 Cor. 2:15; 4:3; 2 Thess. 2:10.
[72]Witherington, *Romans*, 258.
[73]Ibid.
[74]Ibid. 259.
[75]See the Nestle-Aland textual apparatus for the variant reading of Rom. 9:23.
[76]Rightly John Calvin, *Commentary on Paul's Epistle to the Romans*, ed. and trans. John Owen (Grand Rapids: Eerdmans, 1947), 369.

Divine and Human Agency

Romans 9:24-29: God's Calling of a Remnant of Jews and Gentiles to Faith

In Romans 9:24-26, Paul develops his statement in 9:23 regarding the preparation of the vessels of mercy. That the vessels of mercy and the vessels of wrath refer to the eternal destinies of individual groups of people becomes more evident with the relative pronoun ("whom") in 9:24, which (the relative pronoun) connects with vessels of mercy in 9:23.[77] In addition, the personal pronoun "us" in 9:24 refers to both the vessels of mercy in 9:23 and to the "whom" in 9:24. Both "whom" and "us" are the direct objects of the verbal statement "he called." As I argued earlier (Rom. 4:17; 8:30; 9:12), this calling creates life within those who receive it and therefore is effectual. Because of Paul's words in 9:24b-25 that God called some from amongst both Jews and Gentiles to be his people and because of his words in 9:27-29 that some Jews will be saved and would not be destroyed as Sodom and Gomorrah since God left a remnant for himself, Paul's words in 9:24 should be read as soteriological statements about the salvation of some individual Jews and Gentiles, which exegetically suggests that Paul's comments of the vessels of wrath are likewise soteriological since they pertain to the eschatological destruction of those who reject the gospel. Moreover, the important point for my thesis is that God determines the destinies of both groups, and the human agent's destruction is consequent to and the result of God's action to harden his heart. Likewise, the salvation of the vessels of honor is consequent to and the result of God's action to save them in Christ, for God called *only some* Jews and Gentiles to be saved.

Romans 9:30-11:32: Salvation *because of* Faith in Jesus as the Jewish Messiah and Condemnation *because of* Divine Hardening and Unbelief

Romans 9:30-11:32 further supports the point that human agency is consequent to and the result of divine agency in Paul's soteriology. In light of the strong predestinarian theology in 9:6-29, Paul's remarks in 9:30-11:32 may seem puzzling, for he begins the unit by emphasizing the role of the human agent in attaining salvation (Rom. 9:30-10:14), continues by discussing God's divine hardening of some Jews so that they would not believe in Jesus as the Jewish Messiah and be saved (Rom. 10:19-11:24), and he concludes by again emphasizing the role of divine agency in salvation (Rom. 11:25-32). However, a closer look at Paul's argument suggests that God's action surrounds the human agent's action to believe or disbelieve in Jesus as the Jewish Messiah.

In 9:30-10:13, Paul states that the Gentiles who did not pursue righteousness received righteousness by faith, but Israel who pursued righteousness did not pursue it because they did not pursue it by faith. As I argued in chapter 2, righteousness here refers to God's saving righteousness. Thus, Paul expresses that all Gentiles who trust in Jesus as the Jewish Messiah by faith receive God's salvation, but Jews who instead of trusting in Jesus yield to the Mosaic law do not receive God's salvation. This point is established by

---

[77]This is true only at the conceptual level in Rom. 9:23-24, for "vessel" is a neuter singular word and "whom" is a masculine plural word.

Paul's earlier argument in 1:18-3:20 that both Jews and Gentiles are guilty before God apart from faith in Jesus because God requires both groups to obey his Torah in total and not simply to possess it (=Jews) or to obey ignorantly some of its moral norms (=Gentiles). My argument is further established by Paul's previous comments in 9:6-29 regarding the salvation of some Jews and Gentiles and by his statements in 10:5-18 that Torah demands obedience instead of faith (trust in and obedience to Jesus as the Jewish Messiah). But immediately after Paul emphasizes faith in Jesus as the means of receiving God's saving righteousness and disbelief in Jesus as the reason for failure to attain it in 9:30-10:18, Paul begins to emphasize divine agency in 10:19-11:32.

In 10:19, quoting Deuteronomy 32:21, Paul expresses that God would use Gentiles to make Israel jealous and angry. In Romans 10:20, quoting Isaiah 65:1, he expresses that God would be found by Gentiles who do not seek him and who do not ask for him. In Romans 10:21, quoting LXX Isaiah 65:2, he contends that God stretches out his hands all day long to Israel, a disobedient and rebellious people, pleading with them to repent and obey him. He, then, argues that God has not forsaken every Jew, but has chosen only some Jews to be the recipients of his electing mercy unto salvation (Rom. 11:1-6) and that he has hardened other Jews so that they would not receive his soteriological promises by trusting in Jesus as the Jewish Messiah (Rom. 11:7-10). Paul contends that God has done this to some Jews so that their rejection of Jesus would result in the salvation of some Gentiles (Rom. 11:11-16), and he warns the Gentiles not to become arrogant by God's current rejection of many Jews and acceptance of many Gentiles since he will both graft the Jews into his olive tree of salvation again and since he can easily cut Gentiles off again from his olive tree of salvation (Rom. 11:17-24). Yes, Paul affirms that God has cut off some Jews from salvation because of their unbelief and that he has grafted Gentiles into salvation because of their faith (Rom. 11:20). However, he also equally affirms that the reason both groups fall into one of these two groups (unbelief or faith) is God's action, for his hardening of some Jews excludes them from salvation and his election of some Gentiles includes them in salvation (cf. Rom. 9:6-11:10).

The priority of divine agency over human agency is supported by the final section of Romans 9-11. In 11:25-32, Paul again demonstrates that divine agency surrounds human agency.[78] The "for" in 11:25 reveals a connection with 9:30-11:24. In 9:30-10:21, Paul returns to the themes of Jewish rejection of Jesus as the Jewish Messiah and of Gentile salvation. In 11:1-10, he questions God's faithfulness to Israel as a result of the nation's rejection of Jesus as its Messiah. He argues that God is faithful by demonstrating that he chose a remnant of Jews to follow him even in the days of Elijah (cf. 1 Sam. 12:22), and he argues that God's hardening of Israel is the foundational reason for the nation's unbelief. In 11:11-24, Paul promises that God has hardened

---

[78]For a summary of the various issues in Rom. 11:25-32, see Cranfield, *Romans*, 2:576-77; N.T. Wright, *The Letter to the Romans: Introduction, Commentary, and Reflections*, NIB, vol. 10 (Nashville: Abingdon, 2002), 687-95.

Divine and Human Agency

Israel to reject Jesus as the Jewish Messiah to ensure Gentile salvation and to provoke Jews to jealousy because of this. But 11:25 promises that only a partial hardening has come to Israel until the completion of the Gentiles' salvation, after which "all of Israel will be saved" when the deliver comes from Zion to forgive Jacob of his sins (Rom. 11:26-27).[79] Whatever Paul means by "all Israel," [80] he speaks of the Jews' receiving salvation when God completes his work in the Gentiles, because he cites Isaiah 59:20-21 in 11:26, a text that promises that Israel's deliverer will come from Zion to remove her sin due to God's covenant with Israel to forgive her of her sins. Consequently, Jewish salvation and Gentile salvation are consequent to and the result of God's action for them in Jesus.

Romans 11:28-32 further supports the priority of divine agency over human agency in Paul's soteriology. Paul states that the Jews are enemies of the gospel because of the Gentiles, but that they are beloved ones with respect to salvation in accordance with election because of the patriarchs (Rom. 11:28). In 11:29, he states that "God's gifts and calling are irrevocable." In 11:30-32, he expresses that just as the Gentiles were formerly disobedient to God but received God's mercy, likewise the Jews are disobedient and will receive God's mercy, "because God shut out all for disobedience so that he would give mercy to all." He concludes 11:33-36 by expressing that God's ways are incomprehensible. Thus, Romans 9-11 emphasizes that human agency is consequent to and the result of divine agency in Paul's soteriology.[81]

DIVINE AND HUMAN AGENCY IN 1-2 CORINTHIANS

The priority of divine agency over human agency is evident in the Corinthian Correspondence. The evidence that I offer from 1-2 Corinthians consists of statements that refer to God's gracious work *in* the Corinthians regarding both their salvation and sanctification.

1 Corinthians 1:4-9: God's Grace in Christ Enriched the Corinthians

The priority of divine agency over human agency first appears in 1:4-9. After Paul speaks of the Corinthians' salvation experience as something that they

---

[79]For different readings of Rom 11:26, see Longenecker, "Different Answers," 118 n. 35; C.H. Dodd, *The Epistle of Paul to the Romans*, MNTC (New York: Harper & Brothers, 1932), 182; Lloyd Gaston, "Israel's Misstep in the Eyes of Paul," in *the Romans Debate*, ed. Karl P. Donfried (Peabody: Hendrickson, 1977), 319.

[80]For different readings of "all Israel," see Cranfield, *Romans*, 2:576-77; Richard H. Bell, *Provoked to Jealousy: The Origins of the Jealousy Motif in Romans 9-11* (Tübingen: J.C.B., 1994), 140-43; Herman Ridderbos, *Paul: An Outline of His Theology* (Grand Rapids: Eerdmans, 1966), 358; Calvin, *Romans*, 437; Wright, *Romans*, 689; Moo, *Romans*, 722-24.

[81]In Romans 12-15, Paul urges the Romans to obey the gospel because of God's work of salvation in them. The command to obey the gospel follows his explanation of God's action on behalf of them in Jesus.

received from God in 1:1-2,[82] Paul continues to speak of their experience of grace as something that they *received* from God as opposed to something in which they actively participated apart from God's initial action. In 1:4, Paul thanks God for the Corinthians "because of the grace of God, which was given to [them] in Christ Jesus" (brackets mine).[83] In 1:5-7, he presents the reason for his statement in 1:4: "because you were enriched in him in every word and in all knowledge, just as the testimony of Christ was confirmed in you, so that as a result you do not lack in any spiritual gift while you await the revelation of our Lord Jesus Christ." Human agency is certainly present in Paul's words in 1:4-7 in that he states that the Corinthians received God's grace (1 Cor. 1:4), were enriched by God with knowledge and insight (1 Cor. 1:6), received the mystery of Christ (1 Cor. 1:6), and they do not lack any spiritual gift as they await Jesus' return (1 Cor. 1:7). However, Paul presents human agency as a by-product of God's action in Christ both in and on behalf of the Corinthians, for Paul speaks of the Corinthians' participation in God's grace as something they experienced *only after* God worked both in and on behalf of them in Christ. Paul states that God's grace "was given" to them in Christ (1 Cor. 1:4), that they "were enriched" in every word and insight (1 Cor. 1:5), and that the testimony of Christ "was confirmed" in them (1 Cor. 1:6). The result of God's action on behalf of the Corinthians is that they do not lack any spiritual gift (1 Cor. 1:6).

The priority of divine agency over human agency is supported in Paul's subsequent words in 1:8-9. He states that Jesus will "confirm you until the end as blameless in the day of our Lord Jesus Christ" (1 Cor. 1:8). That is, Jesus will prove the Corinthians to be faithful until Jesus returns. Their perseverance and ultimate salvation is not predicated upon their own ability to be blameless until the end but upon God's ability through Christ to prove them to be faithful to the end. In 1:9, Paul elaborates this point by affirming that "God is faithful" and that this God called the Corinthians "into fellowship with his Son, Jesus Christ, our Lord." The Corinthians' confirmation at the revelation of Christ is grounded in God's faithful and effectual work through them in Christ, and their gifts and final salvation are byproducts of God's action on behalf of them.

1 Corinthians 1:18-31: God's Wisdom Versus Man's Wisdom
The priority of divine agency in Paul's soteriology continues in the argument of 1 Corinthians 1:18-31. Paul speaks of those who are perishing (ἀπολλυμένοις) and of those who are being saved (σῳζομένοις) with verbs that could be construed as passive voices. He, then, cites Isaiah 29:14 to emphasize God's action of destroying the wisdom of the wise and rejecting the intelligence of the intelligent (1 Cor. 1:19). Paul continues by rhetorically asking where are the

---

[82]Paul calls the Corinthians "sanctified ones in Christ Jesus" (1 Cor. 1:2), "called saints" (1 Cor. 1:2), "those who are called" (1 Cor. 1:2), and he states that grace and truth come from God the Father and the Lord Jesus Christ (1 Cor. 1:3).

[83]See also 1 Cor. 3:10 where he speaks of receiving God's grace.

Divine and Human Agency

truly wise ones of the world in comparison with God's wisdom (1 Cor. 1:20a), and he again focuses on God's action by stating that "God made foolish the wisdom of the world" (1 Cor. 1:20b). The world does not know God's wisdom, but "God was very pleased to save those who believe through the foolishness of preaching" (1 Cor. 1:21).

Indeed, it is important for Paul's soteriology in this text to acknowledge the human agent's role in experiencing God's salvation in Jesus. After all, Paul states that God saves "those who believe" (1 Cor. 1:21). But the belief of the human action is consequent to and the result of both God's initial action and his desire to provide salvation through the proclamation of the gospel. According to Paul, God's action in the gospel is how he reveals his power after the cross and resurrection via salvation and judgment, and God's action in the gospel is how he destroys the wisdom of the wise of this world. Paul's remarks in 1:22-31 supports the preceding interpretation.

In 1:22-23, Paul expresses that both Jews and Greeks (human agents) reject the gospel and stumble over it for different reasons. But those Jews and Greeks who are called receive the proclamation of the gospel as the means by which they are saved (1 Cor. 1:24). Their acceptance of the gospel reveals God's wisdom and human's folly (1 Cor. 1:25). Paul continues by urging the Corinthians to remember their calling, because not many wise, powerful, or noble are called (1 Cor. 1:26), but that "God chose the foolish things of the world so that he would put to shame the strong things, and God chose the inferior things of the world and the things treated with contempt, the things which are nothing, so that he would abolish the things which are" (1 Cor. 1:27-28). God chose to do this "so that no one would boast in his presence" (1 Cor. 1:29). Paul concludes by stating that the Corinthians are in Christ Jesus "because of [God] (1 Cor. 1:30),[84] so that they have no reason to boast in themselves before God (1 Cor. 1:30). God's work in the Corinthians provides the reason that they should pursue unity in the church throughout the rest of the letter (cf. 1 Cor. 1:4-14:40).

1 Corinthians 2:1-16: A Revelation of God's Power through the Spirit

Paul continues by reminding the Corinthians that he preached the gospel to them by means of God's power and not in his own strength so that their faith would "not be in the wisdom of men but in the power of God" (1 Cor. 2:1-5). At first, human agency may appear to have priority over divine agency in this section since Paul mentions the Corinthians' faith. However, upon a closer look, one should see that Paul's statement about human agency is actually grounded in more fundamental statements about divine agency. For example, Paul states that he did not proclaim the gospel to the Corinthians by means of human wisdom, but he proclaimed Jesus Christ crucified "by means of the demonstration of the Spirit and power" (1 Cor. 2:1-4, esp. 2:4). He further

---

[84] I take the ἐξ in ἐξ αὐτοῦ in a causal sense. The emphasis on divine agency in the context supports this reading.

establishes this point when he states that the Corinthians' faith did not come by means of "man's wisdom" but by means of "God's power" (1 Cor. 2:5).

The priority of divine agency over human agency in Paul's soteriology is developed further in 2:6-16. Paul states that he speaks the wisdom of God and not the wisdom of the rulers in the current age, for the latter fades away (1 Cor. 2:6). God's wisdom was predestined by God before the ages "for our glory" (1 Cor. 2:7), and no ruler in the current age knows this glory (1 Cor. 2:8). He proclaims that no one can grasp what "God has prepared for those who love him" (1 Cor. 2:9). In 2:9, Paul echoes Isaiah 64:4, a text that speaks of God's great acts of salvation and mercy for his people, and he applies this verse to those who have faith in Jesus. Thus, in light of this echo and in light of the context of salvation in 1 Corinthians 1-2, in 1 Corinthians 2:9, Paul specifically states that "God prepared" salvation for those who love him. In 1 Corinthians 2:10, he explains this salvation as God's revelation to them by the Spirit, for only the Spirit knows the mind of God (1 Cor. 2:11). He further expresses that the Corinthians received the Spirit from God so that they would know the things of God, which were given to them (1 Cor. 2:12-13). He concludes that fleshly (i.e. unbelieving) man does not know the things of the Spirit (1 Cor. 2:14-15), but only those who have the mind of Christ know the mind of the Lord.[85]

2 Corinthians 1:3-22: God's Grace, Suffering for Salvation, and the Seal of the Spirit

In 2 Corinthians, Paul expresses the priority of divine agency over human agency in his soteriology. The first place where this develops is in 1:3-22. In 1:3-4, Paul praises God for his comfort in affliction, and he suggests that God comforts them so that they would comfort others who suffer with the same comfort that they received from God. In 1:5, Paul states that he and other Christians share in the sufferings of Christ and they experience comfort through Christ. In 1:6, he connects suffering and comfort with salvation by expressing that he and his colleagues suffer for the Corinthians' comfort and salvation. Paul and his colleagues received mercy and comfort from God, for Paul states that God is the Father of mercies and the God of all comfort and he asserts that God comforts them in every affliction so that they would be able to comfort other Christians who suffer (2 Cor. 1:3-4). Paul also expresses that the suffering comes from God by referring to his sufferings as the "afflictions of Christ" (2

---

[85] Other statements throughout 1 Corinthians support that human agency is consequent to and the result of divine agency. Paul states that the Corinthians are God's temple and that his Spirit dwells in them (1 Cor. 3:16). He states that he and the other apostles were stewards of Christ and of God's mysteries (1 Cor. 4:1). He expresses that everything that the Corinthians had they received from the Lord (1 Cor. 4:7). He states that the Corinthians were washed, sanctified, and justified in the name of the Lord and by the Spirit of God (1 Cor. 6:11). After the preceding statements, Paul urges the Corinthians to flee sexual immorality (1 Cor. 6:18-19) and gives them other moral exhortations (cf. 1 Cor. 7:1-16:20).

Cor. 1:4). In addition, he says that he suffers for their salvation. Thus, God's action through suffering serves as a means by which he imparts salvation to the Corinthians. Paul envisages this point by affirming that although he received the sentence of death in Asia, he trusted in God who raises the dead and that he delivered him from so great an affliction (2 Cor. 1:8-10).

The priority of divine agency in Paul's soteriology continues in 1:12-22. In order to explain his change of travel plans, Paul states that he acted in the world with godly sincerity by God's grace (2 Cor. 1:12). He continues that he and his colleagues did not speak ambivalently about the promises of God in Jesus, but they proclaimed all of the promises of God in Jesus to be yes (2 Cor. 1:15-20). He, then, acknowledges that "God is the one who established us with you in Christ and who anointed us and the one who sealed us and who gave us the down payment of the Spirit in our hearts" (2 Cor. 1:21-22). These latter statements pertain to God's establishment of the Corinthians with regard to salvation since Paul sates that he established them "in Christ" (2 Cor. 1:21) and since he states that God sealed them with the Spirit (2 Cor. 1:22).[86] The emphasis in both of these verses is God's action in and for the Corinthians.

2 Corinthians 2:12-17: God's Triumphant Victory in Christ

In 2 Corinthians 2:12-17, the priority of divine agency in Paul's soteriology is apparent. In 2:12-13, Paul begins by explaining that an open door "for the gospel" was presented to him in Troas. However, he refused to go through it since he had not yet received a word from Titus regarding the Corinthians' response to one of his earlier letters (2 Cor. 2:12-13). In essence, he refused to preach the gospel in Troas due to his despair about the Corinthians' spiritual condition. Thus, he left Troas and went to Macedonia to find Titus. In 2:14, Paul praises God that in spite of his failure to proclaim the gospel faithfully in Troas, God "always conquers us in Christ and manifests the fragrance of his knowledge through us in every place." The imagery in this statement reflects the Greco-Roman context in which Paul lived and wrote his letters. Paul presents God as the sovereign victor who has conquered a people through Christ. Paul suggests that he and all Christians have been conquered by God through Christ, and God puts the conquered on public display in a triumphant march so that everyone can see both the conqueror and the conquered. Paul, of course, is speaking of the sufficiency of God's work of salvation on behalf of Christians, for he states that God conquered "us in/by means of Christ" (2 Cor. 2:14) and he states that "we are an aroma of Christ to God amongst those who are being saved and amongst those who are perishing" (2 Cor. 2:15). To one group, Paul and his colleagues were an aroma unto death and to another group an aroma unto life (2 Cor. 2:16). Paul's emphasis throughout these verses is God's action for him through Christ in spite of his unwillingness to proclaim the gospel in Troas when he circumvented an open door.

---

[86]Paul uses the language of being sealed with the Spirit in other explicit soteriological texts (cf. Rom. 5:1-11, esp. 5:5; Eph. 1:3-14; esp. 1:13-14; 4:30).

2 Corinthians 3:1-18: God's Spirit and the New Covenant

As a means of defending his apostolic ministry, Paul discusses the superiority of the new covenant over the old covenant. As he does this, he highlights the priority of divine agency over human agency in his soteriology. Paul contends that unlike the false apostles, he and his missionary colleagues did not need letters of commendation to or from the Corinthians (2 Cor. 3:1-2), for they are their letters of commendation (2 Cor. 3:2). He continues that the Corinthians reveal that they are a letter of Christ ministered to by Paul and his colleagues and "written not with ink but by the Spirit of the living God, not on stone tablets but on fleshly-heart tablets" (2 Cor. 3:3). This statement especially demonstrates the priority of divine agency over human agency, for Paul states that the Corinthians were the objects of God's work of the Spirit in their hearts. This work is forecast in Jeremiah 31:31-33 and Ezekiel 36-37 where YHWH explicitly foretold the day when he would write his law on the hearts of his people, sprinkle them with clean water, and initiate a new covenant. Paul states in 2 Corinthians 3:1-18 that such a new covenant has been fulfilled in the Corinthians by God through Christ. This point is supported in 3:4 when Paul states that "we have such confidence through Christ in God" and in 3:5 when he states that "we are not sufficient from ourselves but our sufficiency is from God." In 3:6, Paul continues his emphasis on divine agency when he states that God "strengthened us to be ministers of a new covenant, not [a covenant of the] letter but [a covenant of the] Spirit, for the letter kills but the Spirit gives life" (brackets mine). The ministry of Moses brought death and was veiled glory, but the ministry of the Spirit brings life (2 Cor. 3:7-13), for through Christ (Paul argues) the veiled glory is taken away when one turns to the Lord since the Lord is the Spirit and grants liberty and transformation to all who behold his glory (2 Cor. 3:14-18).[87]

2 Corinthians 4:1-5:21: The Ministry of the Gospel in Clay Pots

Paul continues the argument from 2 Corinthians 3 regarding the ministry of the new covenant in 2 Corinthians 4:1-5:21. In the latter unit, Paul focuses on God's bestowment of this ministry to him and his colleagues and upon God's action of reconciling sinners to himself through this new covenant ministry. With these emphases, Paul highlights the priority of divine agency over human agency in his soteriology.

In 4:1, Paul discloses that he received this ministry of the new covenant because he received mercy. In 4:2, he follows this statement by noting that he renounces the hidden things of shame. But this action is achievable *only after* God's action in Christ because Paul received this ministry due to God's mercy and this mercy was God's action of shining in Paul's heart to give the light of the knowledge of the glory of God in the face of Jesus Christ (2 Cor. 4:4-6, esp. 4:6). God gave the treasure of the gospel to clay pots (i.e. to Paul

---

[87]For a detailed exegesis of 2 Corinthians 3, see Scott J. Hafemann, *Paul, Moses, and the History of Israel: The Letter/Spirit Contrast and the Argument from Scripture in 2 Corinthians 3* (Carlisle, UK: Paternoster, 2005).

Divine and Human Agency 177

and his companions) so that he would demonstrate his power (2 Cor. 4:7). Paul and his companions suffered by carrying in their bodies the death of Jesus (2 Cor. 4:8-10), but God worked in them so that they would manifest the life of Jesus and so that life would be manifest in the Corinthians through the resurrection power of God who raised Jesus from the dead (2 Cor. 4:11-15). Their suffering for Christ prepares in them an eternal weight of glory as they look to the eternal treasures of salvation that are not currently seen (2 Cor. 4:16-18), for Paul and his companions groaned in their earthly bodies (2 Cor. 5:1-3), but God clothed them with an immortal hope and gave them the Spirit as the guarantee of this hope (2 Cor. 5:4-5). God's work on behalf of his people enables Paul to rejoice in his present body as he looks by faith to his future hope when he would stand before the judgment seat of Christ (2 Cor. 5:6-10).

In 5:11-21, Paul concludes his discussion about the ministry bestowed upon him by God. In light of God's work in him and in his colleagues (2 Cor. 3:1-5:10), Paul does not commend himself (2 Cor. 5:11-13), for God's love compels them since Jesus died and rose for them (2 Cor. 5:13-15). In 5:17-18, Paul focuses on God's work of new creation in him and all believers. He asserts that God gave him and his companions a ministry of reconciliation and that he has accomplished this new creation through Christ by reconciling the world to himself by not counting the transgressions of the transgressors against them (2 Cor. 5:18-19). In 5:19b-20, he repeats again that God gave them a message of reconciliation that therefore made Paul and his companions to be ambassadors of Christ. Yes, Paul and his companions (human agents) received this ministry of reconciliation and actively participated in the proclamation of the message of reconciliation as ambassadors of Christ (2 Cor. 5:20). Nevertheless, the text still seems to emphasize that human agency was consequent to and the result of God's action in Christ to accomplish reconciliation for the transgressors, for Paul states that God refused to count their transgressions against them because of his work in Christ and God gave to Paul and others this ministry of reconciliation so that they would proclaim to others to be reconciled to God (2 Cor. 5:16-20). In 5:21, Paul clarifies how God successfully reconciled the transgressors to himself through Christ and how he overlooked their transgressions in Christ: "He made the one who knew no sin to be sin for us so that we would become the righteousness of God in him." Regardless of whether one understands Paul to be talking about God's covenantal faithfulness or the imputation of Christ's righteousness,[88] a point that should not to be missed in 5:21 is that the verse focuses on God's action in Christ to deal with the sin-problem. The result of God's action in Christ is that human agents are able to participate in God's righteousness.

---

[88]For examples of each position, see N.T. Wright, "On Becoming the Righteousness of God: 2 Corinthians 5:21," in *Pauline Theology*, ed. David M. Hay (Minneapolis: Fortress, 1993), 1:205-06; Brian J. Vickers, *Jesus' Blood and Righteousness* (Wheaton: Crossway, 2006), 182-83.

DIVINE AND HUMAN AGENCY IN GALATIANS

The priority of divine agency over human agency in Paul's soteriology appears in Galatians. Two themes in particular support this: (1) Paul's discussion of the origin of his apostolic calling and ministry and (2) his discussion of table-fellowship, justification by faith, and sonship.

Galatians 1:1 and 1:11-2:10: The Origin of Paul's Apostolic Calling and Ministry

The Judaizers' assault on the validity of the Galatian Christians' salvation forced Paul to defend the integrity of his gospel. To do this, however, Paul first had to defend his apostolic calling and ministry since the integrity of his gospel cannot be separated from the validity of his apostleship (cf. Acts 9:3-22; Gal. 1:15). Paul begins the letter by affirming that his apostleship came "not from men or through the agency of man, but through Jesus Christ and God the Father who raised him from the dead" (Gal. 1:1). In this one verse, Paul forthrightly announces that God and Jesus were the sole initiators of his apostolic call and that no human agent added anything to it. He continues this line of argumentation in 1:11-2:10.

In Galatians 1:11-12, he states that the gospel that he preached was not "in accordance with man" and that he neither received it nor was taught it "from man," but "through Jesus Christ." He contends that he was advancing in Judaism beyond his contemporaries (Gal. 2:13-14), but that God separated him from his mother's womb and called him through his grace to reveal his son in him, so that he would preach Jesus amongst the Gentiles (Gal. 2:15). Paul speaks of his calling/conversion similarly as Jeremiah when he states that he was separated from his mother's womb by God to preach the gospel (cf. Jer. 1:5), which at least means that God's plan for Paul was prepared before his birth. In addition, Paul explicitly uses language in 1:15 that expresses that human agency is consequent to and the result of divine agency. For example, he says that God "separated me from my mother's womb," that he "called me through his grace," and that he "revealed his son in me" with the result that "I would preach the gospel amongst the Gentiles."

In 1:17-2:10, he argues that no human agent had a hand in his apostolic call. He did not immediately travel to Jerusalem to receive an apostolic affirmation from the other apostles (Gal. 1:17). Instead, he preached the gospel in Arabia and Damascus and went to Jerusalem about 14 years after his conversion and apostolic calling to showcase that his gospel was the same as the gospel of the apostolic pillars, so that he would not be accused of preaching a gospel that competes with them (i.e. as running in vain) (Gal. 1:17-2:2). Once he arrived at Jerusalem nearly 14 years after his conversion and calling, the apostolic pillars of the church did not offer anything to his ministry. To the contrary, they only asked him to remember the poor, which he was already eager to do (Gal. 2:3-10). Thus, Paul's conversion and apostolic calling to preach the gospel suggest that human agency is consequent to and the result of divine agency in Paul's soteriology.

Galatians 2:11-4:7: Table-fellowship, Justification by Faith, and Sonship

In Galatians 2:11-4:7, Paul's argument focuses specifically on table-fellowship, justification by faith, and sonship. In 2:11-14, Paul discusses his rebuke of Peter at Antioch due to Peter's unwillingness to eat with Gentile Christians when some Jews came down from Jerusalem (Gal. 2:11-12). Paul remarks that Peter's actions were hypocritical and that they compelled other Christians likewise to walk in an inappropriate manner with regard to the gospel (Gal. 2:13). But Paul withstood Peter to his face (Gal. 2:14).[89] Because of controversies over table-fellowship, Paul then launches into a discussion in Gal 2:15-21 about justification by faith.

Without trying to discuss or (less likely) to solve the many exegetical difficulties in this unit, I simply note the elements of the text that are pertinent to my thesis regarding the priority of divine agency over human agency. In 2:16, Paul states that "a man is not justified by works of law, but through faith in Christ, and we believed in Christ so that we would be justified by faith." This verse communicates the very point for which I have been arguing: divine agency surrounds human agency. In 2:16b, Paul embeds a statement about human agency ("we believed in Christ") within two statements about divine agency in 2:16a,c ("a man is not justified by works" and "so that we would be justified. . ."), follows these statements with another statement about human agency in 2:16d ". . .by faith in Christ and not by works of law"), and he concludes 2:16e with another statement that emphasizes divine agency ("because by works of law not any flesh will be justified"). In 2:17-21, Paul discusses God's action through Christ. In 2:17, Paul speaks of "seeking to be justified in Christ" and of being found as a sinner. In 2:18-19, he states that "I" did not rebuild what "I" destroyed and that if "I" had done so that "I" would make "myself" to be a transgressor, for "I" died to the law so that "I" would live to God, and "I" was crucified with Christ. Such statements seem to counter my premise about divine agency. However, Paul quickly follows these comments by emphasizing the priority of divine agency: "But I no longer live, but Christ lives in me, and what I live now in the flesh I live by faith in the son of God who loved me and gave himself for me" (Gal. 2:20). Paul affirms that he died to the law by placing faith in Christ, but his death to Torah was due to God's action on behalf of him in Christ. That is, Christ lived "in" Paul, and God gave Christ to die "for" Paul. In 2:21, he attributes his new status in Christ to the "grace of God" and to Jesus' death when he states that he will not nullify God's grace in Christ since this would render Jesus' death for him as needless.

In 3:1-4:7, Paul continues his discussion of salvation by emphasizing sonship. He reminds the Galatians that they received the Spirit by faith and not by works (Gal. 3:1-5), just as Abraham believed God and God counted his belief as righteousness (Gal. 3:6). In 3:7, Paul directly addresses the issue of sonship. He states that "those from faith are sons of Abraham" (Gal. 3:7), but

---

[89]For good reasons, Gal. 2:11-14 is a central text for Paul's theology of justification. For examples, see the essays in James D.G. Dunn, *The New Perspective on Paul* (Grand Rapids: Eerdmans, 2008) and recent critical commentaries.

he also states in 3:8 that the scripture foresaw that "God justifies the Gentiles by faith" and that he told Abraham that "all the nations will be blessed in you." As I have suggested throughout this chapter, faith is fundamental to Paul's soteriology, but Paul states here that "God justifies by faith" not that faith justifies. Therefore, those whom God justifies through faith are blessed with the faithful Abraham (Gal. 3:8).

In 3:10-14, Paul continues to discuss the priority of divine agency over human agency. In 3:10, he states that those from works of the law are cursed because the law must be obeyed. Thus, he emphasizes human agency by stating the human agent's inability to meet the demands of Torah to receive its promise. In 3:11, he emphasizes divine agency when he states that "no one is justified by the law by God. . ." The law is not from faith, but must be obeyed (Gal. 3:12). "Christ," however, "redeemed us from the curse of the law in that he became a curse on behalf of us, because it has been written: everyone who is hanged upon a tree is cursed" (Gal. 3:13).

In 3:13, Paul pits the divine agent's ability to redeem those under the law against the human agent's inability to meet the demands of the divine agent's Torah. The divine agent's action in Christ on behalf of the human agent results in redemption, which in turn imparts the Abrahamic blessing and the Spirit to the Gentiles by means of God's action in Christ. God's action and Abrahamic sonship do not come via Torah or by human action (Gal. 3:15-20), but through God's action in Christ by faith (Gal. 3:21-4:7). Paul reiterates the point of 3:13-14 in 4:4-5 when he states that "God sent forth his son. . . so that he would redeem those under the law so that we would receive the adoption as sons" and in Gal 4:6 when he states that "God sent forth the Spirit of his son into our hearts. . ." Therefore, God's action in Christ on behalf of and in the human agent grants him sonship (Gal. 3:7). This sonship is not hypothetical, but those for whom Jesus died actually receive God's Spirit and those who receive God's Spirit by faith actually experience this new status in Christ because of God's action on behalf of them, and the human agent's response in faith is consequent to God's action for him in Christ.

DIVINE AND HUMAN AGENCY IN EPHESIANS
Paul largely discusses ecclesiological life in Ephesians.[90] In multiple places, Paul emphasizes the priority of divine agency over human agency in his experience of salvation.

---

[90] As I asserted in chapter 2, I am well aware that many scholars continue to reject Pauline authorship of the so-called Prison and Pastoral Epistles. Since these letters bear his name and contain many of the same concepts that appear in the un-contested Pauline epistles, they warrant the same intense investigation as the former letters with respect to my thesis. Regardless of whether Paul wrote these letters or not, they at least reflect a Pauline circle and Pauline theology due to their overlap with themes in the uncontested Pauline letters (e.g. predestination and Jew-Gentile inclusion within the church). For a discussion of the authorship of the contested letters of Paul, see critical commentaries.

Ephesians 1:3-14: God's Spiritual Blessings for Believers in Christ

In Ephesians 1:3-14, Paul praises God with one long Greek sentence for the spiritual blessings that he has bestowed upon all Christians in Christ. Throughout his doxology, the priority of divine agency over human agency with regard to soteriology strongly emerges. In 1:3, Paul begins the sentence by praising "the God and Father of our Lord Jesus Christ, who blessed us with every spiritual blessing in the heavenly places in Christ." That Paul is speaking of the blessings that only believers receive is certain due to the phrases "our Lord Jesus Christ" and "in Christ." That is, these blessings are not universal privileges that God bestows upon all people, but he only grants them to those in Christ. In 1:4-14, he lists some of those spiritual blessings with which God has blessed believers.

In 1:4, Paul states that "God chose us in him before the foundation of the world so that we would be holy and blameless in his presence." The "us" whom God chose in 1:4 is the same group as the "us" whom God blessed with every spiritual blessing in Christ in 1:3, for Paul begins to discuss in 1:4-14 the spiritual blessings that God gave in Christ to the "us" in 1:3. One such blessing is God's election of those who believe to be saved "before the foundation of the world." God's election of the "us" is based exclusively on God's prerogative and not on foreseen effort or faith, for Paul states that "God chose us" without even mentioning the concept of foreknowledge and without mentioning the human agent's action to believe. Instead, Paul simply suggests that the human agent is the object of the divine agent's action in Christ. Another important element of Paul's statement in 1:4 is that the purpose of God's choice was a holy lifestyle ("so that we would be holy and blameless"). There is nothing hypothetical or universal about this statement. Everyone whom God chose to be in Christ will be holy, and the only ones who can currently claim a holy status in the presence of God are those who are in Christ (cf. Eph. 1:3-5). In 1:5, Paul assumes conversion since (in his view) holiness is something that flows from God's work of regeneration (cf. Rom. 8:28-30).

God's action in Christ is further emphasized in 1:5 when Paul states "and he predestined us in love unto adoption through Jesus Christ in him according to the good pleasure of his will." God's choice (i.e. election) and predestination are parallel soteriological concepts in Paul, for he speaks of predestination without speaking of election and vice versa (cf. Rom. 8:28-30; Rom. 9:6-29). As I argued earlier, when the concepts refer to salvation, election and predestination basically mean that God determined/made a choice in advance regarding the eternal, soteriological destinies of individuals (cf. Rom. 9:6-29). The latter points seem to be the case in 1:3-4 since Paul speaks of the soteriological benefits bestowed upon those in Christ by God's divine action. In 1:5, Paul is more specific, however, regarding conversion than in 1:4, for he states in the former that God "predestined us unto adoption." Adoption in Paul means that one has been included into the family of God and counted as a rightful son and heir of God's inheritance, which God makes possible for those in Christ (cf. Rom. 8:12-17; Gal. 3:1-4:7). The reason God predestines "us" in love is simple: "because of the good pleasure of his will" (Eph. 1:5). In other words, God's action to choose and predestined some to be in Christ flowed from the good pleasure of his will.

In 1:6, Paul states that he predestined "us for the praise of the glory of his grace" and that God "bestowed [this grace] upon us in the beloved one" (brackets mine). God's choice to predestine some to be saved results in the praise of "his" glorious grace in Christ. In 1:7, he continues that in Christ "we have redemption through his blood, the forgiveness of transgressions according to the riches of his grace." As he does elsewhere, God attributes the soteriological benefits bestowed upon Christians as the result of God's divine action, and he suggests that God applied these benefits to human agents via Jesus' blood. Thus, Jesus' blood actually accomplished soteriological benefits for those whom God chose to be in Christ.

The argument thus far in Ephesians 1 supports this point, for the entire section has focused on Paul's praise of God for bestowing upon believers every spiritual blessing in the heavenly places in Christ. Paul explicitly states in 1:7 what he has simply glossed with his "in Christ" and "through Christ" language in 1:3-6: namely, that Jesus' blood was the means by which God has accomplished these spiritual blessings for those whom he chose in Christ. In 1:8, he states that God increased grace "in us" in much wisdom and insight. In 1:9-10, he states that God "made known to us the mystery of his will, which he purposed in him" in the fullness of time in order to sum up all things in Christ. In 1:11, Paul proclaims that in Christ "we were given a portion and we were predestined according to the purpose of the one who works all things after the counsel of his will so that we would be to the praise of his glory the first ones who hoped in Christ." Since Paul has already stated in 1:4-5 that God chose and predestined "us" in Christ and since 1:12 states that predestination was so that the "we" would hope in Christ, God then gives the portion to those whom he predestines in Christ in 1:11.

In 1:13-14, Paul now speaks of the role of human agency. He states that in Christ "you heard the word of truth, the gospel of your salvation, in whom also you believed and you were sealed by the Holy Spirit of promise, who is the down payment of our inheritance, resulting in redemption of the possession for the praise of his glory." Human agency is present in 1:13a when Paul speaks of the Ephesians hearing the word and believing it. However, multiple statements about divine agency precede his statement in 1:13a about human agency (e.g. election, predestination), and multiple statements follow in 1:13b-14 Paul's comments about human agency in 1:13. For example, Paul states that the Ephesians "were sealed" with the Holy Spirit (Eph. 1:13), that the Spirit is "the down payment of our inheritance" (Eph. 1:14), and that the Ephesians were redeemed for God's glory (Eph. 1:14). Consequently, human agency (as important as it is) is consequent to and the result of divine agency in Ephesians 1:3-14.

Ephesians 1:15-23: Paul's Prayer for God to work *in* the Ephesians
In Ephesians 1:15-23, Paul prays for the Ephesians based on God's work of salvation in them in Christ. Within this prayer, he emphasizes divine agency.

He acknowledges that both God's work in the Ephesians and their faith motivate him to pray for them (Eph. 1:15-16). But the content of Paul's prayer underlies divine agency. He prays that God would give to the Ephesians a spirit of wisdom and revelation in knowledge (Eph. 1:18), that he would enlighten the eyes of their hearts so that they would know "the hope of his calling, the riches of his glorious inheritance in the saints, and the surpassing greatness of his power in us who believe in accordance with the working of his strength" (Eph. 1:18-19), which is the same power that God worked in Christ to raise him from the dead and seat him at his right hand in heaven above everything (Eph. 1:20-23).[91]

Ephesians 2:1-11: Saved *by* Grace *through* Faith
Paul's discussion of salvation by grace through faith and God's reconciliation of Jews and Gentiles in Christ disclose the priority of divine agency over human agency in his soteriology in Ephesians 2. Paul expresses that the Ephesians were dead in trespasses and sins and that they lived disobediently in those sins prior to their faith in Christ when they served the devil (Eph. 2:1-3). As a result, they were children of God's wrath (Eph. 2:4). Yet, Paul's argument dramatically changes in 2:4-10 with the words "but God" (Eph. 2:4).

Prior to 2:4, the Ephesians were dead in their sins and heading toward God's judgment. However, 2:4 communicates that God acted on behalf of the Ephesians because of his mercy and "because of his great love with which he loved us." The "us" is the same group whom God chose and sealed in Christ in 1:3-14, for there is no textual indicator that Paul now speaks of a different group. The "great love" to which Paul refers in 2:4 refers to that special love that God displays upon those whom he has chosen in Christ. This point is supported by the fact that there is no reason inherent to the individuals mentioned in this text why God would have great love for them, for Paul describes this group as dead in transgressions and sins and destined for God's judgment in 2:1-3. Instead, God chose to display great love toward these whom he chose in Christ for no reason other than his "good pleasure" mentioned in 1:5, 11. This great love is only for God's elect whom he chooses to redeem by and in Christ. Certainly, the New Testament suggests that God loves the world (John 3:16). Still, in 2:4 Paul speaks of a love that transcends a general expression of God's love that he shows to all in that his "great love" is limited to those who are the object of his divine action in Christ.

In 2:5-6, Paul continues that "while we were dead in trespasses and sins, he made [us] alive together with Christ, by grace you are saved, and he raised us and seated us in the heavenly places in Christ Jesus" (brackets mine). Paul's focus here is God's action of saving a people in Christ who would continue to be otherwise dead in their sins. In 2:7, Paul declares that God did this so that he would demonstrate in all times the surpassing riches of his grace "upon us" in Christ. In 2:8, Paul provides a reason for God's action on behalf

---

[91]For a similar prayer, see Eph. 3:14-20.

of the Ephesians when they were dead in trespasses and sins: "for by grace you are saved through faith and this not of yourselves, [it is] the gift of God" (brackets mine). Here Paul merges divine and human agency in a singular statement when he expresses that the Ephesians were saved by grace through faith, but Paul contends here that both grace and faith are gifts from God.

Paul uses the noun χάριτι ("by grace") and the phrase διὰ πίστεως ("through faith") to explain the means by which the Ephesians experienced salvation in 2:8a. But when he asserts that their salvation did not originate with them ("this is not from you"), Paul uses the neuter demonstrative pronoun τοῦτο ("this"). This term can neither only refer to χάριτι since it is a feminine dative singular word nor only to πίστεως since it is a feminine genitive singular word, for (as scholars are well aware) Greek demonstrative pronouns agree with their antecedents in number and gender.[92] Thus, the demonstrative pronoun (τοῦτο) must refer to both grace and faith. Consequently, although faith in Christ is a central component within Paul's soteriology and a central means by which he communicates that Jews and Gentiles participate in God's work of salvation in Christ in Ephesians 1-2, he states in 2:8-9 that both grace and faith are gifts from God. One can conclude, therefore, that at least in Ephesians that an individual has faith in Jesus only because God grants it to him or her as a gift, so that divine agency extends even to the human agent's free agency to believe in Jesus as the Jewish Messiah. In 2:9-10, Paul supports this latter point by expressing that the Ephesians have no reason to boast in themselves and that God created them in Christ to walk in the good works for which he (God) prepared them. In essence, after God works in them, the human agents freely do precisely what the divine agent created them to do: namely, to live in obedience to Christ.

Ephesians 2:11-22: God's Reconciliation of Jews and Gentiles in Christ
Paul's argument in Ephesians 2:11-22 focuses on God's action of reconciling Jews and Gentiles first to himself and second to one another through Jesus' death.[93] In 2:11-12, Paul reminds the Ephesians that prior to God's work for them in Christ, they (Gentile Christians) had no access to God's promises of salvation given to Israel due to their status as Gentiles. But God brought them near by Jesus' blood (Eph. 2:13), for Jesus is their peace and he made the two groups to be one by destroying the dividing wall of Torah between them (Eph. 2:14-15). Furthermore, God through Jesus' death on the cross reconciled both groups into one body to God (Eph. 2:16). Jesus preached peace to Jews and Gentiles during his ministry with the result that Jews and Gentiles have equal access to God (Eph. 2:17-18). Therefore, because of God's work for Jews and especially Gentiles in Christ, Gentiles are no longer aliens to God's promises of salvation (Eph. 2:19). Rather, they are members of God's household and built upon the same apostolic foundation as Jewish Christians (Eph. 2:19-20). They

---

[92]For this rudimentary point, see any introduction to New Testament Greek grammar.
[93]For this precise point, see Williams, *One New Man*, 112-32.

Divine and Human Agency

are fit and joined together with Jewish Christians into a holy temple in the Lord (Eph. 2:21), and they are being built up into a dwelling place of God by the Spirit. Paul's emphasis throughout is God's action for the Ephesians in Christ.

Ephesians 3:1-13: The Grace of God and Paul's Ministry to the Gentiles

In Ephesians 3:1, Paul begins to pray for the Ephesians but stops until 3:14-19. In 3:2-13, he speaks of the ministry to the Gentiles that he received from God. Paul emphasizes divine agency over human agency. He describes this ministry as "God's grace given" to him for the Ephesians (Eph. 3:2). He states that the ministry was a mystery that God made known to him by a revelation (Eph. 3:3). He states that the mystery of the equality of Jews and Gentiles in Christ has not been made known to everyone, but has been revealed by God to God's holy apostles and prophets by God's Spirit (Eph. 3:5-6). He says that he was made a minister of this ministry in accordance with God's free grace given to him by God's power to make known the riches of God's power in Christ in accordance with God's purpose in Christ (Eph. 3:7-13).[94]

DIVINE AND HUMAN AGENCY IN PHILIPPIANS

In Paul's letter to the Philippians, the priority of divine agency over human agency emerges from his message to the Christians and Christian leaders at Philippi. My discussion of divine and human agency here focuses on three texts from Philippians: Philippians 1:6; 2:12-13, and 3:5-11.

Philippians 1:6 and 2:12-13: God's Work *in* the Philippians

Paul's words in Philippians 1:3-11 offer a prayer of thanksgiving for God's work in the Philippians. In 1:3-5, Paul informs them that he is thankful for God's work in them to participate in the gospel from the first day of their conversion to Christ. Their participation was both an initial reception of the gospel and a financial participation whereby they sacrificially gave money for the advancement of the gospel (cf. Phil. 1:6; 2:12-13; 4:15-16). Thus, Paul begins the letter with comments pertaining to human agency: namely, he thanked God for the Philippians' participation in the gospel.

In 1:6, however, Paul reveals the reason for the Philippians' participation in the gospel: "and I am confident with respect to this very thing that the one who began a good work in you will complete it until the day of Christ Jesus." On the one hand, the Philippians voluntarily and even freely chose to participate in the gospel. But, on the other hand, God worked in them to participate, and he will ensure that they will continue to participate until Jesus' return. That God's work in the Philippians pertains to both their conversion and their continual obedience to the Christian gospel seems certain from 1:7-2:30. In 1:7-11, Paul contends that the Philippians stood with him even when he stood trial in defense of the gospel and that he prays that their love for the gospel and for Christian obedience would continue until the return

---

[94]In Eph. 4:1-6:20, Paul exhorts the Ephesians to obey the gospel. The commands flow from his comments about God's action for and in them in Christ.

of Jesus for the glory of God. In 1:27, Paul commands the Philippians to live in a manner worthy of the gospel. In 2:1-11, he commands them to imitate Jesus' obedience and to show mutual and sacrificial love for one another. In 2:19-30, he offers Timothy and Epaphroditus as exemplars of living in obedience to the gospel.

Philippians 2:12-13 is particular important for my thesis in this chapter regarding divine and human agency. In 2:12, Paul commands the Philippians to live in obedience to the gospel by working out their salvation with fear and trembling. Paul speaks in no uncertain terms in 2:12: obedience to the Christian gospel is work; it takes human effort. In 2:13, Paul provides a reason for his command in 2:12 to work out salvation with fear and trembling: "for the one who is working in you both to desire and to work for his good pleasure is God." On the one hand, Paul exhorts the Philippians to obey God and to work hard in their efforts to do so. On the other hand, the reason why the command is achievable for the Philippians is because God has worked in them to obey the gospel. Consequently, because of the divine agent's work in the human agent, Paul commands the Philippians to stop grumbling and bickering with one another and to live as radiant lights in the world for the gospel of Jesus Christ (Phil. 2:14-18).

Philippians 3:5-11: Found in Christ to gain Righteousness
In Philippians 3:5-11, Paul boasts in his former status in Judaism prior to his faith in Christ. He does this to add substance to his commands to beware of the Jewish false teachers who would attempt to lead Gentile Christians away from Christ (cf. Phil. 3:1-4). He says that he was a great Jew born from the highest stock of Jewish religion (Phil. 3:1-6), but he surrendered his prior status within his Jewish community in order to gain Christ (Phil. 3:7). As elsewhere, Paul speaks of salvation as an individual choice that he made to forsake Judaism to gain Christ. He further illuminates the importance of human agency when he states that he considered his Jewish heritage and his previous status as a Jewish persecutor of the Christian church as dung, so that he would gain Christ (Phil. 3:8).

Nevertheless, in 3:9, Paul's remarks reveal the importance of divine agency in his decision to abandon Judaism and to embrace Christianity. He states that he wanted to be found in Christ, because he had no righteousness of his own from keeping Torah, but he wanted to attain God's righteousness through faith in Jesus Christ. God's righteousness here refers to his saving righteousness since Paul joins righteousness with the soteriological concepts of faith and union with Christ in 3:8-9 and since in 3:10-11 he speaks of his knowing Christ and the power of his resurrection, participating in his sufferings, being conformed to his death, and participating in the future resurrection from the dead. The priority of divine agency in this text appears in that Paul asserts that the only way that he could participate in God's saving righteousness is by means of his work through Christ by faith. Thus, Paul conflates divine and human agency in this text, but he seems to put forth the former as the foundation underneath the latter.

DIVINE AND HUMAN AGENCY IN COLOSSIANS

In his letter to the Colossians, Paul speaks of the priority of divine agency over human agency when he discusses God's work in the Colossians and in his prayer that they would continue to progress in their knowledge of and obedience to the gospel. My discussion of divine and human agency in Colossians focuses on Paul's scattered comments throughout the letter pertaining to God's work in the Colossians, their progress in the gospel, and their experience of the gospel.

Colossians 1-3: God's Work *in* the Colossians and Their Progress and Experience of the Gospel

In Colossians 1-3, Paul makes numerous statements that support the priority of divine agency over human agency in his soteriology. He prays for the Colossians to walk in a manner worthy of the gospel "so that they would be filled with the knowledge of God's will in all spiritual wisdom and understanding" and so that they would be strengthened by God's power to persevere in their faith (Col. 1:10-11). He says that God would make them able to participate in a portion of eternal life allotted for the saints (Col. 1:12). He proclaims that God delivered them from darkness (Col. 1:13), placed them in the kingdom of his son (Col. 1:13), and redeemed from and forgave them of their sins by means of King Jesus (Col. 1:14-16). He pronounces that God reconciled all things in Christ and made peace for them through the blood of Jesus on the cross (Col. 1:20). He states that his ministry to the Gentiles was given to him by God (Col. 1:25) and that God desired to make known to the saints the surpassing greatness of the mystery of salvation for the Gentiles (Col. 1:27). He declares that the Colossians received Christ Jesus as Lord (Col. 2:6) and reminds them that they were firmly established, built, and confirmed in the faith (Col. 2:7). They were fulfilled in Jesus (Col. 2:7). They were buried with him in baptism and raised through God's work in them and were given spiritual life when they were dead in transgressions because they received grace from God (Col. 2:12-13). They died and were raised with Christ (Col. 2:20; 3:1). Based on God's work in them through Christ, Paul exhorts them to obey the gospel and live responsibly as Christians in a world that rejects Jesus (Col. 2:20-4:1). Thus, the human agent participates in God's action in Christ, but the divine agent must work in and for the human agent so that he can participate in God's salvation in Christ and so that he can obey the gospel of Christ.[95]

---

[95]The primacy of divine agency in Paul's soteriology occurs elsewhere in the Pauline corpus, but the occurrences are not enough to warrant a detailed investigation since they simply reinforce the same points about divine agency as the texts analyzed above. For examples, see Rom. 12:3, 6; 15:15; 16:20; 1 Cor. 15:10; 16:23; 2 Cor. 6:1; 8:1, 9; 9:8, 14; 13:13; Gal. 6:18; Eph. 4:7, 29; Phil. 4:23; 1 Thess. 1:4; 3:11-13; 5:23-24; 2 Thess. 1:12; 2:10, 13-17; 3:3-5, 16-17; 1 Tim. 1:12, 14; 6:21; 2 Tim. 1:9; 2:1; 4:22.

Conclusion

I have argued in this chapter that in Paul's soteriology, divine agency surrounds human agency. The human agent has an important role in Paul's soteriology, but divine agency is the cause of human agency, and the latter is consequent to and the result of the former in Paul's soteriology. I have endeavored to support this thesis by arguing that Paul's soteriology has strong roots in early Jewish soteriology and that in both early Jewish traditions and in the Pauline corpus, only those who are part of the believing community receive God's soteriological benefits, for the divine agent takes the initiative and works both to accomplish salvation for the human agent and to enable the human agent to receive God's promises that result in salvation. I argued these points by an analysis of a few relevant early Jewish and Pauline texts. In chapter 4, I will consider the purpose and benefits of Jesus' death in Paul's atonement-theology.

Chapter 4

The Purpose and Benefits of Jesus' Death in Paul's Atonement-Theology

Introduction

Chapter 2 considered humanity's spiritual plight in Paul's anthropology. I argued that Paul deems the entire human condition to be under sin's power and incapable of responding to God's great act of salvation in Jesus. Chapter 3 considered divine and human agency in Paul's soteriology. I argued that Paul (similar to many of his Jewish contemporaries) deems human agency to be consequent to and the result of divine agency in his soteriology. This chapter considers the purpose and benefits of Jesus' death in Paul's atonement-theology. I argue that Paul suggests that Jesus' death both actually (not hypothetically) atoned for the sins of all Jews and Gentiles within the Christian community and actually accomplished soteriological benefits for those for whom he died, so that Jesus' death (according to Paul) is the foundational reason why all (and only those) Jews and Gentiles who place faith in him will participate in God's present and future salvation provided in and by Jesus. In addition, this chapter also argues that early Jewish traditions in both the Hebrew Bible and in other sacred texts in early Judaism shaped Paul's conception of Jesus' death, but Paul used those traditions to redefine atonement as something that God accomplished for Jews and Gentiles (i.e. all without distinction) by means of the death of Jesus and not by the sacrifice of animals or by the sacrifice of any other pious Torah-observant Jew besides Jesus.

To defend these points, because of limited space, I investigate only one text from the Hebrew Bible (=Lev. 16), which focuses on animal sacrifices of atonement, selected texts from 2 and 4 Maccabees, which focus on human sacrifices of atonement, and selected texts from the Pauline corpus, which focus on Jesus' death. It is my hope that this line of investigation will help establish the point that just as both animal and human sacrifices of atonement were *restricted* to and offered *specifically* for believing Jews (i.e. God's elect community of faith) in early Jewish religion and not for Gentiles (i.e. the non-elect and unbelieving community) to accomplish soteriological benefits for them, so also Jesus' death in Paul's atonement-theology is *restricted* to and *specifically* for those who identify with the Christian community, and it accomplished soteriological benefits for them. However, whereas atonement in early Judaism was only for Jews and those who converted to Judaism (even

Gentile converts), Paul argues that Jesus' death atoned for the sins of *all* Jews and Gentiles who possess faith in Christ and who unite themselves to the Christian community.

The Purpose of Animal Sacrifices of Atonement in the Hebrew Bible

My investigation of animal sacrifices of atonement in the Hebrew Bible focuses only on Yom Kippur in Leviticus 16. This text is a good representation of the purpose of animal sacrifices of atonement in the Hebrew Bible since YHWH required all Israelites to celebrate Yom Kippur once a fear in spite of the fact that they regularly offered other sacrifices of atonement throughout the year (cf. Lev. 1-5).

Leviticus 16: Yom Kippur
As YHWH prescribed in Leviticus 16,[1] the priests atoned for all of their personal transgressions, the transgressions of the people, and the impurities of the holy place because of the impurities of the people (Lev. 16:3-28). He commanded Aaron to offer specific animals as atonement for sin, so that the people would be purified and cleansed (Lev. 16:3-34).[2] After YHWH tells Moses how Aaron should perform the Day of Atonement, he asserts that this day should be celebrated every year for the cleansing of sin (Lev. 16:29-30). This cleansing through the offering of blood symbolized God's forgiveness (Lev. 16:29-30).[3]

---

[1]Various source critical complexities exist in Leviticus 16 (e.g. authorship, etc.). For source critical discussion, see Karl Elliger, *Leviticus* (Tübingen: Mohr Siebeck, 1966), 202-10; Martin Noth, *Leviticus* (Philadelphia: Westminster, 1965), 118.
[2]See John E. Hartley, *Leviticus*, WBC 3 (Dallas: Word, 1992), 241. Paul House (*Old Testament Theology* [Downers Grove, IL: InterVarsity Press, 1998], 137) asserts that atonement in Leviticus 16 provided expiation for all sin except blasphemy against God.
[3]These sacrifices were not efficacious in and of themselves. The author of Hebrews in his post-cross and post-resurrection interpretation of the OT cult emphatically states that OT sacrifices neither provided forgiveness of nor atonement for sin (Heb. 10:1-11). YHWH did not receive Israel's sacrificial offerings unless they offered them with a pure heart (cf. Psalm 51). For a connection between Israel's sacrifices and repentance, see Jacob Milgrom, *Cult and Conscience: The Asham and the Priestly Doctrine of Repentance* (Leiden: Brill, 1976). Some critical scholars have, therefore, argued that the sacrificial system was not a means by which God would allow Israel to remain in a covenantal relationship with him and that certain Old Testament texts that speak of God rejecting Israel's sacrifices contradict statements in the Pentateuch (e.g., Amos 5:21-22; Hos. 6:6; Isa. 1:10-17; Mic. 6:6-8; Jer. 7:21-23). Cf. H.H. Rowley, "The Unity of the Old Testament," *BJRL* 29 (1946): 5-7; W.O.E. Oesterly, *The Psalms: Translated with Text-Critical and Exegetical Notes* (London: SPK, 1939), 1:274. Although it is true that some Old Testament texts speak rather negatively about the sacrificial system, the fundamental reason that YHWH rejects Israel's sacrifices in those texts was because of the nation's unrepentant heart (1 Sam. 15:22-23; Ps. 51; Isa. 1:10-17). Bruce K. Waltke

Some scholars question whether bloody sacrifice actually satisfied God's wrath in the biblical tradition.[4] Nevertheless, the evidence in Leviticus 16 answers the question in the affirmative. Leviticus 16 begins by stating how one should offer sacrifices before YHWH. He commands Moses to warn Aaron that he should not enter the holy place haphazardly, lest he should die, for YHWH himself would appear in the holy place above the mercy seat (Lev. 16:1-4). Leviticus states that YHWH commands Moses to speak to Aaron "after the death of the two sons of Aaron, when they brought strange fire in the presence of the Lord, and they died" (Lev. 16:1-2). The sons of Aaron died, because they offered an unauthorized sacrifice before YHWH (Lev. 10:2). Immediately after Aaron's sons offered this sacrifice, YHWH consumed them with fire. The fire represents YHWH's judgment and wrath that he would dispense to all who disobeyed his sacrificial stipulations (Lev. 16). YHWH's response to the sons of Aaron contrasts with his response to Aaron and Moses after they offered their sacrifices to YHWH exactly as he had prescribed (Lev. 9:1-24; cf. Lev. 1:1-13). Instead of revealing his wrath by consuming Moses and Aaron with fire, YHWH revealed his glory and consumed their sacrifices (Lev. 9:23-24). Leviticus 16:1, therefore, suggests that YHWH would display his wrath and judgment against disobedience. Aaron's obedience to YHWH spared him and the nation from being the objects of his wrath.[5] The important point not to be missed in Leviticus 16 for my thesis is that YHWH required a bloody sacrifice of animals to be offered for the sins of others; these bloody sacrifices were offered only for those within the believing community of faith known as Israel, and these sacrifices (when offered with a repentant heart) actually provided soteriological benefits for those for whom the sacrifices were offered. That is, when the sacrifices were offered with a repentant heart, YHWH forgave Israel of her sins and preserved the nation from his wrath.

("Atonement in Psalm 51," in *The Glory of Atonement*, ed. Charles E. Hill and Frank A. James III [Downers Grove, IL: InterVarsity Press, 2004], 51-60) convincingly argues this point from Psalm 51.
[4]For example, C.H. Dodd, *The Bible and the Greeks*, 2nd ed. (London: Hodder and Stoughton, 1954), 82-95.
[5]Contra George Buchanan Gray, *Sacrifices in the Old Testament: Its Theory and Practice* (New York: KTAV Publishing House, 1971), 95. Gray asserts that Israel often offered sacrifices with feelings of joy rather than fear or contrition. The truthfulness of Gray's claim, though, does not necessarily extinguish the reality that Israel also offered sacrifices in accordance with Yahweh's prescriptions to appease his wrath. For example, see Exod. 4:24-26; 32:1-34:9; Deut. 4:25-31; 9:1-10:22; 30:1-10; Josh. 7:1-26; Judg. 2:10-23; 3:7-15; 4:6-8, 10-12; 1 Sam. 7:2-14; 12:8-11; 2 Sam. 12:7-23; 21:1-9; 24:1-25; 1 Kgs 8:22-53; 21:17-29; 2 Kgs 13:1-7; 22:14-20; 1 Chr. 21-22; 2 Chr. 6:12-42; 7:12-16; 12:1-12; 15:1-15; 29:1-32:33; 34:20-28).

The Purpose of Human Sacrifices of Atonement in Early Judaism

2 and 4 Maccabees record the noble deaths of the Maccabean martyrs. The authors of these traditions suggest that the Jewish martyrs died vicariously for Israel's sins to purify the nation from its sins, to reconcile God to the nation, and to save the nation from God's wrath. Just as animal sacrifices were offered for the sins of those within the covenant-community of Israel, so also the Jewish martyrs died as vicarious sacrifices of atonement only for the sins of those within the covenant-community of Israel.[6]

2 Maccabees 5:1-8:5: The Sacrifice of the Seven Sons and Reconciliation

2 Maccabees indisputably pre-dates Romans and 4 Maccabees, and it provides strong evidence that supports the soteriological values of the martyrs' deaths.[7] The author of 2 Maccabees presents the martyrdoms of an unknown mother and her seven sons as atoning sacrifices and a saving event for the nation (2 Macc. 7:32-38).[8] After killing Eleazar in 2 Maccabees 6, Antiochus tries to compel a mother and her seven sons to eat unlawful foods (2 Macc. 7:1). They were faced with tortures and punishment (just as Eleazar) if they disobeyed, but each of the seven sons and their mother nevertheless disobey Antiochus. As a result, each suffers torture and death (2 Macc. 7:2-41). While encouraged by his mother to trust God as he faced the prospect of death (2 Macc. 7:28-29), the seventh son echoes the cry of Daniel's three friends in LXX Daniel 3:28-29 and LXX Daniel 3:37 when he states that the nation suffers because of its own sins cf. 2 Macc. 5:17).[9] Just as the confession of Daniel's three friends in LXX

---

[6] Much of the material in this section comes from my recent book *Maccabean Martyr Traditions in Paul's Theology of Atonement: Did Martyr Theology Shape Paul's Conception of Jesus's Death?* (Eugene, Or.: Wipf & Stock, 2010). I have borrowed the overlapping material with permission from Wipf & Stock. I also presented much of this material on 2 and 4 Maccabees in the Function of the Apocryphal and Pseudepigraphal Literature on Early Judaism and Early Christianity study group at the 2010 national meeting of the Society of Biblical Literature in Atlanta, GA. I would like to thank my many colleagues in this group who challenged and help refine many of the points that I enumerate regarding 2 and 4 Maccabees. Many thanks go especially to Daniel P. Bailey, David A. DeSilva, and Amy-Jill Levine for their stimulating, provocative, and challenging remarks during the panel discussion.

[7] Similarly Douglas A. Campbell, *The Deliverance of God: An Apocalyptic Rereading of Justification in Paul* (Grand Rapids: Eerdmans, 2009), 650.

[8] John J. Collins (*Daniel, First Maccabees, Second Maccabees* [OTM 15; 2nd ed.; Wilmington, Del.: Frazier Incorporation, 1989], 310-11) asserts that the martyrdoms of the mother and her seven sons were legendary fables used to elaborate a martyr theology.

[9] Similarly Wolfgan Kraus, *Der Tod Jesu als Heiligtumsweihe: Eine Untersuchung zum Umfeld de Sühnevorstellung im Römer 3:25-26a*, WMANT 66 (Neukirchener-Vluyn: Neukirchener Verlag, 1991), 35. However, Kraus argues against a cultic background behind 2 Macc. 7:32-38.

Purpose and Benefits of Jesus' Death 193

Daniel 3:28-29 and LXX Daniel 3:37, the seventh son's statement appears to be a confession that sin is the reason that the martyrs suffer, because the seventh son also utters that although God is angry with the nation, "he will be reconciled again to his servants" (2 Macc. 7:33; cf. 2 Macc. 1:5; 7:37-38; 8:29).

The seventh son's statement that "we suffer because of our sins" and that "he will again be reconciled to his servants" refers to Israel as a people and the martyrs along with the nation. This seems right because of the first person plural "we" with the phrase "because of *our own* sins," because of the first person plural verb "we suffer," and because when a few in the community sinned against God and suffered the consequences of their sin, the entire community (including the martyrs) would suffer the consequences of this sin in accordance with Deuteronomic tradition (cf. Num. 25:11; 1-2 Kings, 1-2 Chronicles, Isa. 1:1-26; LXX Dan. 3:24-90; Wis. 3:1-6; 1QS DM 1.6-11). The martyrs were not sinless, but they were innocent of religious apostasy unlike their Jewish kinsmen (cf. 1 Macc. 1-2; 2 Macc. 7; 4 Macc. 6). Their suffering was a corollary of their refusal to embrace Greek culture as many of their kinsmen had begun to embrace it (cf. 2 Macc. 5:1-8:5; 4 Macc. 6),[10] and their kinsmen's acceptance of Antiochus' Hellenistic regime resulted in God's judgment of the entire nation through him (cf. 1 Macc. 1). Therefore, the seventh son and the other martyrs offer themselves to God as sacrifices of atonement to pay for the nation's sin, which also became a payment for their sin by virtue of their membership within the nation (cf. 2 Macc. 7:32),[11] and their deaths exclusively brought a soteriological benefit of reconciliation only to Israel and not to the nations. 2 Maccabees 5:27-7:38 supports this.

As a result of the nation's rebellion against God's law, the temple and the land were dishonored (2 Macc. 5:27-6:6). When Antiochus and Menelaus (an apostate Jewish high priest) entered the temple in Jerusalem, they profaned it (2 Macc. 5:15-16). To eradicate God's judgment against the nation, the seven sons voluntarily offer themselves to die for Israel to achieve God's forgiveness (2 Macc. 7:32-38).[12] 2 Maccabees 7:32-38 suggests that the seventh son was

---

[10] A. O'Hagan, "The Martyr in the Fourth Book of the Maccabees," *SBFLA* 24 (1974): 94-120, esp. 108. Against Theofried Baumeister, *Die Anfange der Theologie des Martyriums* (MBT; Münster: Ashendorf, 1980), 41-42.

[11] So Marinus de Jonge, *Christology in Context: The Earliest Christian Response to Jesus* (Philadelphia: Westminster, 1988), 181-82; U. Kellermann, "Zum traditionsgeschichtlichen Problem des stellvertretenden Sühnetodes in 2 Makk. 7:37," *BN* 13 (1980): 63-83, esp. 69; J.W. van Henten, *Maccabean Martyrs as Saviours of the Jewish People* (Leiden: Brill, 1998) 137. Against Sam K. Williams, *Jesus' Death as a Saving Event: The Background and Origin of a Concept*, HTR (Missoula: Scholars Press, 1975), 79 n. 29; David Seeley, *The Noble Death: Greco-Roman Martyrology and Paul's Concept of Salvation*, JSNTSup 28 (Sheffield: Sheffield Academic Press, 1990), 87.

[12] Similarly Eduard Lohse, *Märtyrer und Gottesknecht* (2nd ed.; Göttingen: Vandenhoeck & Ruprecht, 1963), 67-69; J. Gnilka, "Martyriumsparänese und Sühnetod in synoptischen und jüdischen Traditionen," in *Die Kirche des Anfangs: Festschrift für Heinz Schürman* (Leipzig: St. Benno-Verlag, 1977), 223-46; J. Downing, "Jesus and

confident that God would be reconciled again to the nation through the martyrs' deaths because he asserts that God "will be reconciled again to his servants" in 2 Maccabees 7:33 and because 7:37-38 affirms that the seventh son wants God to end his wrath against the nation by means of the deaths of him and his brothers on behalf of the nation.[13] Scholars debate the meaning of the phrase in 7:38.[14] The debate pertains to how one should interpret the seventh son's statement that God's wrath would end "by/in me" (2 Macc. 7:38). Sam K. Williams argues that the seven sons did not avert God's wrath away from the nation by means of their deaths, for the phrases do not suggest the means by which the wrath of God was averted away from Israel, but the point at which the wrath of God was averted.[15] That is, the seventh son simply affirms that the wrath of God would end "with" him and "with" his brothers. Williams maintains his view partly because he rejects that 2 Maccabees teaches vicarious atonement.[16] According to him, 2 Maccabees only presents the martyrs' suffering and death as exemplary for their fellow Jews to imitate when they face their own suffering and death.[17] Williams' analysis is partially correct in two ways. First, the author of 2 Maccabees states that the suffering and deaths of the martyrs were exemplary (2 Macc. 6:28, 31; cf. 2 Macc. 6:24-31). Eleazar's death was an example of nobility for the entire nation to follow (2 Macc. 6:28, 31). Moreover, even 4 Maccabees, where the sacrificial and the soteriological natures of the martyrs' deaths are more explicit, speaks of the martyrs' deaths as exemplary (4 Macc. 6:18-21; 9:23; 10:3, 16; 11:15; 12:16; 13:8-18; 17:23). Second, Williams is correct to note that the preposition ἐν in the phrase "in/by me and in/by my brothers" can convey a variety of meanings (e.g. "in," "with," "by means of," etc.).

In response to Williams' first observation, the exemplary nature of the martyrs' deaths in 2 and 4 Maccabees does not preclude their deaths from functioning as atoning sacrifices and a saving event for the nation. Their deaths

---

Martyrdom," *JTS* 14 (1963): 279-93, esp. 288-89; van Henten, *Maccabean Martyrs*, 140-44. Against a sacrificial reading of 2 Macc 7:32-38, see Williams, *Jesus' Death*, 82-88; Jonathan Goldstein, *2 Maccabees*, ABC 41A (New York: Doubleday, 1983), 316; Seeley, *The Noble Death*, 87-91, 145.

[13] The most important parts of the prayer in 2 Macc. 7:37-38 for my thesis are the seventh son's statements "be merciful quickly to the nation" in 7:37 and "to end the wrath of the almighty in me and in my brothers" in 7:38, but I have cited above the entire Greek text of 2 Macc. 7:37-38 so that the reader can read the seventh son's statement in context. The grammatical construction in 2 Macc. 7:37 is similar to the one in 4 Macc. 6:28. Eleazar asks God in the latter text to provide mercy for the nation through his death. In 2 Macc. 7:37, the seventh son prays that God would "quickly be merciful to the nation" through his death. In both 4 Macc. 6:28 and 2 Macc. 7:37, the martyrs urge God to grant mercy to the nation on the basis of their deaths for it.

[14] Williams, *Jesus' Death*, 83-88; H.W. Surkau, *Martyrien in jüdischer und frühchristlicher Zeit*, FRLANT 36 (Göttingen: Vandenhoeck & Ruprecht, 1938), 59.

[15] Williams, *Jesus' Death*, 83-88.

[16] Ibid.

[17] Ibid., 83-88.

could in fact be both exemplary and sacrifices of atonement (cf. 1 Pet. 2:21-24).[18] In response to Williams' second observation, the preposition likely conveys instrumentality in 2 Maccabees 7:38 ("by means of"), because this meaning occurs in numerous places in 2 Maccabees (2 Macc. 1:28; 5:20; 7:29; 15:11; cf. 4 Macc. 9:22; 16:15); the prepositional phrases occur in a context where the seventh son urges God to be reconciled to the nation again (2 Macc. 7:33);[19] and because the term should be translated as "by means of" in 2 Maccabees 7:29, which is a text in close proximity of 7:38. If the translation "by means of" is correct in 2 Maccabees 7:38, then the seventh son's prayer should be interpreted to mean that he wanted God to end his wrath "by means of" his death and "by means of" the deaths of his brothers. This interpretation would suggest that the seventh son wants his death and the deaths of his brothers to satisfy God's wrath against the nation, just as Eleazar prays regarding his own death in 4 Maccabees 6:28-29.

2 Maccabees 5:1-8:5 supports that God fulfilled the seventh son's expectation through the martyrs' deaths, for the latter text states that God was reconciled to the nation through the martyrs' deaths (2 Macc. 8:1-5). The "only possible means by which this reconciliation could have come about in the context of 2 Maccabees is through the deaths of the martyrs."[20] For example, while Antiochus was invading Egypt a second time, he heard that Judea was in revolt (2 Macc. 5:1-11). He immediately left Egypt and seized Jerusalem while he commanded his soldiers to kill anyone whom they met along the way (2 Macc. 5:11b-14). Antiochus entered the holy temple and profaned it, for he was oblivious that God was using him to defile the temple on account of his anger with Israel (2 Macc. 5:17-18). Just as the temple suffered pollution and judgment because of the nation's sin, it also experienced God's blessings when he pardoned the nation (2 Macc. 5:20a; cf. Lev. 16:16, 30). 2 Maccabees 5:20b

---

[18] 1 Pet. 2:21-24 is the closest biblical parallel where the death of a human is referred to both as exemplary and vicarious for others in the same context.

[19] For other examples where ἐν conveys means or instrumentality, see A.T. Robertson, *A Grammar of the Greek New Testament in the Light of Historical Research* (Nashville: Broadman, 1934), 589-91; Herbert Smyth, *Greek Grammar* (21st ed.; Cambridge, Mass.: Harvard University Press, 2002), 376-77.

[20] J.W. Van Henten, "Tradition-Historical Background of Romans 3:25: A Search for Pagan and Jewish Parallels," in *From Jesus to John: Essays on Jesus and New Testament Christology in Honour of Marinus De Jonge*, JSNTSup 84, ed. Martinus C. de Boer (Sheffield: JSOT Press, 1993), 117-21, esp. 117. Against Williams, *Jesus' Death*, 85-89; Seeley, *The Noble Death*, 88. Cf. Ulrich Kellermann, *Auferstanden in den Himmel: 2 Makkabäer 7 und die Auferstehung der Martÿrer* (Stuttgart: Katholisches Bibelwerk, 1979), 54-55; Stephen Anthony Cummins, *Paul and the Crucified Christ in Antioch* (Cambridge: Cambridge University Press, 2001), 88. William H. Brown ("From Holy War to Holy Martyrdom," in H.B. Huffmon, F.A. Spina, and A.R. Green [eds.], *The Quest for the Kingdom of God: Studies in Honor of George E. Mendenhall* [Winona Lake, IN: Eisenbrauns, 1983], 287-88) states that "Judas and his men are asking God to accept the present national suffering as sufficient, not only to atone for the nation's sins, but as sufficient to invoke his wrath upon the Syrian armies."

states that God's wrath ended, and the glory of Israel was restored to the nation "by means of the reconciliation of the Great Lord" (2 Macc. 8:5; cf. Lev. 9:1-10:2).

After the author describes the other abominations that Antiochus and his companions committed (2 Macc. 5:21-6:11), he subsequently explains why the Jews suffered so severely. He offers this explanation immediately before he writes about the martyrdoms of Eleazar, the mother, and her seven sons (2 Macc. 6:18-8:2). In 2 Maccabees 6:12-17, the author urges his readers not to be discouraged by the grave calamities that had befallen the nation by asserting that God provided the calamities for the nation's benefit. The author also states that God would soon judge the Gentile nations when they reach the full measure of their sins, but he would not deal with Israel in this way. Instead, God was currently judging Israel as the author wrote 2 Maccabees in the calamities that had befallen the nation through Antiochus, and the deaths of the martyrs were representative of his divine judgment. The author explains that God did not, therefore, relinquish his mercy from his people nor did he forsake them (2 Macc. 6:13-16). The author, then, highlights the deaths of the martyrs in 2 Maccabees 6:18-8:2 to demonstrate how God's mercy was achieved for the nation (2 Macc. 5:20; 8:5-7). 2 Maccabees 6:18-8:5 suggests that God reveals his mercy to Israel by his reconciliatory acts toward the nation, because after the seventh son promises God's future judgment of Antiochus (2 Macc. 7:33), he states that he (just as his brothers) offers his life to God with the prayer that he would be merciful to the nation through their deaths (2 Macc. 7:37). Subsequent to the author's presentations of the martyrdoms of Eleazar, the mother, and her seven sons (2 Macc. 6:18-7:42), the author immediately discusses the response of zealous Jews to the martyrs' deaths.

In 2 Maccabees 8, Judas Maccabaeus reappears in the narrative (Israel's leading guerilla fighter). He and other zealous Jews asked God to be merciful to the martyrs, the temple, and the city (2 Macc. 8:2-3). They also pray that the Lord would hear the blood of the martyrs, that he would remember the destruction of the innocent babies, that he would remember the blasphemies against his name, and that he would hate all of the evil committed against Israel (2 Macc. 8:4). The mercy of which the author speaks in 2 Maccabees 5:20 and 6:12-16, the mercy for which the martyrs die (2 Macc. 7:32-38), and the mercy for which Judas prays in 2 Maccabees 8:1-4 becomes a reality when God becomes reconciled again to the nation by removing his wrath away from the Jews and turning it against Antiochus and his army (2 Macc. 5:1-8:5).[21] Yes, the reconciliation for which the seventh son prays that his death and the deaths of his brothers would achieve for the nation becomes a reality for Israel after Judas' prayer, and yes God's glory was again restored to both the temple and the nation through their deaths after Judas' prayer, but God's reconciliation does not take place in the narrative until after the martyrs died for Israel's sin (cf. 2 Macc. 5:20-8:5; 4 Macc. 17:21-22). Therefore, the deaths of the mother and her seven sons reconciled God to Israel.

---

[21]Contra Seeley, *The Noble Death*, 87-88.

Purpose and Benefits of Jesus' Death

4 Maccabees 6:28-29: The Sacrifice of Eleazar, God's Mercy, Satisfaction, and Purification

The martyrdom of Eleazar is the chief example in 4 Maccabees that supports that the deaths of the martyrs functioned as atoning sacrifices and as a saving event for Israel. Eleazar was a scribe of high rank (2 Macc. 6:18), from a priestly family, and an expert in the law (4 Macc. 5:4, 35). Antiochus urges him to disobey the Torah and eat swine (2 Macc 6:18; 4 Macc. 5:6). Instead, Eleazar voluntarily chooses death. As a result, Antiochus severely tortures him (4 Macc 6:1-8). As he bleeds profusely from the scourges that tore his flesh and from being pierced in his side with a spear (4 Macc. 6:6), Eleazar prays that God would use his death to achieve three soteriological benefits for Israel: (1) mercy (4 Macc. 6:28), (2) satisfaction (4 Macc. 6:28), and (3) purification (4 Macc. 6:29).

Eleazar urges God in 4 Maccabees 6:28 to be merciful to Israel through his death (2 Macc. 4:1-6:31; 4 Macc. 5:4-6:40). The mercy for which he prays seems to be deliverance from God's wrath (cf. 2 Macc. 4:16-17), for 1, 2, and 4 Maccabees suggest that God was judging the nation through Antiochus' persecution since many Jews dismissed the Torah as a way of life (cf. 1 Macc. 1). God's judgment of the nation through Antiochus is the reason that the nation suffers in the narrative and the reason that Eleazar requests God's mercy (cf. 1 Macc. 1:1-64; 2 Macc. 7:32).[22]

That Eleazar prays that his death would provide salvation for Israel is elucidated by 4 Maccabees 6:28. In the latter text, Eleazar asks God to be satisfied with the martyrs' judgment for the nation.[23] Since Eleazar's first

---

[22] Other uses of the adjective "merciful" (ἵλεως) elsewhere in 4 Maccabees support that in 4 Macc. 6:28, Eleazar asks God to accept his death as the means through which he would save the nation from his judgment. Prior to Antiochus' torturing of the seven sons in 4 Macc. 8:14, he urged the seven sons to provide mercy for themselves by eating unclean meat. Obedience to Antiochus would have ensured their salvation from his judgment. In 4 Macc. 9:24, as one of the seven sons suffered torture from Antiochus, he exhorted his brothers to follow his example of godliness and he stated that through his godliness God's mercy would save the nation. After the seventh son refuses to obey Antiochus in 4 Macc. 12:4-16, he hurls himself into the fire with which Antiochus threatened him and the other brothers who would not forsake their religion. While entering the fire, the seventh son prays that God would be merciful to save the nation through his death (4 Macc. 12:17). In Exod. 32:12, Moses asks God to be merciful to Israel by asking him not to judge the nation for its idolatry (cf. Exod. 32:33; Num. 14). In Deut. 21:8, Moses urges the nation to pray for God's mercy when an unknown member of the community should wrongly kill a man (cf. Deut. 21:1-8). In 2 Chr. 6:25, Solomon requests that God would be merciful to Israel and forgive the nation for its sin (cf. 2 Chr. 6:27, 39; 7:14). Thus, the LXX connects the adjective with judgment and wrath. For other connections in the LXX between God's mercy and deliverance from judgment, see Amos 7:2; Jer. 5:1, 7; 27:20; 38:34; 43:3.

[23] For other possible substitutionary uses of ὑπερ in atonement texts, see LXX Exod. 21:20; Lev. 26:25; Deut. 32:41, 43; Mic. 7:9; Wis. 1:8; 14:31; 18:11; cf. 1 Macc. 5:32; 2 Macc. 1:26; 3:32; Rom. 5:6-11; 8:32; 1 Cor. 1:13; 11:24; 15:3; 2 Cor. 5:14-15, 21; Gal. 1:4; 2:20-21; 3:13; 1 Thess. 5:10.

request that God would be merciful to the nation is the main clause in the sentence, the adverbial participial clause ("and be satisfied with our judgment for them") is a continuation of the first request in 4 Maccabees 6:28a, and it takes the tone of a prayer of entreaty, as the first part of the prayer. With this request, Eleazar expresses that he offers his life to God as a substitute on behalf of Israel and as a provision for God's mercy, and he hopes that his provision would satisfy God's wrath against the nation. This interpretation seems correct, because Eleazar offers this petition to God while he faces his judgment by means of Antiochus' persecution (4 Macc. 6:28; 17:22; cf. 1 Macc. 6:60; Ps. 68:32; Jer. 18:4; Dan. 4:2) and because δίκῃ consistently refers to divine judgment throughout 4 Maccabees (4 Macc. 4:13, 21; 8:14, 22; 9:9, 15, 32; 11:3; 12:12; 18:22; cf. 2 Macc. 8:11, 13).

In addition to asking God to use his death to achieve mercy and to bring satisfaction to his wrath against Israel, Eleazar also prays that God would make his blood to be Israel's purification (4 Macc. 6:29; cf. 4 Macc. 1:11; LXX Dan. 3:38-40). Since Eleazar has already prayed that God would bring mercy to Israel and end his wrath against Israel through his death, Eleazar's request in 4 Maccabees 6:29 should be interpreted as a request to God to make his death a sacrifice of atonement and a saving event for the nation. The sacrificial nature of Eleazar's request is apparent when he asks God to make his "blood" to be Israel's purification (2 Macc. 5:17-18; 6:15; 7:32; 12:42; 4 Macc. 5:19; 17:21; cf. Lev. 16:16, 30).[24]

Besides 4 Maccabees 6:29, καθάρσιον ("purification") occurs nowhere else in the LXX.[25] However, καθάρισμος ("purification") is a cognate of καθάρσιον. The latter occurs in the LXX and in the New Testament to refer both to the purification of Israel and to Christians. In the respective texts, one receives purification through the blood that the priests offered as atonement (Exod. 29:36; 30:10; cf. 2 Pet. 1:9), through ritual cleansing (Lev. 14:32; 15:13; cf. Mark 1:44; Luke 2:22; 5:14; John 2:6; 3:25), through God's forgiveness (Num. 14:18), through the cleansing of holy utensils (1 Chr. 23:28), through the purification of the temple (2 Macc 1:18; 2:16, 19; 10:5), or through one's piety (4 Macc. 7:6; cf. 1QS 1-3 I, 10). Since Eleazar was an expert in the law, a priest, and from a priestly family (2 Macc. 6:18; 4 Macc. 5:4, 35), he understood the Old Testament background behind purification (cf. 2 Macc. 6:18; 4 Macc. 5:4, 35). Moreover, since Antiochus abolished the sacrificial system, killed anyone who yielded allegiance to the Torah (1 Macc. 1:41-64; 2 Macc. 5:4, 35), controlled the temple, and prohibited any form of worship in compliance with the Torah (cf. 2 Macc. 1:5; 7:32-38; 4 Macc. 6:28-29; 17:20-21), Eleazar's request likely, then, incites God in 4 Macc 6:28-29 to use his death and the deaths of the other martyrs to substitute for the absence of temple sacrifices (which would have included the Yom Kippur ritual since Antiochus forbade all sacrifices [cf. 1 Macc. 1]), so that the nation

---

[24] Against Seeley, *The Noble Death*, 97-98.

[25] Heb. 1:3 is the only other place in the NT where purification is connected to the purification of sins via the death of a human.

Purpose and Benefits of Jesus' Death

would corporately experience God's forgiveness.

In the final part of his prayer in 4 Maccabees 6:29b, Eleazar asks God to receive his death as a ransom for the nation. The occurrence of ἀντίψυχον ("ransom") in 4 Maccabees 6:29b likewise occurs in 17:21. There the term suggests that the martyrs' deaths purified and saved the nation, because the author connects ἀντίψυχον with both the nation's purification from sin and with its salvation. Furthermore, the compound ἀντίψυχον occurs as two different words ἀντὶ ψυχῆς in Leviticus 17 in a context where the author discusses the Day of Israel's atonement (Lev. 16) and the atoning function of blood on behalf of one's life (Lev. 17:11). The function of ἀντίψυχον in 4 Macc 6:29 and 17:21, then, suggests that the blood of the martyrs was the required price paid to achieve both Israel's purification and salvation (cf. 4 Macc. 17:21-22). Consequently, the author of 4 Maccabees appears to be echoing Leviticus 16-17, especially the feast of atonement and the Yom Kippur ritual, when he discusses the martyrs' deaths since he repeatedly uses similar cultic language from Leviticus 16-17 to describe the nature of the martyrs' deaths for the nation in an atonement setting. For example, Eleazar asks God to purify Israel and to satisfy his judgment against the entire nation by means of his "blood" that he offers for the nation (4 Macc. 6:28-29; 7:8; 17:10; 17:21-22; 18:4),[26] and Leviticus 16-17 states that blood was offered for the sins of the entire nation. As with my discussion of 2 Maccabees 5:1-8:5, the important point of which to take note for my thesis is that Eleazar died only for Israel and requests that his death would effect soteriological benefits only for Israel.

4 Maccabees 17:21-22: The Soteriological Effect of the Martyrs' Deaths

In 4 Maccabees 17:21-22, the author of 4 Maccabees explains the soteriological effect of the martyrs' death by offering his interpretation of their deaths: "the tyrant was punished, and the homeland purified-they having become, as it were, a ransom for the sin of our nation. And through the blood of those devout ones and their death as an atoning sacrifice, divine Providence preserved Israel that previously had been mistreated" (NRSV). As one can see from the preceding translation, the author uses cultic language to communicate the soteriological effect of the martyrs' deaths for Israel. The term ἱλαστήριον (translated as "atoning sacrifice") occurs in 4 Maccabees 17:22 with other cultic terminology (e.g. sin, blood, purification), a cultic concept (ransom), and a soteriological term (διασῴζω). The occurrence of ἱλαστήριον in this context is certainly cultic for the above reasons, but also since the term itself is part of a semantic family of ἱλας-words that often occur in cultic contexts in the LXX that speak of atoning sin, and these words often translate form the Hebrew root כפר, which often means "to atone" (cf. Leviticus 16). To clarify, I am not asserting that the ἱλας-word group always translates from the Hebrew root (cf. LXX Exod. 32:14; 2 Kgs 21:3; 1 Chr. 6:34; 2 Chr. 29:24; Ps. 105:30; Zech. 7:2; 8:22), nor am I affirming that the כפר the word group always conveys the idea

---

[26] Against Kraus, *Der Tod Jesu*, 38-39.

of atoning sacrifice (cf. LXX Exod. 32:14; Prov. 16:14).[27] Rather, my point is simply that the ἱλας-word group often occurs in cultic texts and often speaks of sacrificial atonement when this word group occurs with explicit cultic vocabulary, as it does in 4 Maccabees 17:21-22. Thus, 4 Maccabees 17:21-22 speaks of the martyrs' deaths with sacrificial language that closely resembles the Old Testament cult, and 4 Maccabees 17:22 states that the martyrs' sacrificial deaths indeed *only* saved Israel.

Furthermore, 4 Maccabees 17:22 and Romans 3:25 are the only places in available literature where an author applies ἱλαστήριον to the death of a human in a cultic context for the benefit of another. The term refers to the mercy seat in contexts in the LXX where priests atoned for sin through the sacrifice of blood (Lev. 16:14-15), where God commands Israel to put the ἱλαστήριον above the ark of the covenant in the holy of holies, the place where only the high priest could enter (Exod. 25:17-20; 37:6), where God commands the priest to make atonement on the ἱλαστήριον to provide cleansing for sin (Exod. 25:18-22; 31:7; 35:12; 37:6-8; Lev. 16:14-15), and in contexts where God appears above the ἱλαστήριον to show his acceptance of atonement (Exod. 25:22; Lev. 16:2; Num. 7:89). In light of the above arguments regarding the sacrificial context of 4 Maccabees 6:28-29 and 17:21-22 and in light of the occurrence of ἱλαστήριον in this sacrificial text, the term in 17:22 must ascribe a sacrificial function to the martyrs' deaths, which is similar to the term's function in cultic contexts in the Old Testament.

In his unpublished doctoral thesis, Daniel P. Bailey argues that ἱλαστήριον in 4 Maccabees 17:22 and in Romans 3:25 have distinct meanings.[28] The author of 4 Maccabees 17:22 uses the term consistent with its occurrence in the Hellenistic world (i.e. propitiatory), but Paul uses the term consistent with its occurrence in the biblical world (i.e. mercy seat).[29] Thus, according to Bailey, to argue that ἱλαστήριον refers to sacrificial atonement in 4 Maccabees 17:22 is a mistake. After reviewing the evidence in the relevant Hellenistic literature that supports reading the term as propitiatory, Bailey argues that various inscriptions in the Hellenistic world affirm that ἱλαστήρια were offered either to propitiate the wrath of offended deities or to gain their

---

[27]For example, ἐξιλάσκομαι is often cultic and often refers to the cleaning that takes places when sins are atoned (LXX Exod. 30:10; Lev. 1:4; 4:20, 26, 31, 35; 5:6, 10, 13, 16, 18, 26; 6:23; 7:7; Num. 5:8; 6:11; 8:12, 19, 21; 15:25, 28; 17:11, 12; 28:22, 30; 29:5, 11; 31:50; 1 Kgs 3:14; 2 Kgs 2:13; 1 Chr. 6:34; 2 Chr. 29:24; 2 Chr. 30:18; 2 Esdr. 20:34; Ps. 105:30; Ezek. 43:20, 22; 45:17; Sir. 3:3, 30; 5:6; 20:28; 28:5; 34:19; 45:16, 23). However, the one occurrence of ἱλάσκομαι in the LXX is not cultic and void of sacrificial ideas (LXX Exod 32:14). In LXX Exod. 32:14, ἐξιλάσκομαι translates from נחם and highlights YHWH's mercy to Israel in spite of the nation's idolatry.

[28]I am grateful to Daniel P. Bailey for kindly e-mailing me a copy of his dissertation.

[29]Daniel P. Bailey, "Jesus as the Mercy Seat: The Semantics and Theology of Paul's Use of Hilastērion in Romans 3:25" (Ph.D. diss., Cambridge University, 1999), 5-12, esp. 11-12.

favor.³⁰ He also argues that τήριον words do not regularly refer to actions, but to places.³¹ Bailey concludes that the meaning of ἱλαστήριον in 4 Maccabees 17:22 as it relates to the martyrs' deaths "should be sought against a non-sacrificial background."³² According to Bailey, 4 Maccabees nowhere states that the martyrs died as atoning sacrifices for Israel's sin.

Bailey's doctoral thesis is thorough. It provides an extensive lexical analysis of ἱλαστήριον. I agree with his argument that the occurrence of the same term in different texts (i.e. 4 Macc. 17:22 and Rom. 3:25) does not necessitate that the term should be translated the same way in both texts. Nevertheless, as I have argued elsewhere, Bailey's thesis and arguments (if I correctly understand them) seem to pit his lexical analysis against the context within which ἱλαστήριον occurs and therefore prevents the term from conveying its contextual theme.³³ In my view, regardless of how one translates ἱλαστήριον in 4 Maccabees 17:22, since the term occurs in the same context as several atonement vocabulary and concepts found in Leviticus 16-17 (e.g. judgment, purification, ransom, vicarious death, sin, and blood), ἱλαστήριον in 4 Maccabees 17:22 at least alludes to the Yom Kippur ritual and it at least suggests that the martyrs' deaths function as Israel's atonement in the narrative of 4 Maccabees.³⁴

For example, 4 Maccabees 6:28-29 speaks of the martyrs' deaths in the context of blood, purification, and ransom. Likewise, 4 Maccabees 17:21-22 speaks of the martyrs' deaths in the context of purification, ransom, blood, and salvation.³⁵ Therefore, the contextual evidence in 4 Maccabees 6:28-29 and 17:21-22 seems to challenge Bailey's basic conclusion about ἱλαστήριον in 4 Maccabees 17:22: namely, that it should be understood as a pagan reference to a non-cultic/non-sacrificial background. Contrary to Bailey, I suggest that 4 Maccabees 6:28-29 and 17:21-22 together affirm that the martyrs offered themselves to God as atonement for Israel's sin and that their deaths (according to the narrative) actually achieved the nation's salvation, because these texts use cultic language to express that the martyrs' deaths were a ransom, purified the homeland, and provided salvation for the people by turning God's wrath away from Israel (cf. 1 Macc. 1:11; 2 Macc. 5:1-8:5; 4 Macc. 17:20-22).³⁶

---

³⁰For the above analysis and summary of Bailey's view, see David A. DeSilva, *4 Maccabees*, SCS (Leiden: Brill, 2006), 250-51, who cites Bailey ("Mercy Seat," 31-75).
³¹Stephen Finlan, *The Background and Content of Paul's Cultic Atonement Metaphors*, (Atlanta: SBL, 2004), 200-03, who cites Bailey.
³²The above quote comes from DeSilva (*4 Maccabees*, 251), who summarizes Bailey's view.
³³For a similar critique, see also Finlan, *Atonement Metaphors*, 200.
³⁴DeSilva (*4 Maccabees*, 250-51) argues that the author uses the cultic language from the Yom Kippur ritual to describe the effect of the martyrs' deaths.
³⁵DeSilva, *4 Maccabees*, 202.
³⁶DeSilva, *4 Maccabees*, 202-03. Similarly Marinus de Jonge, "Jesus' Death for Others

The Purpose and Benefits of Jesus' Sacrifice in Paul

As I have argued elsewhere, both the Old Testament and martyr theology shaped Paul's conception of Jesus' death because Paul uses either similar or the same cultic and soteriological vocabulary as those traditions to reconstruct these traditions to form his understanding of Jesus' death for others.[37] Because of the limited scope of this monograph, I only focus the following discussion on one similarity and one difference between Paul and these other traditions: Just as the Old Testament and 2 and 4 Maccabees state that animals (=the Old Testament) and pious Jews (=2 and 4 Maccabees) died for Israel and just as they apply the soteriological benefits of those sacrifices only to Israel (i.e. God's elect and believing community), Paul likewise states that Jesus died to achieve soteriological benefits for God's elect and believing community. However, unlike the Hebrew Bible and 2 and 4 Maccabees, Paul contends that Jesus died for the sins of all Jews and Gentiles to accomplish the salvation of all who have faith in Jesus.

Romans 3:24-30: Jesus' Blood and Justification by Faith
In Romans 3:24-30, Paul connects justification by faith with Jesus' blood. In fact, he contends that God justifies sinners by faith because he offered Jesus to die for their sins. In 3:23-24, Paul states that all sinners must be freely justified "by God's grace through the redemption which in Christ Jesus." All who have sinned, to whom Jesus' blood and its benefits apply, refer to Jews and Gentiles, for Paul's argument in 1:18-3:20 focuses on the condemnation of both groups due to their inability to meet Torah's demands. Justification, says Paul, is God's gracious gift and comes to all sinners freely (cf. Rom. 3:23-24), and this justification is possible because Jesus provides redemption for those who are justified.

Paul connects justification by faith in 3:21-22 and in 3:24 with one social term (ἀπολύτρωσις ["redemption," 3:24]) and with 2 sacrificial terms (ἱλαστήριον ["sacrifice of atonement," 3:25] and αἷμα ["blood," 3:25]). "Redemption" (ἀπολύτρωσις) is an economic term.[38] The term appears here for the first time in Romans.[39] Its occurrence at this juncture in Paul's argument

---

and the Death of the Maccabean Martyrs," in T. Baarda, A. Hilhorst, G.P. Luttikhuizen, and A.S. van der Woude (eds.), *Text and Testimony: Essays on New Testament and Apocryphal Literature in Honour of A.F.J. Klijn* (Kampen: Uitgeversmaatschappij J.H. Kok, 1988), 142-51, esp. 150-51.

[37]Williams, *Maccabean Martyrs*; idem "Martyr Theology and Hellenistic Judaism and Paul's Conception of Jesus' Death in Roman 3:21-26," in *Christian Origins and Hellensitic Judaism: Literary and Social Contexts for the New Testament*, eds. Stanley E. Porter and Andrew W. Pitts (Leiden: Brill, Forthcoming).

[38]So Finlan, *Atonement Metaphors*, 164-69.

[39]The term occurs elsewhere in the New Testament in Luke 21:28; Rom. 8:23; 1 Cor. 1:30; Eph. 1:7, 14; 4:30; Col. 1:14; Heb. 9:15, and 11:35. But Paul only connects

Purpose and Benefits of Jesus' Death 203

suggests that in addition to faith, Jesus' redemption is the means through which God justifies all who have sinned (Rom. 3:21-24, esp. 3:23-24). Since Paul uses "redemption" (ἀπολύτρωσις) in 3:24 in the context of blood (3:25) and since the redemption that Jesus has accomplished for Jews and Gentiles by his blood was the means through which God provided justification for them (cf. 3:21-22, 24), "redemption" likely suggests in 3:24 that Jesus' death was some sort of sacrificial payment that was offered to purchase justification for all (Jews and Gentiles) who have sinned (3:23-24).[40] As such, Jesus' death was a ransom since it liberated those who were otherwise guilty before God (cf. 1:18-3:24).[41] Some scholars have rejected the notion that Jesus' death was a ransom since they reject the ransom-theory of the atonement.[42] Nevertheless, notwithstanding the error of the ransom-theory, "redemption" (ἀπολύτρωσις) in 3:24 suggests that Jesus' death was a ransom since it was the necessary price paid for justification (3:24-25).[43] Paul does not state to whom the ransom was paid in

---

ἀπολύτρωσις ("redemption") with blood in Rom. 3:24 and Eph. 1:7. Paul also, however, suggests elsewhere that Jesus' death was a ransom with the words ἀγοράζω ("to buy") (1 Cor. 6:20; 7:23), ἐξαγοράζω ("to redeem") (Gal. 3:13; cf. 4:5; 5:16; Col. 4:5), and λυτρόω ("to redeem") (Titus 2:14).

[40]Adolf Deissmann (*Light from the Ancient East* [New York: Harper, 1927], 319-30) argued that Paul's background for redemption-language was Greco-Roman. He suggested that slaves in the Greco-Roman world could be liberated by the paying or depositing of money in the sanctuary of Apollos' shrine. By such a transaction, the slaves would become the property of Apollos. Scholars subsequent to Deissman questioned his thesis. They argued instead that Paul's background was primarily (even if not exclusively) Jewish. Cf. Leon Morris, *The Apostolic Preaching of the Cross*, 3rd ed. (Grand Rapids: Eerdmans, 1965), 11-64, esp. 9-26; idem, "Redemption," in *Dictionary of Paul and His Letters*, eds. Gerald F. Hawthorne, Ralph P. Martin, and Daniel G. Reid (Downers, IL: InterVarsity Press, 1993), 784-86. I have recently argued that Paul's background is martyrological (cf. Williams, *Maccabean Martyr Traditions*, 60). Paul's assertion that Jesus' death accomplished ἀπολύτρωσις ("redemption") for Jews and Gentiles closely resembles the author's descriptions of the deaths of the Jewish martyrs in 4 Macc. 6:29b and 17:21. In both texts, the author places the term ἀντίψυχον ("ransom"), a synonym for Paul's ἀπολύτρωσις ("redemption"), on the lips of Eleazar (a Jewish martyr) as he prayed that God would receive his death as a sufficient payment for Israel's sin (cf. 4 Macc. 6:28-29; 17:21-22).

[41]Mark A. Seifrid ("Romans," in *a Commentary on the New Testament Use of The Old*, eds. Greg K. Beale and D.A. Carson [Grand Rapids: Baker], 619) does not discount the idea of ransom in Rom. 3:24, but he places the accent on liberation.

[42]For example, see David Hill, *Greek Words and Hebrew Meanings: Studies in the Semantics of Soteriological Terms*, SNTS 5 (Cambridge: Cambridge University Press, 1967), 49-81. Hill primarily rejects the idea of ransom in Rom. 3:24 on lexical grounds. For an explanation of the ransom-theory, see Millard J. Erickson, *Christian Theology*, 2nd ed. (Grand Rapids: Baker, 1998), 810-13.

[43]Cf. Benjamin B. Warfield, "The New Testament Terminology of Redemption," in vol. 2 of *Bible Doctrines: The Works of Benjamin B. Warfield* (Grand Rapids: Baker 2003), 327-98; Morris, *Apostolic Preaching*, 11-64, esp. 9-26; Moo, *Romans*, 229; Finlan, *Atonement Metaphors*, 164-69. Against the idea of ransom, see Frederick R. Swallow, "Redemption in St. Paul," *Sacrament* 10 (1958): 21-27; Hill, *Greek Words*, 49-81.

3:24, but he expressly states in 3:25 that God is the author of the redemption and that the price by which both redemption and justification were accomplished for Jews and Gentiles was Jesus' blood, and his blood actually achieved justification for those for whom he died (cf. 3:24-25).

In 3:25, Paul explains how God justifies sinners through Jesus' redemption. He states that God "offered Jesus to be an atoning sacrifice," that this sacrifice is received "by faith," and that Jesus' "blood" accomplished justification for the one who has faith (Rom. 3:25-26). He continues in 3:27-30 with further comments on justification. In Rom 3:28, he expresses that one is justified by faith and in 3:29-30 that God justifies Jews and Gentiles by faith. Paul's comments in 3:21-31 are embedded between earlier comments in 1:18-3:20 about God's universal condemnation of both Jews and Gentiles due to their inability to meet Torah's demands to the fullest, and they are embedded between a later comment in 4:25 that Jesus "was handed over for our sins and was raised for our justification." Those for whom Jesus died, those who are justified by faith, and those whom God predestines to be in Christ (Rom. 8:29-30) are the same group. Thus, God's offering of Jesus to die for Jews and Gentiles accomplished justification for those whom he died and those for whom he died are those who experience justification by faith and future glorification, and those who experience justification and future glorification are those whom God predestined to be conformed to the image of Christ (cf. Rom. 3:21-8:30). Paul does not speak of Jesus' death as hypothetically accomplishing soteriological benefits for all people via his death, but that Jesus actually effected justification for those for whom God offered him to die. This suggests that the group for whom he died is the same group whom he elected and predestination for justification and glorification to be vessels of mercy (cf. Rom. 8:29-30; 9:23-24) since they are the only ones (not those who die in disbelief) who receive God's soteriological benefits effected by the death of Jesus.

Romans 5:6-11: Jesus' Death, Reconciliation,
Justification, and Salvation
Justification on the basis of Jesus' death is the foundation of the hope that Paul mentions in Romans 5:1-5 (cf. Rom. 5:1-8:39).[44] In 5:6-7, he states that Jesus died for the weak. He, then, explains 5:6-7 in 5:8: "but God demonstrated his own love toward us; namely, while we were sinners, Christ died for us." In 5:6, Paul states that Christ died "for the weak." In 5:7, he states that someone would scarcely die "for a righteous person" and that someone would perhaps die "for a good person." Then, in 5:8, Paul clarifies by stating that Christ died "for us." Christ's death "for us" is a death for sinners since Paul states in 5:8 that Christ's death "for us" occurred "while we were sinners." In 5:9-10, Paul

---

[44] As I have stated elsewhere, many scholars agree that the major theme of Rom. 5:1-8:39 is hope. For example, see Jarvis J. Williams, *One New Man: The Cross and Racial Reconciliation in Pauline Theology* (Nashville: Broadman & Holman, 2010), 80 n. 79.

declares that Jesus' blood accomplished justification, salvation, and reconciliation for those for whom he died.

Moreover, with his inference from 5:8 in 5:9, Paul connects Jesus' death mentioned in 5:8 with salvation: "Therefore, how much more we will be saved through him from wrath, because we were justified by his blood." Jesus' death for sinners is the basis of each soteriological benefit in 5:8-10, for Paul states that Jesus died for sin in 5:8 and in 5:9-10 that Jesus' blood *justifies, saves the ungodly from God's wrath,* and *reconciles* the ungodly to God with the result that the ungodly are no longer enemies of God. This latter point of reconciliation is further elucidated in 5:11 when Paul expresses that those whom God has justified, saves, and reconciles by Jesus' blood have received reconciliation. Therefore, Paul again applies Jesus' blood exclusively to Jews and Gentiles within the believing community, and he states that Jesus' death has accomplished soteriological benefits only for those within the believing community. He does not in this text give any indication that Jesus' death hypothetically accomplished soteriological benefits for all people without exception. Instead, Paul argues that Jesus' death actually justifies, delivers from God's wrath, and reconciles to God all of those for whom he died.

Romans 8:1-4: Jesus' Death and the Fulfillment of the Righteous Requirement of the Law *in Us*[45]

Paul states in Romans 8:1 that "condemnation" no longer exists for those who are "in Christ Jesus." The phrase "in Christ" strongly supports that the benefits of Jesus' death that Paul enumerates in the ensuing verses are only for those "in Christ." That is, no one outside of Christ is without condemnation, but those "in Christ," and those "in Christ" are in him precisely because Jesus died for them. Romans 8:2-4 supports this point. He states in 8:2 the reason why condemnation no longer exists: "For the law of the Spirit of life by means of Christ Jesus freed you from the law of sin and of death." Paul explains 8:2 in Rom 8:3 by stating how those in Christ received such freedom: "For God [did] what the law was incapable [of doing] because it was weak through sinful flesh in that he sent his own son to deal with sin in the likeness of sinful flesh, and he condemned sin in [Jesus'] flesh" (brackets mine).

Paul introduces sacrificial language in Romans 8:1-4 with the phrase περὶ ἁμαρτίας in 8:3. With the latter phrase, many scholars agree that Paul alludes to the "sin-offering" of the Old Testament (cf. LXX Lev. 5:9).[46] Such

---

[45]My discussion of Rom. 8:1-4 overlaps with my discussion in Jarvis J. Williams, "Violent Atonement in Romans: The Foundation of Paul's Soteriology," *JETS* 53 (December 2010): 579-99, esp. 591-95. I have published the overlapping material here with permission from the Journal of the Evangelical Theological Society.

[46]For examples, see Peter Stuhlmacher, *Der Brief an die Römer*, NTD 6 (Göttingen: Vandenhoeck & Ruprecht), 1989), 107; James D.G. Dunn, *Romans 1-8*, WBC 38 (Nashville: Word, 1988), 1:422; N.T. Wright, *The New Testament and the People of God* (Minneapolis: Fortress, 1992), 220-25; Richard H. Bell, "Sacrifice and Christology in Paul," *JTS* 53 (2002): 1-27, esp. 5-8.

an allusion would fit nicely with Paul's argument in Romans 7 that the "I" under the law commits sin ignorantly/unintentionally, for the sin-offering dealt with ignorant/unintentional sins in the Old Testament (cf. LXX Lev. 5:7-8; 6:25 [MT Lev. 6:18]).[47] C.E.B. Cranfield rejects the reading of sin-offering for περὶ ἁμαρτίας in 8:3 in spite of the fact that the LXX often uses this phrase in cultic contexts to refer to a sin-offering (e.g. LXX Lev. 5:9; 14:31; Ps. 39:7).[48] Cranfield argues that a sacrificial reading is forced in 8:3 since the context of Paul's argument does not support such a reading. He argues instead that περὶ ἁμαρτίας in 8:3 should be connected to the statement "in that he sent his son in the likeness of sinful flesh" and not to the verbal clause "he condemned sin in the flesh." According to Cranfield, 8:3 simply refers to Jesus' mission, not to his penal death for sin. Thomas R. Schreiner agrees with Cranfield that περὶ ἁμαρτίας in 8:3 modifies the participle and not the verb, but Schreiner correctly argues that περὶ ἁμαρτίας refers to Jesus as a sin-offering since the phrase refers to a sin-offering 44 of 54 occurrences in the LXX (e.g. LXX Lev. 5:6-11; 7:37; 9:2-3; 12:6, 8; 14:13, 22, 31; 15:15, 30; 16:3, 5, 9; 23:19) and since Paul uses the phrase to refer to Jesus' death for sin in 8:3.[49]

Paul further confirms the purpose and the benefit of Jesus' death for those for whom he died in 8:3 by stating that God "judged/condemned" (κατακρίνω) sin in the flesh. The majority of appearances of this verb in the LXX suggests a penal judgment (cf. LXX Esth. 2:1; Wis. 4:16; Pss. Sol. 4:2; Sus. 1:41, 48, 53), and other occurrences of the verb κατακρίνω or its nominal cognate κατάκριμα in the New Testament supports that those to whom this verb and its cognate are applied would either receive the penalty of judgment (Rom. 2:1; 8:34; 14:23; cf. Matt. 12:41; 20:18; 27:3; Mark 10:33; 14:64; Luke 11:31; Heb. 11:7; 2 Pet. 2:6) or would be delivered from the penalty of judgment (Rom. 8:1; 1 Cor. 11:32).[50] Thus, the concept of sin-offering in 8:3 and Paul's judicial language in 8:1 with κατάκριμα and in 8:3 with κατακρίνω support that Jesus' death was a penal sacrifice of atonement for sin, especially since Leviticus 4:1-35 and 5:9 state that the sin-offering should be slaughtered and its blood should be presented before YHWH in order to provide atonement for sin (cf. Lev. 4:26, 35). Regardless of whether the sin-offering was offered for unintentional/ignorant sins, the important point for my argument is that the sin-offering was nevertheless offered as an expression of God's judgment against sin. YHWH required the animal to be slaughtered for the sins of others and its blood to be shed to make right the

---

[47]Also N.T. Wright, "Romans," NIB 10 (Nashville: Abingdon, 2002), 579.
[48]Cranfield, *Romans* 378-90, esp. 382.
[49]Thomas R. Schreiner, *Romans,* BECNT (Grand Rapids: Baker, 1998), 401-03; Stuhlmacher *Römer*, 107; N.T. Wright, *The Climax of the Covenant: Christ and the Law in Pauline Theology* (Minneapolis: Fortress, 1993), 220-25; Bell, "Sacrifice and Christology in Paul," 1-27, esp. 5-8. Against Barrett, *Romans,* 156; Bradley H. McLean, *The Cursed Christ*, JSNTSupp 126 (Sheffield: Sheffield Academic Press, 1996), 46.
[50]For violent atonement as Paul's central atonement model in Romans, see Williams, "Violent Atonement in Romans," 579-99.

unintentional/ignorant wrongs. Likewise, 8:3 states that Jesus was the sacrificial victim in whom God condemned sin to make right the wrongs of those for whom he died.

Against the idea of penal substitution in 8:3, N.T. Wright stresses that Paul says that God condemned sin, not that he condemned Jesus.[51] Wright correctly acknowledges that Paul states that sin was condemned in Jesus' flesh, but he contends that this does not mean "that God desired to punish someone and decided to punish Jesus on everybody else's behalf."[52] Instead, Wright asserts that in Jesus' cross, God judged sin by rendering it powerless as a power so that sin would no longer take up residence in human beings and consequently produce their death.[53]

Wright is correct to point out that Paul states that God condemned sin, not Jesus. He is also correct to note that contrary to some translations, the phrase "in the flesh" in the clause "God condemned sin in the flesh" refers to Jesus' flesh (not to humanity's flesh), because the entire context of Paul's argument explains why condemnation no longer exists for those in Christ Jesus (cf. Rom. 7:7-8:4). Nonetheless, even if the accent should be placed on God's condemnation of sin in the cross of Jesus in 8:3 instead of on God's condemnation of Jesus, one cannot and indeed must not separate God's condemnation of sin in Jesus' flesh from God's condemnation of Jesus in Rom 8:3 because Paul states that God "judged" sin "in Jesus' flesh." In other words, Wright seems to miss the point in this text that the only way that God's condemnation of sin in Jesus' flesh could have effectively condemned sin and thereby make its power inoperative in humanity is if Jesus paid the penalty that sin brought upon all of humanity: namely, God's judgment in death. This argument fits with Paul's earlier argument in 5:12-21 that Adam brought death to all because of his disobedience, but Jesus brought life to all because of his obedience. In Paul's view, neither God's plan to overcome the power of sin in humanity nor Jesus' obedience was complete until his cross-bearing experience of God's wrath (cf. Rom. 3:25-26; 8:3).

In a way that is similar to Wright, Richard H. Bell does not think that Paul refers to "a satisfaction theory of the atonement" (i.e. penal substitution) in 8:3 when he states that "God condemned sin in Jesus' flesh."[54] Rather, Bell argues that Paul's theory of atonement in 8:3 reflects the P source, which suggests that the sin-offering dealt with the essence of sin in a human, not the human's doing of sin. Bell's view seems to dichotomize falsely between the concept of sin and the doing of sin when in fact Paul himself discusses sin in complex ways in Romans. Paul states that God will repay evil deeds in the judgment with wrath (Rom. 2:6-10), and he affirms that everybody sins (Rom. 3:23). The preceding evidence seems to emphasize the individual doing of sin. Paul also states that sin should not reign over believers (Rom. 6:12), which

---

[51] Wright, "Romans," 578.
[52] Ibid.
[53] Ibid.
[54] Bell, "Sacrifice and Christology in Paul," 6-8 n. 40.

seems to present sin as a power and thereby focuses on the essence of sin. Bell's view neither takes seriously the divine penal language of 5:12-8:4. Adam's disobedience brought "judgment" and "death" upon everyone (Rom. 5:12-21), and the law's entrance only increased the power of sin and the severity of God's judgment (Rom. 5:12-21; 7:1-23), but Jesus' death frees from "condemnation" everyone in him who was under God's "condemnation" of sin increased by the presence of the law (Rom. 7:24; 8:1-3).

Paul's words "in the likeness of sinful flesh" in 8:3 additionally support the specific purpose of Jesus' death and the benefits that his death provided for those for whom he died, because Paul connects God's condemnation of sin in Jesus' death with Jesus' participation within the realm of sinful humanity.[55] Bell rightly argues that the phrase refers to Jesus' "full identity and resemblance" with sinful humanity, for he thinks that Paul is concerned with "the sending of Christ into the area of human existence" and that part of such an existence is indeed sin.[56] Bell does not argue that Jesus committed sin, but correctly identifies functional sinfulness with Jesus.[57] That is, Jesus' participation in the sphere of sin does not mean that he sinned, but that he functioned as a sinner in his wrath bearing death. Jesus' functional sinfulness is supported by the rest of 8:3: "he judged sin in the flesh."

As noted above, the phrase "in the flesh" in the clause "he judged sin in the flesh" in 8:3 refers to Jesus' flesh, not to the sinful flesh of humans. The text of 8:3 does not suggest that Jesus himself was sinful, but affirms that God condemned sin in Jesus' flesh by sending him in the likeness of sinful humanity and by judging him as the guilty sinner in his death on the cross. That Jesus actually died supports this, because death (according to Paul) is both the result of sin's power over humanity and God's judgment of humanity (cf. Gen. 2:17; Rom. 5:12). Although Paul possibly refers both to Jesus' incarnation and to his death in 8:3 with the phrase "in the likeness of sinful flesh (cf. Phil. 2:7),[58] the cross appears to be the emphasis,[59] because the phrase gives the impression that Jesus fully identified with sinful humanity by taking upon himself God's condemnation/judgment for humanity's sin and by being judged/condemned as

---

[55] So Bell, "Sacrifice and Christology in Paul" 7-8. The term ὁμοίωμα ("likeness") in Rom. 8:3 is used elsewhere to mean similar in copy (LXX Deut. 4:15-18, 23, 25; 5:8; Josh. 22:28; 1 Kgs 6:5; Ps. 105:20; Sir. 34:3; Rom. 1:23; 5;13; 6:5). For a detailed analysis of ὁμοίωμα, see Schreiner, *Romans,* 313-14; F.A. Morgan, "Romans 6:5a: United to a Death like Christ's," *ETL* 59 (1983): 267-302.
[56] Bell, "Sacrifice and Christology in Paul," 6-7.
[57] Bell, "Sacrifice and Christology in Paul," 6-7. See in contrast to Bell V.P. Branick ("The Sinful Flesh of the Son of God [Rom 8:3]: A Key Image in Pauline Theology," *CBQ* 47 [1985]: 246-62, esp. 251).
[58] So Bell, "Sacrifice and Christology in Paul," 7-8.
[59] Against Bell, "Sacrifice and Christology in Paul" 8. Bell does not emphasize the importance of the cross-event in Rom. 8:3, but he thinks that Paul refers both to the incarnation and to the cross-event. However, rightly Joseph A. Fitzmyer, *Romans,* ABC 33 (New York: Doubleday, 1993), 486-87; Schreiner, *Romans* 404.

Purpose and Benefits of Jesus' Death 209

a sinner (cf. Gal. 4:5-6; Phil. 2:5-9).[60] Jesus identified with sinful humanity by becoming human, by submitting to the sinful realm of existence, and by going to the cross to take upon himself God's death penalty for humanity's sin (cf. Rom. 5:12-21; 1 Cor. 15:26). Unlike Adam and the rest of humanity, Jesus remained free from the act of committing sin (cf. Rom. 5:12-21; 2 Cor. 5:21), and his sinlessness explains why his death on the cross actually (not hypothetically) delivers from the law those who were condemned by it (cf. Rom. 7:1-8:10). However, like Adam, Jesus paid a severe penalty for the problem of sin: namely, God's judgment in death (cf. Rom. 5:12-21; 8:3).

In 8:4, Paul states that God's purpose of condemning sin in Jesus' flesh was to fulfill the righteous requirement of the law in "us who are not walking according to the flesh but according to the Spirit." Since the entrance of the law into salvation history increased the power of sin (Rom. 1:18-7:25; esp. 3:20, 4:15, 5:12-5:21, 7:7-25, Gal. 3:19),[61] God sent Jesus to overcome the power of sin and death and to fulfill the law's demands "in us" who live according to the Spirit (cf. Rom. 5:12-6:23). Scholars debate whether Christ's active obedience or Christian obedience is in view in 8:4.[62] Because of Paul's remarks in 8:1-3 that the law no longer condemns those "in Christ" since God offered Jesus to die for them to free them from Torah's condemnation, whose death frees those in him by fulfilling the righteous requirement of the law "in us" by means of his condemnation of sin in Jesus' flesh, and because of his comments that those for whom Jesus died have Torah fulfilled in them because of their participation in the Spirit in 8:5-11, Paul speaks to Christian obedience in 8:4 and not to the perfect obedience of Jesus. Jesus' obedience is certainly assumed in light of 8:3.[63] This interpretation is supported by the fact that after 8:3 discusses God's work of defeating the power of sin by condemning sin in Jesus' flesh, 8:4 states that the purpose for which God condemned sin in Jesus' flesh was to fulfill the righteous requirement of the law in us who walk according to the Spirit.

Romans 8:4 expresses that Jesus' life paid a price for those in Christ who were otherwise condemned by the law and his death for those in him fulfilled in them and on their behalf the law's righteous requirement (Rom. 8:1-3), for he took upon himself their condemnation by means of his death for them so that they would receive in themselves the law's fulfillment (Rom. 8:4). This transaction between those in Christ and Jesus is not discussed by Paul as a hypothetical achievement for everyone, but he states forthrightly that those in Christ are not condemned because God offered Jesus to die for them and to free

---

[60]Cf. Jewett, *Romans* 483-84.
[61]For a detailed discussion of this point, see my comments in chapter 2.
[62]For a recent discussion of this debate and for an argument in favor of Christian obedience, see Kevin W. McFadden, "The Fulfillment of the Law's Dikaiōma: Another Look at Romans 8:1-4," *JETS* 52 (2009): 483-97.
[63]I have modified my view of Rom. 8:4 since the publication of my *One New Man*, 82-84. Thus, the view espoused above is different from my explanation of Rom. 8:4 in my earlier monograph.

them from Torah's condemnatory power over them (Rom. 7:24-8:4), and the certainty of their salvation is seen by their actual experience of the Spirit and their liberation from Torah's condemnation. According to Paul, only those who receive the Spirit are liberated from sin's power (cf. Rom. 5:5-8:11). Therefore, only Christians (those who trust in Jesus) receive the benefits of his death.

2 Corinthians 5:14-21: Jesus' Death, Reconciliation, A New Creation, and the Righteousness of God

In 2 Corinthians 5:14-21, the purpose of and the benefits of Jesus' death for those for whom he died are present. Paul states in 5:14 that he endured sufferings for Christ because Christ's love compelled him. The phrase "love of Christ" echoes Paul's statement in Romans 5:8 regarding God's love since he connects both God's love and Christ's love to Jesus' death for the sins of others in both texts. In Romans 5:8, Paul states that God demonstrated his love for humanity in that Christ died for sinners. He likewise states in 2 Corinthians 5:14-15 that Jesus died for others to achieve life for them.[64] The message of Romans 5 and 2 Corinthians 5 is different. Nevertheless, in both texts Paul uses virtually the same vocabulary (e.g. "to die" [Rom. 5:6-8, 2 Cor. 5:14-15]; the death for another formula [Rom. 5:6-9, 2 Cor 5:14-15]; "to reconcile" [Rom. 5:10, 2 Cor. 5:18-20], and "reconciliation" [Rom. 5:11; 2 Cor. 5:18, 19) to highlight the salvation that Jesus achieved by his sacrificial death for those for whom he died. In both Romans 5 and in 2 Corinthians 5, Paul states that a soteriological benefit that Jesus achieved through his death for the ungodly is reconciliation with God.

Paul states in 2 Corinthians 5:18-19 that God reconciled the world to himself in Christ and in 5:19 that he did not count the transgressions of those in the world against them. 2 Corinthians 5:14-15 confirms that Jesus' death was indeed the basis of reconciliation in Christ. These verses also confirm the reason for which God did not count transgressions against the transgressors was Jesus' death. 2 Corinthians 5:21 especially supports that Jesus' death for others in 5:14-15 and reconciliation in Christ in 5:19 should be understood as something actually accomplished for those for whom he died since Paul states that God made Jesus sin for those for whom he died ("God made the one who did not know sin as sin for us. . .").[65]

The preceding statement in 2 Corinthians 5:21 alludes to the Old Testament cult since the statement suggests that Jesus identified in some

---

[64]Against Cilliers Breytenbach, "Salvation of the Reconciled (With a Note on the Background of Paul's Metaphor of Reconciliation)," in *Salvation in the New Testament: Perspectives in Soteriology*, ed. J.G. van der Watt (Leiden: Brill, 2005), 280-81. He rightly acknowledges that the dying formula so prominent in the Greek tradition influenced Paul here. However, he went too far when he stated that the Greek tradition did not teach substitutionary atonement, but that humans died as representatives for the city-state or someone to relieve that person or group form death.

[65]Scholars vigorously debate the meaning of 5:19-21. For a detailed discussion of the text, see Harris, *Second Corinthians*, 439-56.

manner with sin (cf. Rom. 8:3).[66] In Leviticus, the author states that the priest should present a sin-offering when he sins and brings guilt upon the people (Lev. 4:2-3). Likewise, the people as a whole were commanded to sacrifice an animal as a sin-offering when the sin of the people became known to the whole assembly (Lev. 4:13-14). Once the people slaughtered the animal and once they sprinkled the blood in the appropriate places, God would forgive them through this atonement (cf. Lev. 4:20; cf. Lev. 4; 16). Paul does not employ the normal grammatical construction in the LXX (περὶ ἁμαρτίας) to convey the idea of sin-offering (cf. LXX Lev. 5:6-7; 5:11; 7:37; 9:2-3; 12:6, 8; 14:13, 22, 31; 15:15, 30; 16:3, 5, 9; 23:19, Num. 6:11; Rom. 8:3). Nevertheless, the concept of sin-offering is present in 2 Corinthians 5:21 for at least four reasons. First, 5:14-15 suggests that Jesus' death was on behalf of others. Second, 5:17-18 suggests that Jesus brought about a new creation and reconciliation for all who are in him. Third, 5:19 suggests that as a result of the reconciliation that Jesus achieved by means of his death, God does not judge the transgressors for their transgressions. Fourth, God made Jesus sin for others so that they would become God's righteousness in him. When interpreted together, 5:14-15, 19, and 21 suggests that Jesus' death for others was an actual offering for their sin and that his death for their sin was effective in that it actually accomplished their salvation, for his death for the transgressors is the reason why God does not count the transgressions against them (5:19) and the reason why they receive new creation, reconciliation, and the righteousness of God.[67]

Galatians 3:13-14: Jesus' Death, Redemption, and the Promise of the Spirit

In Galatians 3:13-14, Paul's words support that Jesus' death has a specific purpose and that this purpose was effective and accomplished actual benefits for those for whom Jesus died. Galatians 3:13 states that Jesus "redeemed us from the curse of the law in that he became a course on behalf of us: 'because it is written that cursed is everyone who is hanged upon a tree,' so that the blessing of Abraham would come to the Gentiles by means of Christ and so that we would receive the promise of the Spirit by faith."[68] The penal nature of Jesus' death is evident by the phrase "from the curse of the law," by the clause "by becoming a curse for us," and by the Old Testament citation "cursed is everyone who hangs on a tree" (Deut. 21:23). The phrase "from the curse of the

---

[66] Against sin-offering here, see Margaret E. Thrall, "Salvation Proclaimed: 2 Corinthians 5:18-21," *ExT* 93 (1982): 230; Breytenbach, "Salvation of the Reconciled," 276.
[67] Morna D. Hooker ("Interchange in Christ," *JTS* 22 [1974]: 349-61) broadens Paul's statement in 2 Cor. 5:21 (that God made/appointed Jesus as sin) to include the incarnation. Cf. Bell, "Sacrifice and Christology," 14-15.
[68] Stephen Travis ("Christ as the Bearer of Divine Judgment in Paul's Thought about the Atonement," in *Atonement Today*, ed. John Goldingay [London: SPCK, 1995], 21-38; esp. 24) doubts that Gal. 3:13 is about atonement in general or about the salvation of individuals.

law" modifies the verb "to redeem" (ἐξηγόρασεν), and it conveys the idea of separation and liberation.[69] The phrase "by becoming a curse for us" conveys the manner by which Christ "set us free" from the law's curse: "in that he became a curse for us" (cf. Phil. 2:5). The citation from Deuteronomy 21:23 provides scriptural support for the penal nature of Jesus' death for others: "everyone who hangs on a tree is cursed."

The curse of Galatians 3:13 is the result of one's inability to keep the law's demands prescribed in the Mosaic Covenant, a point with which Paul begins in Galatians 3:10-12. This is evident in four ways. (1) Paul uses the phrase "curse of the law" along with "works of the law" in the same context (cf. Gal. 3:10-13). (2) He uses "curse of the law" to describe that the law produces or yields curse-pronouncements to those who disobey. (3) He cites Deuteronomy, which is a recapitulation of the Mosaic Covenant. (4) Deuteronomy 27 begins with an exhortation for Israel to "keep every commandment" that Moses prescribed for them in the law (Deut. 27:1; cf. 27:10).

That the law yields curse-pronouncements to those who disobey is evident from Paul's citation of Deuteronomy 27:26, Habakkuk 2:4, and Leviticus 18:5.[70] Paul cites Deuteronomy 27:26 and Leviticus 18:5 to emphasize that the law demands obedience and anything less results in a curse since the contexts of both texts emphasize the importance of obedience to the covenant for the purpose of remaining in the covenant and since he cites Habakkuk 2:4 to emphasize the importance of believing/faith versus doing (cf. DSS 1QS 5.8, 21, 24; 6.13-23; 8.4, 10, 20). Paul recalls Galatians 3:10-12 in 3:13 with his citation of Deuteronomy 27:26. His entire argument in Galatians 3:10-14 is that the curse-pronouncements of the Mosaic Covenant come upon those who do not obey Torah (Gal. 3:10-12), but Christ has freed all who have faith from those curse-pronouncements by becoming accursed himself on their behalf (Gal. 3:12-13). This latter point should not be missed. Jesus actually delivered those for whom he died from Torah's curse-pronouncements, because he became a curse for them. To elucidate the point further, I will pose a question and provide the answer to it from Paul's comments in Galatians 3:13. For whom did Jesus die according to Galatians 3:13? He died for those whom he redeemed from Torah's curse-pronouncements, because he became a curse on behalf of those for whom he died and whom he delivered from Torah's curse-pronouncements.

The curses of Deuteronomy 27 are the result of disobedience to God's commands given through Moses (Deut. 27:1). Moses prescribes for Israel what they should and should not do when they crossed the Jordon (cf. Deut. 27). If

---

[69]Cf. Daniel B. Wallace (*Greek Grammar Beyond the Basics* [Grand Rapids: Zondervan, 1996], 371) who states that separation is an option for the preposition ἐκ ("from").

[70]For thorough treatments of Paul's citation of Deuteronomy in Second Temple Judaism and in Galatians and Lev. 18:5 in Second Temple Judaism and in Paul, see Pate, *The Reverse of the Curse*; Preston M. Sprinkle, *Law and Life: The Interpretation of Leviticus 18:5 in Early Judaism and in Paul*, WUNT 241 (Tübingen: Mohr-Siebeck, 2008).

Purpose and Benefits of Jesus' Death

Israel disobeyed Yahweh's commands at one point, the individual who disobeyed would be cursed (Deut. 27:15-29:29; cf. Lev. 18:5; DSS 1QS 5.8, 21, 24; 6.13-23; 8.4, 10, 20). Deuteronomy 28:1-68 states that YHWH is the author of the curses since he promises to bless those who obey the covenant (Deut. 28:1-14) and to curse those who disobey the covenant (Deut. 28:15-68). Deuteronomy 21:23, which Paul quotes in Galatians 3:13, specifically elucidates the nature of Jesus' death. Deuteronomy 21:22-23 clarifies that those who commit sin worthy of death should be put to death (i.e. should suffer the death penalty) and that Israel should hang this person on a tree. Moses warns Israel not to leave the dead body of this one on the tree throughout the night, "for a curse of God is the one who is hanged" (Deut. 21:23). The hanging of the dead person promulgates to the entire nation that the one who hangs on a tree has suffered divine judgment; he is rejected by God, and that he is accursed. Since God is the source of the law and of the curse-pronouncements in Deuteronomy, God curses the one who does not do the law since, according to Deuteronomy 27-28, a violation of one of his commandments was worthy of judgment. Jesus, therefore, by becoming a curse "for us" received God's divine death-sentence and took upon himself God's curse that Jews and Gentiles rightly deserved, so that Gentiles would be partakers of the Abrahamic blessing and so that "we" would receive the Spirit by faith (Gal. 3:14-15). The purpose of Jesus' death, then, was to redeem all of those for whom he died from Torah's curses, to extend the promise of salvation given to Abraham to the Gentiles, and to impart to Jews and Gentiles God's Spirit, who is the seal and down payment of salvation. Paul does not suggest here that Jesus' death hypothetically benefits all people without exception. Rather, he applies the purpose and the benefits of Jesus' death to those who have been delivered from Torah's curses-pronouncements and to those who have a personal experience with the Spirit.

Ephesians 1-2 and Colossians 1-2: Jesus' Death, Forgiveness of Sins, and the Reconciliation of 'All' Things *in Christ*

Ephesians 1-2 and Colossians 1-2 support that the purpose of Jesus' death was for the elect community of Jews and Gentiles and the benefits of Jesus' death are applied to the elect community of Jews and Gentiles. Ephesians 1:3-14 is a doxology of praise. As Paul praises God for the spiritual blessings that believers inherit in Christ, he mentions redemption as one of those spiritual blessings. Paul states in Ephesians 1:7 "in [Christ] we have redemption through his blood. . ." Paul's statements in Ephesians 1:7 and Colossians 1:14 are basically the same. The statement "in whom we have redemption" in the above respective contexts suggests that Jesus' redemption achieved salvation for the unredeemed.

The word that Paul uses for "redemption" (ἀπολύτρωσις) in Ephesians 1:7 (Eph. 1:14) and Colossians 1:14 is the same term that he uses in Romans 3:24. In my earlier discussion of Romans 3:24 above, I argued that this term conveys the idea of ransom. This meaning is also present here in Ephesians 1:7 since Paul states in 1:7 that Jesus' blood is the means by which and thus the required price by which the redemption was accomplished: "in [Christ] we have redemption through his blood" (cf. Isa. 53:2-12; Rom. 4:25).[71] The concept of ransom is also present in Colossians 1:14 since Paul states later in Colossians 1:20 that Jesus' blood provided peace and reconciliation for all things and since he states in Colossians 2:13-14 that God forgave trespasses by means of Jesus' cross. The reconciliation of "all things" through the cross of Jesus in Colossians 1:20 does not suggest that Jesus' blood cleanses the sins of all people without exception regardless of whether they trust in him, because Paul states in Colossians 1:14 that "we have redemption in him." The "we" refers to Christians since Paul wrote as a Christian to Christians, since Christians are the only ones whose sins are forgiven by Jesus' death in Paul's view, and since Paul explicitly states in Colossians 1:21-22 that the Colossians were formerly "estranged and enemies with respect to your understanding, but now [Jesus] reconciled [you] by means of his fleshly body through his death to present you to be holy and blameless and irreproachable in his presence." These verses poignantly promulgate that those for whom Jesus died are reconciled to God and present as holy and blameless before him. In Colossians 1:23, Paul's remarks support this point, for he urges the Colossians to remain steadfast in the faith and in the hope of the gospel. Thus, Paul's point in Colossians 1:20 regarding the reconciliation of "all things" via Jesus' death is that the entire creation, which currently groans and awaits its future liberation from the power of sin (cf. Rom. 8:18-25), will experience its liberation thanks to the redeeming death of Jesus, whose death dismantled sin's power over the entire creation.

Redemption through Jesus' blood in Ephesians 1:7 and in Colossians 1:14 (cf. Col. 1:20; 2:13) confirms that Jesus died for a specific purpose and that this purpose was effected in the lives of those who believe, for his death actually (not hypothetically) wiped away sins and even canceled out the transgressions of those who violated God's specific commands. But his comments about redemption in Ephesians 1:7 are especially helpful to my thesis in this chapter since he connects Jesus' redemption with election (Eph. 1:4), predestination (Eph. 1:5, 11), forgiveness of sins (Eph. 1:7), hearing the gospel and personal faith in the gospel (Eph. 1:13), and the reception of the Spirit (Eph. 1:13-14). Thus, one can infer that those who receive redemption and forgiveness of sins through Jesus' blood, those who respond to the gospel in faith, and those who receive the seal and down payment of the Spirit are those whom God has chosen and predestined to be in Christ before the foundation of the world, for Paul lists these soteriological benefits as the spiritual blessings inherited by Christians in Christ, for which he praises God, and since he states that all those in Christ have received from God these

---

[71]See I. Howard Marshall, "The Development of the Concept of Redemption in the New Testament," in *Reconciliation and Hope: Essays in Honor of Leon Morris,* ed. R.J. Banks (Exeter: Paternoster, 1974), 153-69; Harold W. Hoehner, *Ephesians* (Grand Rapids: Baker, 2002), 206. Against Andrew T. Lincoln, *Ephesians*, WBC 42 (Nashville: Nelson, 1990), 28.

Purpose and Benefits of Jesus' Death 215

benefits (Eph. 1:3-14). Therefore, according to Ephesians 1:3-14 and Colossians 1-2, the purpose of Jesus' death was to atone the sins of the elect and the benefits of his death were applied to all of those for whom he died. This is supported by the fact that only they actually receive and participate in those blessings that exist as a result of Jesus' death for them.

Conclusion

This chapter has considered the purpose and benefits of Jesus' death in Paul's atonement-theology. I have argued that Paul suggests that Jesus' death both actually (not hypothetically) atoned for the sins of all Jews and Gentiles within the Christian community and that his death actually accomplished soteriological benefits for those for whom he died, so that (according to Paul) Jesus' death is the foundational reason why all (and only those) Jews and Gentiles who place faith in Jesus as the Jewish Messiah will participate in God's present and future salvation provided in Jesus. In addition, this chapter has also argued that early Jewish traditions in both the Hebrew Bible and in other sacred texts in early Judaism shaped Paul's conception of Jesus' death, but Paul used those traditions to redefine atonement as something that God accomplished for his people by means of the death of Jesus and not by the sacrifice of animals or any other pious human besides Jesus.

To defend these points, because of limited space, I investigated only one text from the Hebrew Bible (=Lev. 16), which focuses on animal sacrifices of atonement, selected texts from 2 and 4 Maccabees, which focus on human sacrifices of atonement, and selected texts from the Pauline corpus. This line of investigation sought to establish the point that just as both animal and human sacrifices of atonement were *restricted* to and offered *specifically* for believing Jews (i.e. God's elect community of faith) in early Jewish religion and not Gentiles (i.e. the unbelieving community) to accomplish soteriological benefits for them, so also Jesus' death in Paul's atonement-theology is *restricted* to and *specifically* for the elect community of faith, i.e., for those who identify with the Christian community, and his death accomplished soteriological benefits exclusively for them. However, whereas atonement in early Judaism was only for Jews and those who converted to Judaism, I have argued that Paul suggests that Jesus' death atoned for the sins of all Jews and Gentiles within the believing community who possess faith in Jesus as the Jewish Messiah.

Chapter 5

Conclusion

Chapter 2 considered humanity's spiritual plight in Paul's anthropology. I argued that Paul deems the entire human condition to be under sin's power and incapable of responding to God's great act of salvation in Jesus. Chapter 3 considered divine and human agency in Paul's soteriology. I argued that Paul (similar to many of his Jewish contemporaries) deems human agency to be consequent to and the result of divine agency in his soteriology. Chapter 4 considered the purpose and benefits of Jesus' death in Paul's atonement-theology. I argued that Paul suggests that Jesus' death actually (not hypothetically) atoned for the sins of all elect Jews and Gentiles within the Christian community and that his death actually accomplished soteriological benefits for those for whom he died, so that Jesus' death (according to Paul) is the foundational reason why all (and only those) Jews and Gentiles who place faith in him will participate in God's present and future salvation provided in Jesus. In addition, chapter 4 also argued that early Jewish traditions in both the Hebrew Bible and in other sacred texts in early Judaism shaped Paul's conception of Jesus' death, but Paul used those traditions to redefine atonement as something that God accomplished for Jews and Gentiles by means of the death of Jesus and not by the sacrifice of animals or by the sacrifice of any other human besides Jesus. In this chapter, I tie together the arguments presented in chapters 2-4 and infer conclusions from them.

The Extent of the Atonement and Human Depravity in Paul

If my exegesis and arguments in chapter 2 are correct regarding the spiritual plight of humanity in Paul's anthropology, Paul thought that both Jews and Gentiles are sinners, are guilty before God, are slaves to sin's power, and that they are incapable of meeting the demands set forth in Torah. Consequently, God's Torah cannot bring life to them, contrary to the promise in Leviticus 18:5 and Deuteronomy 30:15-20, but it only brings death due to sin's reign over them and due to their inability to meet Torah's demands. As I argued in chapter 2, according to Paul, apart from God's action in and on behalf of Jews and Gentiles in Jesus, humanity's spiritual plight remains in its dismal state of bondage, of moral inability, and of condemnation (cf. Rom. 1:18-8:39). Although the demands to pursue Christ and to believe in the gospel as the power of God unto salvation are set before Jews and Gentiles through the proclamation of the gospel (cf. Rom. 1:16-17; 9:30-11:36), Paul strongly contends that Jews and Gentiles are morally incapable of pursuing those demands and receiving those promises of salvation found in the gospel due to their slavery to sin's power. Thus, Paul deems it necessary for God to act *on behalf of* Jews and Gentiles and *in* Jews and Gentiles through Christ to liberate them from sin's power and to emancipate them from Torah's condemnation (cf. Rom. 8:1-4), for they would otherwise continue to be slaves to sin's power (Rom. 6) and dead in their trespasses and sins (Eph. 2:1-3).

The Extent of the Atonement and Divine and Human Agency in Paul

In Paul's view, God acted on behalf of Jews and Gentiles firstly by choosing some before the foundation of the world from both groups to be in Christ and to be conformed into his image (cf. Rom. 8:29-30; Eph. 1:4-5, 11). Paul's view of election and predestination is both corporate and individual, for those whom God chose and predestined to be in Christ are part of a collective group of the redeemed, and they actually experience God's soteriological blessings as both individuals and as a corporate group (cf. Rom. 8:28-30; 9:6-29). That is, God chose them to be part of the group of the justified and glorified ones (Rom. 8:29-30). This group of individuals whom God chose to believe actually believe and freely choose to be united to Christ by faith (cf. Rom. 10:8-13; Eph. 1:4-14), but the reason that they believe is because the divine agent takes the initiative and works on their behalf before the foundation of the world apart from their works so that they would respond to the gospel by faith (Rom. 9:6-29; Eph. 1:4-14; 2:8-9). God's initial action on behalf of some Jews and Gentiles was necessary since they were otherwise dead in trespasses and sins and since they were otherwise slaves to sin's power (Rom. 6; Eph. 2:1-3). Thus, Paul argues that God chose some Jews and Gentiles to be in Christ and to believe in Christ before the foundation of the world, and through the proclamation of the gospel about Jesus the Jewish Messiah he "made them alive together with Christ," saved all Jews and Gentiles who believed "by grace through faith," and worked in them by his grace by granting them the gift of faith to believe the gospel and the gift of obedience to the gospel (Eph. 2:8-10).

Paul, however, nowhere communicates that the human agent looses his freedom to the divine agent with respect to salvation or that the freedom of the divine agent and the freedom of the human agent are in competition with one another with respect to salvation. Instead, Paul's view seems to be that divine and human agency exists in tension with one another, for in many contexts where he emphasizes divine agency he likewise emphasizes human agency without any explanation as to how both can be true (cf. Rom. 9:6-10:13). But, for Paul, the only reason that the human agent can be a free agent with respect to salvation is if/when the divine agent works *in* him to liberate him from sin's power (cf. Rom. 7:1-8:11). The human agent otherwise does not possess the moral capacity to be a free agent with respect to salvation even though God presents him with real moral commands and expectations with regard to the gospel of Jesus Christ.

Some (and perhaps many) may criticize that my reading of divine and human agency in Paul makes him contradictory since (they would say) it is illogical to argue that Paul believed that the human agent possesses real moral freedom, on the one hand, if he believed that the divine agent determined the actions of the human agent in advance, on the other hand, or if I contend that Paul believed that the human agent only becomes a free moral agent when God works in him the moral capacity to pursue and embrace the promises of salvation in Christ. My response to this criticism is that it does not matter if Paul seems contradictory! Whether Paul's view of divine and human agency is contradictory is a separate question from how does Paul view divine and human agency. Rather, the question at hand for any serious reader of Paul is simply what does Paul say about divine and human agency? I have offered exegetical evidence and arguments that I think support the priority of divine agency in Paul's soteriology. Philosophical objections to the position argued in this monograph do not refute my thesis or make unlikely its plausibility, and such objections must be substituted and abandoned for a serious and rigorous reading of Paul that concerns itself with what he actually says about agency.

The Extent of the Atonement and the Soteriological Experience in Paul

As I argued in chapter 4, Paul states that Jesus' death for Jews and Gentiles actually (not hypothetically) accomplished soteriological benefits for them and that he never applies either Jesus' death or those soteriological benefits achieved by his death to those outside of the Christian community. Instead, when writing to Christian communities, Paul states that Jesus died "for us" (cf. Rom. 5:6-8; Gal 3:13), "for sins" (cf. 1 Cor. 15:3), or "for me" (cf. Gal. 2:20). He never states that Jesus died for the world (regardless of how one may understand world). Rather, he applies Jesus' death and its benefits to those already within the Christian community, and he speaks of Jesus' death as accomplishing very specific soteriological benefits for them. He does not apply Jesus' death to the sins of those who live or die in disbelief of the gospel, but only to those Jews and Gentiles who participate in and experience God's great act of salvation in Jesus (cf. Rom. 3:21-5:11; Eph. 2:13). Even when he speaks of God accomplishing reconciliation for the "world" via Jesus' death in Romans 11:15, his use of "world" is restricted to all Jews and Gentiles who believe in Jesus as the Jewish Messiah. "World" in Romans 11:15 does not apply to all people without exception who live and die in disbelief of Jesus, for Paul arduously argues in Romans 9-11 that God fulfills his soteriological promises to Jews and that he includes Gentiles within these promises by means of his great act of salvation in Jesus, the Jewish Messiah, with the result that the world would be reconciled to God through Christ by faith (cf. Rom. 11:15). The entire world *without exception* (in Paul's view) is not reconciled to God,

Conclusion

for he laments that a large number of Jews chose to disbelieve the gospel (cf. Rom. 9:1-5: 10:1). But the "world" is reconciled to God through Jesus in that *some* Jews and Gentiles will be saved by faith.

In addition, when Paul states that Jesus died as a ransom for "all" (1 Tim. 2:6), this inclusive statement pertains not to *everyone without exception* but to *everyone without distinction*, for Paul begins 1 Timothy 2:1 by urging Timothy to pray for "all men." He defines the phrase "all men" in 1 Timothy 2:2 as kings, leaders, and all who are in authority. Thus, the "all men" whom God desires to be saved in 1 Timothy 2:4, and the "all" for whom Jesus died as a ransom must contextually be the all types of people for whom Paul exhorts Timothy to pray: i.e. kings and rulers in authority. Paul thought that some from this group (or maybe even all) would participate in and experience salvation, would live in obedience to the gospel, enjoy the current blessing of the Spirit, and would participate in the future resurrection to live with Christ (cf. Rom. 12:1-15:13; 1 Cor. 15; Eph. 1:4-14).

Suggestions to New Testament Scholars and Theologians for Future Scholarly, Dialogue about the Extent of the Atonement in Paul

I have endeavored throughout this monograph to argue that Paul views Jesus' death to be specifically for and only for those Jews and Gentiles who unite themselves to Jesus by faith, who identify with the Christian community, and who thereby participate in God's great act of salvation in Jesus via an investigation of selected texts in early Jewish literature and in Paul. In light of the analysis and investigation that I have herein put forth, I think that it simply will not suffice in scholarly discussion about the extent of the atonement for New Testament scholars (whether Calvinistic or Arminian, whether confessional or non-confessional, and whether Christian or non-Christian) to reject my thesis *a priori* without first listening carefully to what I am and what I am not saying or without responding to it point by point with a serious critique of my exegesis of these texts and the arguments developed from the texts. In addition, it will no longer suffice for theologians (whether Calvinistic or Arminian, whether confessional or non-confessional, and whether Christian and non-Christian) to supply technical philosophical and theological arguments as to why the thesis argued here is incorrect. To rebut my thesis, theologians must replace convoluted and confusing theories of the extent of the atonement with a detailed analysis and critique of the exegesis of the relevant texts presented in the earlier chapters. All biblical scholars and theologians must deal with the arguments found in and made about the biblical text. Just because one may identify himself or herself as a theologian instead of a biblical scholar does not mean that he or she can circumvent serious biblical exegesis in response to exegetical arguments when doing theology.

Books and articles that continue to be written either against or for a certain view of the extent of the atonement (a few were published both in the last and the current decade) and polemical conferences on the extent of the atonement that are uninformed by careful exegesis, unfamiliar with the scholarly discussion, and dominated by an impervious spirit or *ad hominem* rhetoric offer no serious exegetical arguments about the issue, for they only linger in the philosophical, theological, or emotional realms. Thus, such endeavors are absolutely void of substantial, exegetical freshness and make no contribution to (what should be) a serious scholarly, exegetical dialogue about the extent of the atonement. In part, this means that phrases like "limited," "particular," "definite," "unlimited," "general," or "universal" atonement should be abandoned and substituted for Pauline language and categories, for the preceding phrases were unknown to Paul and impose post-Pauline and post-Reformational vocabulary onto Pauline texts, thereby make Paul speak modern interpreters' post-Reformational theological language, and therefore hinder contemporary readers of Paul from both seeing with his 1st century and Jewish-Christian eyes and from speaking with his 1st century Jewish-Christian voice.

As I stated above, the philosophical and theological problems that one may find with the view presented here of Paul's view of the extent of the atonement (or with any Pauline view for that matter) is a separate issue from the issue of seeking to determine what the relevant Pauline texts actually say about the extent of the atonement (or any given Pauline issue). New Testament scholars and theologians must not conflate or confuse these two matters. Regardless of how loudly New Testament scholars or theologians (or preachers!) vociferate against the idea that Paul viewed Jesus' death to be only for those Jews and Gentiles who unite themselves to Jesus by faith and who identify with the Christian community by participating in God's plan of salvation by trusting in Jesus as the Jewish Messiah by faith and by living in communal obedience in the world with other Christians are precisely the ones (and the only ones) for whom Paul thought Jesus died, their vociferations will continue to be a "noisy song" and a "clanging symbol" until New Testament scholars and theologians take seriously what the relevant texts in Paul actually say about the extent of Jesus' death. The same goes for those New Testament scholars and theologians (and preachers!) who simply appeal to John 3:16, 1 John 2:2, or 2 Peter 2:1 in response to the position argued in this monograph. The preceding verses neither prove nor say anything about the extent of the atonement in Paul, for Paul did not write them. To cite these texts as the end all verses in the discussion only adds to the current confusion regarding the extent of the atonement.

Furthermore, it will no longer suffice for New Testament scholars and theologians (and preachers!) to be fundamentally concerned with protecting their own theological presuppositions regardless of how Arminian or Reformed, Conservative or Liberal, confessional or non-confessional, Christian or non-Christian, and Protestant or Catholic that they are. But the task of the serious investigator of the extent of the atonement and the task of all critical readers of Paul should be to engage rigorously the relevant texts that speak to the issue. Therefore, the first question that "we" readers of Paul should ask is not how can "we" (regardless of our presuppositions, faith or lack of faith)

Conclusion

protect or defend what "we" believe to be or not to be true or how can "we" vindicate or disprove what "we" have always been taught to be or not to be true before "we" even read Paul. Rather, serious readers of Paul and of this monograph should begin with the question of what does the biblical text say (and in my case, what does Paul say?) about the extent of the atonement, and does this monograph actually reflect Paul's view? When Calvinists, who appeal to the Reformed tradition, Arminians, who appeal to the Wesleyan tradition, and other biblical scholars whether Christian or non-Christian, who appeal to the enlightenment, post-enlightenment, and post-colonial traditions, let their traditions determine how Paul must have understood Jesus' death instead of appealing to the relevant Pauline texts, they provide no substantial, scholarly contribution to the discussion of the extent of the atonement in Paul. Instead, they provide only baseless talk about "their" ideas of the extent of the atonement.

To clarify, I do not claim that my discussion of the extent of the atonement in Paul in this monograph is a neutral investigation. I readily admit that I am part of a biblical and theological tradition that I deeply appreciate and value, and this tradition has both consciously and subconsciously shaped the way that I read Paul. I neither claim that I have provided a "purely objective" investigation of the extent of the atonement in Paul. The harsh (and troubling) reality for us "modernist" and anti "post-modernist" readers of Paul is *no* scholar can be purely objective about Paul's view of the extent of the atonement or of any Pauline text that speaks to the issue, because every scientific and objective investigation is subject to the subjective art of interpretation. Yet, although my thesis argued here should certainly (and hopefully will) be subject to serious, rigorous, and critical interrogation by every scholar and student who reads it, as any thesis should be, and although it certainly is not without its own exegetical problems and historical and theological presuppositions and biases, I have at least attempted throughout this monograph to do what no other New Testament scholar or theologian has done: namely, to provide a book length biblical monograph that provides an answer to the question for whom did Christ die according to Paul. I have endeavored to answer this question by offering a detailed analysis of selected early Jewish and Pauline texts. In my view, Paul's answer seems to be that Jesus died for all elect Jews and Gentiles who unite themselves to Christ by faith and who live in obedience to the Christian gospel within the Christian community. Consequently, Paul endured all suffering for Christ throughout his missionary endeavors for the sake of the gospel for the salvation of the elect because he believed that he was an apostle of the elect for whom Jesus died (cf. 2 Tim. 2:10; Tit. 1:1).

Bibliography

Primary Sources

Biblia Hebraica Stuttgartensia. Edited by A. Schenker. (Stuttgart: DeutcheBibelgesellschaft, 1967/77).
Charlesworth (ed.), James H. *The Old Testament Pseudepigrapha*, 2 vols. (New York: Double Day, 1983 & 1985).
The Greek New Testament. Edited by Barbara Aland, Kurt Aland, Johannes Karavidopoulos, Carlo M. Martini, and Bruce M. Metzger. 4th rev. ed. Stuttgart: Deutsche Bibelgesellschaft, 1998.
Septuaginta. Edited by A. Rahlfs. Stuttgart: Deutsche Bibelgesellschaft, 1979.
Vermes (trans.), Geza. *The Complete Dead Sea Scrolls in English*, Revised Edition (London: Penguin, 2004).

Secondary Sources

Abasciano, Brian J. *Paul's Use of the Old Testament in Romans 9:1-9: An Intertextual and Theological Exegesis*, JSNTSup/LNTS 301 (London: T&T Clark, 2005).
— *Paul's Use of the Old Testament in Romans 9:10-18: An Intertextual Exegesis*, LNTS 317 (London: T&T Clark, 2010).
Agersnap, Søren. *Baptism and the New Life: A Study of Romans 6:1-14* (Aarhus: Aarhus University Press, 1999).
Alexander, Philip S. 'Predestination and Free Will in the Theology of the Dead Sea Scrolls,' in *Divine and Human Agency in Paul and His Cultural Environment*, LNTS 335, eds. John M.G. Barclay and Simon J. Gathercole (New York: T&T Clark, 2006), 27-49.
Armstrong, Brian G. *Calvinism and the Amyraut Heresy* (Madison: University of Wisconsin Press, 1969).
Arnold, Clinton E. 'Returning to the Domain of the Powers: Stoicheia as Evil Spirits in Galatians 4:3, 9,' *NovT* 38 (1996), 55-76.
Aquinas, Thomas. *Summa Theologiae.* (Notre Dame: Ave Maria Press, 1981).
Augustine. *Basic Writings of Saint Augustine*, vol 1, ed. Whitney J. Oates (New York: Random House, 1948).
— *Letters of Saint Augustine*, ed. John Leinenweber (Tarrytown, NY: Triumph Books, 1992).
— 'Tractate on John's Gospel,' in *Nicene and Post-Nicene Fathers*, series 1, ed. P. Schaff (1186-89, repr. Peabody, MA: Hendrickson, 1994).
Bailey, Daniel P. 'Concepts of Stellvertretung in the Interpretation of Isaiah 53,' in *Jesus and the Suffering-Servant: Isaiah 53 and Christian Origins*, eds. W. H. Bellinger and W. R. Farmer (Harrisburg, PA, 1998), 223-50.
— 'Jesus as the Mercy Seat: The Semantics and Theology of Paul's use of Hilastērion in Romans 3:25' (Ph.D. diss., Cambridge University, 1999).

Barclay, John M.G. 'By the Grace of God I am What I am: Grace and Agency in Philo and Paul,' in John M.G. Barclay and Simon J. Gathercole (eds.), LNTS 335, *Divine and Human Agency in Paul and His Cultural Environment* (New York: T&T Clark, 2006), 140-57.
Barnes, Tom. *Atonement Matters: A Call to Declare the Biblical View of the Atonement* (Webster, NY: Evangelical Press, 2008).
Barth, Karl. *A Shorter Commentary on Romans* (London: SCM Press 1959).
— *The Epistle to the Romans*, trans. Edwyn C. Hoskyns, 7th edition (Oxford: Oxford University Press, 1965).
Barth, Markus. *Was Christ's Death a Sacrifice?* Scottish Journal of Theology Papers 9 (Edinburgh: Oliver & Boyd, 1961).
Bartlett, Anthony W. *Cross Purposes: The Violent Grammar of Christian Atonement* (Harrisburg, PA: Trinity International Press, 2001).
Bassler, Jouette M. 'Divine Impartiality in Paul's Letter to the Romans,' *NovT* 26 (1984), 43-58.
— *Divine Impartiality: Paul and a Theological Axiom*, SBL Dissertation 59 (Chico: Scholars Press, 1982).
Baumeister, Theofried. *Die Anfänge der Theologie des Martyriums*, MBT (Münster: Aschendorf, 1980).
Beale, G.K. 'Reconciliation in 2 Corinthians 5-7 and Its Bearing on the Literary Problem of 2 Corinthians 6:14-7:1,' *NTS* 35 (1989), 550-81.
Becker, J.C. *Paul, the Apostle: The Triumph of God in Life and Thought* (Philadelphia: Fortress, 1980).
Becker, U. 'Gospel,' in *Dictionary of New Testament Theology*, ed. Colin Brown (Grand Rapids: Zondervan, 1986), 2:104-114.
Beilby and Paul R. Eddy (eds.), James. *The Nature of the Atonement: Four Views* (Downers Grove: InterVarsity Press, 2006).
Bell, Charles. 'Calvin and the Extent of the Atonement,' *EQ* 55 (1983), 115-23.
Bell, Richard H. 'Sacrifice and Christology in Paul,' *JTS* 53 (2002), 1-27.
— *No One Seeks for God*, WUNT 106 (Tübingen: Mohr Siebeck, 1998).
— *Provoked to Jealousy: The Origins of the Jealousy Motif in Romans 9-11* (Tübingen: J.C.B., 1994).
Ben Ezra, Daniel Stökl. *The Impact of Yom Kippur on Early Christianity*, WUNT 163 (Tübingen: Mohr Siebeck, 2003).
Berkhof, Louis. *Systematic Theology*, 4th ed. (Grand Rapids: Eerdmans, 1977).
Bird and Preston M. Sprinkle (eds.), Michael F. *The Pistis Christou Debate* (Peabody, MA: Hendrickson, 2009).
Blacketer, Raymond A. 'Definite Atonement in Historical Perspective,' in *The Glory of the Atonement: Biblical, Theological, and Practical Perspectives*, eds. Charles E. Hill and Frank A. James III (Grand Rapids: Baker, 2004), 304-23.
Boettner, Loraine. *Studies in Theology*, 4th ed. (Grand Rapids: Eerdmans, 1957).
Boyce, P. *Divine Initiative and Human Response in Ezekiel* (Sheffield: JSOT Press, 1989).
Branick, Bell V. P. 'The Sinful Flesh of the Son of God (Rom 8:3): A Key Image in Pauline Theology,' *CBQ* 47 (1985), 246-62.
Breytenbach, Cilliers. 'Christus starb für uns: Zur Tradition und paulinischen Rezeption der sogennanten Sterbeformeln,' *NTS* 49 (2003), 447-75.
— 'Salvation of the Reconciled (With a Note on the Background of Paul's Metaphor of Reconciliation),' in *Salvation in the New Testament:*

Perspectives on Soteriology, ed. J. G. van der Watt (Leiden: Brill, 2005), 271-86.
— 'Versöhnung, Stellvertretung und Sühne: semantische und traditionsgeschichtliche Bemerkungen am Beispiel der Paulinischen Briefe,' *NTS* 39 (1993), 59-79.
— *Versöhnung: Eine Studie zur paulinischen Soteriologie*, WMANT 60 (Neukirchener-Vluyn: Neukirchener Verlag, 1989).
Brondos, David A. *A Fortress Introduction to Salvation and the Cross* (Minneapolis: Augsburg Fortress, 2007).
— *Paul on the Cross: Reconstructing Paul's Story of Redemption* (Minneapolis: Augsburg Fortress, 2006).
— *Redeeming the Gospel: The Christian Faith Reconsidered* (Minneapolis: Augsburg Fortress, 2010).
Brown, William H. 'From Holy War to Holy Martyrdom,' in H.B. Huffmon, F.A. Spina, and A.R. Green [eds.], *The Quest for the Kingdom of God: Studies in Honor of George E. Mendenhall* (Winona Lake, IN: Eisenbrauns, 1983), 287-88.
Bruce. F.F. *The Epistle to the Galatians*. NIGTC. (Grand Rapids: Wm. B. Eerdmans Publishing Co., 1982).
Buchanan, George Wesley. 'The Day of Atonement and Paul's Doctrine of Redemption,' *NovT* 32 (1990), 236-49.
Bultmann, Rudolph. 'Adam and Christ according to Romans 5,' in *Current Issues in New Testament Interpretation: Essays in Honor of Otto A. Piper*, eds. and trans. W. Klassen and G. F. Snyder (New York: Harper & Brothers, 1962), 143-65.
— *The Theology of the New Testament*, trans. Kendrick Grobel, First Published in 1951 and in 1955 as 2 vols (Waco: Baylor University, 2007).
Burnett, Gary W. *Paul & the Salvation of the Individual* (Leiden: Brill, 2011).
Burton, Ernest De Witt. *Galatians*, ICC, 2nd ed. (Edinburgh: T. & T. Clark, 1975).
Byrne, Brendan. 'The Problem of ΝΟΜΟΣ and the Relationship with Judaism in Romans,' *CBQ* 62 (2000), 294-309.
Byron, John. *Slavery Metaphors in Early Judaism and Pauline Christianity*, WUNT 162 (Tübingen: Mohr Siebeck, 2003).
Calvin, John. *Commentary on Paul's Epistle to the Romans*, ed. and trans. John Owen (Grand Rapids: Eerdmans, 1947), 369.
— *Concerning the Eternal Predestination of God*, trans. J.K.S. Reid (Louisville: Westminster John Knox, 1997).
— *Institutes of the Christian Religion*, trans. Henry Beveridge (Grand Rapids: Eerdmans, 1997).
— *Tracts and Treatises*, trans. Henry Beveridge (Edinburgh: 1849).
Cambier, J.'Péchés des hommes et péches d' Adam en Rom v. 12,' *NTS* 11 (1964-65), 246-53.
Campbell, Douglas A. *The Deliverance of God: An Apocalyptic Rereading of Paul* (Grand Rapids: Eerdmans, 2009).
Campbell, W.W. 'The Freedom and Faithfulness of God in Relation to Israel,' *JSNT* 13 (1981), 27-45.
Carter, T.L. *Paul and the Power of Sin*, SNTSM 115 (Cambridge: Cambridge University Press, 2003).
Chalke, Steve. 'The Redemption of the Cross,' in *The Atonement Debate: Papers from the London Symposium on the Theology of Atonement*, eds.

Derek Tidball, David Hilborn, and Justin Thacker (Grand Rapids: Zondervan, 2008), 36-45.
— *The Lost Message of Jesus* (Grand Rapids: Zondervan, 2003).
Chang, Hae-Kyung. 'The Christian Life in a Dialectical Tension? Romans 7:7-25 Reconsidered,' *NovT* 49 (2009), 257-280.
Collins, John J. *Daniel, First Maccabees, Second Maccabees* (OTM 15; 2nd ed.; Wilmington, Del.: Frazier Incorporation, 1989).
Cone, James H. *God of the Oppressed* (Maryknoll, NY: Orbis, 1997).
Cosgrove, Charles H. 'Justification in Paul: A Linguistic and Theological Reflection,' *JBL* 106 (1987), 653-670.
Cousar, Charles B. *A Theology of the Cross: The Death of Jesus in the Pauline Letters* (Minneapolis: Augsburg Fortress, 1990).
Cranfield, C.E.B. *Romans*, ICC, 11th edition (New York: T. & T. Clark, 2004).
Crysdale, Cynthia S.W. *Embracing Travail: Retrieving the Cross Today* (New York: Continuum, 1999).
Cummins, Stephen Anthony. *Paul and the Crucified Christ in Antioch* (Cambridge: Cambridge University Press, 2001).
Dabney, R.L. *Systematic Theology*, 2nd ed. (St. Louis: Presbyterian Publishing Co., 1878).
Daly, Robert J. 'Images of God and the Imitation of God: Problems with Atonement,' *Theological Studies* 68 (2007), 36-51.
— *Christian Sacrifice: The Judaeo-Christian Background before Origen* (Washington, DC: The Catholic University of America, 1978).
— *Sacrifice Unveiled: The True Meaning of Christian Sacrifice* (New York: T&T Clark, 2009).
Danker, Frederick W. 'Rom V.12: Sin under Law,' *NTS* 14 (1967-68), 428.
Das, A. Andrew. 'Paul and Works of Obedience in Second Temple Judaism: Romans 4:4-5 as a 'New Perspective' Case Study,' *CBQ* 71 (2009), 795-812.
— *Paul, the Law, and the Covenant* (Peabody, MA: Hendrickson, 2001).
— *Solving the Romans Debate* (Minneapolis: Fortress, 2007).
Davis, Christopher A. *The Structure of Paul's Theology: 'The Truth Which is the Gospel'* (Lewiston, NY: Mellen Biblical Press, 1995).
de Jonge, Marinus. 'Jesus' Death for Others and the Death of the Maccabean Martyrs,' in *Text and Testimony: Essays on New Testament and Apocryphal Literature in Honour of A.F.J. Klijn*, ed. T. Baarda et al. (Kampen: J.H. Kok, 1988), 142-51.
— 'Jesus' Death for Others and the Death of the Maccabean Martyrs,' in *Jewish Eschatology, Early Christian Christology and the Testaments of Twelve Patriarchs: Collected Essays* (Leiden: Brill, 1991), 125-34.
— *Christology in Context: The Earliest Christian Response to Jesus* (Philadelphia: Westminster, 1988).
— *God's Final Envoy: Early Christology and Jesus' Own View of His Mission* (Grand Rapids: Eerdmans, 1998), 12-33.
— *Jesus, the Servant-Messiah* (New Haven: Yale University Press, 1991), 37-48.
de Roo, Jacqueline C.R. *Works of the Law at Qumran and in Paul*, NTM 13 (Sheffield: Sheffield Phoenix Press, 2007).
Deissmann, Adolf. *Light from the Ancient East* (New York: Harper, 1927).
DeSilva, David A. *4 Maccabees*, SCS (Leiden: Brill, 2006).
Dever and J.I. Packer, Mark. *In My Place Condemned He Stood* (Wheaton: Crossway, 2007).

Dodd, C.H. *The Bible and The Greeks*, 2nd ed. (London: Hodder and Stoughton, 1954).
— *The Epistle of Paul to the Romans*, MNTC (New York: Harper & Brothers, 1932).
Downing, J. 'Jesus and Martyrdom,' *JTS* 14 (1963), 279-93.
Dunhill, John. 'Communicative Bodies and Economies of Grace: The Role of Sacrifice in the Christian Understanding of the Body,' *Journal of Religion* 83 (2003), 79-93.
Dunn, J.G. 'The New Perspective: whence, what and whither?' in *The New Perspective on Paul* (Grand Rapids: Eerdmans, 2008), 1-97.
— 'Paul's Understanding of Jesus' Death,' in *Reconciliation and Hope*, ed. Robert Banks (Grand Rapids: Eerdmans 1974), 76-89.
— *Romans 1-8*, WBC 38A (Nashville: Word, 1988).
— *The Theology of Paul, the Apostle* (Grand Rapids: Eerdmans, 1998).
Eisenbaum, Pamela. *Paul Was not a Christian* (New York: HarperCollins, 2009).
Eldon Ladd, George. *A Theology of the New Testament*, revised edition (Grand Rapids: Eerdmans, 1974).
Elliger, Karl. *Leviticus* (Tübingen: Mohr Siebeck, 1966).
Erickson, Millard. *Christian Theology*, 2nd ed. (Grand Rapids: Baker, 1998).
Finlan, Stephen. *Problems with Atonement: The Origins of, and Controversy about, the Atonement Doctrine* (Collegeville, Minn.: Liturgical Press, 2005).
— *The Background and Content of Paul's Cultic Atonement Metaphors* (Atlanta: SBL, 2004).
Fitzmyer, Joseph. 'The Consecutive Meaning of ἐφ ᾧ in Romans 5.12,' *NTS* (1993), 321-39.
— *Romans*, ABC 33 (New York: Doubleday, 1993).
Forster and V. Paul Marston, Roger T. *God's Strategy in Human History* (Wheaton: Tyndale House, 1974).
Friedrich, Gerhard. *Die Verkündigung des Todes Jesu im Neuen Testament*, BThSt (Neukirchener-Vluyn: Neukirchener Verlag, 1982).
Fryer, Nicole S.L. 'The Meaning and Translation of Hilastērion in Romans 3:25,' *EvQ* 59 (1987), 99-116.
Garland, David E. *1 Corinthians*, BECNT (Grand Rapids: Baker, 2003).
Garlington, Don B. *'The Obedience of Faith:' A Pauline Phrase in Historical Context*, WUNT 2/38 (Tübingen: Mohr Siebeck, 1991).
Gaston, Lloyd. 'Israel's Misstep in the Eyes of Paul,' in *the Romans Debate*, ed. Karl P. Donfried (Peabody: Hendrickson, 1977), 319.
Gathercole, Simon J. 'A Law unto Themselves: The Gentiles in Romans 2:14-15,' *JSNT* 85 (2002), 27-49.
— *Where is Boasting? Early Jewish Soteriology and Paul's Response in Romans 1-5* (Grand Rapids: Eerdmans, 2002).
Geisler, Norman L. *Chosen But Free*, 2nd ed. (Bloomington, Minn.: Bethany House, 2001).
Getty, Mary Ann. 'Paul and the Salvation of Israel: A Perspective on Romans 9-11,' *CBQ* 50 (1988), 456-69.
Gnilka, J. 'Martyriumsparänese und Sühnetod in synoptischen und jüdischen Traditionen,' in *Die Kirche des Anfangs: Festschrift für Heinz Schürman* (Leipzig: St. Benno-Verlag, 1977), 223-46.
Goldstein, Jonathan. *2 Maccabees*, ABC 41A (New York: Doubleday, 1983).
Gosnell, Peter W. 'Law in Romans: Regulation and Instruction,' *NovT* 51 (2009), 252-71.

Gray, George Buchanan. *Sacrifices in the Old Testament: Its Theory and Practice* (New York: KTAV Publishing House, 1971).
Grayston, Kenneth. 'Atonement and Martyrdom,' in *Early Christian Thought in Its Jewish Context*, ed. John Barclay and John Sweet (Cambridge: Cambridge University Press, 1996), 250-63.
Green and Mark Baker, Joel B. *Rediscovering the Scandal of the Cross: Atonement in New Testament & Contemporary Contexts* (Downers Grove, IL: InterVarsity Press, 2000).
Grudem, Wayne H. *Systematic Theology* (Grand Rapids: Zondervan, 2000).
Hafemann, Scott J. *Paul, Moses, and the History of Israel: The Letter/Spirit Contrast and the Argument from Scripture in 2 Corinthians 3* (Carlisle, UK: Paternoster, 2005).
Hall, Basil. 'Calvin against the Calvinists,' in *John Calvin*, ed. G.E. Duffield (Grand Rapids: Eerdmans, 1966), 19-37.
Hanson, A.T. 'Vessels of Wrath or Instruments of Wrath? Romans 9:22-2, *JTS* 32 (1981), 443-44.
— *The Wrath of the Lamb* (London: SPCK, 1957).
Hardin and Brad Jersak (eds.), Michael. *Stricken By God? Non-Violent Identification and the Victory of Christ.* (Grand Rapids: Eerdmans, 2007).
Harrill, J. Albert. 'Paul and Slavery,' in *Paul in the Greco-Roman World: A Handbook*, ed. J. Paul Sampley (Harrodsburg, PA: Trinity Press International, 2003), 575-607.
Harrison, J. *Paul's Language of Grace in Its Graeco-Roman Context*. WUNT 2.172 (Tübingen: Mohr Siebeck, 2003).
Hartley, John E. *Leviticus*, WBC 3 (Dallas: Word, 1992).
Hawthorne, Ralph P. Martin, and Daniel G. Reid (eds.), Gerald F. *Dictionary of Paul and His Letters.* (Downers Grove, IL: InterVarsity Press, 1993).
Hays, Richard. *The Faith of Jesus Christ*. 2nd ed. (Grand Rapids: Wm. B. Eerdmans Publishing Company, 2001).
Heim, S. Mark. *Saved from Sacrifice: A Theology of the Cross.* (Grand Rapids: Eerdmans, 2006).
Helm, Paul. *Calvin and the Calvinists* (Edinburgh: Banner of Truth 1982; reprint Edinburgh: Banner of Truth, 1998).
Hengel, Martin. *The Atonement: A Study of the Origins of the Doctrine in the New Testament*. trans. John Bowden. (London: SCM, 1981).
Hill and Frank A. James III (eds.), Charles E. *The Glory of the Atonement* (Downers Grove, IL: InterVarsity Press, 2004).
Hill, David. *Greek Words and Hebrew Meanings: Studies in the Semantics of Soteriological Terms*, SNTS 5 (Cambridge: Cambridge University Press, 1967).
Hoehner, Harold W. *Ephesians* (Grand Rapids: Baker, 2002).
Hofius, Otfried. 'The Fourth Servant Song in the New Testament Letters,' in *The Suffering Servant: Isaiah 53 in Jewish and Christian Sources*, trans. Daniel P. Bailey, eds. Bernd Janowski and Peter Stuhlmacher (Grand Rapids: Eerdmans, 2004), 172-83.
Hogeterp, Albert L.A. '4QMMT and Paradigms of Second Temple Jewish Nomism,' *Dead Sea Discoveries* 15 (2008), 359-79.
Holland, Tom. *Contours of Pauline Theology: A Radical New Survey of the Influences on Paul's Biblical Writings* (Scotland, UK: Mentor, 2004).
Hooker, Morna D. 'Interchange in Christ,' *JTS* 22 (1974), 349-61.
— *Not Ashamed of the Gospel: New Testament Interpretations of the Death of Christ* (Grand Rapids: Eerdmans, 1994).

House, Paul. *Old Testament Theology* (Downers Grove, IL: InterVarsity Press, 1998).
Hunt and James White, David. *Debating Calvinism* (Multnomah, Or.: Multnomah, 2004).
Hunt, David. *What Love is This: Calvinism's Misrepresentation of God* (Bend, Or.: The Berean Call, 2004).
Janowski, Bernd. *Sühne als Heilsgeschen*, WMANT 55, 2nd ed. (Neukirchener-Vluyn: Neukirchener Verlag, 2000).
Jefferey, Mike Ovey, and Andrew Sach, Steve. *Pierced for Our Transgressions: Rediscovering the Glory of Penal Substitution* (Nottingham, UK: Inter-Varsity Press, 2007).
Jersak, Brad. 'Non-violent Identification and the Victory of Christ,' in *Stricken by God?: Nonviolent Identification and the Victory of Christ*, eds. Brad Jersak and Michael Hardin (Grand Rapids: Eerdmans, 2007), 18-53.
Jervis, L. Ann. 'The Commandment which is for Life (Romans 7:10): Sin's Use of the Obedience of Faith,' *JSNT* 27 (2004), 193-216.
Jewett, Robert K. *Anthropological Terms: A Study of Their Use in Conflict Settings* (Leiden: Brill, 1971).
— *Romans*, Hermeneia (Minneapolis, Fortress, 2007).
Käsemann, Ernst. 'Some Thoughts on the Theme of the Doctrine of Reconciliation in the New Testament,' in *The Future of Our Religious Past: Essays in Honour of Rudolph Bultmann*, ed. James M. Robinson, trans. Charles E. Carlston and Robert P. Scharlemann (London: SCM, 1971), 49-64.
— 'The Saving Significance of the Death of Jesus in Paul,' in *Perspectives on Paul*, trans. Margaret Kohl (Philadelphia: Fortress, 1971), 32-59.
— *Commentary on Romans*, trans. Geoffrey Bromiley (Grand Rapids: Eerdmans, 1980).
Keathley, Kenneth. *Salvation and Sovereignty: A Molinist Approach* (Nashville: Broadman & Holman, 2010).
Keck, Leander. *Romans*, ANTC (Nashville: Abingdon, 2005), 217.
Kellermann, Ulrich. 'Zum traditionsgeschichtlichen Problem des stellvertretenden Sühnetodes in 2 Makk 7:37,' *BN* 13 (1980), 63-83.
— *Auferstanden in den Himmel: 2 Makkabäer 7 und die Auferstehung der Martÿrer* (Stuttgart: Katholisches Bibelwerk, 1979).
Kendall, R.T. *Calvin and English Calvinism to 1649* (New York: Oxford University Press, 1979).
Kim, Seyoon. '2 Cor 5:11-21 and Reconciliation,' *NovT* 38-39 (1996-1997), 360-84.
— *The Origin of Paul's Gospel*, 2nd ed., WUNT 2 (Tübingen: Mohr Siebeck, 1984).
Kirk, J.R. Daniel. 'Reconsidering Dikaiōma in Romans 5:16,' *JBL* 126 (2007), 787-92.
Knöppler, Thomas. *Sühne im Neuen Testament*, WMANT 88 (Neukirchener-Vluyn: Neukirchener Verlag, 2001).
Kraus, Wolfgan. *Der Tod Jesu als Heiligtumsweihe: Eine Untersuchung zum Umfeld de Sühnevorstellung im Römer 3:25-26a*, WMANT 66 (Neukirchener-Vluyn: Neukirchener Verlag, 1991).
Kümmel, W.G. *Römer 7 und das Bild des Menschen im Neuen Testament* (Munich: Kaiser Verlag, 1974).

Lampe, Peter. 'Human Sacrifice and Pauline Christology,' in *Human Sacrifice in Jewish and Christian Tradition*, ed. Karin Finsterbusch, Armin Lange, and K. F. Diehard Römheld (Leiden: Brill, 2007), 191-209.
Leahy, Frederick S. 'Calvin and the Extent of the Atonement,' *Reformed Theological Journal* 8 (1992), 54-64.
Leithart, Peter J. 'Adam, Moses, and Jesus,' *CTJ* 43 (2008), 264-65.
Leitzmann, Hans. *Die Briefe des Apostels Paulus I: Die vier Hauptbriefe*, HNT 3 (Tübingen: J.C.B. Mohr, 1910).
Lincoln, Andrew T. *Ephesians*, WBC 42 (Nashville: Nelson, 1990).
Lohse, Eduard. *Märtyrer und Gottesknecht* (2nd ed.; Göttingen: Vandenhoeck & Ruprecht, 1963).
Lombard, Peter. *The Sentences: Book 3—On the Incarnation of the Word*, trans. Giulio Silano (Toronto: Pontifical Institute of Mediaeval Studies, 2008).
Longenecker, Bruce W. 'Different Answers to Different Issues: Israel, the Gentiles, and Salvation History in Romans 9-11,' *JSNT* 35-37 (1989), 95-123.
Luther, Martin. *Luther's Works*. American edition, ed. H.T. Lehmann et al. Vol 25 (St. Louis: Concordia), 1955-86.
Lyonnet and Léopold Sabourin, Stanislas. *Sin, Redemption, and Sacrifice: A Biblical and Patristic Study* (Rome: Biblical Institute Press, 1970).
Mann, Alan. *Atonement for a Sinless Society: Engaging with an Emerging Culture* (Carlisle, UK: Paternoster, 2005).
Manson, T.W. 'Hilastērion,' *JTS* 46 (1945), 1-10.
Marshall, I. Howard. 'The Death of Jesus in Recent New Testament Study,' *WW* 1 (1983), 12-21.
— 'The Development of the Concept of Redemption in the New Testament,' in *Reconciliation and Hope: Essays in Honor of Leon Morris*, ed. R.J. Banks (Exeter: Paternoster, 1974), 153-69.
— 'The Meaning of Reconciliation,' in *Unity and Diversity in New Testament Theology: Essays in Honor of George E. Ladd*, ed. Robert A. Guelich (Grand Rapids: Eerdmans, 1978), 117-32.
— *Aspects of the Atonement: Cross and Resurrection in the Reconciling of God and Humanity* (London, UK: Paternoster, 2008).
Martin, Ralph P. *Reconciliation: A Study of Paul's Theology* (Atlanta: John Knox, 1981).
Maston, Jason. *Divine and Human Agency in Second Temple Judaism and Paul: A Comparison of Sirach, Hodayot, and Romans 7-8*, WUNT 297 (Tübingen: Mohr Siebeck, 2010).
Mathews, Kenneth A. *Genesis 1-11:26*. NAC (Nashville: B&H, 1996).
McFadden, Kevin W. 'The Fulfillment of the Law's Dikaiōma: Another Look at Romans 8:1-4,' *JETS* 52 (2009), 483-97.
McKnight, Scot. *A Community Called Atonement* (Nashville: Abingdon, 2007).
— *Jesus and His Death: Historiography, the Historical Jesus, and Atonement Theory* (Waco, TX: Baylor University Press, 2005).
McLean, Bradley H. 'Christ as Pharmakos in Pauline Soteriology,' *SBLSP* (1991), 187-207
— 'The Absence of an Atoning Sacrifice in Paul's Soteriology,' *NTS* 38 (1992), 531-53.
— *The Cursed Christ*, JSNTSup 126 (Sheffield: JSOT Press, 1996).

Melancthon, Phillip. *Commentary on Romans*, ed. and trans. Fred Kramer (St. Louis: Concordia, 1992).
Milgrom, Jacob. *Cult and Conscience: The Asham and the Priestly Doctrine of Repentance* (Leiden: Brill, 1976).
Moo, Douglas. *The Epistle to the Romans*. NICNT (Grand Rapids: Wm. B. Eerdmans Publishing Co., 1996).
Moore, Jonathan D. 'Calvin Versus the Calvinists? The Case of John Preston (1587-1628),' *RRR* 6.3 (2004), 327-48.
Morris, Leon. 'Redemption,' in *Dictionary of Paul and His Letters*, eds. Gerald F. Hawthorne, Ralph P. Martin, and Daniel G. Reid (Downers, IL: InterVarsity Press, 1993).
— 'The Meaning of Hilastērion in Romans 3:25,' *NTS* 2 (1955-1956), 3-43.
— *Romans*, PNTC (Grand Rapids: Eerdmans, 1988).
— *The Apostolic Preaching of the Cross*, 3rd ed. (Grand Rapids: Zondervan, 1965).
— *The Cross in the New Testament* (Grand Rapids: Baker, 1965).
Muller, Richard A. *Dictionary of Latin and Greek Theological Terms* (Grand Rapids: Baker, 1985).

Murray, John. 'Calvin on the Extent of the Atonement,' *Banner of Truth* 234 (1983), 20-22.
— *Redemption Accomplished and Applied*. (Grand Rapids: Wm. B. Eerdmans Publishing Co., 1955).
— *The Imputation of Adam's Sin* (Phillipsburg, NJ: P&R, 1959).
Nicole, Roger. 'Particular Redemption,' in *Our Savior God: Man, Christ, and the Atonement*, ed. J.M. Boice (Grand Rapids: Baker, 1980), 165-78.
— 'C.H. Dodd and the Doctrine of Propitiation,' *WTJ* 17 (1954-1955), 117-57.
— 'John Calvin's View of the Extent of the Atonement,' *WTJ* 47 (1985), 197-25.
— 'John Calvin's View of the Extent of the Atonement,' in *Standing Forth: Collected Writings of Roger Nicole* (Fearn, Ross-shire, Christian Focus Publications, 2002), 283-312.
Noth, Martin. *Leviticus* (Philadelphia: Westminster, 1965).
Nygren, Anders. *Commentary on Romans*, trans. Carl C. Rasmussen (Philadelphia: Muhlenberg Press, 1949).
O'Hagan, A. 'The Martyr in the Fourth Book of the Maccabees,' *SBFLA* 24 (1974), 94-120.
Oesterly, W.O.E. *The Psalms: Translated with Text-Critical and Exegetical Notes* (London: SPK, 1939).
Ortlund, Dane C. 'Justified by Faith, Judged according to Works: Another Look at a Pauline Paradox,' *JETS* 52 (2009), 323-39.
Owen, John. *The Death of Death in the Death of Christ* (Edinburgh: Banner of Truth, 1959).
Owen, Paul L. 'The 'Works of the Law' in Romans and Galatians: A New Defense of the Subjective Genitive,' *JBL* 126 (2007), 560-61.
Packer, J. I. 'What Did the Cross Achieve? The Logic of Penal Substitution,' *Tyndale Bulletin* 25 (1974), 3-45.
Pelagius. *Pelagius' Commentary on St. Paul's Epistle to the Romans*, ed. and trans. Theodore De Bruyn (Oxford: Clarendon Press, 1993).
Pohle, J. *The Catholic Encyclopedia* (New York: Encyclopedia Press, 1913).
Porter, Stanley. 'The Pauline Concept of Original Sin, in Light of Rabbinic Background,' *Tyndale Bulletin* 41 (1990), 3-30.

— *Katallassō in Ancient Greek Literature, with Reference to the Pauline Writings* (Cordoba: Ediciones El Almendro, 1994).
Powers, Daniel G. *Salvation through Participation: An Examination of the Notion of the Believer's Corporate Unity with Christ in Early Christian Soteriology*, Biblical Exegesis and Theology 29 (Leuven: Peeters, 2001).
Rainbow, Jonathan. *The Will of God and the Cross: An Historical and Theological Study of John Calvin's Doctrine of Limited Atonement* (Allison Park, PA: Pickwick, 1990).
Rainbow, Paul A. *The Way of Salvation: The Role of Christian Obedience in Justification* (London, UK: Paternoster, 2005).
Räisänen, Heikki. *Paul and the Law* (Philadelphia: Fortress, 1983).
Raitt, Jill. 'St. Thomas Aquinas on Free Will and Predestination,' *Duke Divinity School Review* 43 (1978), 188-95.
Rashdall, Hastings. *The Idea of Atonement in Christian Theology: Being The Bampton Lectures for 1915* (London: Macmillan, 1925).
Reid (ed.), Daniel G. *The IVP Dictionary of the New Testament* (Downers Grove, IL: InterVarsity Press, 2004).
Ridderbos, Herman. *Paul: An Outline of His Theology* (Grand Rapids: Eerdmans, 1966).
Rigby, Cynthia L. 'Taking Our Place: Substitution, Human Agency, and Feminine Sin,' *International Journal for the Study of the Christian Church* (2004), 220-34.
Robertson, A.T. *A Grammar of the Greek New Testament in the Light of Historical Research* (Nashville: Broadman, 1934).
Röhser, G. *Metaphorik und Personifikation der Sünde* (Tübingen: J.C.B. Mohr, 1987).
Rolston III, Holmes. *John Calvin versus the Westminster Confession* (Richmond, VA: John Knox, 1972).
Roumendal, P.L. 'Calvin's Forgotten Classical Position on the Extent of the Atonement: About Sufficiency, Efficiency, and Anachronism,' *WTJ* 70 (2008), 317-35.
Rowley, H.H. *The Biblical Doctrine of Election*, 2nd ed. (London: Lutterworth, 1950).
Sanders (ed.), John *Atonement and Violence: A Theological Conversation* (Nashville: Abingdon, 2006).
Sanders, E.P. *Paul and Palestinian Judaism* (Minneapolis: Fortress, 1977).
— *Paul, the Law, and the Jewish People* (Minneapolis: Fortress, 1983).
Schlatter, Adolf. *The Theology of the Apostles: The Development of New Testament Theology*, trans. Andreas J. Köstenberger (Grand Rapids: Baker, 1999; First published in 1922), 228-51.
Schnabel, Eckhard J. *Law and Wisdom from Ben Sira to Paul*, WUNT 2/16 (Tübingen: Mohr Siebeck, 1985).
Schnelle, Udo. *Apostle Paul: His Life and Theology*, trans. M. Eugene Boring (Grand Rapids: Baker, 2005).
Schreiner, Thomas R. 'Does Romans 9 teach Individual Election unto Salvation?' in *Still Sovereign: Contemporary Perspectives on Election, Foreknowledge, and Grace*, eds. Thomas R. Schreiner and Bruce A. Ware (Grand Rapids: Baker, 2000), 89-106.
— 'Justification: The Saving Righteousness of God in Christ,' *JETS* 54 (2011), 19-34.
— *New Testament Theology: Magnifying God in Christ* (Grand Rapids: Baker, 2008).

— *Paul: An Apostle of God's Glory in Christ* (Downers Grove, IL: InterVarsity Press, 2001).

— *Romans*, BECNT (Grand Rapids: Baker, 1998), 245-49.

Schwager, Raymond. *Banished from Eden: Original Sin and Evolutionary Theory in the Drama of Salvation*, trans. James G. Williams (London: Gracewing, 2005).

— *Jesus in the Drama of Salvation: Toward a Biblical Doctrine of Redemption*, trans. James G. Williams and Paul Haddon (New York: Crossroad, 1999).

Seeley, David. *The Noble Death: Greco-Roman Martyrology and Paul's Concept of Salvation*, JSNTSup 28 (Sheffield: Sheffield Academic Press, 1990).

Seifrid, Mark A. 'Romans,' in *a Commentary on the New Testament Use of The Old*, eds. Greg K. Beale and D.A. Carson (Grand Rapids: Baker).

— 'Unrighteousness by Faith: Apostolic Proclamation in Romans 1:18-3:20,' in *Justification and Variegated Nomism: The Paradoxes of Paul*, eds. D.A. Carson, et al., WUNT 2.140 (Tübingen: Mohr Siebeck, 2004), 106-45.

Smyth, Herbert. *Greek Grammar* (21st ed.; Cambridge, Mass.: Harvard University Press, 2002).

Snodgrass, Klyne R. 'Justification by Grace—to the Doers: The Place of Romans 2 in the Theology of Paul,' *NTS* 32 (1986), 72-93.

Spencer, Duane Edward. *TULIP: The Five Points of Calvinism in Light of Scripture*, 7th ed. (Grand Rapids: Baker, 2007).

Sprinkle, Preston M. *Law and Life: The Interpretation of Leviticus 18:5 in Early Judaism and in Paul*, WUNT 241 (Tübingen: Mohr-Siebeck, 2008).

St. Jerome. *Commentary on Matthew*, trans. Thomas P. Scheck (Washington, DC.: The Catholic University Press of America, 2008).

Stauffer, Ethelbert. *The Theology of the New Testament*, trans. John Marsh (London: SCM, 1955).

Steele, Curtis C. Thomas, S. Lance Quinn, David N. *The Five Points of Calvinism: Defined, Defended, and Documents*, 2nd ed. (Phillipsburg, NJ: P&R, 2004).

Stott, John. *The Message of Romans: God's Good News for the World*, TBST (Downers Grove, IL: InterVarsity Press, 1994).

Stowers, Stanley K. *A Rereading of Romans*: *Jews Justice, and Gentiles* (New Haven: Yale University Press, 1994), 251-55.

— *The Diatribe and Paul's Letter to the Romans*, SBLDS 57 (Chico: Scholars Press, 1981).

Stuhlmacher, Peter. *Der Brief an die Römer*, NTD 6 (Göttingen: Vandenhoeck & Ruprecht), 1989).

Surkau, H.W. *Martyrien in jüdischer und frühchristilicher Zeit*, FRLANT 36 (Göttingen: Vandenhoeck & Ruprecht, 1938).

Swallow, Frederick R. 'Redemption in St. Paul,' *Sacrament* 10 (1958), 21-27.

Tanner, Kathryn. 'Incarnation, Cross, and Sacrifice: A Feminist-Inspired Reappraisal,' *ATR* (2004), 35-56.

Thielman, Frank. 'God's Righteousness as God's Fairness in Romans 1:17: An Ancient Perspective on a Significant Phrase,' *JETS* 54 (2011), 35-48.

— 'The Atonement,' in *Central Themes in Biblical Theology: Mapping Unity in Diversity*, eds. Scott J. Hafemann and Paul R. House (Grand Rapids: Baker, 2007), 102-27.

— *From Plight to Solution: A Jewish Framework for Understanding Paul's View of the Law in Galatians and Romans,* NovT Supp LXI (Leiden: Brill, 1989).
— *Theology of the New Testament: A Canonical and Synthetic Approach* (Grand Rapids: Zondervan 2005).
Thorsteinsson, Runar M. *Paul's Interlocutor in Romans 2: Function and Identity in the Context of Ancient Epistolography,* ConBNT 40 (Stockholm: Almqvist & Wiksell, 2003).
Thrall, Margaret E. 'Salvation Proclaimed: 2 Corinthians 5:18-21,' *ExT* 93 (1982).
Tidball, David Hilborn, and Justin Thacker (eds.), Derek. *The Atonement Debate* (Grand Rapids: Zondervan, 2008).
Tidball, Derek. *The Message of the Cross* (Downers Grove: InterVarsity, 2001).
Torrance, J.B. 'The Incarnation and 'Limited Atonement,'' *EQ* 55 (1983), 83-94.
Travis, Stephen. 'Christ as the Bearer of Divine Judgment in Paul's Thought about the Atonement,' in *Atonement Today,* ed. John Goldingay (London: SPCK, 1995), 21-38.
— *Christ and the Judgment of God: The Limits of Divine Retribution in New Testament Thought* (Peabody, MA: Hendrickson, 2008).
Trueman, Carl. 'Puritan Theology as Historical Event: A Linguistic Approach to the Ecumenical Context,' in *Reformation and Scholasticism,* 253-75.
— *The Claims of Truth: John Owen's Trinitarian Theology* (Carlisle: Paternoster, 1998).
Turner, D.L. 'Adam, Christ, and US: The Pauline Teaching of Solidarity in Romans 5:12-21' (Th.D. diss, Grace Theological Seminary, Winona Lake, Ind., 1982).
Turretin, Francis. *Institutes of Eclectic Theology,* trans. George Musgrave Giger, ed. James T. Dennison, Jr. (Phillipsburg, NJ: P&R, 1994).
Umbach, H. *In Christus getauft—von der Sünde befreit: Die Gemeinde als sündenfreier Raum bei Paulus* (Göttingen: Vandenhoeck & Ruprecht, 1999).
van Henten, J.W. 'Jewish Martyrdom and Jesus' Death,' in *Deutungen des Todes Jesu im Neuen Testament,* WUNT 181, ed. J. Frey and J. Schröter (Tübingen: Mohr Siebeck, 2005), 139-68.
— 'The Tradition-Historical Background of Romans 3:25: A Search for Pagan and Jewish Parallels,' in *From Jesus to John: Essays on Jesus and New Testament Christology in Honour of Marinus de Jonge,* JSNTSup 84, ed. Martinus C. de Boer (Sheffield: Sheffield Academic Press, 1993), 101-28.
— *Maccabean Martyrs as Saviours of the Jewish People* (Leiden: Brill, 1998).
VanLandingham, Chris. *Judgment and Justification in Early Judaism and the Apostle Paul* (Peabody, MA: Hendrickson, 2006).
Versnel, Henk S. 'Making Sense of Jesus' Death: The Pagan Contribution,' in *Deutungen Todes Jesu im Neuen Testament,* WUNT 181, ed. Jörg Frey and Jens Schröter (Tübingen: Mohr Siebeck, 2005), 213-94.
Vickers, Brian J. 'Grammar and Theology in the Interpretation of Rom 5:12,' *TrinJ* 27 (2006), 271-88.
—. *Jesus' Blood and Righteousness* (Wheaton: Crossway, 2006).
Vining, Peggy. 'Comparing Seneca's Ethics in Epistulae Morales to those of Paul in Romans,' *Restoration Quarterly* (2005), 83-104.

Wallace, Daniel B. *Greek Grammar Beyond the Basics: An Exegetical Syntax of the New Testament* (Grand Rapids: Zondervan, 1996).
Walls and Joseph R. Dongell, Jerry L. *Why I Am Not A Calvinist* (Downers Grove, IL: InterVarsity Press, 2004).
Waltke, Bruce K. 'Atonement in Psalm 51,' in *The Glory of Atonement*, ed. Charles E. Hill and Frank A. James III (Downers Grove, IL: InterVarsity Press, 2004), 51-60.
Warfield, Benjamin B. 'Atonement,' in the *Works of Benjamin B. Warfield*, vol. 9 (Grand Rapids: Baker, reprinted 2003), 261-309.
— 'The New Testament Terminology of Redemption,' in vol. 2 of *Bible Doctrines: The Works of Benjamin B. Warfield* (Grand Rapids: Baker 2003), 327-98.
— *Calvin and Calvinism*, vol. 5 in the Works of Benjamin B. Warfield (Grand Rapids: Baker, 2003).
Wasserman, Emma. 'Paul among the Philosophers: The Case of Sin in Romans 6-8,' *JSNT* 30.4 (2008), 387-415.
— 'The Death of the Soul in Romans 7: Revisiting Paul's Anthropology in Light of Hellenistic Moral Psychology,' *JBL* 126 (2007), 793-816.
Watson, Francis. *Paul, Judaism, and the Gentiles: Beyond the New Perspective* (Grand Rapids; Eerdmans, Revised Edition 2007).
Weaver, David. 'From Paul to Augustine: Romans 5:12 in Early Christian Exegesis,' *St. Vladimir's Theological Quarterly* 27 (1983), 187-206.
Weaver, David. 'The Exegesis of Romans 5:12 Among the Greek Fathers and Its Implications for the Doctrine of Original Sin: The 5th-12th Centuries,' *St. Vladimir's Theological Quarterly* (1985), 133-59.
Weaver, Denny. *The NonViolent Atonement* (Grand Rapids: Eerdmans, 2001).
Wengst, K. *Christologische Formeln und Lieder des Urchristentums*, SNT 7 (Gütersloh: Mohn, 1972).
Westerholm, Stephen. *Perspectives Old and New on Paul: The 'Lutheran' Paul and His Critics* (Grand Rapids: Eerdmans, 2004).
Williams, David J. *Paul's Metaphors: Their Context and Character* (Peabody, MA: Hendrickson, 1999).
Williams, Delores S. 'The Color of Feminism: Or Speaking the Black Woman's Tongue,' *JRT* 43 (1986), 42-58.
Williams, Delores S. *Sisters in the Wilderness: The Challenge of Womanist God-Talk* (Maryknoll, NY: Orbis, 1993).
Williams, Jarvis J. 'Martyr Theology in Hellenistic Judaism and Paul's Conception of Jesus' Death in Romans 3:21-26,' in *Christian Origins and Hellenistic Judaism: Literary and Social Contexts for the New Testament*, eds. Stanley E. Porter and Andrew W. Pitts (Leiden: Brill, Forthcoming).
Williams, Jarvis J. 'Penal Substitution in Romans 3:25-26?' *PTR* 13 (2007), 73-81.
Williams, Jarvis J. 'Violent Atonement in Romans: The Foundation of Paul's Soteriology,' *JETS* 53 (2010), 579-99.
Williams, Jarvis J. *Maccabean Martyr Traditions in Paul's Theology of Atonement: Did Martyr Theology Shape Paul's Conception of Jesus' Death?* (Eugene, Or: Wipf and Stock, 2010).
Williams, Jarvis J. *One New Man: The Cross and Racial Reconciliation in Pauline Theology* (Nashville: Broadman & Holman, 2010).
Williams, Sam K. *Jesus' Death as a Saving Event: The Background and Origin of a Concept*, HTR (Missoula: Scholars Press, 1975).

Williams, Sam K. *Jesus' Death as Saving Event: The Background and Origin of a Concept*, HDR 2 (Missoula: Scholars Press, 1975).
Witherington III, Ben. *The Problem with Evangelical Theology: Testing the Exegetical Foundations of Calvinism, Dispensationalism, and Wesleyanism* (Waco: Baylor University Press, 2005).
Witherington, III and Darlene Hyatt, Ben. *Paul's Letter to the Romans: A Socio-Rhetorical Commentary* (Grand Rapids: Eerdmans, 2004).
Wright, N.T. '4QMMT and Paul: Justification, 'Works,' and Eschatology,' in *History and Exegesis: New Testament Essays in Honor of Dr. E. Earle Ellis for His 80th Birthday*, ed. Aang-Won (Aaron) Son (New York: and London: T & T Clark, 2006), 104-132.
Wright, N.T. 'Justification: Yesterday, Today, and Forever,' *JETS* 54 (2011), 49-63.
Wright, N.T. 'On Becoming the Righteousness of God: 2 Corinthians 5:21,' in *Pauline Theology*, ed. David M. Hay (Minneapolis: Fortress, 1993).
Wright, N.T. 'The Law in Romans 2,' in *Paul and the Mosaic Law*, ed. James D.G. Dunn (Grand Rapids: Eerdmans, 2001), 131-150.
Wright, N.T. *Justification: God's Plan & Paul's Vision* (Downers Grove, IL: InterVarsity Press, 2009).
Wright, N.T. *The Climax of the Covenant: Christ and the Law in Pauline Theology* (Minneapolis: Fortress, 1991).
Wright, N.T. *The Letter to the Romans: Introduction, Commentary, and Reflections*, NIB, vol. 10 (Nashville: Abingdon, 2002).
Wright, N.T. *The New Testament and the People of God* (Minneapolis: Fortress, 1992).
Wright, N.T. *What Saint Paul Really Said: Was Paul of Tarsus the Real Founder of Christianity?* (Grand Rapids: Eerdmans, 1997).
Yearly, Lee H. 'St. Thomas Aquinas on Providence and Predestination,' *AThR* 49 (1967), 409-23.
Yinger, Kent L. *Paul, Judaism, and Judgment According to Deeds*, SNTSMS 105 (Cambridge: Cambridge University Press, 1999): 152-53).
Young, Frances M. *The Use of Sacrificial Ideas in Greek Christian Writers from the New Testament to John Chrysostom* (Philadelphia: The Philadelphia Patristic Foundation, 1979).
Zahn, T. *Der Brief des Paulus an die Römer ausgelegt*, 3rd ed. (Leipzig: Deichert, 1925).

Scripture Index
Old Testament
Genesis

1-3, 35
2-3, 35, 50
2:10 LXX, 141
2:17, 35, 89, 91, 156, 211
3, 35
3:1-24, 35
3:8, 35
3:14, 35
3:14-21, 35
3:16, 35
3:17, 35
3:17-19, 35
3:19, 35
4:1, 35
4:3 LXX, 165
4:3-5, 35
4:6, 35
4:7, 35
4:9, 36
5:1-6:1, 36
6, 36, 154
6:2, 36
6:4, 36
6:5-6, 36
10:5 LXX, 141
12, 150, 152, 153
12-50, 150
12:1-3, 97
12:3, 21
12:7, 97
13:14-16, 97
15, 152, 153
15:1-5, 21, 151
15:6, 85, 150, 152
15:6 LXX, 76, 78, 85, 150
15:6 MT, 85
17, 151-153
17:1-4, 75
17:1-9, 150
17:1-14, 76, 78, 87, 152
17:2-8, 97
18:10, 167
18:14, 167
18:19, 162
18:19 LXX, 83
20:5 LXX, 83
20:13 LXX, 83
21:12, 167
21:23 LXX, 83
22:18, 21
24:7, 97
24:27 LXX, 83
24:29 LXX, 83
26:4, 21
27:19 LXX, 165
38:26 LXX, 84
44:16 LXX, 84
47:7 LXX, 168

Exodus

3-4, 108
3-14, 109
3-15, 171
3:7-8, 109
3:7-9, 107
3:10, 107
3:10-22, 108
3:11, 107
3:17, 108
3:20, 108
3:21, 108
4:1, 108
4:2-5, 108
4:6-7, 108
4:9, 108
4:10-17, 108
4:20-21, 109
4:20-21 MT, 108-109
4:22-23, 108
4:24-26, 193
5-11, 36
5:1-14:30, 109
6:14, 165
7:13-14, 109
7:22, 109
8:15 MT, 109
8:19, 109
8:28, 109
8:32, 109
9:7, 109
9:12, 109
9:16, 167
9:16 LXX, 167
9:35, 109
10:1, 109
10:20, 109
10:27, 109
11:10, 109
12-13, 36
12:33-14:31, 36
12:48, 75-76
13:2, 165
14, 36
14:8, 109
14:8 MT, 109
15, 109, 171
15:1-8, 109
15:1-21, 36
15:9, 109
15:10-20, 109
15:13 LXX, 83
16:2, 36
16:3, 36
17:1-2, 36
17:3, 36
19:3, 37
19:3-32:19, 37
20, 58-59
20:1-6, 37
20:2-3, 38
20:3-6, 37
21:20 LXX, 200
23:7 LXX, 84
24, 37, 74, 87
24:18, 131

25:17-20 LXX, 203
25:18-22 LXX, 203
25:22 LXX, 203
29:36 LXX, 201
30:10 LXX, 201-202
31:7 LXX, 203
32, 57, 63
32-34, 91, 170
32:1, 37
32:1-34:9, 193
32:2-4, 37
32:4, 37
32:5, 37
32:5-6, 37
32:7-8, 37
32:9, 37
32:12, 200
32:14 LXX, 202
32:33, 200
33:3, 62
33:5, 62
33:19, 167
34:6-7, 171
34:7 LXX, 83
34:9, 62
34:29, 171
35:12 LXX, 203
37:6 LXX, 203
37:6-8 LXX, 203

Leviticus
1-5, 192
1:1-13, 193
4, 214
4:1-35 LXX, 209
4:2-3, 213
4:13-14, 214
4:20, 214
4:20 LXX, 202
4:26, 209
4:26 LXX, 202
4:31 LXX, 202
4:35, 209
4:35 LXX, 202
5:6 LXX, 202
5:6-11 LXX, 209
5:6-7 LXX, 214
5:7-8 LXX, 208
5:9 LXX, 208, 209
5:10 LXX, 202
5:11 LXX, 214
5:13 LXX, 202
5:16 LXX, 202
5:18 LXX, 202
5:26 LXX, 202
6:18 MT, 208
6:23 LXX, 202
6:25 LXX, 208
7:7 LXX, 202
7:18 LXX, 76
7:37 LXX, 209, 214
9:1-10:2, 198
9:1-24, 193
9:2-3 LXX, 209, 214
9:23-24, 193
10:2, 193
12:3, 75-76
12:6 LXX, 209, 214
12:8 LXX, 209, 214
14:4 LXX, 202
14:11, 168
14:13 LXX, 209, 214
14:22 LXX, 209, 214
14:31 LXX, 208-209, 214
14:32 LXX, 201
15:13 LXX, 201
15:15 LXX, 209, 214
15:30 LXX, 209, 214
16, 31, 191-193, 202, 214, 218
16 LXX, 201
16-17 LXX, 201, 204
16:1, 193
16:1-2, 193
16:1-4, 193
16:2, 91
16:2 LXX, 203
16:3 LXX, 209, 214
16:3-28, 192
16:3-34, 192
16:5 LXX, 209, 214
16:9 LXX, 209, 214
16:14-15 LXX, 202-203
16:16, 198, 200
16:29-30, 192
16:30, 198, 200
17 LXX, 201
17:4 LXX, 76
17:11 LXX, 201
18:4-5, 75
18:5, 159, 215, 220
19:15 LXX, 83
20:22, 75
23:19 LXX, 209, 214
25:18, 75
25:44 LXX, 140
26:13 LXX, 140
26:25 LXX, 200

Numbers
4:16, 168
5:8 LXX, 202
6:11 LXX, 202, 214

238

7:89 LXX, 203
8:12 LXX, 202
8:19 LXX, 202
8:21 LXX, 202
11:1, 36
12:1-9, 36
13:25-33, 36
13:32-33, 36
14, 200
14:1, 36
14:2, 36
14:3, 36
14:9, 37
14:10, 36
14:11, 37
14:18, 201
14:18-19, 37
15:25 LXX, 202
15:28 LXX, 202
16:11, 36
16:41, 36
17:11 LXX, 202
17:12 LXX, 202
18:27 LXX, 76, 78
18:30 LXX, 76
24:4 LXX, 80
24:16 LXX, 80
25, 57, 91
25:11, 195
28:22 LXX, 202
28:30 LXX, 202
29:5 LXX, 202
29:11 LXX, 202
31:21 LXX, 62, 75
31:50 LXX, 202
36:13 LXX, 62, 75

Deuteronomy
4:1, 65
4:1 LXX, 62, 75
4:5 LXX, 62, 75
4:5-6, 65

4:6-8, 81
4:13-14, 65
4:15-18 LXX, 211
4:23 LXX, 211
4:25 LXX, 211
4:25-31, 193
4:26, 65
5-6, 65
5:8 LXX, 211
6, 57, 66
6-28, 75
6-30, 58
6:1, 74
6:4-25, 66
7:6-8, 162, 164
8:19-20, 65
9, 91
9:1-10:22, 193
9:4-6 LXX, 83
9:6, 62
9:13, 62
9:27 LXX, 63
10:16, 62-63, 77
11:17, 65
21:1-8, 200
21:8, 200
21:22-23, 216
21:23, 214-216
25:1 LXX, 84
27, 91, 215
27-28, 216
27:1, 215
27:15-29:29, 215
27:26, 215
28:1-14, 215
28:1-68, 215
28:15-68, 67, 215
28:20, 65
28:22, 65
28:24, 65
28:25, 65
28:52, 65
28:53 LXX, 69

28:55 LXX, 69
28:57 LXX, 69
30:1-10, 193
30:6, 77-78
30:11-14, 65
30:15, 87
30:15-16, 58
30:15-20, 160, 220
30:16, 60, 75
30:16 LXX, 75
30:18, 65
32:21, 172
32:41 LXX, 200
32:43 LXX, 200
33:4 LXX, 81
33:9 LXX, 81
33:9-10 LXX, 80
33:10 LXX, 81
33:19 LXX, 83
33:21 LXX, 83

Joshua
2:28 LXX, 211
5:2, 75-76
7:1-26, 193
24:14 LXX, 83
24:30 LXX, 140

Judges
2:8 LXX, 140
2:10-23, 193
3:7-15, 193
4:6-8, 193
4:10-12, 193
5:11 LXX, 83
14:10, 76
16:25, 168

1 Samuel
7:2-14, 193
9:1-2, 37
9:15-16, 37
10:17-24, 37

11, 37
12:8-11, 193
12:22, 173
14:47-52, 37
15, 37
15:1, 37
15:1-3, 37
15:6, 37
15:8-9, 37
15:11, 37
15:19, 37
15:22-23, 193
15:23, 37
15:24, 38
15:25, 38
15:26, 38
16:14, 38
16:14-15, 38
16:16, 38
16:23, 38
17, 38
18:10, 38
18:10-19, 38
19:2, 38
19:9, 38
24:1-22, 38
26:1-25, 38
28:1-25, 38

2 Samuel
4:10 MT, 142
11:1-5, 38
11:6, 38
11:8-13, 38
11:27, 38
12:7-23, 193
21:1-9, 193
24:1-25, 193

1 Kings
9:6, 38
9:6-7, 38
11:4-13, 38
11:26-40, 38
12:1-15:3, 39

1:38-53, 38
2:10 LXX, 83
3:14 LXX, 202
3:16-18, 38
4:1-19, 38
4:20-34, 38
5:1-12, 38
6-8, 38
6:1-8:66, 38
6:5 LXX, 211
8:22-53, 193
8:32 LXX, 84
9:4, 38
11:1, 38
11:14-25, 38
12:7 LXX, 83
12:16-24, 38
16:7, 39
16:30-32, 39
21:17-29, 193
26:23 LXX, 83
31:9, 142

2 Kings
2:1-3 LXX, 202
2:13 LXX, 202
3:1-7, 193
3:2-3, 39
4:10 LXX, 142
8:15 LXX, 83
13:1-7, 193
13:2, 39
15:8-9, 39
15:17-18, 39
15:23-24, 39
15:27-28, 39
16:1-2, 39
17:7-23, 39
18:9, 142
18:26 LXX, 142
18:31 LXX, 142
21:1-9, 39
21:19-22, 39
22:14-20, 193
22:21 LXX, 83

22:25 LXX, 83
23:31-32, 39
24:8-9, 39

3 Kings
1:42 LXX, 142

4 Kings
9:7 LXX, 140
10:33 LXX, 140
18:12 LXX, 140

1 Chronicles
6:34 LXX, 202
18:14 LXX, 83
21-22, 193
23:28, 201
29:13 LXX, 148
29:17 LXX, 83

2 Chronicles
1:14-17, 38
2:1-7:10;14, 38
6:12-42, 193
6:23 LXX, 83
6:25, 200
6:27, 200
6:39, 200
7:12-16, 193
7:14, 200
8:13-30, 38
9:8 LXX, 83
10:1-19, 39
10:26, 39
10:34, 39
11:14-17, 39
12:1-12, 193
15:1-15, 193
22:51-53, 39
29:1-32:33, 193
29:24 LXX, 202
30:18 LXX, 202
34:20-28, 193

Nehemiah
   1:1-6 LXX, 143

Esther
   1:1 LXX, 113
   2:1 LXX, 209
   2:20 LXX, 113
   4:8 LXX, 113
   4:17 LXX, 113-114
   5:1 LXX, 114
   5:9-14 LXX, 114
   6:1 LXX, 113
   6:1-3 LXX, 114
   6:13 LXX, 113
   8:1-10:3 LXX, 114
   10:3 LXX, 114

Job
   2:9, 169
   34:11, 64
   38:14, 169

Psalms
   2:9, 169
   4:2 LXX, 83
   4:6 LXX, 83
   5:9, 50, 82
   5:9 LXX, 83
   7:9 LXX, 83
   7:18 LXX, 83
   9:5 LXX, 83
   9:9 LXX, 83
   10:7, 50, 82
   10:7 LXX, 83
   11:7 LXX, 80
   14:1-3, 50, 82
   14:2 LXX, 83
   16:1 LXX, 83
   16:15 LXX, 83
   17:21 LXX, 83
   17:25 LXX, 83
   17:28, 78
   17:28 LXX, 76
   17:31 LXX, 80
   24:8 LXX, 61
   28:4, 64
   31 LXX, 150-151
   31:1-2 LXX, 150-151
   32, 150-152
   32:1-2, 150-151
   32:1-2 MT, 150
   32:10, 151
   32:10-11, 151
   33:9 LXX, 61
   35:1 LXX, 140
   36:1, 50, 82
   39:7 LXX, 208
   50:6 LXX, 81
   51, 192, 193
   53:1-3, 50, 82
   61:13 LXX, 64
   68:17 LXX, 61
   68:32, 200
   85:5 LXX, 61
   95 LXX, 142
   95:2 LXX, 142
   95:10 LXX, 142
   96 MT, 142
   96:2 MT, 142
   96:10 MT, 142
   99:5 LXX, 61
   104:19 LXX, 80
   105:1 LXX, 61
   105:20 LXX, 211
   105:30 LXX, 202
   105:31, 78
   105:31 LXX, 76
   106:1 LXX, 61
   106:11 LXX, 80
   108:21 LXX, 61
   115:2 LXX, 81
   118:11 LXX, 80
   133:1 LXX, 140
   135:1 LXX, 61
   140:3, 50, 82
   142:2 LXX, 83
   144:9 LXX, 61

Proverbs
   1:16, 50, 82
   16:14 LXX, 202
   16:27, 64
   24:12 LXX, 64

Ecclesiastes
   7:20, 50, 82

Isaiah
   1, 74
   1:1-26, 195
   1:4, 39
   1:7 LXX, 84
   1:10-17, 193
   1:21, 39
   5:23 LXX, 84
   13:6, 64
   13:6-16, 58, 60
   13:9, 64
   28:13, 80
   29:16-17, 169
   29:17 LXX, 76
   32:15, 78
   32:15 LXX, 76
   34:8, 58, 60
   40:9 LXX, 143
   42:6-7, 74, 87
   43:8, 74
   43:9 LXX, 84
   45:9-11, 169
   49:6, 74, 87
   52:5, 74
   52:7, 144
   52:7 LXX, 143
   53, 4
   53:2-12, 216
   53:12 LXX, 76
   56:10, 74

59:7-8, 50, 82
59:9-10, 74
59:20-21, 173
60:6, 143
60:6 LXX, 143
61:1, 143
61:1 LXX, 143
64:4, 176
64:8, 169
65:1, 172
65:1-3, 39
65:2 LXX, 172
29:14, 175
49:1, 144

Jeremiah
1:5, 144, 162, 181
2:2-37, 39
2:3, 39
3:6-10, 39
4:4, 62-63
5:1 LXX, 200
5:7 LXX, 200
7:21-23, 193
7:25, 140
17:10, 64
18, 169
18:4, 200
20:15 LXX, 142
25:14, 64
27:20 LXX, 200
30-31, 109, 111
30:3, 109
30:8, 109
30:9, 110
30:10, 110
30:10-31:40, 110
30:11, 110
30:15, 110
30:16, 110
30:17-23, 110
31, 110
31:1, 110
31:3, 110
31:4-6, 110
31:8-9, 110
31:11, 110
31:12-14, 110
31:19, 110
31:21, 110
31:23, 110
31:31-32, 110
31:31-33, 159, 178
31:31-34, 70-71, 77, 79, 110, 159-160
31:33, 110
31:34, 110
32:19, 64
38:31-34 LXX, 70-71, 79
38:34 LXX, 200
43:3 LXX, 200
51:24, 64

Lamentations
2:21-22, 64

Ezekiel
1:1-3, 39
3:7, 62, 63
5:1-7:9, 39
7:10, 64
7:20, 39
11, 110-111, 160
11:2, 39
11:16, 110
11:17-19, 110
11:20, 111
11:21, 111
13:2, 39
14:1-11, 39
22:1-31, 39
33:20, 64
34:1-10, 39
36, 111
36-37, 79, 111, 159-160, 178
36:1-15, 111
36:20, 74
36:22-23, 111
36:22-37:28, 77-78
36:24, 111
36:25, 111
36:26-27, 78, 111
36:27, 111
36:28, 111
36:29-38, 111
37, 111
37:1-28, 111
43:20 LXX, 202
43:22 LXX, 202
45:17 LXX, 202

Daniel
1:35 Th, 127
1:37 Th, 127
1:38 Th, 127
3:24-90 LXX, 195
3:24-90 Th, 127
3:28-29 LXX, 195
3:37 LXX, 195
3:38-40 LXX, 200
4:2, 200
7:9-11, 58, 60
9:6, 140

Hosea
6:6, 193
6:7, 39

Joel
1:15, 63
2:1, 63
4:14, 63
2, 79
2:1-17 LXX, 142

2:1-2, 58, 60
2:18-3:2 LXX, 142
2:32 LXX, 80
3:3-4 LXX, 142
3:5 LXX, 142-143

Amos
2:6, 39
3:2, 162
3:3, 39
3:7, 140
5:21-22, 193
7:2 LXX, 200

Obadiah
1:15, 64

Jonah
1:9, 140

Micah
2:1, 39
6:6-8, 193
7:9 LXX, 200

Nahum
1:7, 61
1:7 LXX, 143
1:8-14 LXX, 143
2:1 LXX, 143, 144
2:1-3:19 LXX, 143

Habakkuk
1:3, 39
2:4, 215

Zephaniah
1:12-16, 64
1:14, 64
1:14-2:3, 58, 60

1:17, 74
1:18, 64
3:8, 58, 60

Zechariah
7:2 LXX, 202
8:22 LXX, 202

Malachi
1:2-3, 167
4:1, 58, 60, 64

New Testament
Matthew
23, 74
1, 18, 20, 34
1:21, 18, 20
3:15, 83
4:21, 166
6:24, 103
7:1-2, 58
8:9, 140
12:37, 84
12:41, 209
13:13, 34
19:8, 62
20:18, 209
20:28, 166
20:28, 10
23, 57
24, 56
24:44, 34
25:32, 141
27:3, 209
27:32-44, 101

Mark
1:44, 201
7:9-13, 56
7:21-22, 56
10:5, 62
10:33, 209
12:24, 34
14:64, 209
15:21-32, 101

Luke
2:7, 165
4:18-19, 143
6:13, 141
6:22, 141
11:31, 209
11:49, 141
21:28, 205
23:26-43, 101
2:22, 201

5:14, 201
9:10, 141
13:37, 102
16:13, 103

John
2:6, 201
3:16, 186, 223
3:25, 201
5:16, 34
5:18, 34
6:37, 21
8:47, 34
10:15, 20
10:17, 34
10:26, 11
11:52, 20
12:18, 34
12:39, 34
14:2, 11
15:13, 20
16:7, 21
17:2, 21
17:6, 21
17:11-12, 11

Acts
1:26, 141
2:23, 163
2:42, 141
2:43, 141
4:28, 164
7:8, 40
7:28, 81
8-9, 94
9, 141
9:3-22, 180
10:35, 83
13:2, 141
13:38-39, 84
14:12, 141
17:31, 83
19:9, 141
19:17-27, 101
20:28, 20

24:25, 83
26:5, 162
27:44, 40

Romans
1, 43, 48, 86-87, 174, 208
1-2, 82
1-4, 54
1-8, 168
1:1, 140-144, 146
1:1-2, 146
1:1-5, 73
1:1-7, 140-141
1:1-3:8, 82
1:2, 141, 144
1:2-3, 141
1:2-4, 144-145
1:2-6, 145
1:2-7, 144
1:2-9, 144
1:3, 45, 52
1:5, 142, 145
1:6, 141, 145
1:6-7, 145
1:7, 141-142, 145
1:8-15, 145
1:9, 142-144
1:15, 47, 146
1:15-17, 47, 140
1:16, 47, 55, 57, 69, 142, 144-146
1:16-17, 73, 84, 145-146, 220
1:16-5:11, 43
1:17, 69, 84, 144-146
1:18, 47, 59, 146, 170
1:18-3:20, 47, 56
1:18-5:11, 34
1:18-23, 58, 146

1:18-31, 63, 71, 74, 79, 82,
1:18-32, 47-48, 54-56, 59, 70-71, 83, 104
1:18-2:29, 77
1:18-3:8, 82
1:18-3:18, 83
1:18-3:20, 56, 61, 63, 83-85, 95, 146, 156, 172, 205-206
1:18-3:24, 206
1:18-7:25, 212
1:18-8:39, 220
1:19-20, 147
1:19-23, 147
1:19-32, 147
1:20, 55
1:21, 72, 94
1:21-25, 57
1:21-23, 147
1:23, 211
1:24, 55, 57, 72, 142, 146
1:24-31, 55-57
1:24-32, 55, 147
1:25, 48, 59
1:26, 34, 48, 57, 142, 146
1:26-27, 57
1:26-31, 57
1:27, 48
1:27-31, 75
1:28, 48, 146
1:29, 57
1:29-30, 57
1:29-31, 49, 57-58
1:30, 57
1:32, 49, 55, 57-58, 69, 75, 80, 91
1:32-2:3, 62
2, 77

2-3, 105, 154
2:1-3:3, 81
2:1-3:8, 49, 63
2:1-3:9, 94
2:1-3:19, 87
2:1-3:20, 49, 54, 56, 58, 62, 82, 87-90, 104, 147, 154
2:1-4:25, 41
2:1, 55- 58, 76, 81, 209
2:1-3, 54-55, 62
2:1-2, 59
2:1-4, 62
2:1-5, 61, 68
2:1-10, 55
2:1-13, 69
2:1-16, 55-56, 60, 85, 147
2:1-29, 56-57, 76, 80, 83, 89, 148
2:2, 58- 60
2:3, 57, 60
2:3-4, 61
2:3-16, 59
2:4, 60-62
2:4-16, 75
2:5, 62-64, 72, 170
2:5-3:20, 62
2:5-12, 65
2:5-13, 69
2:5-14, 72
2:5-16, 47
2:6, 64, 68, 72, 75-76, 87
2:6-10, 47, 67, 210
2:6-12, 65, 71
2:6-13, 68, 71, 76
2:6-16, 55, 67, 72

2:6-25, 75
2:7-10, 68
2:7, 64
2:7-12, 71
2:7-16, 72
2:8, 59, 64, 170
2:8-9, 64, 67
2:9-10, 55, 58, 63
2:9, 64
2:10, 55, 64
2:11, 55, 64-65, 69
2:12, 65, 69
2:12-14, 64
2:12-14, 70
2:12-16, 64, 69, 72
2:12-29, 64, 68, 148
2:12-3:20, 105
2:13, 65-66, 67-71, 75-76, 81, 83-84, 87, 102
2:13-15, 69
2:13-15, 73
2:14, 56, 58, 65, 69, 70-72, 80
2:14-15, 70-72
2:15, 65, 70-74
2:15-16, 71-72
2:16, 65, 72-73, 77, 142, 144
2:16-29, 73, 148
2:17, 56, 62, 74, 148
2:17-18, 49
2:17-3:8, 59
2:17-3:9, 89
2:17-20, 69, 74, 81, 86, 94
2:17-3:19, 147
2:17-29, 148
2:18, 59, 74, 94
2:19, 74

2:19-29, 49
2:20, 59, 74
2:21-22, 75
2:21-23, 74, 78
2:21-24, 74, 86
2:23, 74, 86, 148
2:24, 74
2:25, 62, 75-76, 78, 86, 148
2:25-29, 73, 74
2:25-26, 75, 78, 148, 153
2:25-29, 77-78, 80
2:26, 62, 75-76, 78-80
2:26-29, 77, 79
2:27, 62, 70, 79-80, 86, 93
2:28, 45, 52, 77, 83
2:28-29, 77, 79, 159
2:29, 72, 77, 79-80, 93
3, 85, 95, 203, 206
3-4, 153
3:1, 80, 82, 92, 148
3:1-2, 49
3:1, 58
3:1-6, 59
3:1-8, 80
3:1-18, 83
3:1-9, 89
3:2, 49, 80
3:3, 81-82, 102
3:4, 59, 81-82, 84
3:4-8, 82
3:5, 47, 81, 170
3:5-8, 81
3:7, 59, 142
3:8, 82

3:10-12, 92
3:9, 44, 46, 49, 82, 92
3:9-20, 49, 82, 154
3:9-18, 49-50
3:10-11, 50
3:10-12, 50, 82
3:10-18, 50, 82, 86
3:10-19, 59
3:12, 50
3:13, 50, 82
3:13-14, 50
3:14, 50, 82
3:15-16, 50
3:15-17, 50, 82
3:17, 50, 94
3:18, 50, 82
3:19, 49, 58, 82-83
3:19, 58
3:19-20, 83, 87, 152
3:20, 45, 49, 50, 52, 65, 68-69, 71, 81, 83-88, 102, 147, 153, 212
3:20-21, 149
3:20-22, 153
3:21, 149
3:21-22, 84, 144, 147, 149
3:21-26, 73, 85, 146-147, 156
3:21-4:25,83, 85, 147. 154
3:21-5:1, 84, 102
3:21-31, 149, 206
3:21-22, 153, 205
3:21-4:12, 153
3:21-5:19, 156

3:21-24, 205
3:21-8:30, 207
3:21-5:11, 222
3:22, 92
3:33, 85
3:23, 43, 50, 84, 95, 105, 156, 210
3:23-24, 205
3:24, 84, 102, 149, 153, 205-206, 216
3:24-25, 153, 206
3:24-26, 147
3:24-30, 205
3:25, 202-203, 205-206
3:25-26, 149
3:25-31, 149
3:25-26, 206, 210
3:26, 61, 84, 102, 147, 149
3:27, 148-149
3:27-28, 149
3:27-30, 153, 206
3:27-31, 148
3:28, 84, 102, 149, 153, 206
3:29-30, 206
3:30, 84, 102, 149
3:31, 102, 149
4, 77, 85
4:1, 45, 52, 149
4:1-25, 76, 79, 85, 149, 152
4:1-5, 153
4:1-6, 153
4:2, 84, 102, 149-150
4:3, 85, 148, 149-150

4:3-6, 76, 151
4:4, 150
4:4-5, 66, 150
4:4-8, 150
4:5, 84, 149-150
4:6, 149, 151
4:6-8, 150
4:7, 151
4:7-8, 149, 151
4:8, 151
4:9, 76, 149, 151, 153
4:9-11, 76
4:9-25, 151
4:9-12, 151
4:10, 76, 151
4:11, 149, 151, 152, 153
4:11-12, 149, 152
4:13, 21, 149, 152-153
4:13-14, 149
4:13-25, 152
4:14, 102, 149, 153
4:15, 47, 88-89, 92, 153-154, 170, 212
4:16, 21, 149
4:16-20, 154
4:17, 166, 171
4:19, 149
4:20, 149
4:22, 55, 76, 149
4:23, 76
4:24, 154, 157
4:24-25, 149
4:25, 21, 43, 149, 152, 154, 206, 216
5-8, 103
5:1, 102, 154
5:5, 84

5:1-11, 33, 177, 154
5:1-5, 207
5:1-8:39, 207
5:1-8:39, 207
5:2, 154
5:3, 58
5:3-4, 154
5:3-5, 154
5:5, 72, 177
5:5-8:11, 212
5:6, 155, 207
5:6-11, 155, 200
5:6-7, 155, 207
5:6-8, 155, 213, 221
5:6-9, 213
5:7, 155, 207
5:8, 19, 155, 207, 213
5:8-10, 155, 207
5:9, 15, 47, 84, 102, 155-156, 170, 207
5:9-10, 207
5:9-11, 155
5:10, 22, 84, 155-156, 213
5:11, 155-156, 207
5:12, 34-36, 40-43, 90-91, 100-101, 103, 211
5:12-13, 41
5:12-14, 160
5:12-16, 42
5:12-21, 33-35, 43, 60, 90, 95-96, 98-101, 156-157, 210-212
5:12-6:23, 88, 90, 157, 212
5:12-7:25, 94

5:12-19, 98
5:12-8:4, 210
5:13, 41, 89-90
5:13-14, 42, 88-89, 153
5:13-17, 34
5:13-21, 42
5:14, 34-35, 44, 88, 91, 100, 105, 156
5:14-21, 90
5:15, 34-35, 42, 100
5:15-21, 42
5:15-16, 35
5:15-17, 43
5:16, 42, 43
5:16, 34
5:16-21, 42
5:16, 100
5:16, 156
5:17, 34-35, 42-43, 44, 91, 100, 156, 157
5:17-21, 43
5:17-22, 102
5:18, 34-35, 37, 43, 100
5:18-19, 21, 35
5:18-21, 34
5:19, 34-35, 43, 100
5:20, 44, 88, 89, 98
5:20-21, 43, 98, 157, 160
5:20-6:23, 96
5:21, 44
6, 44, 95, 97-98, 100, 157, 220
6:1, 44, 98, 101, 103, 157
6:1-7:6, 45
6:1-8:11, 34
6:1-3, 157

6:1-5, 98
6:1-7, 102
6:1-10, 157
6:1-11, 101, 157
6:1-23, 90, 98,
   100-101, 158
6:1-8:39, 92
6:1-14, 103
6:2, 100, 102
6:2-4, 44, 100,
   157
6:2-5, 98
6:2-8:17, 44
6:2-10, 101
6:3, 100, 102,
   157
6:4, 44, 100, 102,
   157-158
6:5, 101-102,
   157
6:5-7, 157
6:6, 8, 21, 44, 94,
   98, 100-101-
   102, 157
6:6-7, 98
6:6-11, 101
6:7, 44, 84, 102-
   103
6:7-9, 44
6:8, 44, 101-102,
   157
6:8-11, 102, 157
6:9, 100
6:9-10, 102
6:10, 44, 102
6:11, 44-45, 102,
   157
6:11-13, 157
6:12, 44, 101,
   210
6:12-23, 101-102
6:14, 44, 52, 102,
   104, 157
6:14-15, 46
6:14-16, 44

6:14-20, 44
6:15, 101, 103
6:15-23, 103
6:15-17, 157
6:16, 83, 91, 103
6:16-18, 101
6:16-23, 103
6:17, 72, 103
6:18, 102-103,
   157
6:18-19, 44
6:19, 45, 52, 103
6:19-20, 157
6:20, 103
6:20-23, 101
6:21, 91
6:21-22, 103
6:22, 44, 103
6:22-23, 157
6:23, 44-45, 91,
   103
7, 45, 88- 90, 92,
   105, 153-154,
   208
7-8, 158
7:1, 45, 89, 92,
   94
7:1-3, 158
7:1-4, 93
7:1-5, 46
7:1-6, 45, 88,
   159
7:1-10, 90
7:1-23, 210
7:1-25, 88, 105,
   154, 158-160
7:1-8:10, 211
7:2, 45, 102
7:2-3, 93
7:3, 45
7:4, 46, 93, 158
7:4-5, 158
7:5, 45, 46, 52,
   89, 91, 93, 95,
   158

7:5, 45
7:6, 46, 77, 80,
   93, 102, 158
7:7, 93- 95, 158
7:7-9, 89
7:7-12, 93
7:7-13, 93, 95
7:7-21, 95
7:7-23, 88, 95
7:7-25, 89-90,
   94, 146, 158,
   212
7:7-24, 44
7:7-8:4, 210
7:8, 44, 90, 95-
   96, 158
7:8-9, 90
7:8-11, 93, 95
7:9, 44, 90-91,
   158
7:9-10, 95
7:10-11, 96
7:9-12, 90
7:10, 89-91, 95,
   158-159
7:11, 44, 91, 159
7:12, 91, 93
7:12-13, 93
7:13, 91- 93, 95
7:13-14, 92
7:13-23, 159
7:14, 44, 58, 91-
   93, 95
7:14, 58
7:15, 92-94, 159
7:15-16, 92-93
7:15-24, 93
7:15-25, 93
7:5, 93
7:15-20, 96
7:15-21, 94, 96
7:15-23, 95, 159
7:15-25, 96
7:16, 94, 159
7:16-18, 92

7:16-20, 92
7:17, 44, 92, 94-95, 159
7:18, 45, 52, 92, 94-95, 101, 159
7:18-21, 159
7:19, 92, 95
7:19-20, 92-93, 159
7:20, 44, 92, 95
7:21, 95-96
7:21-23, 93
7:22, 95-96, 159
7:22-23, 95
7:23, 44, 96, 99, 159
7:24, 90-91, 96, 101, 159, 210
7:24-25, 93
7:24-8:4, 212
7:25, 44-45, 52, 90, 96, 101, 159
7:25-8:11, 159
8, 79, 159, 170
8:1, 90, 91, 159, 208-209
8:1-11, 73
8:1-4, 62, 77, 79, 89, 92
8:1-11, 93, 101
8:1-4, 160, 208
8:1-3, 210, 212
8:1-4, 220
8:2, 91, 159, 208
8:2-11, 90
8:2-3, 80
8:2, 44
8:2-4, 208
8:2-7, 159
8:3, 159, 163, 208-212, 214
8:3-9, 45, 52

8:4, 80, 83, 160, 212
8:4-11, 160
8:5-11, 160, 212
8:6, 91
8:8-9, 45
8:9, 21, 45
8:10, 44, 83
8:10-11, 101
8:11, 163
8:12, 45, 52
8:12-17, 160, 184
8:13, 45, 52, 101
8:17, 160
8:17-18, 160
8:18, 160
8:18-25, 166, 217
8:18-39, 160
8:19, 44
8:21-23, 44
8:22, 44, 58, 161
8:23, 101, 161, 205
8:24, 161
8:26, 161
8:26-27, 161
8:27, 72
8:28, 58, 141, 161, 164, 166
8:28-30, 161, 163, 184, 220
8:29, 161-165
8:29-30, 161, 166, 206-207, 220
8:30, 84, 102, 141, 161, 163-166, 171
8:31, 161, 164
8:31-39, 161
8:32, 21, 161, 164, 200

8:33, 84, 102, 163
8:33-34, 161
8:34, 21, 209
8:35-36, 161
8:39, 45, 154
9-11, 80-81, 164, 167, 170, 173-174, 222
9:1-11:36, 73, 81-83
9:1-5, 167, 170, 220
9:1-8, 167
9:1-9, 167
9:1-18, 167
9:2, 72
9:3, 45, 52
9:5, 45, 52
9:6, 167
9:6-8, 76
9:6-11:32, 167
9:6-15, 167
9:6-29, 168, 172, 184, 220
9:6-11:10, 173
9:6-10:13, 221
9:6-11:32, 170
9:7, 21, 141, 166
9:7-9, 167
9:8, 21, 45, 52, 76
9:10-12, 167
9:10-18, 168
9:10-24, 164
9:11-12, 164
9:11-13, 164
2:12-16, 69
9:12, 141, 166, 171
9:13, 167
9:14-15, 167
9:14-18, 171
9:15-16, 170
9:15-17, 170

9:16, 167
9:16-17, 168
9:17, 164, 167-168, 170
9:17-18, 169-170
9:18, 168
9:19, 168
9:19-21, 171
9:19-23, 169
9:20, 57, 168
9:20-21, 169
9:20-29, 168
9:21, 170
9:22, 61, 169
9:22-23, 61, 169-170
9:22-24, 164
9:23, 6, 60, 170-171
9:23-24, 171, 207
9:24, 141, 171
9:24-25, 164, 171
9:24-26, 61, 171
9:24-29, 166
9:25, 141
9:26, 141
9:27, 61
9:27-29, 171
9:30, 80
9:30-10:3, 80
9:30-10:13, 77, 80, 92, 172
9:30-10:14, 172
9:30-10:18, 172
9:30-10:21, 84
9:30-33, 94
9:30-11:32, 172
9:30-11:34, 173
9:30-11:36, 168, 220
10:1, 72, 170, 222
10:1-13, 143

10:3, 80
10:4, 81
10:5-13, 80
10:5-18, 172
10:6, 72
10:8, 72
10:8-9, 80
10:8-16, 144
10:8-13, 146, 220
10:9, 72
10:10, 72
10:11, 21
10:13, 80
10:14-11:36, 80
10:15, 141, 143
10:15-16, 144
10:16, 142
10:19, 94, 172
10:19-11:24, 172
10:19-11:32, 172
10:20, 172
10:21, 172
11, 60
11:1-10, 60
11:1-2, 167
11:1-6, 172
11;1-10, 173
11:1-24, 164
11:2, 21, 164
11:7-10, 172
11:11-16, 172
11:11-24, 60, 173
11:12, 60
11:14, 45, 52
11:15, 222
11:17-24, 173
11:20, 173
11:22, 60
11:25, 173
11:25-32, 172-173
11:26, 40, 60, 173

11:26-27, 173
11:28, 142, 174
11:28-32, 173
11:29, 174
11:30-32, 174
11:33-36, 164, 174
11:33, 60
11:34, 94
12:1-15:12, 165
12:1-2, 165
12:1-15:13, 222
12:3, 190
12:5, 45
12:6, 190
13:2, 72
13:5, 55
13:6, 34
13:14, 45, 52
14:1, 50
14:2, 50
14:22, 73
14:23, 209
15:1, 50
15:1-13, 50
15:7, 51, 55
15:7-9, 50
15:8, 50, 59
15:8-12, 59
15:9, 50
15:9-12, 50, 59
15:15, 190
15:15-20, 140
15:16, 142, 144
15:17, 148
15:19, 142, 144
15:22, 55
15:22-33, 140
15:27, 92
16:20, 190
16:25, 142, 144
16:26, 144

1 Corinthians
1, 209
1-2, 176
1:1-2, 174
1:2, 45, 174
1:3, 145, 174
1:4, 174
1:4-9, 174
1:4-7, 174
1:4-14:40, 176
1:5, 174
1:5-7, 174
1:6, 174-175
1:7, 174
1:8, 175
1:8-9, 175
1:9, 141, 166, 175
6:9-11, 56
1:11, 51
1:12-13, 51
1:12-4:13, 51
1:13, 200
1:17, 141-142
1:18, 12, 143
1:18-19, 65, 170
1:18-31, 175
1:19, 175
1:20, 175
1:21, 175
1:22-23, 175
1:22-31, 175
1:24, 175
1:25, 175
1:26, 45, 52, 175
1:27-28, 176
1:28, 102
1:29, 45, 52, 176
1:30, 45, 176, 205
2:1-4, 176
2:1-5, 176
2:4, 176
2:5, 176
2:6, 102, 176
2:6-16, 176
2:7, 164, 176
2:8, 176
2:9, 176
2:10, 176
2:11, 176
2:12-13, 176
2:14-15, 176
3:3, 92
3:10, 174
3:16, 176
4:1, 176
4:4, 84
4:5, 72
4:7, 177
4:15, 142
5, 51
5:1, 56
5:5, 45, 52
5:7, 148
6:1-11, 51
6:9, 51, 57
6:10, 51, 57
6:11, 51, 84, 177
6:13, 102
6:16, 45, 52
6:18-19, 177
6:20, 51, 205
7:1-16:20, 177
7:17-24, 166
7:23, 205
7:28, 45, 52
7:37, 72
8-10, 51
8:1, 51, 58
8:11, 170
9:11, 92
9:12, 142
9:14, 142
9:15-16, 148
9:16, 142
9:18, 142
10:1-22, 57
10:6-7, 51
10:8, 51
10:9-10, 170
10:18, 45, 52
11:17-21, 51
11:20, 51
11:21, 51, 52
11:22, 52
11:24, 200
11:28, 40
11:32, 209
11:33, 51
12-14, 51-52
12-15, 52, 174
12:3, 55
13:8, 102
13:10, 102
13:11, 102
14:25, 40, 72
15, 43, 52, 222
15:1-2, 144
15:1-58, 43
15:3, 200, 221
15:10, 190
15:11, 40
15:18, 65, 170
15:20, 43
15:21, 43, 91
15:21-22, 43
15:22, 21, 43
15:23-58, 43
15:24, 102
15:26, 91, 102, 211
15:31, 148
15:39, 45, 52
15:39-40, 45
15:50, 45, 52
15:54-55, 91
15:56, 44, 91
16:23, 190

2 Corinthians
1:3-4, 177
1:2, 145
1:3-22, 177
1:4, 177

1:5, 177
1:6, 177
1:8-10, 177
1:12, 92, 148, 177
1:12-22, 177
1:14, 148
1:15, 177
1:17, 45, 52
1:21, 177
1:21-22, 177
1:22, 177
2:8, 55
2:12, 144
2:12-17, 177
2:12-13, 177-178
2:14, 45, 178
2:15, 65, 170, 178
2:15-16, 143
2:16, 178
3, 179
3:1, 78
3:1-2, 178
3:1-6, 78
3:1-18, 178
3:1-5:10, 179
3:2, 78, 178
3:3, 78, 178
3:4, 178
3:5, 178
3:6, 77-78, 93, 96, 178
3:6-18, 159
3:7, 93, 102
3:7-8, 91
3:7-10, 91, 92
3:7-13, 179
3:11, 102
3:13, 102
3:14, 102
3:14-18, 179
4:1, 179
4:1-5:21, 179
4:2, 179

4:3, 65, 170
4:4-6, 179
4:6, 179
4:7, 179
4:8-10, 179
4:11, 45, 52
4:11-15, 179
4:12, 91
4:16-18, 179
5:1, 58
5:1-3, 179
5:4, 41, 42
5:4-5, 179
5:6-10, 179
5:11-13, 179
5:11-21, 179
5:12, 148
5:13-15, 179
5:14, 213
5:14-15, 21, 200, 213-214
5:14-21, 213
5:15, 21
5:16, 45, 52
5:16-20, 180
5:17, 45
5:17-18, 179, 214
5:18, 213
5:18-19, 179, 213
5:18-20, 213
5:19, 213-214
5:19-20, 179
5:20, 180
5:21, 45, 180, 200, 211, 213-214
6:1, 190
6:7, 83
6:17, 141
7:1, 45, 52, 77
7:4, 148
7:5, 45, 52
7:10, 61, 91

7:14, 148
8:1, 190
8:9, 190
8:23, 141
9:3, 148
9:8, 190
9:9-10, 83
9:13, 144
9:14, 190
10:2-3, 45, 52
10:3, 52
10:4, 92
10:7-8, 52
10:10, 52
10:14, 144
11:7, 144
11:15, 83
11:18, 45, 52
11:23, 52
11:33, 52
12:7, 45, 52
13:13, 190

Galatians
1, 180
1:1, 180
1:3, 145
1:4, 200
1:6, 104
1:11-2:10, 180
1:15, 141, 166, 180-181
1:16, 45, 52
1:17, 181
1:17-2:2, 181
1:17-2:10, 181
1:22, 45
2:3-10, 181
2:4, 45
2:11-12, 181
2:11-14, 181
2:11-4:7, 181
2:11-5:14, 104
2:12, 141
2:13, 181

2:13-14, 181
2:14, 181
2:15, 181
2:15-16, 141
2:15-21, 181
2:16, 45, 52, 85, 181, 182
2:16-17, 84, 102
2:16-3:9, 85
2:17, 182
2:17-21, 182
2:18-19, 182
2:20, 20, 45, 52, 182, 221
2:20-21, 200
2:21, 182
3, 77
3-4, 97
3-5, 92
3:1-4:7, 182, 184
3:1-5:1, 97
3:1-5, 182
3:3, 45, 52
3:6, 76, 182
3:7, 182-183
3:8, 16, 21, 84, 102, 182
3:10, 92, 182
3:10-12, 215
3:10-13, 46, 215
3:10-14, 182, 215
3:11, 84, 102, 182
3:12, 182
3:12-13, 215
3:13, 182, 200, 205, 214-215, 221
3:13-14, 183m 214
3:14-15, 216
3:15, 97
3:15-20, 183
3:15-21, 104

3:15-25, 97
3:16, 97
3:17, 97, 102
3:18, 97
3:19, 81, 97, 212
3:19-20, 92
3:21, 97
3:21-22, 104
3:22, 44, 92, 97
3:22-23, 46
3:23, 97, 104
3:24, 84, 102
3:24-25, 97
3:28, 45
4:3, 92, 104
4:4, 6, 21
4:4-5, 183
4:4-25, 46
4:5, 104, 205
4:5-6, 211
4:6, 183
4:9, 104
4:13-14, 45, 52
4:17, 148
4:21, 104
4:21-5:1, 97
4:23, 45, 52
4:25, 92
4:29, 45, 52
4:31, 55
5, 52
5:1, 104
5:2-4, 75
5:3, 104
5:4, 84, 102
5:6, 45
5:11, 102
5:13, 45, 52, 166
5:16, 45, 52-53, 205
5:16-17, 45, 52
5:16-26, 52
5:17, 45, 53
5:18, 52
5:18-21, 48

5:19, 45, 52-53
5:19-21, 56
5:19-26, 53
5:20, 53
5:21, 53
5:24, 45, 52-53
5:24-26, 53
5:25, 53
5:26, 53
6:2, 40
6:4, 148
6:8, 45, 52
6:12-13, 45, 52
6:18, 190

Ephesians
1, 184
1-2, 187, 216
1:2, 145
1:3, 21, 45, 183
1:3-4, 19
1:3-5, 184
1:3-6, 185
1:3-14, 99, 164, 177, 183, 185-186, 217
1:4, 183-184, 217
1:4-5, 185, 220
1:4-14, 183, 220, 222
1:5, 165, 184, 186, 217
1:5-6, 15
1:6, 184
1:7, 184, 205, 216-217
1:9-10, 185
1:11, 165, 185, 217, 220
1:13, 144, 185, 217
1:13-14, 177, 185

1:14, 185, 205, 216
1:15-16, 185
1:15-22, 99
1:15-23, 185
1:18, 185
1:18-19, 185
1:20-23, 185
2, 186
2:1, 44, 46, 104
2:1-3, 53, 186, 220
2:1-10, 99
2:2, 104
2:2-3, 46
2:3, 45, 47, 52-53, 64, 104
2:4, 186
2:4-10, 186
2:5, 44, 46, 104
2:5-6, 186
2:7, 45, 186
2:8, 186
2:8-9, 187, 220
2:8-10, 221
2:9-10, 187
2:11, 45, 52, 55
2:11-12, 79, 99, 187
2:13, 187, 222
2:14, 45, 52
2:14-15, 187
2:15, 102
2:16, 187
2:17-18, 187
2:19, 187
2:19-20, 187
2:21, 187
3:1, 52, 187
3:2, 187
3:2-13, 187
3:3, 187
3:5-6, 188
3:6, 45
3:7-13, 188

3:14-19, 99, 187
3:14-20, 185
3:16, 96
3:16-17, 96
3:16-19, 96
3:19, 96
4:1, 166
4:1-6:20, 99, 188
4:1-14, 183
4:4, 166
4:7, 190
4:17, 53, 99
4:17-5:8, 57
4:17-19, 100
4:17-20, 57
4:17-24, 53
4:18, 53, 99
4:18-20, 99
4:19, 53, 99
4:20-21, 99
4:21, 99
4:22, 98
4:22-5:20, 53, 56
4:22-24, 99
4:24, 83, 99-100
4:29, 190
4:30, 177, 205
5:3, 52
5:6, 47, 64
5:9, 83
5:17, 99
5:23, 20
5:25, 20
5:26, 20
5:29, 45
5:31, 45, 52
6:5, 45, 52
6:12, 45, 52
6:13, 34
6:14, 83
6:15, 144

Philippians
1:1, 45
1:2, 145

1:3-5, 188
1:3-11, 188
1:6, 188
1:7-11, 188
1:7-2:30, 188
1:11, 83
1:13, 52-53
1:15, 53
1:17, 53
1:22, 45, 52
1:24, 45, 52
1:26, 148
1:27, 144, 188
1:28, 170
2, 54
2:1-11, 54, 188
2:5, 214
2:5-9, 211
2:7, 211
2:12, 188-189
2:12-13, 188
2:13, 188
2:14-18, 189
2:16, 148
2:19-30, 188
3, 77
3:1-4, 189
3:1-6, 189
3:3, 77
3:3-4, 45, 52
3:5-6, 148
3:5-11, 188-189
3:6, 83
3:7, 189
3:8, 189
3:8-9, 94, 189
3:9, 189
3:10-11, 189
3:12, 41, 42
3:19, 170
3:20, 165
3:21, 165
4:2, 54
4:10, 41, 42
4:15-16, 188

4:23, 190

Colossians
1-2, 216-217
1-3, 190
1:2, 45, 145
1:3-4, 100
1:5, 144
1:10-11, 190
1:12, 190
1:13, 190
1:13-14, 100
1:14, 205, 216-217
1:14-16, 190
1:15, 165
1:18, 165
1:20, 190, 217
1:21-22, 217
1:22, 45, 52
1:23, 144, 217
1:24, 45, 52
1:25, 190
1:27, 190
2:1, 45, 52
2:4, 99
2:5, 45, 52, 100
2:6, 190
2:6-4:1, 100
2:7, 190
2:8, 99, 104
2:11-12, 77-78
2:12, 100
2:12-13, 100, 190
2:13, 44-46, 52, 104, 217
2:13-14, 217
2:18, 45, 52
2:20, 100, 104, 190
2:20-3:17, 54, 56
2:20-4:1, 190
2:23, 45, 52
3:1, 100, 190
3:1-4, 100
3:1-10, 100
3:2, 54
3:3, 100
3:5, 54, 57, 100
3:5-9, 100
3:5-17, 100
3:6, 47, 64
3:8, 54
3:9, 54, 98-100
3:9-10, 100
3:11, 21
3:12-17, 100
3:16-19, 99
3:22, 45, 52
4:5, 205

1 Thessalonians
2, 34
1:1, 145
1:4, 190
1:10, 47
2:2, 144
2:8-9, 144
2:12, 166
2:13, 34
2:16, 47, 64
3:2, 144
3:7-8, 34
3:11-13, 190
4:1-6, 57
4:7, 166
4:16, 45
4:17, 40
5:9, 47
5:10, 200
5:11, 55
5:23-24, 190

2 Thessalonians
1:2, 145
1:8, 144
1:12, 190
2:3, 170
2:8, 102
2:10, 65, 170, 190
2:11, 34
1:13-17, 190
2:14, 166
3:3-5, 190
3:16-17, 190

1 Timothy
1:2, 145
1:12, 190
1:14, 190
1:16, 34
2:1, 222
2:2, 222
2:3-5, 34
2:4, 12, 16, 222
2:4-6, 21
2:6, 222
3:16, 45, 52
4:10, 20
6:9, 170
6:11, 83
6:12, 166
6:21, 190

2 Timothy
1:2, 145
1:8, 144
1:9, 166, 190
1:10, 102
2:1, 190
2:8, 144
2:10, 17, 34, 224
2:22, 83
2:25, 61
3:15, 93
3:16, 83
4:8, 83
4:22, 190

Titus
1:1, 224
1:4, 145

2:14, 20, 205
3:5, 83
3:5-6, 34
3:7, 84, 102

Philemon
1:1, 52
1:15, 34
1:16, 45, 52, 140

Hebrews
1:3, 201
1:6, 165
1:9, 83
2:1, 34
2:14, 102
3:6, 148
5:13, 83
6:15, 40
7:2, 83
9:15, 34, 205
10:1-11, 192
11:7, 83, 209
11:28, 165
11:33, 83
11:35, 205
12:11, 83
12:23, 165

James
2:12, 40
2:21, 84
2:23, 76
2:25, 84
3:18, 83
4:16, 148

1 Peter
2, 197
2:11, 92
2:21-24, 197
2:23-24, 45
2:24, 83
3:14, 83

4:1-4, 57

2 Peter
1:1, 83
1:9, 201
2:1, 223
2:5, 83
2:6, 209
2:21, 83
3:13, 83
3:17, 162

1 John
2:2, 12, 18, 223
2:29, 83
3:1, 34
3:7, 83
3:10, 83
3:24, 21

Revelation
1:5, 165
9:17, 40
14:10, 64
16:19, 64
19:11, 83
20:1-15, 64
22:1, 83

Early Christian Authors and Writings

1 Clement
5.1-6.1, 4
7.1, 3
7.1-3, 3
7.1-4, 4
7.4, 3-4
7.5, 4
7.6, 4
7.6-7, 4
7.7, 4
8.5, 4
12.7, 4
16.4, 4
16.5, 4
16.7, 4
16.9, 4
21.6, 4
29.1, 4
36.1, 4
38.1, 4
46.4, 4
46.6, 4
46.7, 4
49.1-50.1, 4
49.5, 4
49.6, 4
50.2, 5
50.3, 5
50.6-7, 5

2 Clement
1.1, 5
1.1-5, 5
1.2, 5
1.4, 5
1.6, 5
1.7, 5
1.8, 5
2.1, 5
2.1-6, 5
2.3, 5
2.4, 5
2.7, 5
9.1-11, 5
14.5, 5
17.4, 5
17.4-5, 5
17.5, 5

Epistle of Barnabas
1.1-4.14, 8
5.1, 8
7.2, 8
7.5, 8
7.10-11, 9
11.1-12.11, 8
14.4, 9
14.5, 9
14.6, 9
14.7-9, 9
14.8, 9
14.9, 9

Epistle of Mathetes to Diognetus
7.2, 9
8.1-9.2, 9, 10
9.2, 10
9.3-4, 10
9.3-6, 10
9.5-6, 10
9.6, 10

Ignatius to the Ephesians
1.1, 6
9.1, 6
10.1, 6
16.2, 6
17.1, 6
18.1, 6

Ignatius to the Trallians
2.1, 7
11.2, 7

Ignatius to the Smyrnaeans
1.1-2, 7
2.1, 7
6.2, 7

Polycarp to the Philippians
1.1, 7
1.2, 7
1.3, 7
9.2, 7

Martyrdom of Polycarp
16.1-2, 7
17.1-2, 7
17.2, 8
22.1, 8

Old Testament Apocrypha

1 Esdras
2:1-22, 112
2:10, 169
3:26, 140
4:58-60, 112
5:7, 112
6:5, 112
6:15, 112
6:23-24, 112
8:10, 112
8:12, 69
8:21, 69
8:25-27, 112
8:77-78, 112
8:83, 112
8:84, 112
9:39, 69

2 Esdras
1-2, 112
1:4-7, 112
1:7, 112
1:10-23, 112
2:10, 113
3:3-4, 112
3:7-8, 35
3:20, 113
3:27, 113
5:4, 113
5:21-30, 113
6:1-6, 113
6:19, 64
6:38-53, 112
7:17, 64, 113
7:18, 112
7:19-24, 112
7:22-24, 112
7:33-35, 64
7:45-61, 113
7:71-73, 112
7:77, 113
7:79-80, 113
7:105, 113
7:129, 113
8:6, 113
8:7-17, 113
8:33, 113
8:56-58, 113
9:26-36, 113
15-16, 112
20:34, 202

Judith
1:1-16, 114
2:1-13, 114
2:14-3:9, 114
3:4, 140
4:1-12, 115
4:3, 169
4:13-15, 115
5:11, 140
5:21, 115
6:1-10, 115
6:10, 140
6:17-21, 115
8:11-17, 115
8:32-35, 115
9:1-14, 162
9:5-6, 115
9:7, 115
9:8, 115
9:9, 115
9:10, 115
9:11, 115
9:13, 115
9:14, 115
10:8-9, 115
10:11-16, 116
11:5-23, 116
12:4, 116
12:10-13:3, 116
13:3, 116
13:4-8, 116
13:11, 116
13:14-16, 116
13:17, 116
14:10, 75-76, 78, 116
15:1-10, 116
16:1-5, 116
16:2, 116
16:3-4, 116
16:5, 116

Tobit
1:3, 67, 83, 149
1:5-18, 67
1:5-7, 149
1:8, 69, 149
1:11-12, 149
1:16, 149
2:11-14, 149
2:14, 83
3:1-6, 149
3:1-6 BA, 116
3:2-6, 149
3:6, 149
3:16 BA, 116, 117
4:5-11, 67
4:5-7, 83
4:5-14, 149
4:9-10, 62
6:13, 69
6:18 BA, 117
7:11 S, 117
7:13, 69
11:7-15 BA, 117
11:17 BA, 117
12:6-18 BA, 117
12:8-9, 83
13:1-17 BA, 117
13:6, 83
14:6, 83
14:11, 83

Additions to Esther
14:15, 75

1 Maccabees
1, 57, 74, 195
1-2, 195
1:1, 199
1:1-64, 199
1:11, 204
1:15, 76
1:16-62, 117
1:41-64, 201
1:48, 75
1:60-61, 75
2:21, 62, 75
2:26, 76, 78
2:46, 75
2:52, 76, 78, 150
2:67, 65
3:16-22, 117
3:23-25, 117
4:10-11, 117
4:12-25, 117
4:30-33, 118
4:33, 118
4:34, 118
4:49, 169
5:32, 200
6:60, 200
7:37-42, 118
12:25, 61
14:35, 83

2 Maccabees
1:3-4, 74
1:5, 195, 201
1:11-12, 118
1:16-17, 118
1:18, 201
1:24, 61
1:26, 200
1:28, 197
2:16, 201
2:17-18, 118
2:19, 201
3:22-28, 118
2:23-42, 118
3:31-34, 118

3:32, 200
3:35-39, 118
4:16-17, 199
4:35-38, 118
5:1-11, 198
5:1-8:5, 195, 197, 199, 201, 204
5:4, 201
5:11-14, 198
5:15-16, 196
5:17, 195
5:17-18, 198, 200
5:17-26, 118
5:20, 197, 198, 199
5:20-8:5, 199
5:21-6:11, 198
5:27-7:38, 196
5:35, 201
6, 194
6:1-11, 118
5:27-6:6, 196
6:10, 75
6:12-16, 199
6:12-17, 118, 198
6:13-16, 198
6:15, 200
6:18, 199, 201
6:18-7:42, 198
6:18-8:2, 198
6:18-8:5, 198
6:24-31, 197
6:28, 197
6:31, 197
7, 195
7:1, 195
7:2-41, 195
7:9, 118
7:23, 119
7:28-29, 195
7:29, 197
6:31, 197

7:32, 195, 200
7:32-38, 57, 194-196, 199
7:33, 195, 196, 197, 198
7:37, 196, 198
7:37-38, 195, 196
7:38, 196, 197
8:1-4, 199
8:1-5, 197
8:2-3, 199
8:4, 199
8:5, 198
8:5-7, 198
8:11, 200
8:13, 200
8:29, 195
8:36, 119
9:5, 119
10:1, 119
10:5, 201
12:11, 119
12:15, 119
12:28, 119
12:42, 200
13:4, 119
13:9-17, 119
14:34, 119
15:7-8, 119
15:11, 197
15:21, 119
15:25-36, 119

3 Maccabees
1:16, 119
1:27, 119
2:1-23, 119
4:20-21, 119
5:7-9, 119
5:1-13, 119
5:25-30, 119
5:35, 119
5:51, 119
6:1-29, 119

259

6:32, 119
6:36, 119
6:39, 119
7:6, 119
7:9-23, 119

4 Maccabees
1:1-2:18, 119-120
1:4, 83
1:6, 83
1:11, 200
1:18, 83
2:6, 83
4:8-14, 120
4:13, 200
4:21, 200
5:4, 199, 201
5:4-6:40, 199
5:6, 199
5:19, 200
5:24, 84
5:35, 199, 201
6, 195
6:1-8, 199
6:1-7:23, 120
6:1-17:22, 120
6:6, 199
6:18-21, 197
6:28, 196, 199-200
6:28-29, 57, 197, 201, 203-204, 206, 120
6:29, 199-201, 206
7:6, 201
7:8, 201
7:21-22, 201
7:32-38, 201
8:14, 200
8:15-13:1, 120
8:22, 200
9:9, 120, 200
9:15, 200
9:22, 197
9:23, 197
9:24, 120, 200
9:32, 200
10:3, 197
10:16, 197
11:3, 200
11:15, 197
12:12, 200
12:14-16, 200
12:16, 197
12:17, 200
13:8-18, 197
15:3, 120
16:15, 197
17:10, 201
17:20-21, 201
17:20-22, 204
17:21, 200-201, 206
17:21-22, 57, 120, 199, 201-204, 206
17:22, 200, 202-204
17:23, 197
18:4, 201
18:22, 200

Prayer of Manasseh
1:1-13, 120
1:1-15, 120
1:14, 120
1:15, 120

Wisdom of Solomon
1:1, 84
1:1-2, 121
1:3, 121
1:5, 121
1:7, 121
1:8, 200
1:11-12, 121
1:15, 84
2:11, 84
2:24, 39
3:1-6, 195
4:15, 121
4:16, 209
5:6, 84
5:16, 121
5:18, 84
7:9, 76
7:15, 121
7:17-22, 121
7:25-26, 121
8:7, 84
8:21, 121
8:21-9:18, 121
9:3, 84
9:6, 76
9:9, 121
11-15, 63
11-16, 64
11:1-16:1, 55-56, 74
11:23, 61, 62
12:10, 62
12:12-18, 121
12:16, 84
12:19, 121
14:7, 84
14:31, 200
15:1, 61
15:1-2, 62
15:2-3, 74
15:7, 121, 169
15:8, 57
15:18-19, 121
16:2, 121
16:7, 121
18:1-8, 121
18:4, 74, 87
18:11, 200
19:1-5, 121
19:22, 121

Sirach
1:1-10, 122
1:14, 122
1:18, 122
1:20, 122
1:22, 84
1:28, 122
2:1-10, 122
2:11, 122
2:15-18, 122
3:3, 202
3:30, 202
4:14, 122
5:4-7, 62
5:6, 202
6:37, 122
7:3, 84
9:12, 84
10:12-18, 122
10:19-24, 122
10:29, 84
11:14, 123
11:26, 67, 87, 122
11:21-28, 123
13:22, 84
15, 123
15:11-20, 122-123
15:16-17, 122
15:19-20, 122
16:10, 63
16:11-14, 122
16:12, 64
16:14, 64
16:22, 84
17:11, 74
17:23, 67, 87
20:28, 202
22:27-23:6, 123
23:1, 123
23:2-3, 123
23:4, 123
23:4-6, 123
23:5, 123

23:6, 123
23:11, 84
24:1-17, 123
24:19-22, 123
24:27, 74, 87
25:24, 39
26:28, 84
26:29, 84
27:5, 169
28:5, 202
31:5, 84
31:10, 148
33:7-13, 123
33:13, 123, 169
34:3, 211
34:14-20, 124
34:19, 202
35:19, 87
35:22-26, 122
37:15, 124
38:1, 124
38:4-6, 124
38:7-8, 124
38:9, 124
38:10, 124
38:11, 124
38:12, 124
38:29-30, 169
39:6-11, 124
42:2, 84
42:15-50:24, 123
44:10, 84
44:19, 150
45:5, 74, 88
45:8, 169
45:16, 202
45:23, 202
45:26, 84
46:1, 124
46:9-10, 124
47:12-22, 124
50:9, 169
51:13-30, 124

Psalms of Solomon
1:2, 84
1:3, 124
3:1-8, 124
2:1-37, 124
2:15, 84
2:16-18, 64
2:33-35, 64, 124
2:36, 61
4:2, 209
4:23-25, 124
5:6-7, 125
8:1-13, 125
8:1-34, 82
8:6, 84
8:14-34, 125
8:24, 84
8:25, 84
8:26, 84
9:1-11, 82
9:2-5, 84
9:3-5, 62
9:4, 125
9:4-5, 64
9:5, 125
11, 142
11:1, 142
14:2, 84, 88
14:2-3, 67
14:10, 67
15:4, 67
15:8, 60
15:16, 67
16:1-11, 125
16:3, 125
16:12-15, 125
17, 60
17:1, 74
17:8-9, 64
17:23, 84, 169
17:37, 84
18:1, 60
18:1-12, 60

Baruch
  1:1-14, 125
  1:1-2:10, 126
  1:15, 84
  1:15-3:8, 126
  2:6, 84
  2:11-26, 126
  2:12, 62, 75
  2:18, 84
  2:27-35, 126
  3:1-8, 126
  3:6, 126
  3:7, 126
  3:9-4:4, 72, 126
  3:36, 74
  4:1-2, 67
  4:1-4, 74
  4:1-29, 126
  4:4, 56, 74, 87
  4:5-5:9, 126
  4:13, 84
  4:30-5:9, 126
  4:34, 66
  5:2, 84
  5:4, 84
  5:9, 84

Epistle of Jeremiah
  1:17, 169

Suzanna
  1:7, 140
  1:22-23, 75
  1:41, 209
  1:42-64, 126
  1:44-46, 126
  1:44-46 Th, 127
  1:48, 209
  1:53, 209

Odes of Solomon
  7:35, 150
  11:1-3, 77

Pseudepigrapha

1 Enoch
1:1-9, 127
1:7-9, 64
5:2, 127
5:9, 127
9:5, 127
16:3, 63
45:6, 127
50:4-5, 127
90:20-27, 58, 60
105:1, 74

2 Enoch
2:2-4, 127

4 Ezra
3:7-22, 39
3:13-14, 128
3:20, 128
3:21, 35, 43
3:32-36, 56
4, 39
4:4, 128
5:22-30, 128
5:49, 128
6:1-6, 128
6:5, 62
6:7-9:25, 67, 75
7, 39
7:21, 128
7:22-24, 82
7:34, 59
7:61, 128
7:68, 128
7:72-74, 128
7:77, 62
7:90-99, 128
7:102-105, 128
7:102-140, 128
7:116-118, 128
7:125-131, 128
7:132-140, 128
8, 39

8:4-36, 128
8:33, 62
8:36, 62
8:59-60, 128
10:10, 128

2 Apocalypse of Baruch
13:8, 64
14:12, 62
21:20, 61
48:22-24, 74
48:46-47, 65
85:9, 59
44:2-15, 74
44:4, 64
54:15, 41
54:19, 39, 41
54:21, 64
13:9, 128
23:4, 129
32:1, 129
38:1-2, 129
48:15-16, 129
48:18-24, 129
51, 87
51:3, 83
54:5, 129
54:21-22, 129

2 Apocolypse of Abraham
2:1-5, 129
10:17, 129
22:1-5, 129
23:1-4, 129

Letter of Aristeas
15-16, 129
17, 130
18, 130
19, 130
20, 130
32, 130

35, 130
57, 130
87-202, 130
139, 58, 87-88
142, 56, 58, 87-88
152-53, 56
195, 130
196, 130
197, 131
199-200, 130
200, 130
208, 130
216, 130
224, 130
231, 130
234, 130
236-238, 130
242, 130
243, 131
244, 131
246, 131
248, 131
266, 131
292, 131
271-272, 131

Jubilees
1, 131
2-50, 131
1:7, 131
1:7-11, 131
1:12-14, 131
1:15-18, 131
1:19-22, 131
1:22-25, 78, 132
1:23, 77, 132
1:24, 132
3:17-32, 39
5:10-16, 58, 60
5:13-19, 64
5:16-19, 64
5:17-19, 132
10:4, 132
11:16-17, 132

12, 150
12:1-14, 150
12:2-5, 132
12:19, 150
12:19-21, 132
14:10, 87
15:1-34, 75-76, 78, 87
15:26, 75
15:29-33, 132
17:15-18, 150
21:4, 64
21:21-22, 50
21:21-26, 132
22:9, 132
22:10, 132
22:10-12, 132
22:15-23, 87
22:16-23, 55-56, 63-64, 74
24:10-13, 132
30:7-12, 75
30:21-22, 67
33:18, 64

Joseph and Aseneth
8:9-15:11, 133
19:5, 133
19:9, 133
20:7, 133
27:10, 133

Life of Adam and Eve
1:149 ApMos, 87
12:10-11 ApMos, 64
27:1-3 Vita, 133
28:3-4 ApMos, 133
41:3 Vita, 133

Pseudo Philo

9:7-8, 133
9:9, 133
11.1-2, 65
19:8-9, 134
21:9, 134
21:10, 134
23:1-14, 134
32:14, 134

Aristobulus
2, 134

Hellensitic-Judeo Poets, Fragment of Orphica
43, 134

Martyrdom and Ascension of Isaiah
1:13, 134
2:1-6, 134
3:11-12, 134
5:1-2, 134
5:14-16, 134
11:41, 134

Jannes and Jambres
25, 134

Testament of Job
5:1, 134
7:13, 134
19:4-20:3, 134

Lives of the Prophets
10:6, 134

History of the Rechabites
1:1-5, 134

Sibylline Oracles
3.70, 66
3.702, 64
3.194-95, 74
3.195, 87
3.595-606, 55
4.183-85, 64

Testaments of the 12 Patriarchs

Testament of Asher
2:1-10, 66
6:1-5, 66

Testament of Benjamin
10:7-9, 64

Testament of Dan
5:1, 66

Testament of Gad
7:4-5, 64
5:7, 63

Testament of Isacchar
5:1-2, 66

Testament of Joseph
9:2, 134
11:1, 66, 134

Testament of Judah
13:105, 66
13:1-5, 66

26:1, 66

Testament of Levi
3:2, 63, 64
4:1-2, 64
14:1-8, 74
14:3-8, 74
14:4, 57
14:5-6, 57
14:6, 57
14:7, 57
14:8, 57
15:2, 63

Testament of Naphtali
3:3, 56
4:1-2, 56

Testament of Reuben
4:1, 134

Testament of Simeon
6:2, 63

Testament of Zebulun
1:4-5, 134

Dead Sea Scrolls
1QH
  1:21, 169
  2, 39, 136
  2:9, 74, 87
  3 V.17, 137
  4 VI, 137
  4 VI.10, 137
  4 VI.12, 137
  4 VI.25, 137
  4 VII.10-11, 137
  4 VII.11, 137
  4 VII.11-14, 137
  4 VII.15-16, 137
  4 VII.17-18, 137
  4 VII.18-20, 137
  4 VII.20-25, 137
  5 VIII.1, 137
  5 VIII.2-4, 137
  5 VIII.5-9, 137
  5 VIII.10-12, 138
  7, 81
  9, 81
  9:14-16, 87
  14, 81
  15:13-19, 163
  19 XVIII, 138
  23 XX.10-15, 138

1QM
  1:1, 74
  1:7, 74
  1:11, 74
  1:13-15, 74
  XIII.8-11, 136
  XII.11-5, 136
  13:5, 39
  XIV.7-10, 136

1QpHab
  7:4-5, 74
  8:1-2, 64

1QS
  10:16-18, 64
  1-3 I, 201
  I.1-25, 135
  1.5-2.3, 75
  1:9, 74
  II.1-4, 135
  2:16, 74
  III.7-10, 135
  III.11-4:1, 136
  3:13, 74, 87
  III.16-20, 135
  3:18-25, 163
  3:24-25, 74
  4:11, 63
  4:12-14, 63
  4:19-20, 59
  4:20-21, 39
  5:8, 215
  5:12, 63
  5:21, 215
  5:24, 215
  6:13-23, 215
  8:4, 215
  8:10, 215
  8:20, 215
  10, 201
  11, 163
  11:22, 169

1QS DM
  1.6-11, 195

4Q215
  aii 2-7, 67

4Q257
  2i 3-6, 87

4Q393
  I.5, 138
  II.4, 138
  II.5-10, 138

4Q504
  V.15, 138
  VI.5-10, 138

4Q504-6
  II.10-15, 138

4Q521
  II.11, 138

4QMMT
  85

CD
  3:14-16, 87
  5:13-17, 82
  16:4-6, 75
  20, 81
  20:30, 59

Philo

Abr.
98, 74, 87
275-76, 70, 72

Against Flaccus
6.36-39, 101
10.75, 101

Cher.
98-101, 139

Conf.
182, 139

Deus
108, 139
109, 139

Ebr.
105-10, 139

Fug.
166-76, 139

Her.
102-11, 139

Leg.
1.82, 139
1.305, 63
3.105-06, 64
3.137, 139
3.166, 139
3.219, 139

Leg. All.
3.106, 62

Mig.
26-35, 139

Migr.
30, 139

Mut.
51-53, 139
3.166, 139

Sac.
52-58, 139

Sacr.
42, 139
124, 139

Somn.
2.75-78, 139

Spec.
1.43, 139
4.187, 139

Virtues
100-200, 139

Josephus
Ag. Ap.
2.291-95, 74
2.293, 87

Ant.
5.107, 66
6.5.3.302-304, 101
13.257, 75
13.257-58, 75
13.318-319, 75
13.397, 75
20.139, 75
20.145, 75

Wars
2.14.9, 101

Seutonius, *Domitian*
11, 101

Subject Index

Adam 35, 37-42, 44-51, 54-55, 63, 93, 104-105, 107-118, 120, 122-124, 149, 154-155, 179, 181-182, 184, 245, 247

Adoption 212, 214

Anthropology, 36-38, 104, 223, 256-257

Atonement 1-4, 7-8, 10, 12-21, 23, 25, -28, 30-37, 40, 100, 138, 143, 222-226, 228-229, 233-237, 239-240, 244-245, 249-250, 254-257, 260-262

Blood 3-5, 7, 10-14, 16-22, 24, 26-27, 60, 98, 100, 128, 140, 177, 181, 190, 214-215, 217, 221, 225, 231, 233-242, 244, 249, 253-254

Boasting 101-102, 171-173, 180, 181, 204, 217

Church 1, 2, 6-8, 10, 14, 21, 23-24, 27, 33, 60, 132, 164, 167, 204, 210, 213, 220

Circumcision 53, 59, 61, 87-93, 97, 101-102, 123, 171-172, 174-176

Commandment 43, 66, 76, 84, 87, 105, 106, 107, 108, 114, 141-144, 153, 159-160, 251-252

Covenant 5, 10-11, 27, 43-44, 73-74, 76, 81, 87-94, 97, 99, 102-103, 110, 114, 127, 130, 150, 155, 157-159, 176-177, 186, 190, 202, 207-208, 236, 251-252

Creation 6, 18, 39-41, 46, 48, 51-52, 56-57, 63, 68-69, 82, 97, 120, 124, 151, 159, 161, 169-170, 187, 190, 194, 198, 209, 250, 254

Cross 7, 8, 15-16, 25, 26-27, 31, 70, 106, 204, 217, 221, 225, 244-247, 253

Divine/Human Agent 125, 127-129, 131, 134, 138, 144, 146-148, 155, 170-171, 173, 179-181, 183-186, 188, 193-194, 196-197, 200-201, 204, 213-214, 218, 220

Elect/Election 1-2, 5-9, 13-22, 25, 27-28, 36, 88, 141, 144, 148, 150, 153-154, 157, 188-189, 192, 216, 223-224, 238, 252, 254-256, 262

Eternal Life 7-8, 13-15, 49-50, 62, 65, 74, 77-78, 104, 116-120, 123, 133, 140, 149, 154, 160, 166, 170, 184, 194, 220

Expiation 30, 224

Faith 7-8, 15, 17, 19, 25-27, 36-37, 39, 53, 55, 59, 62, 70, 78, 84-85, 87-90, 92-94, 97-100, 104, 106, 111, 113-123, 125, 143, 163, 166-169, 171, 173-181, 184, 186-187, 192-194, 200-201, 205, 208-209, 211-213, 215-217, 219-221, 223-224, 226, 238-241, 250-256, 258, 260-262

Flesh 5, 8, 10, 21, 45, 52-54, 61-62, 79, 82, 89-90, 93, 97, 103, 105, 109, 111-113, 120, 124, 130, 158-159, 173, 178, 184-187, 211, 232, 242-248

Foreknowledge 19, 135, 188-192, 213

Gospel 9, 14, 37, 55, 61, 63, 74, 83-85, 92, 99-100, 123-124, 162-164, 166-169, 184, 186, 196, 198, 200, 202, 204-208, 210-211, 215, 218-221, 253-254, 257-260, 262

Hebrew Bible 36, 126-127, 131, 192, 223-224, 238, 255, 257

Hope 5, 7, 15, 39, 103, 132, 135, 147, 151, 161, 166, 177, 179-180, 188, 190, 194, 208, 215, 223, 241, 253

Justification 12, 15, 17, 24-25, 47, 49-50, 74, 77-82, 85, 88-89, 95, 97-100, 103, 106, 168, 170-171, 173, 177-182, 188, 194, 209, 211, 238-241

Law 38, 40, 43-44, 48, 50-54, 57, 61, 63, 65-66, 68-69, 75-88, 90, 92-95, 97-110, 112-116, 121-124, 132-134, 140, 146, 149-152, 155-156, 160, 172, 176-179, 181, 183-186, 191, 194, 200, 207, 211-212, 228, 232, 234, 242-248, 250-252

Martyr Theology 227, 238

Nachwirgung 38, 46, 51, 53, 64, 108, 120, 122

Obedience 10, 12, 25, 28, 39-40, 42, 45-50, 54, 65, 69, 71, 73, 75-78, 80-82, 86-88, 93-95, 99-102, 104, 106, 109, 111, 113, 115, 118-119, 122, 127, 130, 140-144, 149, 152-153, 155-158, 160, 167, 170, 172, 178, 182, 184-185, 187, 196, 200, 202, 217, 219-220, 226, 245, 247-248, 251-252, 258, 260-262

Old Man/New Man 25, 52, 116-122, 183

Old Testament 1, 10, 19, 46, 58, 66, 68, 73-74, 77, 86, 90, 92-93, 95-96, 107, 110, 139, 148, 150, 155, 162, 166, 189, 195-196, 224-226, 234, 236, 238, 243, 249-250

Predestination 7, 13, 18-21, 37, 150, 157, 188, 191-193, 198, 205, 213-215, 241, 254, 258

Purification 10-11, 232-235, 237

Qumran 45, 101

Ransom 11-12, 15, 17, 129, 234-235, 237, 239-240, 253, 260

Reconciliation 17-18, 22, 28, 32, 98, 181, 209, 216, 228, 230- 232, 241, 242, 249-250, 253, 259

Redemption 2, 5-6, 11-13, 15-17, 22, 27-28, 51-53, 98, 130, 137, 158, 188, 212, 214-216, 238-240, 250, 252-254

Reformed Theology 17, 20-21, 25-27, 261- 262

Remonstrants 19, 23, 26

Repentance 3-5, 7, 69-72, 130, 140, 142, 146, 148-149, 152, 154, 199, 201, 225

Resurrection 9, 15, 50-51, 60, 106-107, 116, 118-120, 122, 132-133, 138-139, 149, 154-155, 159, 167, 179, 181, 183-184, 187, 204, 208, 220, 225, 260

Righteousness 8, 50, 55, 62, 78, 88-89, 93, 98-100, 102, 104, 111, 116-120, 122-123, 141, 145-146, 149, 153, 156, 159-160, 166, 168-179, 182-184, 197, 200, 209, 212, 220, 250

Sacrifice 14, 28, 223, 225, 233, 235-236, 239-240, 244, 249, 255, 257

Salvation History 38, 40, 47-48, 51, 53, 63, 85, 94, 111, 103-104, 106, 109-111, 114-115, 119, 122, 124, 174, 179, 185, 195, 247

Second Temple Judaism 1, 36, 45-46, 77, 100, 142, 161, 189, 251

Septuagint 71, 73-75, 79-81, 83, 87-89, 92, 94-95, 97-98, 100, 133, 144, 150, 162, 164-166, 171, 174-175, 193, 195, 201, 227, 232-233, 235-236, 243, 246, 249

Sin 5-8, 10-11, 14-18, 23, 25, 28, 32, 35, 37-55, 57-59, 61-65, 67, 75, 78, 80-81, 90, 93, 96-97, 100, 102-125, 129-132, 136, 140, 142-147, 153, 155, 158, 171, 173, 175-176, 179, 182-187, 191, 202, 209, 223-225, 227-228, 230, 232, 234-237, 240, 242-250, 252, 254, 256-258

Soteriology 6-7, 12, 21, 33, 36-38, 70, 79, 88, 121, 125-127, 150, 161-162, 167-168, 170, 179, 181-183, 187, 191, 193-195, 200- 210, 212-214, 216-217, 220-221, 223-224, 226-229, 232, 235, 238, 241-242, 249, 254-256, 258-259

Spirit 5, 7, 25, 27-28, 44, 52, 54-55, 57, 61-62, 71, 78, 82, 84, 89, 90, 92-93, 97, 107-109, 113, 117, 131, 155, 158-160, 164-165, 179-180, 184-188, 204-208, 212, 215, 218, 242, 247-248, 250, 252, 254, 260

Synod of Dort 2, 23, 26

Torah 38, 47, 48, 51, 53-54, 63,-65, 67-69, 71-74, 76-77, 80-98, 100-104, 106-114, 117, 119, 122-124, 130, 132, 137, 140-143, 146, 148-150, 170-174, 176-178, 184-186, 200, 211-212, 217, 220, 232, 234, 238, 241, 247-248, 251-252, 257

Transgression 35, 37-38, 40-42, 44-46, 48-51, 63, 86, 104-105, 107-108, 111, 114-116, 118-120, 124-125, 179, 181-182

Westminster Confession of Faith 20, 26-27, 29, 224, 228

Works 3, 19, 28, 30, 33-35, 53, 61-62, 74-75, 77-79, 83-84, 88-89, 97-103, 125-126, 132-133, 141-142, 145, 151, 155, 159-160, 171, 173-175, 177, 178-179, 187-188, 191, 195, 211-212, 215, 217, 221, 251, 258

Wrath 23, 36, 55-57, 63, 69, 70-75, 85, 98, 118, 124, 135, 138, 140, 155, 159-160, 169-171, 178, 180-181, 190-191, 196-199, 216, 225-226, 228-233, 236-237, 242, 245-246

www.ingramcontent.com/pod-product-compliance
Lightning Source LLC
Chambersburg PA
CBHW061436300426
44114CB00014B/1703